Financial Advisor Series

Foundations of Financial Planning: The Process

Second Edition

Allen C. McLellan
Kirk S. Okumura
Glenn E. Stevick, Jr.

THE AMERICAN COLLEGE PRESS

FA263.02.1

270 S. Bryn Mawr Avenue
Bryn Mawr, PA 19010
(888) AMERCOL (263–7265)
theamericancollege.edu

Library of Congress Control Number 2009908145
ISBN-10: 1-932819-90-8
ISBN-13: 978-1-932819-90-8
Printed in the United States of America

The American College

The American College® is an independent, nonprofit, accredited institution founded in 1927 that offers professional certification and graduate-degree distance education to men and women seeking career growth in financial services.

The Center for Financial Advisor Education at The American College offers both the LUTCF and the Financial Services Specialist (FSS) professional designations to introduce students in a classroom environment to the technical side of financial services, while at the same time providing them with the requisite sales-training skills.

The Solomon S. Huebner School® of The American College administers the Chartered Life Underwriter (CLU®); the Chartered Financial Consultant (ChFC®); the Chartered Advisor for Senior Living (CASL®); the Registered Health Underwriter (RHU®); the Registered Employee Benefits Consultant (REBC®); and the Chartered Leadership Fellow® (CLF®) professional designation programs. In addition, the Huebner School also administers The College's CFP Board—registered education program for those individuals interested in pursuing CFP® certification, the CFP® Certification Curriculum.[1]

The Richard D. Irwin Graduate School® of The American College offers the master of science in financial services (MSFS) degree, the Graduate Financial Planning Track (another CFP Board-registered education program), and several graduate-level certificates that concentrate on specific subject areas. It also offers the Chartered Advisor in Philanthropy (CAP)® and the master of science in management (MSM), a one-year program with an emphasis in leadership. The National Association of Estate Planners & Councils has named The College as the provider of the education required to earn its prestigious AEP designation.

The American College is accredited by:

The Middle States Commission on Higher Education
3624 Market Street
Philadelphia, PA 19104
267.284.5000

The Middle States Commission on Higher Education is a regional accrediting agency recognized by the U.S. Secretary of Education and the Commission on Recognition of Postsecondary Accreditation. Middle States accreditation is an expression of confidence in an institution's mission and goals, performance, and resources. It attests that in the judgment of the Commission on Higher Education,

1. Certified Financial Planner Board of Standards, Inc., owns the certification marks CFP®, CERTIFIED FINANCIAL PLANNER™, and CFP (with flame logo)®, which it awards to individuals who successfully complete initial and ongoing certification requirements.

based on the results of an internal institutional self-study and an evaluation by a team of outside peer observers assigned by the Commission, an institution is guided by well-defined and appropriate goals; that it has established conditions and procedures under which its goals can be realized; that it is accomplishing them substantially; that it is so organized, staffed, and supported that it can be expected to continue to do so; and that it meets the standards of the Middle States Association. The American College has been accredited since 1978.

The American College does not discriminate on the basis of race, religion, sex, handicap, or national and ethnic origin in its admissions policies, educational programs and activities, or employment policies.

The American College is located at 270 S. Bryn Mawr Avenue, Bryn Mawr, PA 19010. The toll-free number of the Office of Professional Education is (888) AMERCOL (263-7265); the fax number is (610) 526-1465; and the home page address is theamericancollege.edu.

Contents

Financial Advisor Series

Sales Skills Techniques

Techniques for Exploring Personal Markets
Techniques for Meeting Client Needs
Techniques for Prospecting: Prospect or Perish

Product Essentials

Essentials of Annuities
Essentials of Business Insurance
Essentials of Disability Income Insurance
Essentials of Employee Benefits
Essentials of Life Insurance Products
Essentials of Long-Term Care Insurance
Essentials of Multiline Insurance Products

Planning Foundations

Foundations of Estate Planning
Foundations of Financial Planning: An Overview
Foundations of Financial Planning: The Process
Foundations of Investment Planning
Foundations of Retirement Planning

Preface

The mission of this book is to develop your professionalism as a financial advisor who counsels prospects and clients about the need for financial planning. We intend to do this by teaching you the eight-step selling/planning process. Each chapter covers one or two steps of the process and/or skills, techniques, or knowledge that facilitate its use. To gain an understanding of the selling/planning process, you need to read the entire book. This will give you both an overview of the whole process and an in-depth look at each step of the process.

Although much of the text material will be new to you, some will, no doubt, refresh knowledge you acquired in the past. In either case, all of the text material is both valuable and necessary if you aspire to be a successful financial advisor. The benefits you gain from studying the text material will be directly proportional to the effort you expend. So read each chapter carefully and answer the essay and multiple-choice review questions for the chapter (preferably before looking in the back of the book for the answers); to do less would be to deprive yourself of the unique opportunity to become familiar with the selling/planning process and all that it entails.

The book includes numerous educational features designed to help you focus your study of the selling/planning process. Among the features found in each chapter of the book are

- learning objectives
- examples, figures, and lists
- key terms and concepts
- review questions (essay format)
- self-test questions (multiple-choice format)

Features located in the back of the book are a(n)

- answers to questions section
- glossary

- index

Finally, all of the individuals noted on the acknowledgments page made this a better book, and we are grateful. In spite of the help of all these fine folks, however, some errors have undoubtedly been successful in eluding our eyes. For these we are solely responsible. At the same time, we accept full credit for giving those of you who find these errors the exhilarating intellectual experience produced by such discovery. Nevertheless, each of the authors acknowledges that any errors discovered are the fault of one of the other authors.

Acknowledgments

This book was written by Allen McLellan, Kirk Okumura, and Glenn Stevick of The American College. Original contributors also included Richard Dulisse and Bruce Worsham, formerly of The American College.

The College wishes to thank Dr. Larry Barton, president and CEO of The American College, and David Woods, CEO of the National Association of Insurance and Financial Advisors (NAIFA), for their roles in creating the Financial Services Specialist (FSS) designation in which this book is required reading. Also, The College wishes to thank Walt Woerheide, vice president and dean of The American College, for providing continued support and encouragement in writing this book.

The College would also like to thank the following individuals for their substantial contributions to materials that were included in the book:

Bob Cooper	Dale Johnson
Dave Cordell	Lewis Morgan
Ron Duska	Mike Roszkowski

To all of these individuals, without whom this book would not have been possible, The College expresses its sincere appreciation and gratitude.

About the Authors

Allen C. McLellan, LUTCF, CLU, ChFC, CASL, CFP, is an assistant professor of insurance at The American College. His responsibilities include writing and preparing text materials for LUTC and FSS programs. He also teaches financial planning courses at The College.

Mr. McLellan is editor of *Foundations of Financial Planning: An Overview, Foundations of Financial Planning: The Process,* and *Foundations of Investment Planning,* published by The American College Press. He also writes for *Advisor Today*, the national magazine distributed to members of NAIFA.

Before joining The College, Mr. McLellan served over 21 years as an Air Force Officer. During his military career, he taught mathematics at the Air Force Academy and served as the Director of Evaluation for the Air Force's Squadron Officer School. After his military retirement, he worked for nearly 16 years as an insurance agent, registered representative, and financial planner.

Mr. McLellan earned his BS degree from the U.S. Air Force Academy and his MS in aeronautical engineering from the Air Force Institute of Technology. He is a member of NAIFA, the Air Force Association, and the Military Officers Association of America.

Kirk S. Okumura is an author/editor at The American College. His responsibilities at The College include writing and preparing text materials for the LUTCF and FSS programs. He also teaches insurance and financial planning courses at The College.

Mr. Okumura is co-author of *Essentials of Long-Term Care Insurance* and *Techniques for Exploring Personal Markets;* he is author of *Essentials of Employee Benefits.* All of these books are published by The American College Press. Mr. Okumura also writes articles for *Advisor Today,* the national magazine distributed to members of NAIFA.

Before joining The College, Mr. Okumura worked for State Farm Insurance Company as a supervisor in a regional life/health office and as a trainer in the Pennsylvania regional office's agency training area.

Mr. Okumura earned a BS degree from The Pennsylvania State University.

Glenn E. Stevick, Jr., LUTCF, CLU, ChFC, is an author/editor and assistant professor of insurance at The American College. His responsibilities at The College include writing and preparing text materials for the LUTCF and FSS programs. He also teaches insurance and financial planning courses at The College.

Mr. Stevick is co-author of *Essentials of Long-Term Care Insurance, Techniques for Exploring Personal Markets,* and *Essentials of Life Insurance Products;* he is author of *Techniques for Meeting Client Needs* and *Essentials of Business Insurance.* All of these books are published by The American College. Mr. Stevick also writes articles for *Advisor Today*, the national magazine distributed to members of NAIFA.

Before joining The College, Mr. Stevick worked for New York Life as a training supervisor for 15 years in its South Jersey office. He also served as an agent with New York Life for more than 2 years. Prior to his insurance industry experience, Mr. Stevick taught psychology at the college level and worked in various educational and mental health programs.

Mr. Stevick earned his BA degree from Villanova University and his MA degree from Duquesne University. Mr. Stevick is a 20-year member of NAIFA and a 16-year member of the Society of Financial Service Professionals.

About the Financial Advisor Series

The mission of The American College is to raise the level of professionalism of its students and, by extension, the financial services industry as a whole. As an educational product of The College, the Financial Advisor Series shares in this mission. Because knowledge is the key to professionalism, a thorough and comprehensive reading of each book in the Series will help the practitioner-advisor to better service his or her clients—a task made all the more difficult because the typical client is becoming ever more financially sophisticated with each passing day and demands that his or her financial advisor be knowledgeable about the latest products and planning methodologies. By providing practitioner-advisors in the financial services industry with up-to-date, authoritative information about various marketing and sales techniques, product knowledge, and planning considerations, the books of the Financial Advisor Series will enable many practitioner-advisors to continue their studies so as to develop and maintain a high level of professional competence.

When all books in the Financial Advisor Series are completed, the Series will encompass 16 titles spread across three separate subseries, each with a special focus. The first subseries, *Sales Skills Techniques,* will focus on enhancing the practitioner-advisor's marketing and sales skills but will also cover some product knowledge and planning considerations. The second subseries, *Product Essentials,* will focus on product knowledge but will also delve into marketing and sales skills, as well as planning considerations in many of its books. The third subseries, *Planning Foundations,* will focus on various planning considerations and processes that form the foundation for a successful career as a financial services professional. When appropriate, many of its books will also touch upon product knowledge and sales and marketing skills. Current and planned titles are listed earlier in this book.

Overview of the Book

Foundations of Financial Planning: The Process is structured around the eight-step selling/planning process. It is designed to guide the student through each step of the process to show him or her what financial planning is all about. Chapter 1 begins by identifying the eight steps of the selling/planning process and explaining what financial planning is and how it is conducted. The chapter ends by examining step 1 (identify the prospect) and step 2 (approach the prospect) of the process.

The focus of Chapter 2 is on step 3 (meet the prospect) of the process. The advisor's overriding objective in this step is to establish a relationship with the client that is conducive to financial planning. To achieve this objective, the advisor must be able to communicate effectively with the client.

Chapter 3 addresses step 4 (gather information and establish goals) of the process. With the aid of a fact-finder form, the advisor is able to gather personal and financial information about the client and help the client establish goals. Establishing reasonable, achievable goals is as critical to developing a successful financial plan as information gathering.

Chapter 4 examines several tools and techniques used to develop financial plans. The chapter begins with a discussion of the time value of money and its application to financial planning. It then explores the concept of financial risk tolerance. Financial plans are often developed in conjunction with investment portfolios that are tailored to fit the client's level of risk tolerance. The management of these portfolios is the final topic of this chapter.

The first part of Chapter 5 discusses the preparation of personal financial statements. These statements are used in step 5 (analyze the information) to analyze the client's existing financial situation and to develop a plan to improve that situation. The second part of Chapter 5 identifies the components of the financial plan and explains how they can be used in step 5 to help analyze information. Chapter 6 concentrates on step 6 (develop and present the plan) of the process. Using the components of the plan identified in Chapter 5 , it describes how financial plans are developed and presented to the client.

Chapter 7 deals with step 7 (implement the plan) and step 8 (service the plan), the final two steps of the process. The chapter begins by discussing some issues involved in implementing a plan such as client resistance and the involvement of other professionals. The chapter concludes with a discussion on servicing the plan—that is, monitoring and evaluating the plan on an ongoing basis.

Chapter 8 , the last chapter in the book, discusses funding a college education and the regulation of advisors. Funding a college education is included in the book to illustrate the application of many of the concepts covered in earlier chapters and some of the steps of the process. The final topic is the regulation of advisors, a subject important to all participants in the selling/planning process.

1

The Planning Process and Prospecting

Learning Objectives

An understanding of the material in this chapter should enable the student to

1-1. Describe the eight-step selling/planning process.

1-2. Describe how financial planning is conducted.

1-3. Define the product that financial advisors offer to clients.

1-4. Create an ideal client profile.

1-5. Identify target markets.

1-6. Explain how to position his or her practice.

1-7. Describe methods to build prestige and create awareness.

1-8. Select appropriate prospecting methods.

1-9. Determine an approach method.

1-10. Write and implement an approach script.

Chapter 1 introduces the eight-step selling/planning process (around which the book is structured) and compares it to the traditional six-step financial planning process. The chapter then explains what financial planning is and how it is conducted. The chapter concludes by examining the first two steps of the selling/planning process. Together, these two steps address the critical objective of attracting new clients, the lifeblood of a financial advisor's practice.

WHAT IS FINANCIAL PLANNING?

One factor that has hampered the development of financial planning as a discipline and a profession is that there has been very little agreement among advisors as to what exactly it is. Indeed, it sometimes seems that there are as many definitions of financial planning as there are people who believe they are engaged in it.[2]

---

2. Shelley A. Lee, "What Is Financial Planning, Anyway?" *Journal of Financial Planning*, December 2001, pp. 36–46.

Financial Planning Is a Process

financial planning

Despite this ongoing debate among advisors, *financial planning* can be defined conceptually as a process that accomplishes both of the following:

- determines the client's financial problems and/or financial goals
- develops a plan to solve the client's problems and/or achieve the client's goals

selling/planning process

Whether a single financial problem or goal is being addressed or a comprehensive financial plan is being developed, the financial planning process has six steps: (1) establish and define the advisor-client relationship, (2) determine goals and gather data, (3) analyze and evaluate the data, (4) develop and present a plan, (5) implement the plan, and (6) monitor the plan. Advisors who primarily sell financial products generally view the financial planning process as a *selling/planning process* that has eight steps—that is, six steps similar to steps in the financial planning process preceded by two additional steps. These eight steps are to (1) identify the prospect, (2) approach the prospect, (3) meet the prospect, (4) gather information and establish goals, (5) analyze the information, (6) develop and present the plan, (7) implement the plan, and (8) service the plan. (See Table 1-1 for a comparison of the eight-step selling/planning process with the six-step financial planning process.) Thus, the six-step financial planning process is an integral part of the eight-step selling/planning process.

Table 1-1
Comparing the Eight-Step Selling/Planning Process with the Six-Step Financial Planning Process

Step	Selling/Planning Process	Financial Planning Process	Step
1	Identify the Prospect		
2	Approach the Prospect		
3	Meet the Prospect	Establish and Define the Advisor-Client Relationship	1
4	Gather Information and Establish Goals	Determine Goals and Gather Data	2
5	Analyze the Information	Analyze and Evaluate the Data	3
6	Develop and Present the Plan	Develop and Present a Plan	4
7	Implement the Plan	Implement the Plan	5
8	Service the Plan	Monitor the Plan	6

Although not all financial advisors sell financial products, we have chosen to structure this book around the eight-step selling/planning process because the financial plans that advisors develop are themselves considered products that must be marketed and sold. Except for the few advisors who have prospects calling them for appointments, even fee-only advisors have to market and sell their financial planning expertise in developing plans. In other words, the eight-step selling/planning process reflects the necessity of having to market and prospect that the overwhelming majority of financial advisors face.

comprehensive approach

multiple-purpose approach

single-purpose approach

Advisors who use the selling/planning process in their practices find it accommodating because it can be applied to the full range of a client's financial problems and/or goals using a *comprehensive approach,* and it can also be applied to a smaller subset of those problems and/or goals using a *multiple-purpose approach.* In fact, it can even be applied to a single client problem or goal using a *single-purpose approach.* It is not, however, the range of client problems and/or goals addressed that determines whether an advisor is engaged in financial planning. Rather, it is the advisor's use of the process to address the client's problems and/or goals that is the determining factor.

Steps in the Selling/Planning Process

What follows is a brief description of the selling/planning process. This will give you a bird's-eye perspective of the whole process before we swoop down for a closer look at each step in the process.

In steps 1 and 2 of the selling/planning process, you identify and approach prospects. Step 1 requires marketing and prospecting skills such as defining your product(s) and your ideal client, identifying your target market(s), positioning your practice in your target market(s), building prestige and creating awareness in your target market(s), and selecting your prospecting methods. Step 2 entails asking a prospect for an appointment. Steps 1 and 2 are explored later in this chapter.

In step 3 of the process, you meet with the prospect to mutually determine whether to establish an advisor-client relationship. This requires you to begin developing rapport and establishing credibility with the client. You also need to disclose information to the client about your background, business philosophy, and method of compensation. Communication skills are critical in this step and subsequent steps where you interact with the client.

Once you and the client agree to continue the process, you begin step 4, where you gather information and establish goals. This typically involves the use of a fact-finder form designed to collect information about the client's personal and financial situation, including his or her goals and their priorities.

In step 5 of the process, you review all of the information about the client. You analyze and evaluate the strengths and weaknesses in the client's present financial situation as they affect your ability to solve the client's financial problems and/or achieve the client's financial goals. This may require that some or all of the client's goals be revised. The major tools and techniques that you can use in your step 5 analysis are (1) the time value of money, (2) financial risk tolerance, and (3) personal financial statements.

Step 6, developing and presenting the plan, consists of developing several recommendations as to how the client can best solve his or her financial problems and/or achieve his or her financial goals. Your recommendations are then presented to the client for review and approval.

After you present the plan recommendations to the client for his or her review and approval, your challenge in step 7 is to motivate the client to take action and implement those recommendations. Here, you need to help the client acquire all the products and/or services necessary to implement the plan.

Step 8, servicing the plan, includes responding to client inquiries, evaluating the performance of all implementation vehicles, reviewing changes in the client's circumstances and the financial environment, and meeting on a regular basis to monitor the progress of the plan and to make any necessary changes to it.

The selling/planning process described above is depicted schematically in Figure 1-1. The blocks on the left represent the eight steps in the process; the blocks on the right indicate the main substantive activities that occur in each step.

A specialized application of financial planning is college funding. An additional topic of importance is the regulation of financial advisors.

HOW IS FINANCIAL PLANNING CONDUCTED?

Although many clients could benefit from comprehensive financial planning, they typically are unwilling to invest the time and money that it requires. In fact, except for the wealthy, most clients cannot afford to have a comprehensive plan developed at one time. Moreover, they find it difficult to deal with the totality of their financial problems and/or goals all at once. Instead, they prefer the multiple-purpose approach to financial planning because they have to concentrate on the most pressing of their problems and/or goals during any one consultation. Besides, if these clients participate in several multiple-purpose planning meetings over a period of years, they will eventually have a fairly comprehensive plan in place.

In this book, we refer to this drawn-out planning approach as sequential multiple-purpose financial planning. It encompasses a series of multiple-purpose planning consultations that generally take place over a period of years as the client progresses through the stages of his or her financial life cycle. In fact, some advisors view this approach as a less pure form of comprehensive financial planning because the ultimate goal is for the client to have a comprehensive plan in place after the final multiple-purpose planning meeting.[3]

3. The pure form of comprehensive financial planning occurs when the financial advisor (and his or her team of specialists) completes a comprehensive plan for the client all at one meeting or, more realistically, at several meetings that take place over a relatively short period of time.

Figure 1–1 The Selling/Planning Process

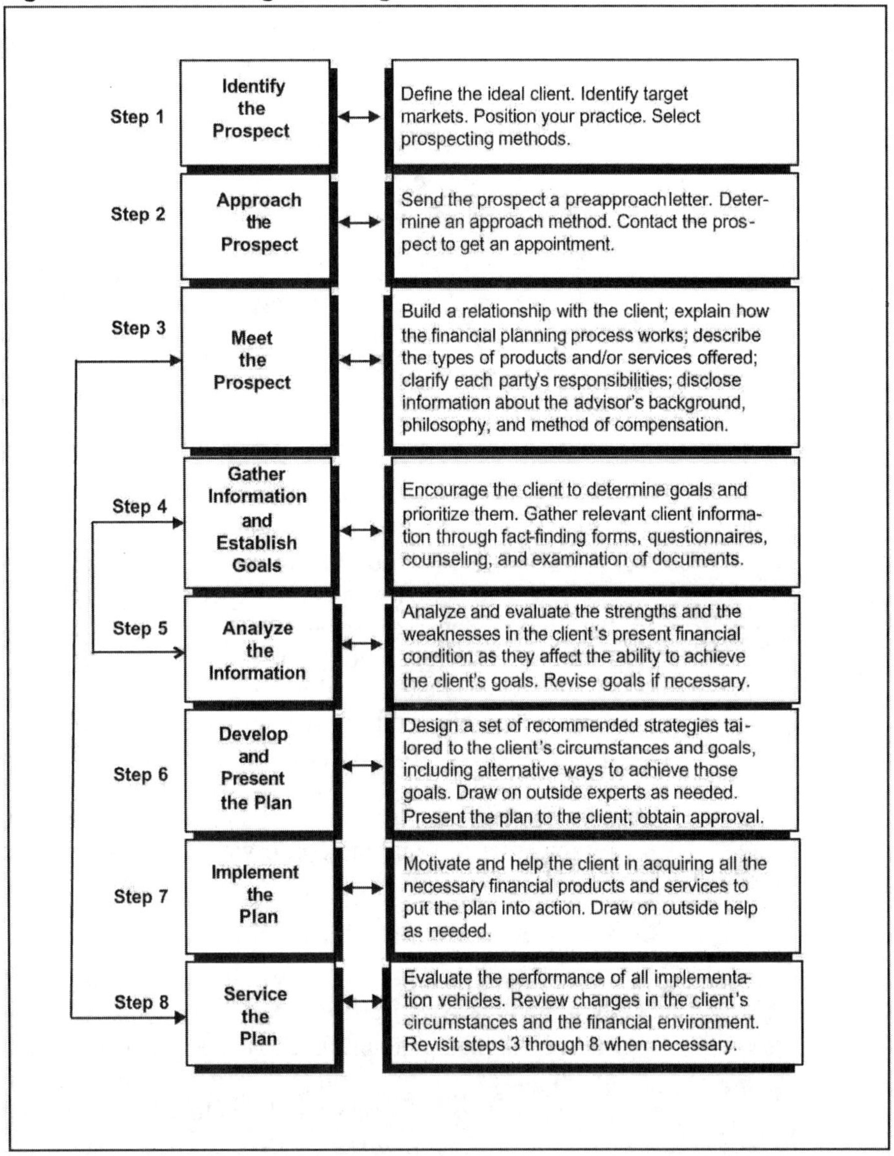

Step 1
Identify the Prospect
Define the ideal client. Identify target markets. Position your practice. Select prospecting methods.
Step 2
Approach the Prospect
Send the prospect a preapproach letter. Determine an approach method. Contact the prospect to get an appointment.
Step 3
Meet the Prospect
Build a relationship with the client; explain how the financial planning process works; describe the types of products and/or services offered; clarify each party's responsibilities; disclose information about the advisor's background, philosophy, and method of compensation.
Step 4
Gather Information and Establish Goals
Encourage the client to determine goals and prioritize them. Gather relevant client information through fact-finding forms, questionnaires, counseling, and examination of documents.
Step 5
Analyze the Information
Analyze and evaluate the strengths and the weaknesses in the client's present financial condition as they affect the ability to achieve the client's goals. Revise goals if necessary.
Step 6
Develop and Present the Plan
Design a set of recommended strategies tailored to the client's circumstances and goals, including alternative ways to achieve those goals. Draw on outside experts as needed. Present the plan to the client; obtain approval.
Step 7
Implement the Plan
Motivate and help the client in acquiring all the necessary financial products and services to put the plan into action. Draw on outside help as needed.
Step 8
Service the Plan
Evaluate the performance of all implementation vehicles. Review changes in the client's circumstances and the financial environment. Revisit steps 3 through 8 when necessary.

Financial Planning Pyramid

financial planning pyramid

One tool that you can use to help clients understand the sequential approach to multiple-purpose financial planning is the *financial planning pyramid* pictured in the following figure. The pyramid illustrates how this approach to financial planning can build a comprehensive plan from the ground up in three sequential stages of multiple-purpose planning. This type of comprehensive plan typically requires several meetings with the client over a period of years.

Figure 1–2 Financial Planning Pyramid

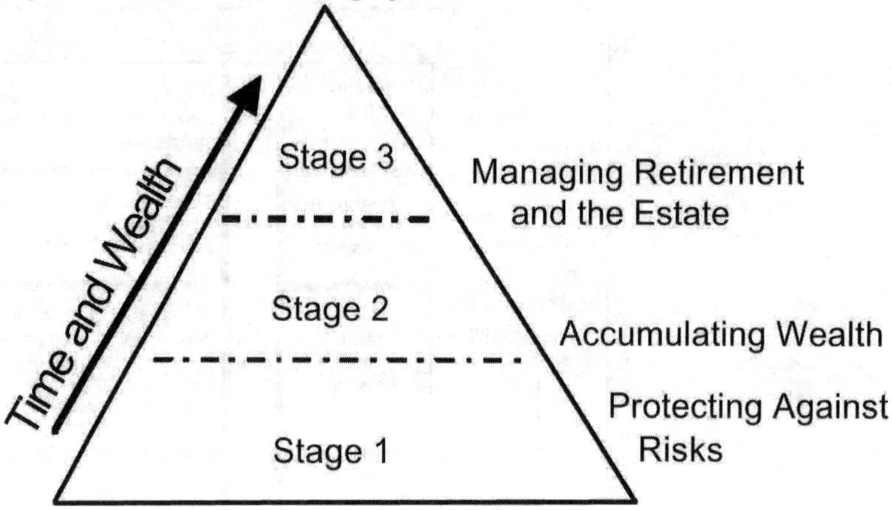

At the first stage of plan development, you concentrate your efforts on protecting the client against unexpected occurrences that could cause financial hardship. You develop a relatively simple plan with emergency savings, insurance coverages, and a properly drawn will. At the second stage, you focus on the client's wealth accumulation objectives. In other words, as the client's financial well-being improves, the focus of the plan shifts from income protection needs to wealth accumulation goals. This typically involves growing money through various types of investments. At the third and final stage, you address retirement and estate goals. These goals focus on the management of retirement assets and the conservation and distribution of the estate.

Content of a Financial Plan

When you prepare a comprehensive financial plan for a client, whether entirely in one consultation or incrementally over a period of time, what should the plan contain? Clearly, comprehensive financial planning is such an ambitious and complex undertaking that it must cover numerous subjects. At a minimum, these subjects should include the major planning areas listed below:

- general principles of financial planning (for example, personal financial statements, client attitudes and behavioral characteristics, and so forth)
- insurance planning and risk management
- employee benefits planning
- investment planning
- income tax planning
- retirement planning
- estate planning

A comprehensive financial plan should address all of these planning areas as they relate to your client. If you do not have the expertise to personally address each of these planning areas in the development of the plan, you should form a team of specialists and serve as its manager. Your role would then be to coordinate the efforts of the team and to contribute expertise in your own field of specialization. If, for some reason, one of these planning areas does not apply to your client, the plan should spell out this fact. This will indicate that you did not overlook an important planning area in the development of the plan but that you investigated and found it not to apply to your client at this time.

In addition to the major planning areas that pertain to almost every client, there are a number of more specialized areas that are relevant to many. These specialized areas are, for the most part, subsets of, and typically involve several of, the major planning areas. However, because all of these specialized areas are unique, they merit separate treatment. They should be part of your client's comprehensive financial plan only if he or she is affected by them. Typically, a single-purpose or multiple-purpose financial plan that is focused on a particular planning need deals with these specialized areas.

The most important of these specialized areas in terms of the number of people it affects is education funding, a topic covered in greater depth in chapter 8. The other specialized areas worthy of mention are those that can be categorized as financial planning for special circumstances. These areas typically include planning for

- divorce
- terminal illness
- nontraditional families
- job change and job loss, including severance packages
- dependents with special needs

As previously mentioned, all of these specialized planning areas are subsets of one or more of the major planning areas. For example, divorce planning could affect every single one of the major planning areas but, nevertheless, should not be part of a comprehensive financial plan unless your client is contemplating divorce. Even then, divorce planning would be better handled under a single-purpose or multiple-purpose financial plan because of its unique aspects and shorter planning horizon than the major planning areas.

FOCUS ON ETHICS
Ethical Behavior and Financial Success

A question that many advisors have asked is, "Is the highly ethical advisor financially rewarded for being ethical?" The answer is maybe, but there is no guarantee. There are certainly some illustrations of the shady advisor reaping significant financial gains. Disciplined ethical conduct by itself does not guarantee financial success.

Perhaps the question should be addressed from a different perspective. Do clients want to do business with someone who really understands financial planning but who has questionable morals? Do clients want to do business with someone whose integrity is unassailable but whose financial planning skills are marginal? The answer to both questions is no.

The skilled financial advisor who is client focused and ethically well-disciplined clearly has the attributes that clients desire and deserve. Again, the practice of ethics provides no guarantees of financial success. It is clear, however, that clients want to do business with financial advisors who have earned their trust and are technically competent.

Format of a Financial Plan

A financial plan, whether comprehensive or not, is essentially a written report to the client regarding your findings and recommendations. This report results from the application of the selling/planning process to the client's present situation to assist the client in solving his or her financial problems and/or achieving his or her financial goals. Although there are as many different formats for a financial plan as there are financial advisors, it is easy to agree that every comprehensive plan should include certain types of information. For example, every comprehensive plan should cover all of the major planning areas. Every plan should be based on SMART goals (that is, goals that are Specific, Measurable, Achievable, Relevant, and have Target date) set by the client. And every plan should be structured around strategies to solve the client's problems and/or achieve his or her goals. In addition, in the process of formulating strategies, assumptions have to be made and should be spelled out in the plan documents. Typical assumptions include the interest rate, the rate of inflation, and the client's financial risk tolerance, to name a few. Finally, every plan is developed around information gathered during a fact-finding process. Much of this information, such as financial statements, should also be included in the plan.

Recognizing that there are many possible formats for organizing all of this information into a written report for the client, one possible format is the order of the 13 components that every comprehensive plan and most complex multiple-purpose plans should include. These components, discussed at length in chapter 5, 6, and 7 are as follows:

1. client goals
2. identification of concerns and problems

3. planning assumptions
4. financial position statement
5. cash flow statement
6. insurance planning and risk management
7. employee benefits planning
8. specialized financial planning goals
9. investment planning
10. income tax planning
11. retirement planning
12. estate planning
13. recommendations

Regardless of the format you adopt for organizing a plan, the important point to remember is that the format of the plan should make it easy for the client to understand and evaluate what is being proposed. Careful organization, as well as the use of graphs, diagrams, and other visual aids, can help in this regard.

Life Cycle Financial Planning

financial life cycle

There are five distinct phases in an individual's *financial life cycle*. Starting at a relatively young age (age 25 or younger), a career-minded person typically will pass through four phases en route to phase five, retirement. These five phases and their corresponding age ranges are as follows:

1. early career (age 25 or younger to age 35)
2. career development (age 35 to age 50)
3. peak accumulation (age 50 to ages 58–62)
4. preretirement (3 to 6 years prior to planned retirement)
5. retirement (ages 62–66 and older)

Together these five phases span a person's entire financial life. Although some people will not experience all of the phases or will spend more or less time in any one phase, the vast majority of career-minded people will go through all five.

As previously indicated, the third step in developing a financial plan is to meet the prospect and establish an advisor-client relationship. Once you have set the ground rules for the financial planning sessions and gathered information about the client, your next task is to lead the client through the goal-setting process. Goal setting requires clients to recognize that there are several phases in their financial life; for young clients, the early career phase is the beginning of that life. The goals that young clients who are in this phase typically set reflect this fact. For example, a client who is in the early career phase often is newly married and has young children, and the client and/or his or her spouse are establishing employment patterns. The client probably is concerned about accumulating funds for a home purchase if he or she has not already done so. As the children grow older, the client begins to think about saving for college. Protecting his or her family from a potential financial disaster due to death or disability is also important, as is building a cash reserve or emergency fund to meet unexpected contingencies. However, the client's goals that pertain to retirement and estate planning generally will not have a very high priority in the first few years of the early career phase, but they still need to be considered if the financial plan is to be a truly comprehensive one.

Once the client has a financial plan, it is incumbent on you to service and monitor that plan. As the client moves into the career development phase of his or her financial life cycle, some goals may need revision. This phase is often a time of career enhancement, upward mobility, and rapid growth in income. The phase usually includes additional accumulation and then expenditure of funds for children's college educations. Moreover, you should recommend coordinating the employee benefits of the client and his or her spouse and integrating them with insurance and investment planning goals.

As the client moves into the peak accumulation phase, you should be servicing the plan in case changes are needed. In this phase, the client is usually moving toward maximum earnings and has the greatest opportunity for wealth accumulation. The phase may include accumulating funds for special purposes, but it is usually a continuation of trying to meet the goals set for the major planning areas.

The preretirement phase often involves winding down both the career and income potential, and restructuring investment assets to reduce risk and enhance income. There is a further emphasis on tax planning and evaluating retirement plan distribution options relative to income needs and tax consequences. Throughout this phase, you should be actively involved in keeping the client's financial plan on target to meet all of his or her goals.

The final phase in the client's financial life cycle is retirement. If you have kept the client's financial plan fine-tuned, then this phase should be a time of enjoyment for the client, with a comfortable retirement income and sufficient assets to preserve purchasing power. While all of the major planning areas should have been receiving attention throughout the client's financial life cycle, now is the time for you to make certain that the client's estate plan is in order.

life cycle financial planning

The advisor who services a client's personal financial plan throughout the client's financial life cycle is practicing *life cycle financial planning*. A financial plan that is developed for a relatively young client needs to be reviewed and revised periodically as the client ages and passes through the phases of the financial life cycle. Many of the client's financial goals will need adjusting as life's circumstances change; having the right goals is critical to creating a successful financial plan. Your role as an advisor in setting goals is to help the client establish SMART goals and to set a positive tone for the entire selling/planning process. The process encompasses not only the development of the client's first financial plan but also any future revisions and/or modifications to that plan.

The content of a comprehensive financial plan should, as already mentioned, include a discussion of each of the major planning areas. Financial planning is a process that should be ongoing throughout the client's financial life. That is why financial planning over the client's financial life is often called life cycle financial planning. Whichever phase of the financial life cycle the client is currently in strongly influences the priority given of goals for each planning area.

IDENTIFY THE PROSPECT

As we have seen, the first step in the selling/planning process is to identify the prospect. A haphazard approach to identifying prospects will most likely result in a dearth of prospects and a great deal of frustration. Therefore, it is important for you to create and implement a marketing plan that will generate a flow of the types of prospects you want to approach. This will require you to

- define the product
- create an ideal client profile
- identify target markets
- position your practice
- build prestige and create awareness
- select prospecting methods

Define the Product

A marketing plan begins with defining the product you are selling from your clients' perspective. What are your clients really buying? Think of a financial plan as a product that has three parts: (1) a tangible written document or documents, as evidenced by a report and perhaps a will, trust, and/or insurance policy, (2) the solution to a problem or the attainment of a goal that the written document addresses, and (3) the knowledge, ideas, and skills of the advisor. All three parts of the product are important, and a marketing plan should take all three of them into account.

Tangible Written Document(s)

At the end of the selling/planning process, your client will own a tangible written document or documents that spells out the specifics of the personal financial plan. This, however, is not what your client is paying for. Your client is paying for the financial security and success that comes from implementing and servicing the plan. And this can only come from the other two parts of the product.

Solution to a Problem or Attainment of a Goal

In addition to the tangible written document(s), a financial plan has an intangible part that manifests itself in the solution to your client's financial problems and/or the attainment of financial goals. As a financial advisor, it is critical for you to understand that the products and/or services you sell to implement the plan are the means that enable your client to solve financial problems and/or attain financial goals. Moreover, problems and goals have two dimensions. There is the obvious financial one and the not so obvious emotional one. However, even though the emotional dimension is less obvious, it is more important than the financial dimension in terms of marketing, because it determines whether your client will act or even be interested in solving problems and/or attaining goals. For example, it is much easier for you to market mutual funds if your client believes that investing in them is his or her ticket to financial freedom.

Advisor

The third part of the product is the advisor. Arguably, the greatest difference between a financial plan your competitor prepares and one you prepare is you, beginning with your knowledge, ideas, and skills. How well do you know your client's financial problems and goals? What ideas do you have to help him or her address them? How skilled are you in carrying out the selling/planning process?

However, in the competitive field of financial planning, you may find that your knowledge, ideas, and skills alone are not enough to differentiate you from the competition. Your personality, life experiences, hobbies, and so forth may also play a role in distinguishing you. In fact, marketing gurus Peter Montoya and Tim Vandehey argue in *The Brand Called You* that you should focus on marketing yourself and not the products you sell. They say that "you should highlight those characteristics which make you stand out from the crowd ...."[4]

Practical Application

Marketing your products and/or services begins with making an inventory of each of the three parts of your financial plans. A good approach is first to list the products you sell and/or the services you provide to implement plans. Next, for each product or service you listed, indicate the problem(s) it solves and/or the goal(s) it helps to attain. For each of these problems and/or goals, identify any special knowledge, ideas, and/or skills needed. Then, list your knowledge, ideas, and skills. Finally, take stock of your personality, life experiences, hobbies, and so on that make you unique and set you apart from other advisors.

Completing this inventory will help you identify the needs of your target market that you can satisfy. In addition, it will enable you to pinpoint knowledge and skill gaps that you must address to maximize other marketing opportunities within your target market. Finally, it will allow you to define your unique value, build prestige, and create awareness to distinguish yourself from the competition in your target market.

---

4. Peter Montoya and Tim Vandehey, *The Brand Called You.* (Costa Mesa, CA: Millennium Advertising, 1999), p. 30.

Example

Melanie sells mutual funds. Here is how she might complete an inventory of her target market's problems/goals and her knowledge/skills:

Problems/Goals	Knowledge/Skill
• saving for retirement	• retirement funding vehicles • retirement income gap calculation • retiree health insurance • long-term care insurance • cash flow analysis • risk tolerance • asset allocation • diversification • knowledge of fund family details

If Melanie's knowledge and skills match those needed for saving for retirement, she would be well suited to market mutual funds as a retirement savings vehicle.

Create an Ideal Client Profile

Next, you need to identify the type of prospect you want to approach. This will enable you to focus your prospecting and allow you to work with prospects who will become long-term clients. The advantages of doing this include

- making your job easier because you will receive more referrals
- working with prospects who are likely to become clients
- avoiding those prospects with whom an advisor-client relationship would be difficult
- making your business more profitable

Now, let us look at how you create an ideal client profile.

How to Create an Ideal Client Profile

Think about your most recent clients. Then make a list of the 20 best clients in terms of their profitability and the enjoyment you received from working with them, indicating the basic demographic information and personal attributes that made working with each one so enjoyable. (Note: If you are shifting the focus of your practice, your ideal client profile should reflect this shift if it means that the type of clients you want to work with will change.)

Demographic information is fairly easy to identify. It typically includes age, gender, marital status, geographic location, family size, religion, and so forth. With the demographic information, you should also include the financial value of each client to your business (as well as the amount of business he or she referred to you). In contrast, identifying personal attributes takes more thought because you are trying to determine why you enjoyed working with the client. Here are some questions to ask yourself that can help with this task:

- What personality traits make working with this client so enjoyable?
- What does this client think is important about life? What does he or she value?
- What are this client's attitudes toward financial planning and related topics?
- What type of lifestyle does this client have (modest, moderate, or luxurious)?
- What needs of this client were you able to satisfy? (Express his or her needs in terms of problems you are helping to solve and goals you are helping to achieve.)

To create the most accurate client profile, you should also consider the characteristics and attributes your best clients do not have. This entails profiling the 10 worst clients you recently worked with to determine why you did not enjoy working with them.

Once you have completed profiling both your best and worst clients, take a piece of paper and make a chart with two columns. The first column heading should be "What I Want." The second column heading should be "What I Don't Want." Then examine your profiles for trends. Demographics and attributes that repeatedly show up in the best and worst profiles should be placed in the appropriate column. For example, if four of your worst clients are overanalytical, that characteristic should appear in the "What I Don't Want" column. The following is an example of characteristics and attributes of one advisor's best and worst clients.

Example

What I Want	What I Don't Want
• has household income of $65,000 or more	• overanalytical
• understands basic principles of investing	• unreliable
• desires face-to-face interaction	• dishonest
• values family	• price shopper
• needs help with retirement and education planning	• do-it-yourselfer
• has investable assets of $70,000 or more	

You can now create a profile of your ideal client from the lists of traits you want your ideal client to have and those you do not want him or her to have. As you create the profile, translate the list of negative traits you do not want your client to have into positive ones you desire. For instance, if you do not want a do-it-yourselfer, then you want a delegator or someone who seeks advice. Using the two columns in the example above, the ideal client can be described as shown in the example below.

Example

My ideal client is someone who

- has a household income of $65,000 or more
- has investable assets of $70,000 or more
- understands basic principles of investing
- wants a face-to-face relationship
- desires advice from a competent professional about retirement and education planning
- is family oriented
- appreciates the value of good advice and is willing to pay for it
- is reliable and honest

Practical Applications

The most obvious application for your ideal client profile is to focus your prospecting activity. Compare your new or current prospects with the profile to determine whether you should continue to pursue them, eliminating those who do not match the profile. In addition, you should periodically repeat the profiling process to see if your ideal client has changed. For example, you may discover that you are now working predominantly with prospects who have investable assets of $150,000 or more instead of the $70,000 or more you originally listed on the profile.

Another application is to determine who your "A" clients are—that is, those clients to whom you provide your top level of service. This will enable you to create a service strategy that caters to these top clients.

Additional worthwhile applications (some of which are discussed later in this chapter) are as follows:

- Use the profile to guide you in your marketing strategies and materials.
- Post your ideal client profile on your website and in your office.
- Give the profile to friends, family, centers of influence (defined later in this chapter), and current clients so they know with whom you want to work.

Identify Target Markets

target market

Now that you have developed your ideal client profile, you need to identify your target markets—that is, large groups of people who match your ideal client profile. A *target market* is an identifiable and accessible group of people with common characteristics and common needs who regularly communicate with one another. The group must be sufficiently large so that you do not run out of prospects but small enough so that your reputation as a trustworthy and competent advisor precedes you. Chances are, you are already working with one or more target markets.

The process of identifying target markets involves the following steps:

- Identify and segment your natural markets.
- Research potential target markets.
- Write a description of your potential target markets.
- Test potential target markets.

Identify and Segment Your Natural Markets

natural market

When you read the section on creating an ideal client profile, you may have felt that you were identifying your *natural market*—that is, a group of people to whom you have a natural affinity or to whom you have access because of similar values, lifestyles, experiences, attitudes, and so on. There is a difference, however. Your ideal client profile is generally a subset of your natural market. There are people in your natural market who do not meet your ideal client profile. For example, you may have a great deal in common with people from a certain profession, but they may not meet the income and net worth requirements of your ideal client profile.

The Natural Market: Affinity and Access
Affinity refers to the part of your natural market formed by your friends, family, and acquaintances. You have a certain comfort level with them because of certain commonalities. In fact, many of them are in your ideal client profile. Your natural market, however, is not limited to people you know. It also refers to people to whom you have access for reasons other than a personal relationship or acquaintance.
Access means that you can approach these people and gain entry to their group because of something in common. For example, you may have young children. Part of your natural market is the parents of your children's friends or perhaps the parents of all of the children in the school your children attend (if you think big).

Because of the relationship between your ideal client profile and natural market, your natural market is where you should begin in defining your target market. To do this, use the information you compiled when you created your ideal client profile and list the following for each prospect:

- interests (community interests, hobbies, social organizations, religious groups, clubs, alumni organizations, sororities, fraternities, and so on)
- ethnicity or culture (if there is a larger market reflecting these)
- occupation or profession
- employer

market segments

Now divide your natural market into different *market segments*—that is, groups of people with common characteristics and common needs. The people of each group should be distinct in terms of their characteristics and/or needs. There generally are four factors used to segment markets: geography, demography, psychography, and behavior.

Geography

For the financial services industry, geographic segmentation is typically based on county, city, borough, neighborhood, and so forth. Many times, however, geography is not a factor, but keep your eyes open in case it is.

Demography

Demographic segmentation includes variables such as age, gender, education, ethnicity, occupation, income, size of family, marital status, religion, generational cohort, (baby boom, generation X, the silent generation, and so forth), and family situation (single, married with kids and a single income, married with no kids and two incomes, empty nester(s), divorced, and so on).

Psychography

Psychographic segmentation groups people by lifestyle. Variables include activities, attitudes, values, interests, and hobbies. For example, you may have a few clients who are running enthusiasts, play in a softball league, participate in a bowling league, and so forth.

Behavior

Finally, behavioristic segmentation groups people by their buying and usage behaviors. This type of segmentation categorizes people according to life events (birth of a child, marriage, divorce, and so on), type of user (soloist, collaborator, delegator), brand loyalty, benefits sought (convenience, price, quality), and so forth. For example, you could find that upcoming nuptials triggered a few of your best clients to seek your financial advice. It could be a coincidence, but then again, it may be a great target marketing opportunity.

Buying behaviors are probably the greatest predictor of future purchases. A good way to explore this marketing concept is to ask your clients about life events that are occurring now or are expected to occur before or during the planning process. After the financial plan is implemented, ask your clients why they chose to do business with you. Then track their answers to both of these questions to see if there are any trends.

The task of dividing your natural market into different market segments can be a challenge. Here are some helpful hints to make it easier:

- Consider using a computer spreadsheet program to conduct your analysis. Code each characteristic and indicate if your top clients have it.
- Look for common needs or reasons for using your financial products and/or services. If there is no commonality, you do not have a good market segment.
- Analyze your top clients to see if there are any characteristics that the majority of them possess.
- One or more characteristics should reflect possible ways to identify and access a market segment. Such characteristics might include occupation or profession, employer, activities (working out at the same gym, joining the same club, and so on), neighborhood, and so forth. If there are no distinguishing characteristics that enable you to identify and access the market segment, you do not have a target market.

Research Potential Target Markets

In this step, the first objective is to determine whether a market segment is a target market. You know that the market segment already has common characteristics and common needs. What you need to determine are the following:

- Does the size or value of the potential target market warrant your time and effort?
- Are you able to identify members easily, and are they accessible for you to approach them for an appointment?
- Do members communicate with one another either formally (newsletter, association magazine, and so on) or informally (word of mouth)? If so, how?

A good first step to answering these questions is to conduct initial research on the Internet, at a library, or a local chamber of commerce (see the box titled "Market Research Aids"). Ideally, you can answer these questions before you conduct a market survey because market surveys require a commitment of time and resources.

Example

Cecil is looking at targeting real estate agents in Chester County, Pennsylvania. He does a search for a realtor association in Chester County, using an Internet search engine. He discovers the Suburban West REALTORS® Association, which covers Chester and Delaware counties. Through this website, he learns that there are 4,400 members. Some members are not realtors but businesspeople who provide products and services related to the real estate industry.

From this website, Cecil has determined that the target market is large enough to warrant his time and effort. The existence of the website gives him reason to believe there is a communication network. Also, he has access to a database of names, numbers, and addresses of real estate agents for market research and, ultimately, prospecting.

Once you have conducted your initial research and eliminated market segments that are too small, have low profitability potential, do not have a communication network, and/or have members who are not easily identifiable and accessible, the remaining market segments should meet the strict definition of a target market. From these, select your best potential target markets and prepare to conduct a market survey. Surveys can provide a number of benefits. For example, you can get firsthand information about the members of the market, not just outdated statistics from a commercial or government source. Moreover, the members of the market you interview may notice your efforts, which will let them know that you can help solve their problems. This alone can build your prestige and create awareness of you in your role as an advisor. In fact, it is an excellent first step to prospecting within your target market. You can meet prospective clients and build advisor-client relationships.

The primary purpose of your market survey is to gather enough information about the market to enable you to decide if it is worth penetrating. Thus, you must first determine exactly what information you need to collect. At a minimum, you should collect enough information to allow you to accomplish the following:

- Confirm the distinguishing characteristics of members of the target market.
- Understand the problems and goals common to most members, especially financial problems and goals.
- Determine how members communicate with one another, especially about financial problems and goals.
- Understand how members perceive the financial products and/or services you provide.
- Determine the competition's marketing efforts and success within the target market.

Market Research Aids

An excellent resource is *The Lifestyle Market Analysis*, which gives demographic and psychographic information for 210 designated market areas all over the United States. One report gives demographic information about designated market areas such as the percentage of the population that has a certain occupation, household income, children, and so forth. Another report gives psychographic information about designated market areas such as the percentage of the population who invest, participate in certain sports, have certain hobbies and interests, and so on. You may be able to find a copy of *The Lifestyle Market Analysis* at your public library. For more information, see srds.com.

In addition, there are many other Internet resources:

Free Sites

U.S. Census Bureau	census.gov
Statistical Abstract of the U.S.	census.gov/prod/www/statistical-abstract-us.html
County and City Data Book	census.gov/statab/www/ccdb.html
The Social Statistics Briefing Room	whitehouse.gov/fsbr/ssbr.html (varies by state)
State Chamber of Commerce	

Search Engines (Free)

Google	google.com
Hotbot	hotbot.com

Pay Sites

The American Marketing Association	ama.org
ESRI Business Information Solutions	esribis.com
American Demographics	adage.com

Therefore, design your survey questions accordingly. The survey should be thorough but concise; you do not want to overwhelm your participants. Keep the number of questions under 10 if you can. (A list of sample questions appears in the box below.)

Speak to individuals in your target market so your information comes directly from the source. Ask several market members to participate in your survey, assuring them that your purpose is not to sell them something but to find out more about them and the target market to which they belong. Offer each participant the opportunity to see the results of your survey. This may help you set up your first appointments with market members.

Market Survey Sample Questions

These sample questions have worked well in past market surveys.

Questions regarding characteristics

- What attitudes and interests do you share with others in your market?
- If an outsider went to a convention for members of your market, what impressions would he or she get from meeting members?
- Is there something special or interesting that members in your market have in common? Why is this common to your market?

Questions regarding the common needs of market members

- What is your number one financial concern? What do people like you do to solve this concern?
- What are your common problems and concerns?
- If you could have a day's fee paid that would allow you to hire a good financial advisor to solve a problem for members of your market, what would you have that person do? Why?
- What kind of articles or topics do you read about in your market's newsletter or magazine?
- What type of financial articles would you like to see? Why?

Questions regarding how the market communicates within itself

- What do people in your market read to keep up with the latest information?
- What industries, associations, or clubs support your market?
- How often do you get together with other market members, and what do you do when that happens?

Questions about the perception of the products and services you sell

- How do you feel about [type of product or service]? How important do you feel it is? Why?
- What determines how you buy [product or service]? Price? Quality? Brand name? Customer service? Convenience? Other?
- Who or where would you go to find information about [product or service]?

Questions regarding competition

- Who comes to mind when members in your market think of [your products and services]?
- How do you know about [name of a competitor]? Does [competitor] send you mail or e-mail? Does [competitor] advertise? Where?
- What reputation does [competitor] have among members in your market?

Write a Description of Your Potential Target Markets

Once you have completed your research, write a description of your potential target market. Your description should highlight common characteristics and needs and identify how members communicate with each other, as shown in the following example.

Example

Target market: math teachers in the Philadelphia area who are also parents

Common characteristics: analytical, concerned about their children's educations, and somewhat risk averse; average salary for Pennsylvania teachers around $45,000 per year

Common needs: education planning and retirement planning

Communication network: 1,100-member organization for math teachers (ATMOPAV) that meets regularly and publishes a quarterly newsletter (focusing on teaching concepts and ideas) and has a website (atmopav.com)

Test Potential Target Markets

Before you spend time and money targeting a market in earnest, test it out. Identify several prospects in the market and approach them. Evaluate them as a sample of the market to determine the following:

- How much income can you expect to generate from members of this market?
- How many referrals can you expect members of this market to provide?
- How responsive are the members of this market to your products and services?
- How accessible are the members of this market?
- What are the members' success ratios (calls per initial meetings, initial meetings per fact-finding sessions, and so forth)?
- How much do you enjoy working with members of this market?

In addition, you should keep gathering information about your potential target market to determine how to position your practice, effectively build prestige and create awareness, and prospect efficiently.

Position Your Practice

Thus far, you have defined the product, created an ideal client profile, and identified target markets. Now you need to decide how to position your practice in your target market.

Study the Competition

As part of your market research, you should inquire about your competition. Your position in the market is always relative to the competition. At a minimum, you need to know the following:

- Who is your competition?
- What are they identifying as their unique value? In other words, what are they giving as the reason to do business with them?
- How long have they been targeting this market?
- How are they gaining access to the market?
- How are they building prestige within the market?
- What are their strengths and weaknesses?
- How does the market view them?

Remember, your goal is to present a unique value to your target market that only you can offer. Be aware that if you are successful, your competition will try to mimic your approach. Therefore, stay on top of your competition so you can keep yourself distinct in your target market.

Define Your Unique Value

You are now ready to define how you will provide value to your target market. To do this, you need to determine what distinguishes you from the competition and what you can do that others cannot do. This is why you need to take inventory of all you bring to the table. The more your product (that is, the tangible written document(s), the solutions, and you) uniquely meets the needs of your target market, the more you will stand out from the competition.

Another important way for you to offer value is through relationships with other professionals. At a basic level, you may be able to provide greater value through strategic alliances with other noncompeting financial advisors. You may be a gifted networker who seems to know everyone. If so, you can offer value by referring clients to professionals outside of the financial services arena.

The bottom line is that you must define yourself in a way that differentiates you from the competition in your target market.

Define How You Want to Be Perceived

Related to defining your unique value is defining how you want to be perceived in your target market. What do you want your reputation to be? It is important to establish yourself in the minds of the prospects in your target market as the advisor of choice. Identify personal characteristics and interests to which prospects in your target market will respond favorably. These are your personal brands for your target market.

Build Prestige and Create Awareness

After you have identified your unique value and defined what you want your reputation to be, you need to build your prestige and create awareness in your target market. The following are some of the standard ways to accomplish this.

Public Persona

Although your reputation is built over time, prospects typically decide whether to do business with you based on their first impression. They judge you by your dress, posture, tone of voice, and behavior. Because you get only one chance to make a good first impression, know what image you want to present to your target market.

Start with your personal appearance. Look professional and successful with well-groomed hair, clean hands and nails, polished shoes, and well-kept clothes. However, the way you do this depends on your market. A Rolex wristwatch and expensive three-piece suit would not be appropriate if your target market consists of middle-class families.

Make sure that your office is professional and clean. Matching furniture and an organized desk communicate success and a businesslike persona. If your desk is cluttered, the prospect may be concerned about the safeguarding of his or her personal information.

Finally, and most important, the public perception of your character matters. This means that you must treat people with respect and dignity and watch what you say. If you cannot say anything nice, do not say anything at all. Avoid questionable jokes and remarks that touch on topics that offend others. Always maintain the utmost integrity.

Personal Brochure

You may want to use a one-page personal brochure or résumé to introduce yourself to a prospect. In many cases, this is the prospect's first impression of you, so the brochure should not only communicate the desired perception you want projected, but it should also cater to your ideal client. To effectively do this, you need to understand what your ideal client would want to know.

Although no two brochures are exactly the same, there are some standard pieces of information you should have in yours:

- your name and contact information, including website, if applicable
- your biographical information (the length depends on what your ideal client would want to know about you)
- your professional experience and credentials (designations, business licenses, and so forth)
- the products and/or services you offer

10-Second Commercial

Socializing provides an opportunity for you to create awareness and interest in what you do. When people ask, "What do you do for a living?" you should have a short response that is relevant and interesting. A response like "I am a financial planner" tells people how you make money and what you can do for them. However, it is neither interesting nor attention grabbing. In contrast, consider a response like this, "Do you know what cartographers do? [People typically respond with a no, but even if they say yes, you give your answer.] They make maps that help people reach their destinations. Well, I do something similar for people. I make financial maps that help people reach their financial destinations. Do you have such a map?"

Here are some tips for creating a 10-second commercial:

- Ask a question that pertains to a prospect's need for your services. The question should position your response to be a solution to a problem or question that the prospect might be asking.
- Follow up your commercial by stating your value in terms of the results you achieve for clients.
- Be creative and interesting, but follow your company guidelines. They may restrict the way you can describe your work. Because of today's compliance issues, exercise caution and do not misrepresent the products and/or services you sell or what you do.
- End with a question that measures the prospect's interest.
- Have a business card with you to give the prospect if you feel it is appropriate.

The key is to customize your commercial to the prospects and refer to a need that they might have. By doing so, you are not only creating awareness about your products and services; you are also creating interest—and interest will eventually get you an appointment.

Local Organizations

Get involved in a local civic or service organization about which you (and your target market) are passionate. Involvement can be at various levels, ranging from sponsorship to leadership. At a low end of the involvement continuum is sponsorship. It typically requires some monetary expenditure but minimal time commitment. In the middle of the involvement continuum is an active member. If you join an organization, you should be enthusiastic about its cause and make the necessary commitment of time, interest, and money. At the high end of the involvement continuum is leadership. Obviously, this requires a much higher level of commitment. Therefore, if you seek a leadership position in an organization, make sure your involvement will not hinder your business activities and other important personal relationships.

Local Media

Make yourself available to the local media (print, radio, and TV). Contact journalists and let them know that you can provide expert opinions and quotes on a list of financial planning issues. By helping them, you can showcase your expertise and competence. Furthermore, if you enjoy writing, see if local newspapers and organizations with newsletters need financial planning articles to fill their copy. You may be able to obtain reprints of these articles to send to prospects to build your prestige and credibility.

Mail

Mass mailing to the general public is expensive and inefficient. Mailing to prospects in your target market, however, can precondition them to meet with you when you approach them. Make sure that the message you are sending them is appropriate for their situation.

Speaking to Groups

If you have public speaking skills, giving speeches or teaching classes is a great way to showcase your financial planning expertise with minimal expense. In fact, in the case of adult education classes, you could even earn a few dollars to compensate you for your time and effort. The primary goals of these speaking and teaching engagements are to promote your reputation and expertise as a financial advisor who can help people solve their financial problems and/or attain their financial goals. It is important, however, not to overtly prospect or showcase your products while giving speeches or teaching classes. In fact, in many cases it would be inappropriate. However, placing your contact information on handouts is a subtle and acceptable way of marketing your practice.

Advertising

If you determine that specific advertising can reach your target market, it is money well spent. Otherwise, advertising to the undifferentiated general public is not a good use of your money.

Internet Website

Is an Internet presence critical to your success? Most likely it is, because the number of households with Internet access increases every year. As a governing principle, your Internet presence should reflect the wants, needs, and tastes of your ideal client.

At a bare minimum, your website should contain information about you and your staff, your products and/or services, how to contact you, your philosophy on financial planning, and practical information that a prospect and client can use. This practical information can include helpful articles or links to articles on financial planning topics, as well as other items of interest for your target market such as

- a question-and-answer page (an advice column)
- case studies (describing the financial benefits you provided for a few of your ideal clients)
- worksheets (to help clients do budgeting, retirement planning, education planning, and so on)
- a calendar of events such as seminars, client appreciation days, community events you sponsor, and other events that may be of interest to your target market

As you (or a professional) design your website, you should be aware of any regulations that may apply. For example, if you are a registered representative with a broker/dealer, you probably need to receive approval for the materials you plan to post on your website. Make sure you know any limitations that apply to you.

The Right Methods to Build Prestige and Create Awareness

The methods you choose to build prestige and create awareness depend on several factors, including access to the target market, receptiveness of the methods, cost in both time and money, and your personal abilities. To gain access to your target market, begin by asking yourself several questions about its members, such as the following:

- Where do they shop?
- Where do they exercise?
- To which organizations do they belong?
- What publications and newspapers do they read?
- Who is influential in their financial decision-making process?

With this information, identify possible methods to use, rejecting those that would not be well received or that would be cost prohibitive in time or money. In general, work toward your strengths and passions; avoid using methods that are inconsistent with who you are. The inconsistencies will be obvious and will have a negative effect on your reputation.

Select Prospecting Methods

There are several tried-and-true prospecting methods. With your creativity, you should be able to adapt them to fit your market and personality. The guiding principle for selecting methods is to use those methods that generate the best clients. All things being equal, the most effective method over the years has been referrals.

Referrals

referrals

Successful advisors have found referrals, or recommendations, to be a very efficient and effective means to generate an endless list of prospects. *Referrals* are people to whom you are introduced by someone who knows and values your work. In their highest form, referrals are unsolicited and come to you because of the enthusiastic recommendations they received from your satisfied clients. Until your practice evolves to this level, you will have to ask for referrals.

You should pave the way for referrals early on in the selling/planning process by creating the expectation of receiving them from the prospect if he or she appreciates what you are doing. For example, during the initial meeting, you might say, "Mr. and/or Ms. Prospect, as we work together, if you find what we are talking about to be important and valuable, then give me the opportunity to meet with people you know and care about so that I may help them, too." Then when you ask the prospect for referrals, it will not come as a surprise.

The best time to ask the prospect for referrals is when he or she indicates an appreciation for you and/or your products and services. It could be after the plan is implemented. Or it could be anytime during the planning process after the prospect makes a positive comment like, "I am so glad you told me that. I did not know that mutual fund was available to me." Even if the prospect does not implement the plan, ask him or her about the value of the process. If he or she has a favorable opinion of you and the process, ask for referrals.

Life Events

There are certain life events that create a heightened awareness of financial needs. These events are

- graduating from college
- starting the first job
- receiving a promotion
- changing employers
- getting married
- purchasing a home
- having children
- getting a divorce
- starting a business
- retiring

When you ask the prospect for referrals, use your ideal client profile to indicate the type of referral you are looking for. You could even give the prospect a copy of your client profile and explain that this is the type of client you service best. In addition, you may find it helpful to describe several life events to the prospect that cause people to be more open to discussing financial matters. Ask the prospect if he or she knows any people who are experiencing one of these life events. If the prospect knows someone, ask him or her for a referral.

Center of Influence (COI)

center of influence (COI)

By definition, a *center of influence (COI)* is an influential person who knows you favorably and agrees to introduce or recommend you to others. Although a client may become an effective COI, just as a COI may become a client, neither is necessary for your relationship with a COI to be beneficial.

In general, you will find that COIs

- are active in the community or a sphere of influence
- are sought out for advice by the community or within their sphere of influence
- seek to communicate with others
- are givers, not takers

Good COIs know the people in your target market regardless of their occupation or profession. However, there are some occupations and professions that deal directly with your target market and finding COIs in these could prove very profitable. Examples include

- attorneys
- CPAs
- other advisors whose products do not compete with yours
- members of a golf club
- members of a volunteer organization

After you have identified some possible COIs, you will need to set up meetings with them. These meetings are as important as appointments with clients. Therefore, plan your presentation. Keep it brief and consistent with your approach. For example, if you are meeting with a community leader, the goal of your presentation should be to show how the COI can help others by referring them to you. To accomplish this objective, be prepared to do the following:

- Explain the negative impact that the particular issue you are highlighting will have on individuals and, if applicable, society as a whole.
- Illustrate the impact of the issue with personal stories.
- Explain how purchasing your products and/or services can prevent people from experiencing this negative impact.
- Give the COI some practical actions that he or she can take to help.

You will probably want to ask the COI for referrals. If so, give him or her a copy of your ideal client profile. Although referrals are important, there may be other ways the COI can help you. For example, if the COI is the leader of a local business association, you can approach him or her about giving an educational presentation to the association.

Networking

networking

Networking is the mutual sharing of ideas and clients with other professionals whose work does not compete with yours. For networking to be successful, there must be open lines of communication among all parties.

Most networking groups have the same general rules. Membership is limited to one person from each profession, whether insurance, real estate, stock brokerage, and so forth. Each person attending the meeting is required to bring a prescribed number of names.

If you can find an existing networking group in your community, it might be worthwhile to investigate joining it to provide you with a steady stream of prospects.

Seminars

Seminars are a prospecting method in which you conduct an educational and motivational meeting for a group of people who are interested in your topic. They generally are effective because they accomplish three key objectives. First, they enable you to increase participants' awareness of their financial needs. Second, they cast you in the role of a financial expert who can help the participants meet those financial needs. Third, and most important, because of your success in accomplishing the first two objectives, seminars enable you to identify several prospects at one time from among the participants.

If you recall from our earlier discussion, it may be inappropriate to ask attendees at group presentations for contact information. Seminars, however, are different from group presentations. Seminar participants expect you to ask them for contact information so you can follow up and approach them for appointments.

APPROACH THE PROSPECT

Until you have the luxury of a constant stream of prospects calling you for appointments, you will have to be proactive. Thus, the second step in the selling/planning process is approaching the prospect. This step requires you to contact the prospects you identified so you can set up appointments with them for initial meetings. The tasks involved in completing this step are to

- send a preapproach letter
- determine an approach method
- write an approach script
- implement the approach

Send a Preapproach Letter

The purpose of sending a preapproach letter to the prospects you identified is to create awareness of who you are and what you can do for them. You want to precondition them to meet with you when you call. They will be less inclined to do so if they have no idea who you are and what you can do for them.

How do you feel when you receive a call without any prior warning? If you react like most people, you are suspicious and defensive and do not listen to what the caller says. You are too busy thinking, "Who is this and how can I get rid of him or her?" The use of a preapproach letter introduces you to the prospect before you call.

In cases where the prospect's name is a referred lead, the preapproach letter should also mention the name of the referrer, if possible. This will give more legitimacy to your phone call.

Determine an Approach Method

There are two main ways to approach a prospect for an appointment: by telephone and face-to-face. The most common (and the one that we will spend time discussing) is the telephone approach. Everyone has a telephone, and in the time you contact one prospect using a face-to-face approach, you could have contacted several prospects using a telephone approach. Note, however, that a face-to-face approach may work better for prospecting small businessowners.

Write an Approach Script

In either case, you will need to know what you will say. Many advisors balk at the words "telephone script." They feel that a script will restrict them or cause them to sound mechanical. Actually, the opposite is true. Scripts help you feel more comfortable and enable you to project a more confident phone personality. They free you to focus on the prospect and listen for clues to gauge his or her level of interest in what you are saying.

The remainder of this section will focus on the basics of writing an approach script. Keep in mind that your objective for calling the prospect is to get an appointment. With this in mind, put together a script that has a greeting, creates interest, asks for the appointment, and ends the call. In addition, be prepared for resistance to your call. Be ready to exit gracefully should resistance persist.

Your conversation should last only a few minutes. A good script is short and generates interest. As always, remember to follow company guidelines, obtain any necessary compliance approval, and observe all federal and state do-not-call rules.

Know the Objective

Your objective in making the call is to more thoroughly introduce yourself to the prospect and set the appointment. Obviously, you will not need to introduce yourself to existing clients, but you will want to reestablish rapport if you have not spoken to them for some time. If you are calling new prospects, your preapproach letter should have preconditioned them to who you are. Also, they may have some idea of who you are from having attended one of your seminars where they gave you contact information.

Sometimes a prospect or client may ask you a question related to a product or service. One you probably hear often is, "How much will this cost me?" Some advisors cannot resist the temptation to answer these questions over the telephone. Resist it. Save your answers for when you meet with the prospect. Remember, your objective in making the call is simply to get the appointment.

Greet the Prospect

You want to make a good first impression. Open your conversation with something upbeat like, "Good morning/good afternoon." Identify yourself and the company you represent. Consider adding a phrase such as "I will only take a moment of your time" or "Do you have a moment to speak?" This demonstrates that you are sensitive to the prospect's busy schedule.

Create Interest

Remember, you are trying to motivate the prospect or client to see you. Tell why you are calling. Cite an example of how you helped other people in your target market solve their financial problems and/or achieve their goals.

Ask for the Appointment

This is why you are calling. Explain the purpose of the meeting in terms of the results you hope to achieve for him or her. Personalize these results. Avoid using the word "appointment." Use "meet," "see," or "get together."

End the Call

First and most recent impressions are memorable. Therefore, it is important that you know how to end the call. There are some things you must do, such as give directions (if the prospect is unfamiliar with the location of your office). In addition, reconfirm the appointment and affirm your desire to meet the prospect or client. The following example illustrates how to end a prospecting call effectively.

Example

"Good afternoon, Prospect, this is Joe Advisor from ABC Financial. I will take only a moment of your time. I work with people like you who dream about a comfortable retirement. I would like to meet with you to see if I could help you create a plan so you can realize your dream. Would some time during the day work for you, or are evenings better?"

Managing Prospect Resistance

Unfortunately, some people may have objections to purchasing your products and/or services. You will find that these objections usually fall into one of four categories:

- no hurry
- no money
- no need
- no trust

Rather than being caught off guard with no idea how to handle objections, write a script for each category that makes you sound confident. The perception of confidence will help you address their resistance. Although resistance is covered in more depth in chapter 7, here are some general guidelines:

- Acknowledge the concern. Let the prospect know that it is okay to feel the way he or she feels.
- Clarify the concern. Ask a question if needed.
- Resolve the concern. Make sure you have answered the concern before you request an appointment again.
- Reposition your request for an appointment.

Keep the Door Open

Sometimes the prospect's resistance remains after your best attempt to overcome it. In these situations, you need a way to end the call that leaves the door open. While high pressure and badgering may get you an appointment, you should not try to debate someone into an appointment. If you detect that the prospect has no interest after you have attempted twice to schedule an appointment, make sure that you

- acknowledge the prospect's position
- keep the door open by asking the prospect if there is a better time to call or if he or she would be interested in receiving mail. Most important, let the prospect know that if he or she should change his or her mind to give you a call.
- thank the prospect for his or her time and end the call

Example

"Okay. If you change your mind or know someone who needs help understanding how to protect his or her financial future, give me a call. I am in the phone book under Kelly Martin Financial. Thanks for your time. Have a good evening."

Caller ID and Voice Mail

You have new challenges with caller ID and voice mail. These technologies have increased the number of calls you need to make to actually talk to someone. For caller ID, the solution after one attempt at calling with no answer and no voice mail is to send a follow-up preapproach letter in which you again explain who you are and that you will be calling to set up a meeting. If this does not work, then you have to assume that this prospect is not interested in your products and/or services.

For voice mail, you need to be creative. One approach is to utilize the 10-second commercial concept and describe the results you can help your client achieve. The easiest thing to do is to use the positioning statement you were going to use in asking for the appointment. For example, you could leave a message like this.

Example

"Good evening, Jane. This is Kelly Martin from ABC Financial. I specialize in helping young adults like you create strong foundations on which to build their financial dreams. I would love to get together with you to see if you may want to use my services. I will give you a call back sometime next week."

Most advisors would not leave their own number with the request that the prospect return the call. Initiating the contact helps you feel more confident and comfortable because you know what you will say. If the prospect initiates the call, you may not remember where the lead came from or you may be tempted to ad lib rather than follow your script.

Practice, Practice, Practice

Once you have written your scripts, practice them. Read them to other advisors and get their feedback. You can also record yourself and hear what you sound like. Does it sound like you are reading?

Implement the Approach

After you have sent out preapproach letters and practiced your scripts, it is time to pick up the phone and call. Once you have set the appointment, send out a confirmation letter, along with your personal brochure (if you have not already sent a brochure). A few days prior to the appointment, call to confirm it.

SUMMARY

In the first two steps of the selling/planning process, you work with prospects, first to identify them and then to approach them. Technically, the prospect does not become a client until after he or she purchases a product and/or service from you. For commission-based advisors, the transition occurs in step 7 of the process when the plan is implemented. For fee-based advisors, the transition typically occurs in step 3 or 4 of the process when the fee is paid. However, for the sake of simplicity, in this book we refer to the prospect as a client beginning in chapter 2 where we discuss step 3 of the process.

CHAPTER REVIEW

Key Terms and Concepts are explained in the Glossary. Answers to the Review Questions and Self-Test Questions are found in the back of the textbook in the Answers to Questions section.

Key Terms and Concepts

financial planning
selling/planning process
comprehensive approach
multiple-purpose approach
single-purpose approach
financial planning pyramid
financial life cycle
life cycle financial planning
target market
natural market
market segments
referrals
center of influence (COI)
networking

Review Questions

1-1. Define financial planning.

1-2. What are the steps of the selling/planning process?

1-3. Identify the major planning areas to include in a comprehensive financial plan.

1-4. What is the multiple-purpose approach to financial planning?

1-5. What are the advantages of creating an ideal client profile?

1-6. What are the steps for identifying target markets?

1-7. List seven questions to answer when studying your competition.

1-8. List nine ways to build prestige and create awareness.

1-9. List four prospecting methods.

1-10. What are the four categories of objections?

Self-Test Questions

Instructions: Read the chapter first, then answer the following questions to test your knowledge. There are 10 questions; circle the correct answer, then check your answers with the answer key in the back of the book.

11. Tasha is working with a young couple who have no emergency savings and only mandatory coverages for auto insurance. On which stage of the financial planning pyramid will Tasha help her clients focus?

(A) protecting against risks
(B) accumulating wealth
(C) paying off debt
(D) managing retirement and the estate

12. Which of the following best fits the definition of a target market?

(A) single women ages 20–35
(B) parents of children who go to the same school as your daughter
(C) brain surgeons in Podunk, a small town
(D) subscribers to the *Daily Planet*, the local newspaper

13. The objection "I'm too young to worry about planning for retirement" falls into which category of objections?

(A) no hurry
(B) no money
(C) no trust
(D) no value

14. Which of the following advertisements is the most cost effective for a target market of young parents?

(A) a commercial spot on a local radio show about computers
(B) personal brochures at the local senior center
(C) an ad in a private school's newsletter to parents
(D) a full-page ad in the national magazine *Tomorrow's Parents*

15. Which of the following major planning areas is (are) addressed in a comprehensive financial plan?

I. investment planning
II. income tax planning

(A) I only
(B) II only
(C) Both I and II
(D) Neither I nor II

16. Ways to build prestige and create awareness include which of the following?

    I. Speak about personal finances at a Rotary Club meeting.
    II. Buy a list of members in your target market.

    (A) I only
    (B) II only
    (C) Both I and II
    (D) Neither I nor II

17. Approach methods include which of the following?

    I. sending a postcard
    II. calling on a telephone

    (A) I only
    (B) II only
    (C) Both I and II
    (D) Neither I nor II

READ THE FOLLOWING DIRECTIONS BEFORE CONTINUING

The questions below differ from the preceding questions in that they all contain the word EXCEPT. So you understand fully the basis used in selecting each answer, be sure to read each question carefully.

---

18. All the following are guidelines for handling resistance when contacting a prospect for an appointment EXCEPT

    (A) Acknowledge the prospect's concern.
    (B) Clarify the prospect's concern.
    (C) Review features and benefits of your product.
    (D) Reposition your request for an appointment.

19. All the following are characteristics found in centers of influence EXCEPT

    (A) They are active in the community.
    (B) They seek to communicate with others.
    (C) They are takers, not givers.
    (D) They are sought for advice within their sphere of influence.

20. All the following are distinct phases in an individual's financial life cycle EXCEPT

    (A) early career
    (B) peak accumulation
    (C) preretirement
    (D) generation X

2

Meeting and Communicating Effectively with Clients

Learning Objectives

An understanding of the material in this chapter should enable the student to

2-1. Explain the importance of communicating effectively with clients throughout the financial planning process.

2-2. Explain the three main types of structured communication used in financial planning.

2-3. Explain the importance of structuring communications, building rapport, establishing credibility, handling resistance, disclosing information, and scheduling the second meeting in communicating with clients.

2-4. Explain the attributes of an advisor that facilitate meeting and communicating with clients.

2-5. Describe several basic communication principles.

2-6. Explain the importance of attending and listening skills to communicating effectively with clients.

2-7. Describe several types of leading responses.

2-8. Compare the advantages and disadvantages of several types of questions used in financial planning.

The focus of this chapter is on meeting the client, step 3 of the eight-step process. The financial advisor's overriding objective in this step of the process is to establish a relationship with clients that is conducive to financial planning. To achieve this objective, the advisor must be able to communicate effectively with his or her clients.[5]

IMPORTANCE OF COMMUNICATING EFFECTIVELY WITH CLIENTS

Many people take communication for granted. After all, it is an activity that most of us have engaged in since our childhood years, so why not take it for

5. Portions of this chapter have been drawn from chapters 2 and 3 of the third edition of *Readings in Financial Services: Environment and Professions,* edited by Dale S. Johnson (Bryn Mawr, PA: The American College, 1984). Chapter 2 is titled "Effective Communication in Financial Counseling" and was authored by Lewis B. Morgan. Chapter 3 is titled "Practical Communications Skills and Techniques in Financial Counseling" and was authored by Dale S. Johnson. Chapter 3 was also published with the permission of The American College as a two-part article in *The Financial Planner,* Vol. 11, no. 6 (June 1982): pp. 98–105, and Vol. 11, no. 7 (July 1982): pp. 62–71.

granted? The sad truth is that many of us are ineffective communicators simply because we make that very assumption.

Communication is far too important a skill to treat lightly. This is especially true in the field of financial planning. It is the single most critical skill that you as a financial advisor bring to a financial planning session. Ineffective communication is an obstacle to a strong advisor-client relationship. The failure of clients and advisors to communicate fully and clearly with each other can result in improperly identified financial goals and the formulation of inappropriate planning strategies. The result for the client is not being able to achieve his or her financial goals. The communication process is the starting point from which you help your client to establish financial goals and then design a plan to achieve those goals. Simply put, effective communication between you and your client is crucial to the selling/planning process.

As stated previously, the focus of this chapter is on meeting and establishing a relationship with clients that is conducive to financial planning. This requires you to learn how to communicate effectively with your clients. Thus, we need to examine the communication process as it typically exists in an advisor-client relationship. Our goal is to help financial advisors become better communicators. Perhaps you already consider yourself an effective communicator; however, there are probably aspects of the communication process in which you can improve. This chapter will attempt to bring these aspects into sharper focus and provide you with techniques for becoming the best communicator/advisor that you are able to be.

TYPES OF STRUCTURED COMMUNICATION USED IN FINANCIAL PLANNING

Lay people often use the terms interviewing, counseling, and advising interchangeably. Yet each of these forms of structured communication has characteristics that are uniquely its own and that differentiate it from the other two. We will describe these three forms of structured communication and discuss how you can use them in the selling/planning process.

Interviewing

interviewing

Interviewing is one of the most common forms of structured communication. Interviewing can be defined as a process of communication, most often between two people, with a predetermined and specific purpose, usually involving asking and answering questions designed to gather meaningful information. For example, a critical step in the selling/planning process (step 4 of the process depicted in Figure 2–1) requires you to gather complete data and information about a client relevant to the client's personal and financial situation. To gather this information, you typically schedule a fact-finder session, usually the second meeting with a client, in which you interview the client by asking a series of questions designed to help fill in the blank spaces on a fact-finder form. (See chapter 3.) There is a specific purpose to the interview: to gather relevant information through a question-and-answer dialogue.

directive interview

Stewart and Cash in their book, *Interviewing: Principles and Practices*, refer to two basic types of interviews: directive and nondirective.[6] In a directive interview, you direct and control both the pace and the content to be covered. This is a formal and structured style of interaction. You complete a fact-finder form as the client answers pointed questions. Many of the questions are asked and answered rapidly in an almost staccato fashion. What is your date of birth? Where do you live? What is your occupation? What is the highest level of education you completed? The advantages of the directive interview are its brevity and its organized collection of data. Its disadvantages are its inflexibility and the limited opportunity for your client to expound on any of the questions you ask.

nondirective interview

In a *nondirective interview,* both your client and you can discuss a wider range of subject areas, and the client usually controls the pacing of the interview through the depth of his or her responses. Thus, the advantages of the nondirective interview include greater flexibility, more in-depth analysis, and the potential for a closer relationship between you and your client. Its disadvantages are that it consumes more time and often generates data that are subjective in nature.

Both types of interviews are commonly used in the selling/planning process. Segments of the initial meeting with clients often resemble a nondirective interview, while both types of interviews often take place in the same fact-finding meeting. Moreover, all interviews, whether directive or nondirective, share common characteristics. They typically take place in a formal and structured setting. The question-and-answer format is the primary method of communication. The subject matter discussed is specific to the overall purpose of the interview, and digressions from the subject are usually not encouraged. Finally, the interview by itself usually requires only a relatively short meeting of the parties.

Counseling

counseling

The second term, *counseling,* connotes an offer of help. Your job as a financial advisor is to provide assistance to clients as they explore their present financial situations, begin to understand where they are in relation to where they would like to be, and then act to get from where they are to where they want to be. Even though this may sound like a simple process, it is not. Counseling, as used in financial planning, usually takes time and is typified by discussion, reflection, and eventually insights that help the client select a financial plan from among the suggested or recommended alternatives.

---

6. Charles J. Stewart and William B. Cash, *Interviewing: Principles and Practices*, seventh ed. (Dubuque, IA: Brown & "Benchmark, 1993).

While your role as a financial counselor takes place over a period of time, the interview, as a form of structured communication, is usually of relatively short duration. In counseling, you and the client develop an interpersonal relationship, something that generally does not occur in a solitary interview. When we discussed interviewing, we stated that the question-and-answer format was the primary method of communication. Although you also ask questions in counseling, they are not your primary method of communication. In counseling, you may paraphrase what the client has said, reflect a feeling, share feedback or perceptions, clarify, summarize, interpret, provide information, and confront. In short, counseling is not as stylized as interviewing because it is less formal and less structured. Much more of the humanness of both you and the client comes into focus, all with the purpose of providing help to the client.

Advising

advising

The third type of structured communication is *advising*, which involves giving specific guidance or suggestions to clients. Advising is often confused with counseling. In fact, many clients who are unfamiliar with counseling think that what they will receive is advice. Perhaps one reason for this misconception stems from the journalistic proliferation of advice such as is offered in the "Dear Abby" type of newspaper columns. This is not to say that financial advisors who are counseling their clients never offer advice because they do, but most financial advisors believe that the best kind of advice for their clients is self-advice, rather than advice from an expert.

Several situations might require that financial advisors give advice. For example, a tax advisor might provide advice on tax shelters, capital gains, tax deferral, and so on. Or an investment advisor might recommend a particular stock or mutual fund because he or she believes that it is consistent with both the client's risk tolerance level and financial ability to handle risk. In each of these instances, the advisor knows much more about his or her field of expertise than the client does, and the client uses this knowledge to help make a decision.

To reiterate, there are several occasions when financial advisors are called on to give advice. After all, financial advisors are the experts and thus their advice has proven value. However, there is a danger for advisors in offering advice too soon in the advisor-client relationship. This danger is that the client's ability to make decisions becomes discounted in favor of the expert's opinion. In fact, advice giving has been criticized by some counseling experts who maintain that advice fosters dependency and robs clients of the right to make decisions for themselves. Moreover, they believe that advisors who provide quick answers to somewhat complex financial problems are often guilty of projecting their own needs, problems, and/or values into the advice. So how do financial advisors give advice to clients without assuming responsibility for their clients' financial lives?

Perhaps the best way for you to give advice to clients is by using the eight-step selling/planning process depicted in the figure below) to address client concerns. Advisors who adhere to the selling/planning process systematically analyze their clients' financial situations. They work alongside their clients as partners to help them take control of their financial lives. Although the role of advisors in the selling/planning process is geared more toward counseling clients than advising them, advising is still an important form of structured communication. The inherent danger of advising clients is minimized when the advice is given within the confines of the selling/planning process. In this case, any advice given to a client is the result of a thorough analysis of the client's financial situation. Advisors generally give advice to clients in the form of suggestions or recommendations, but the clients are encouraged to make decisions for themselves and assume responsibility for their own financial lives.

FOCUS ON ETHICS
How Ethical Behavior Improves Communication

Many clients misunderstand the specifics of the plans their financial advisors suggest or recommend. This problem is compounded when complex financial instruments are required to implement the plans. It is much like drivers and automobiles. Most drivers really need transportation, and cars solve this problem. However, that does not mean that drivers understand how their cars operate.

A financial advisor once stated that there are two essential rules for effectively dealing with clients. The first is to earn their trust because trust breaks down communication barriers. Different advisors may accomplish this in different ways, but the goal is for advisors to feel free to ask challenging questions and continue probing until a satisfactory level of understanding is achieved. When there are limits to what clients can understand, earned trust is essential.

The second rule is to maintain trust, a critical factor in the advisor-client relationship. Although clients may not fully understand, they should not fail to act. Indeed, if clients understood every aspect of financial planning, they would not need their advisors. Clients often make decisions based solely on their trust in their advisors.

There is no better way to earn and maintain trust than to develop an unassailable reputation for ethical and professional behavior. A valuable side benefit is improved communication.

Types of Structured Communication

- Interviewing
- Counseling
- Advising

Because there is frequent interaction between you and your clients in the selling/planning process, the distinctions among interviewing, counseling, and advising are often blurred. As the discussion about the three types of structured communication indicates, financial advisors use all three types in the selling/planning process, and those advisors who routinely use the selling/planning process perform their jobs in a wholly professional and ethical manner.

CONSIDERATIONS IN MEETING AND COMMUNICATING WITH CLIENTS

In the preceding section, we differentiated the three types of planned and purposeful communication: interviewing, counseling, and advising. Each one is used in the selling/planning process. For instance, step 4 of the selling/planning process utilizes interviewing to facilitate the completion of fact-finder forms. Counseling occurs in several steps of the selling/planning process, including step 4 where clients set their financial goals. Advising frequently takes place in step 6 of the process where advisors recommend or suggest several alternative strategies for their clients to consider. In other words, financial advisors generally rely on all three types of structured communication; each type is more or less appropriate for particular tasks. Let us now examine some specific communication and meeting issues you must deal with in your relationships with clients.

As stated previously, your overriding objective in step 3 of the selling/planning process is to meet and establish a relationship with clients in order to get their agreement to continue the process and perform fact finding. This is facilitated by developing rapport with clients in the hope of eventually gaining their trust. Trust is the intangible aspect of the selling/planning process that you must gradually cultivate and earn, and the first step in earning clients' trust is to establish a relationship with them. The process of establishing a relationship with clients normally begins with the initial meeting, which lays the foundation for an advisor-client relationship that ideally will span each client's entire financial life. Let us begin our discussion of meeting and communicating with clients with the first element that must be attended to in any kind of planned and purposeful communication setting.

Structuring Communications with Clients

The first element that needs to be attended to in any kind of planned and purposeful communication setting is structuring. Structuring serves to determine both the format and the subject matter of the interaction that is to follow. As a financial advisor, your task is to make the purpose of each meeting clear to the client at the outset. This includes introductions, an explanation of the process involved, a discussion of forms that are used and the amount of time that will be required to complete them, a discussion of the confidential nature of the relationship, and some prediction of what kinds of outcomes the client might reasonably expect. This structuring need not be lengthy and cumbersome; in fact, it is far better to structure in a clear, straightforward, and succinct fashion.

Consider the following example of structuring in which the advisor's approach is friendly and promises cooperation. The client is made to feel important, that he or she is the focal point of the meetings. The statement offers hope to the client that the results of the selling/planning process will help him or her achieve the desired goals.

Example

Advisor: For me to be able to provide the best possible service for you, we'll probably need to meet at least three or four more times, although I want you to know that I'm available to meet with you as often as you need me. Today, I thought we'd start by discussing the selling/planning process. To put this in proper perspective, I'll explain the products and services that we provide and how they might help you. In the next meeting, we'll gather some information about your financial situation. To do this, I'll help you fill out a fact-finder form, which will remain confidential between the two of us. As we go about our business together, I will develop and present to you some alternatives that will be sensible and help you meet your goals. Do you have any questions?"

In step 3 of the selling/planning process, the client may be apprehensive or uncertain about the whole process and how to begin. A good guide for you to follow is to begin where the client is. If the client is, in fact, anxious at the outset, you should take the time to discuss the difficulty of merely getting started. Talking about this will not only alleviate most of the client's anxieties, it will also help to build rapport with the client. It is important to keep in mind that whenever feelings emerge, it is best to focus on those feelings rather than ignore them. If, for example, in the middle of a meeting, a client appears distressed over some aspect of his or her financial situation (for example, an impending divorce), you should spend some time discussing these feelings. Until you address and deal with those feelings, a further discussion of content is unproductive and meaningless.

Developing Rapport with Clients

As a financial advisor, you should seek to develop rapport with your clients. Rapport, another way of describing a comfortable and harmonious relationship, is best developed through actions you initiate. The most important component in developing rapport is your acceptance of the client and the client's awareness of this acceptance. This attitude stems from a sincere desire on your part to respect the uniqueness of each client and a genuine wish to help. Clients want to do business with advisors they feel understand them, with whom they share something in common, who are competent, who listen to what they want to accomplish, and whom they can believe and trust. Having something in common increases the client's level of comfort about doing business with you and facilitates the development of a relationship. Engaging the client in conversation that builds warm, positive feelings of trust and rapport is also a plus.

If you develop rapport in step 3 of the selling/planning process, the products and/or services you recommend will more likely reflect the clients' real needs and values. However, in order for clients to buy products and/or services from you, they must first trust you. Trust, as previously noted, is the intangible aspect of selling that you must gradually cultivate and earn. You must prove that you are there to help clients, not simply to sell them something. To do this, you must create an environment that promotes openness and builds rapport by

- alleviating the concerns of clients
- responding to the social style of clients
- communicating effectively with clients

Alleviating the Concerns of Clients

Various barriers that can create tension between you and your clients during an initial meeting, as well as throughout the selling/planning process, must be removed if you are to develop rapport. These barriers can be divided into four categories:

- distrust of salespeople. Many people have a negative image of people who sell products and/or services and avoid meeting with them for fear of being talked into buying something they do not want or need.
- fear of making a decision. Decisions involve risk, and many people avoid risk, especially when money is involved. Also, fear of making the wrong purchase decision (that is, buyer's remorse) can cause people to avoid stressful decision-making situations.
- need for stability. Many people are complacent and resist change because they prefer familiarity.
- time constraints. At today's increasingly hectic pace of life, busy people are reluctant to commit their time.

Being aware of client stress can help you identify opportunities to alleviate it and build rapport. Here are some tips:

- Do not impose on clients. Schedule the initial meeting (as well as future ones) at times that are convenient for clients.
- Watch your verbal pace. Talk in an unhurried, businesslike manner, and never interrupt when clients are speaking. Listen carefully to what clients are saying because listening is a necessary component in good communication.
- Be aware of nonverbal behaviors. You might be surprised to learn that as little as 7 percent of a first impression is based on what is actually said. The remaining 93 percent is based on nonverbal behaviors, such as body positions, gestures, eye contact, and voice tone.
- Encourage clients to talk. Having clients talk is not only a great tool for getting feedback, but it is also a common way to relieve stress. Encourage clients to do most of the talking.

- Control your anxiety. Studies have shown that a person who is already anxious becomes even more so when talking to someone who displays nervousness or anxiety.

Responding to the Social Style of Clients

social styles

As a financial advisor, building rapport is your responsibility. You should be able to detect what each client wants from an advisor-client relationship and to use your communication skills to shape the discussion to satisfy those wants. Identifying the client's needs in the relationship is easier if you can identify the client's social style.

Psychologist David W. Merrill described the following four *social styles:*

- driver
- expressive
- amiable
- analytical

The American population is evenly divided among the four social styles. Each person has a dominant social style that influences the way he or she works. According to David W. Merrill and Roger H. Reid, "We all say and do things as a result of certain habit patterns, and people make predictions about us because they come to expect us to behave in a particular way—the fact is that even though each of us is unique, we tend to act in fairly consistent, describable ways. All of us use habits that have worked well for us, habits that make us comfortable, and these habits become the social style that others can observe.[7]

People are like thermostats; they are constantly seeking to reach a state of equilibrium or comfort. They seek out social situations that reinforce their behavior and avoid situations that cause discomfort. As soon as another person enters the picture, tension is produced, and each one must reestablish his or her balance and comfort zone. The challenge for each of us is to determine the proper amount of tension and stress that will provide the proper balance.

You can achieve better communication when you understand your clients and treat them the way they want to be treated. Adapting to clients' social styles in order to make them feel at home and less threatened can help you establish more effective communications and better advisor-client relationships. By listening to and observing clients during step 3 of the selling/planning process, you can learn how to communicate with them. Effective communication occurs when you are able to respond to the client's social style as you continue with the selling/planning process. The following table summarizes the characteristics of each social style and how best to respond to a person who engages that style.

7. David W. Merrill and Roger H. Reid, *Personal Styles and Effective Performance* (CRC Press LLC, 1999).

Table 2-1
Responding to Social Styles

Social Style	Style Characteristics	How to Respond
Driver	• Forceful, direct • Will not waste time on small talk • Wants power • Is controlling	• Be efficient • Move right along • Support his or her conclusions and actions • To encourage decisions, provide options and probabilities
Expressive	• Outgoing, enthusiastic • Enjoys telling about personal projects and dreams • Wants recognition • Is energizing	• Be interesting • Take time to listen • Support his or her visions and intuitions • To encourage decisions, provide testimony and incentives
Amiable	• Easygoing, dependent • Enjoys telling about personal relationships • Wants approval • Is supportive	• Be cooperative • Find areas of common involvement • Support his or her relationships and feelings • To encourage decisions, provide assurances and guarantees
Analytical	• Logical, quiet • Is uncomfortable with small talk • Wants respect • Is systematic	• Be accurate • Stick to an agenda • Support his or her principles and thinking • To encourage decisions, provide evidence and service

Communicating Effectively with Clients

financial life planning

Financial advisors must build rapport with clients in order to help them solve their problems. One aspect of rapport building is communicating effectively, an emphasis of this chapter. Some advisors, however, think effective communication means only that they have to explain their products and/or services to clients. In fact, effective communication involves much more. At a minimum, it requires you to learn how to listen. Failing to hear what the client is really saying can cost you dearly. Developing good listening skills will result not only in increased sales and the sense of a job well done, but also in clients who are more likely to accept your suggestions or recommendations because you demonstrate an interest in them by listening to what they have to say, especially about their personal goals and life dreams. Bringing clients' personal goals and life dreams into the advisor-client relationship and developing financial strategies around them is called *financial life planning*.

Today, financial advisors increasingly need to take account of the true values and motivations in their clients' lives. They need to take time to know their clients, to be real with them, to ask them questions that a caring friend would ask, and to help them figure out what is really important to them. They need to do this up front at the initial meeting, as well as at the second meeting where information is gathered and goals determined, because what clients think is really important to them is the foundation upon which their financial goals are set and priorities established.

Most advisors, however, are not comfortable about interviewing, counseling, and advising their clients in nonfinancial matters. They are concerned that they will be called upon to step outside their areas of expertise and be all things to all clients. Not to worry. The financial life planning approach only requires financial advisors to conversationally explore life issues as they relate to financial matters and to facilitate a dialogue in a way that communicates their interest in each client as a whole person. You can accomplish these two objectives without sinking into the quicksand of psychological counseling.

Establishing Credibility with Clients

As a financial advisor, it is important for you to establish credibility with your clients as quickly and as early as possible in the relationship. There is the danger that if you fail to establish your credibility at the initial meeting with the client, you may not get another chance because the client may decide not to proceed to the next step in the selling/planning process. A client-focused advisor is well aware of this time constraint and plans ways to establish and communicate his or her credibility. By anticipating a client's expectations, listening carefully to the client, and observing the client's behavior, you can attempt to overcome negative responses from the client, while at the same time improving your credibility and hastening the development of rapport.

The following four factors build on one another and culminate in your establishing credibility:

- **propriety.** There are many ways to describe this factor: appropriateness, correct appearance, proper image, and suitability. It centers on meeting the expectations of what the client considers proper business customs, dress, and behavior; it encompasses looking the part, appearance, manners, protocol (greetings, shaking hands, recognition of the client's status), and appropriate speech. Although first impressions play a relatively small role in long-term relationships, they definitely matter. As a financial advisor, your manners, appearance, and confidence speak volumes about your attitude toward yourself, the client's business, and the client. The client will be asking himself or herself, "Does the advisor walk, talk, and look like he or she is a competent planner? Is the advisor going to communicate his or her intention to be helpful?" Your words must match your body language and tone of voice. The propriety factor could be considered an initial screening by the client. It avoids a negative assessment and early dismissal before you can demonstrate your skills. Arriving on time, looking the part, being well-groomed, and dressing professionally are good ways to get started.

- **competence.** Language that captures this factor includes skillful, knowledgeable, inspires confidence, experienced, capable, expert, and "puts my mind at ease." One way for you to establish your competence is through disclosure. Most clients want to know something about their advisors' educational backgrounds, professional certifications and licenses held, professional experience, business philosophies, and training. They also want to know how their advisors are being compensated and whether they have any possible conflicts of interest. Although clients generally are not inclined to ask their advisors outright about these topics, they nonetheless expect their advisors to provide this type of information, and advisors generally do furnish it in the form of a disclosure statement they hand out and explain at the initial meeting. You can also use a disclosure statement to outline your repertory of products and services to help clients establish their financial plans.

  You do not need to claim expertise in every planning area. You can establish your competence by explaining that colleagues are available to provide technical support or work with clients on subjects that require a specialist.
- **commonality.** This factor includes shared harmony, agreement, comfort level, camaraderie, companionship, friendship, and a good "gut" feeling. Commonality is the foundation of trust and rapport. The client asks himself or herself, "Is this the kind of person I want to do business with?" Often, a common understanding and respect for one another's attitudes and values is present, either initially or over time, through sharing and disclosure. This is the basis and value of a third-party referral: You come well regarded and respected. It is natural that clients feel more comfortable with advisors who share common interests with them.
- **intent.** Intent involves the client's perception of your motives and your interest in helping and benefiting him or her. Do you put the client's best interest before your own? The client must decide whether you have a true problem-solving attitude or are just trying to make a sale for your benefit. Intention is perceived in more than words. It is perceived through your body language, tone of voice, and follow-through on commitments. This is perhaps the most important factor in developing credibility. As the saying goes, the client does

not care what you know until he or she knows that you care. If you state your purpose in a clear and understandable manner and back it up with actions, this will help to establish your intent and the client's ability to believe and trust you.

Factors That Establish Credibility

- Propriety
- Competence
- Commonality
- Intent

Your level of confidence, enthusiasm, and openness will affect how you are perceived. Be positive and do not apologize. Avoid statements like, "I'm new at this" or "I'm not really too good at this." If you are not enthusiastic about your work, how can your clients be convinced to rely on you? If you do not think you can do the job, why should your clients think you can? Demonstrate your enthusiasm through your voice, body language, and speech. Carry yourself with assuredness. Openness means you are genuine, that you do not try to fake expertise. There is no façade, no role-playing of what a professional advisor is considered to be. You are yourself; if you do not know something, admit it and find the answer. Following through on a promise is another way to establish your credibility.

Dealing with Client Resistance

resistance

Resistance often occurs in even the best advisor-client relationships. Resistance can be expressed as either overt or covert hostility toward the advisor. Overt hostility generally is easier to recognize and handle than covert hostility. In addition, there are several other types of resistance behaviors that advisors might encounter during the selling/planning process.

Recognizing Client Resistance

Open or overt hostility is the easiest type of resistance to recognize and, in most cases, to handle. We all know what angry people look and sound like: Their faces become flushed; their jaws tighten; they clench their fists; their voices rise; their language becomes more expressively angry. The only effective thing to do at this point is to reflect this anger by saying, "I can sense your anger. You don't like what I've just said, do you?" This allows clients to vent whatever pent-up feelings of anger they have; the anger slowly begins to dissipate, and their behavior becomes more rational.

Covert hostility is more difficult to recognize and can be more difficult to deal with because clients themselves may not even be aware of their anger. Some indications of the client's covert hostility are missing appointments, arriving late for appointments, being sarcastic or cynical, acting overly genteel or polite, and not getting down to business. Whatever way the client demonstrates covert hostility, the best approach is not to interpret the behavior as latent hostility or passive-aggressiveness but simply to focus on the behavior itself and let the client analyze or interpret it. For instance, you might say, "I've noticed that whenever we talk about your spouse's handling the family budget, you become sarcastic. What do you think might be going on?" Your recognition of client resistance helps the client focus on his or her behavior and allows the client to vent angry feelings. You must address resistance as directly as possible if any successful planning is to come out of the advisor-client relationship.

Other types of resistance behaviors that you might encounter during the selling/planning process include withdrawal or passivity, dwelling in fantasy or nonreality, ambivalence or vacillation, and the use of inappropriate humor, to name a few. As mentioned, you should not analyze or interpret a client's resistance behavior because analysis tends only to make the client defensive. Instead, you should be aware of what is occurring, note whether it is a recurrent pattern, and at an appropriate point, share such observations in a nonjudgmental manner with the client.

Sources of Client Resistance

Client resistance is almost a given in the financial planning environment, probably because clients, when they enter into an advisor-client relationship, yield a certain amount of their privacy and personal power over the situation to their advisors. Resistance is a way of defending or restoring some of the balance of power. Certain topics, because of their sensitive nature, seem to be particularly vulnerable to client resistance.

One such sensitive topic is death and dying. Because of the uncertainty of its timing, death is extremely anxiety producing to most people. Dr. Elisabeth Kubler-Ross, an eminent authority on death and dying, postulated that there are five stages that a person facing death passes through: denial, anger, bargaining, depression, and acceptance.[8] The first four of these stages are different forms of resistance that the person uses for self-protection. As a financial advisor, you need to be particularly sensitive to the feelings of your older clients when discussing future plans with them. You must listen and observe very closely what they communicate when discussing death and dying. You must be empathetic to their feelings, communicate accurately what you hear and observe, and manifest a genuine concern for their feelings and attitudes. You must also be aware of and have control over your own feelings about death, so that you do not impose them on what clients are attempting to communicate.

During the selling/planning process, you can help to restore some control over the future by involving your clients fully in decision making and planning for contingencies. This allows them to feel useful, worthwhile, and somewhat in control of their situation.

---

8. Elisabeth Kubler-Ross, *Death and Dying* (New York: Macmillan, 1968)

Another area where you may encounter resistance involves marital tensions, such as separation/divorce, parent-child disputes, the empty-nest syndrome, and mid-life crises. Although you are not expected to be a qualified marriage or family counselor, you should be astute enough to recognize when a married couple is resisting because of an underlying, unexpressed marital problem. And once it is recognized, you should be willing and able to focus with the couple on the problem area. Otherwise, if you ignore the problem, whatever decisions you and the couple reach will be less valid than those that you would reach after a full airing of the problem. Besides providing a possibly welcome catharsis for the couple, focusing on the problem can enable them to muster their forces to arrive at a mutually satisfactory solution. In planning sessions with couples who disagree on a crucial subject, you need to listen closely to what both partners have to say. Letting the dominant partner do more of the talking and deciding is far too common, unfortunately. Because the outcome of the decision affects both partners, both should be involved in the discussion. To do any less almost guarantees an unsatisfactory conclusion.

Another sensitive area involves executive clients who have failed to attain the degree of success they had dreamed of in their professions. Their dreams shattered and unfulfilled, they may resort to cynicism, biting sarcasm, or empty humor in an attempt to endure it. Rather than laugh hollowly along with them, you need to reflect their underlying feelings to let them know that you understand their disappointment. A simple statement like, "I suppose it's a bitter pill to swallow when you've worked so hard to see your personal hopes go unfulfilled," allows your clients to feel understood and appreciated. More often than not, the clients will begin to discuss more openly how they feel. And once people are able to express their feelings, they are well on the way to addressing their problems in an effective manner.

Resistance behaviors, in any case, are a certain tip-off that clients are having difficulty subscribing to your line of reasoning. It does no good for you to proceed with business as usual, ignoring the obvious resistance; you can accomplish nothing as long as the resistance continues. You must deal with resistance openly and objectively if there is any chance that it will diminish, allowing the participants to get on with the business at hand.

Disclosing Information to Clients

disclosure statement

Your initial meeting with a client sets the stage for future meetings. If you do not live up to the client's expectations during the first meeting, there will be no second or follow-up meeting, and you will not get an opportunity to continue the selling/planning process with the client. To help ensure that there will be a second meeting, you need to disclose certain kinds of information to your clients during the course of the first meeting. Clients, as indicated in our earlier discussion of advisor competence, want to know something about their advisors' educational backgrounds, professional certifications and licenses held, professional experience, business philosophies, training, method of compensation, and possible conflicts of interest. A *disclosure statement* handed out and discussed at the first meeting can provide much of this information to clients.

The disclosure statement should answer several questions that clients would like to ask you in your role as a financial advisor if they were interviewing you. This is to say that you should think of yourself as a client and formulate a battery of questions that you would like your advisor to answer. The disclosure statement can then function as the vehicle for communicating the answers to many of these questions. Although not an exhaustive list, the kinds of questions that the client would like the answers to are as follows:

- What experience do you have as a financial advisor?
- What is your educational background?
- What certifications and licenses do you hold?
- Will you educate me about your available products and/or services?
- Is your financial planning practice limited in scope?
- What is your approach to financial planning?
- Will you listen to me?
- Will you answer my questions?
- Will you be the only person working with me?
- How much will I pay for your products and/or services?
- How long will it take you to go through the selling/planning process with me?
- What are your and my responsibilities under the planning process?
- Are you giving me a sense of steady service, or are you interested only in a one-time sale?
- Do you come recommended by others?
- Are you up-to-date?
- Will you provide me with a written agreement?

If the information requested by any of these questions cannot, for whatever reason, be included in the disclosure statement, you should verbally communicate this information to your clients when explaining the purpose and contents of the disclosure statement to them. In addition, you should verbally explain how you are compensated for your work and what clients are required to pay for your products and/or services. These additional explanations should be forthcoming even if both topics are fully explained on the disclosure statement.

Financial advisors are compensated for their work in several ways:

- a salary paid by the advisor's employer. The advisor's employer receives payment from the client in the form of fees and/or commissions in order to pay the advisor's salary.
- fees that are based on an hourly rate, on a percentage of the client's assets and/or income, or on a flat rate
- commissions paid by a third party from the products sold to the client to implement the financial plan
- a combination of fees and commissions. Clients are charged fees by the advisor for the work done to develop the financial plan. Commissions are paid to the advisor by third parties from the sale of

their products to the client to implement the plan. Many advisors offset a portion of the fees charged clients if they receive commissions in the course of implementing the plan.

Advisors who practice the pure form of comprehensive financial planning operate on a fee-only basis. These advisors are few in number and are not the focus of this book. Salaried advisors, likewise, are few in number and also not the focus of this book. Advisors who practice either single-purpose, multiple-purpose, or the less pure form of comprehensive financial planning, which is tantamount to multiple-purpose planning done on a periodic basis, typically are compensated by the receipt of commissions or by a combination of fees and commissions. These advisors make up the majority of the financial planning profession and are the focus of this book.

Scheduling the Second Meeting with Clients

As noted at the beginning of this chapter, the advisor's overriding objective in step 3 of the selling/planning process is to meet and establish a relationship with clients in order to get their agreement to continue the process. The initial client meeting is the venue for achieving this objective.

The initial meeting typically begins with you in your advisor role, explaining both the format and the subject matter of the interaction that is to follow. Your task here is to make the purpose of the selling/planning process clear to clients at the outset. Next, you should spend some time getting to know the clients, finding out what is really important to them and what they have in common with you. Although this brief interval of life planning is crucial for building rapport and establishing relationships with clients, it will not establish your credibility. To do this, you must disclose information about your educational background, professional certifications and licenses held, professional experience, business philosophy, training, and method of compensation. If the meeting proceeds according to your agenda, the clients' need for financial planning should be clear, and you will be able to wrap up the meeting by scheduling a follow-up meeting to do fact finding.

When you ask your clients about scheduling a follow-up meeting, they may say no and voice their concerns about some aspect of the process. If this happens, you should address their concerns immediately; if you can satisfactorily resolve them without taking up much time, the clients will in all likelihood want to continue with the process. However, if you are unable to overcome their concerns (chapter 7 has a detailed discussion about client concerns), whatever they may be, perhaps it is best that the process end now for these clients. You have other clients who need your expertise and are eager to receive it. So do not waste your time and effort on clients who are unappreciative of your planning skills.

For those clients looking forward to continuing the process, schedule the second meeting for the near future and tell them that you will be sending them a letter confirming the time and location. Follow-up letters are a key component of a successful advisor-client relationship. They let clients know that you are thinking about them and their needs and that you are serious about meeting their expectations.

In addition to confirming the time and location of the second meeting, the follow-up letter should thank the client for taking time out of his or her busy schedule to meet with you. The letter should also briefly explain that the second meeting will be an information-gathering and goal-setting session, and that to facilitate these efforts the client will need to complete as much of a fact-finder form as possible. You should point out the checklist for documents on the last page of the fact finder with a request that the client supply you with copies of all those items that are relevant. You can either hand the fact finder to the client at the end of the initial meeting or enclose it with the letter. If possible, you can arrange to have the client's planning documents picked up before the fact-finding meeting so that you will have time to review their contents. In any event, the client certainly needs to bring the fact-finder form with him or her to the second meeting and supply the items noted on the checklist no later than that time. In addition, the follow-up letter should explain that after you have had an opportunity to analyze the information collected at the second meeting and develop a plan for reaching the client's goals, you will need to schedule a third meeting to present and discuss the proposed plan.

ATTRIBUTES OF AN EFFECTIVE ADVISOR

The main component that you bring to a meeting with a client is yourself. You, first and foremost, must be yourself in your relation to and interaction with clients. You are a human being, complete with strengths and weaknesses. But you are also a professionally trained individual, a person who, ideally, enjoys listening to and trying to understand other people and accept them as they are. To be effective, you must also be sincere and genuine in attempting to help others learn how to help themselves. This attitude generates interesting, challenging, and highly gratifying work; it is—more than anything else—hard work when done professionally.

Carl Rogers, in his classic book, *Client-Centered Therapy: Its Current Practice, Implications and Theory*, postulated that there are three conditions necessary to bring about constructive client change: (1) unconditional positive regard, (2) accurate empathy, and (3) genuineness.[9] Most experts on the subject agree that if an effective advisor-client relationship is to exist, you must value the client as a unique individual (unconditional positive regard), be able to perceive and understand what the client is experiencing (accurate empathy), and be open and spontaneous (genuine).

A constructive advisor-client relationship serves not only to increase the opportunity for clients to attain the goals that are important to them, but also as

9. Carl R. Rogers, *Client-Centered Therapy: Its Current Practice, Implications and Theory* (Boston, MA: Houghton Mifflin, 1951).

a model of a good interpersonal relationship. Some questions that all financial advisors ought to ask themselves from time to time are the following:

- Knowing myself, do I think it will be possible to value my clients, especially those who think, feel, and act differently than I do?
- How easy or difficult will it be for me to view the world from another's perspective without imposing my own standards, beliefs, and attitudes on that person? Will my own values, ideas, and feelings hinder my understanding of another person?
- How open do I care, or dare, to be with a client? Will I be able to be myself and still adapt to the client's social style?

These are important questions for you to consider before engaging in the dynamics of an advisor-client relationship. Far too many financial advisors assume that they have the right kind of personality to counsel others without ever scrutinizing themselves in the same way.

Let us examine the three core conditions to which Rogers refers, along with a fourth condition, self-awareness.

Unconditional Positive Regard

unconditional positive regard

Unconditional positive regard is an attitude of valuing the client, or being able to express appreciation of the client as a unique and worthwhile person. Liking and respecting another person has a circular effect. When you value clients, your sense of liking will be communicated to them; this by itself will enhance the clients' self-esteem and add to their appreciation of themselves as worthwhile human beings.

Accurate Empathy

accurate empathy

Accurate empathy means that your sense of the client's world fits the client's self-image. This gives clients the feeling that you are in touch with them. When clients say something like, "Yes, that's it," or "That's exactly right," it indicates that you are on target, and that clients feel you are closely following and understanding them.

Learning to understand clients, however, is not an easy process. It involves your capacity to put aside your own set of experiences in favor of those of the client; you must be able to see the client's problems through the client's eyes instead of your own. It requires skillful listening so you can hear not only the obvious but also the subtleties of which even the client may be unaware.

Developing accurate empathy also requires you to identify and resolve your own needs so they do not interfere with understanding the client's feelings and concerns. However, you must be careful not to identify so strongly with the client that it impedes rather than facilitates the counseling objective.

Genuineness

genuineness

Genuineness means simply that you are a "real" person—there is no facade, no stereotypical role-playing of what a professional advisor is considered to be. As a professional advisor who is genuine, you are wholly aware of yourself and your feelings, thoughts, values, and attitudes. You are not afraid to express yourself openly and honestly at all times. You communicate in an expressive manner and do not conceal anything. You are open and willing to listen to whatever the clients want to discuss. In other words, being genuine means that you are able to be yourself without having to sacrifice your integrity or compromise your principles.

And yet, in order for advisor-client relationships to work, you must learn how to accommodate client personalities by adapting to each client's social style. As discussed earlier in this chapter, this typically takes place in step 3 of the selling/planning process when you are busy establishing and defining your relationship with clients. Adapting to a client's social style is an important component in building rapport with the client, and an advisor-client relationship built on rapport is much more likely to be a productive and ongoing relationship than one missing this ingredient.

Self-Awareness

self-awareness

There is general consensus among counselor—educators that advisors should possess *self-awareness*, especially with regard to their attitudes and values. Advisors who are aware of their own value systems have a better chance of avoiding the imposition of their values on their clients. This quality is vitally important because you want to help clients make decisions that stem from the clients' own value systems rather than from yours. The more you know about yourself, the better you can understand, interpret, evaluate, and control your behavior, and the less likely you are to attribute aspects of yourself to clients—a rather common defense mechanism known as projection. Before you can be aware of others, it is essential that you be solidly grounded in self-awareness.

In her book, *Effective Helping: Interviewing & Counseling Techniques*, Barbara Okun suggests that an advisor should continually try to determine his or her own needs, feelings, and values by answering the following questions:[10]

- Am I aware when I find myself feeling uncomfortable with a client or with a particular subject area?
- Am I aware of my avoidance strategies?
- Can I really be honest with the client?
- Do I always feel the need to be in control of situations?
- Do I often feel as if I must be omnipotent in that I must do something to make the client "get better" so that I can be successful?

10. Barbara F. Okun, *Effective Helping: Interviewing & Counseling Techniques*, fourth ed. (Pacific Grove, CA: Brooks-Cole Publishing Co., Division of Wadsworth, Inc., 1992)

- Am I so problem oriented that I'm always looking for the negative, for a problem, and never responding to the positive, to the good?
- Am I able to be as open with clients as I want them to be with me?

The adage "know thyself" should apply to financial advisors and other helping professionals even more than it does to the population at large. A very large part of your responsibility as an advisor is to know yourself as thoroughly as possible, so you can provide the very best kind of objective, informed counseling for clients. Advisors who have many blind spots about themselves will surely be less effective in a helping situation than advisors who are comfortably self-aware. This is not to say that you must be a problem-free, completely self-actualized individual; rather, it means that you are a human being with a multitude of strengths and some weaknesses—but weaknesses that are known and will not interfere with the dynamics of counseling another person.

Orientation to Values

People have value systems that are the result of years of living on this planet. Many of these values are inculcated in them by their parents, their schools, their religions, their peers, and society. However these values came to them, they are as much a part of them as their physical and psychological characteristics. This is not to say that they are a permanent, static part of their being because values can, and do, change.

The point is that values, while deeply internalized, are not immutable. You need to remind yourself of this as you work with clients who are confused and afraid in approaching important decisions. Although people are in many ways a reflection of their past history, they are—or can be—much more than that. There is no need to be shackled to the past. People can, if they choose, overcome their past and live new lives based on who they are in the present and what they believe in and hold to be valuable both now and in the future. This is a liberating concept that frees people to think, feel, and behave in ways that are compatible with their present being, rather than dooming themselves to repeat the past and live in ways that are no longer meaningful.

As a financial advisor, your role in this situation is to act as a catalyst rather than as a maintainer of the status quo. The implied danger, of course, is that you might try to force change in your clients' values and attitudes where none is desired or sought, or that you might subtly or not so subtly try to impose your values on clients. You must consciously guard against both of these dangers. What advisors must do is listen carefully to clients as they sift through the various value choices they face so that when they finally make a choice, they can do so freely without encumbrances from the past. Clients must actually be opened up to the freedom of making choices that are relevant and meaningful to their existence. Good advisors have a knack for being able to do this.

Differences in Values

Each person has a hierarchy of values that makes order of his or her life. An older client facing retirement might, for example, rank security above risk taking when deciding how to invest money. On the other hand, a younger financial advisor might rank risk taking above security in the hierarchy of values. What happens, then, when the risk-taking advisor sits down to counsel his or her security-minded client? If the advisor is sensitive and understanding, he or she will listen to the client and try to get a sense of what is important to the client and what the client is willing and unwilling to do. The effective financial advisor does not try to sell the client a product and/or service that the advisor believes is right for the client but the client believes is wrong, unsafe, or risky.

Counseling is caring, and caring means that you care enough—have enough faith in the client's worth as a unique human being—to permit the client to make value choices that fit the client's value system. As a financial advisor, you can and should provide information that will help the client make the choice, but the choice ultimately belongs with the client, not you. Only in this way are you truly counseling the client.

In addition to differences in values, which often reflect the differences in age between advisors and clients, we should consider two other "isms"—sexism and racism—and how they impinge on the advisor-client relationship. Let us look first at sex differences.

Attributes of an Effective Advisor

- Unconditional positive regard
- Accurate empathy
- Genuineness
- Self-awareness

Sexist counseling occurs when you use your own sex ideology as a framework for counseling. In the field of financial planning, this might take place when a male advisor discourages a female client from doing something that has traditionally been thought by many men to be inappropriate, such as returning to work when there is an infant at home to be cared for. This kind of subtle advice giving, besides reflecting the obvious sex-role bias of the advisor, is not in keeping with what is happening in many households today. More important, it is intrusive in that the responsibility for making the decision is clearly the client's and not the advisor's. As an advisor, you must learn to recognize your own biases and sex-role stereotypes and not inflict them on people whom you are trying to help.

In the case of married couples, you should typically counsel both husband and wife. It is important to understand what both spouses have to say. In the past it was far too common to defer to the husband, the perceived "breadwinner," without taking into consideration what the wife had to contribute. Today that is not the case. When both husband and wife are in complete agreement, no problem exists. But when they disagree—and this is often communicated through nonverbal signals like a sigh, a frown, or an angry glance—it is important to bring the subject up for a full discussion. It is far better to spend whatever time and energy it takes to help both spouses reach a mutually acceptable decision than to proceed with one spouse's plan of action, knowing that it does not satisfy the other one.

Regarding racism in the financial planning profession, you should not limit your choice of clients based on race or make assumptions about your client's needs based on race.

The issue of whether white advisors can be effective in a relationship with African American or Hispanic clients has been the subject of much research, although no conclusive findings exist. An effective advisor, regardless of his or her race, should be able to work with clients of all races because all people have the same basic psychological needs and problems. As an advisor, you need to be conscious of your own biases regarding race and to guard against allowing biases to adversely affect the quality of the advisor-client relationship. The counseling strategies employed should not differ with regard to the race of the client any more than they should differ with regard to the sex, age, or religion of the client.

BASIC COMMUNICATION PRINCIPLES

In the previous section, we discussed the attributes of an effective advisor. In this section, we will explore communication as a process and attempt to relate fundamental principles of communication to effective counseling in the selling/planning process. An effective advisor is also an effective communicator.

Communication is often thought of as one person sending a message through both verbal and nonverbal channels to another person or persons with the intention of evoking a response. A speaker asks, "How are you?" and the listener (or receiver of the communication) answers, "Just fine—except for my back." Effective communication takes place when the receiver interprets the sender's message in precisely the same fashion in which the sender intended it. Difficulties in communication arise when the receiver misunderstands and/or misinterprets the sender's message. Because any individual's intentions are private and rarely clearly stated, the receiver of the message has the difficult job of decoding the message without knowing for a fact what the sender's intentions are.

In addition, communication failures can be attributed to the wide variety of stimuli with which individuals are bombarded during the course of a conversation. People try to communicate while watching television or listening to a CD, or they attempt to conduct two conversations simultaneously. But all noise is not auditory; some is emotional in nature. For example, labor-management negotiations are often fraught with suspicion and mistrust. Prejudices and biases, then, are emotionally built-in stimuli that interfere with objective listening and effective communication.

Related to this communication failure is the sad but simple truth that individuals listen in order to evaluate and render judgment about the speaker, which, in turn, makes the speaker guarded and defensive about what he or she is attempting to communicate. A good example of this type of ineffective communication is a city council meeting where one side advocates raising taxes while the other side interrupts, casts aspersions, and generally fights mightily against the tax hike. Whenever there are two people or two groups, each with a strong vested interest in an emotional issue, the likelihood of there being clear communication is virtually nil.

Even in the best of circumstances, communication should not be taken for granted. Let us look now at some basic principles of communication.

- Communication is learned through experience, but experience itself does not necessarily make us effective communicators. As children, we learn how to communicate by imitating our models—parents, siblings, neighbors, playmates, and baby sitters. Unfortunately, not all of our models are effective communicators. Thus, we acquire poor habits of communication early, and those habits, like all habits, are difficult to break. A child reared in a home where everyone talks at the same time and no one listens carries this model when leaving the home.
- The meaning of words is illusory. Words do not mean—people do. Words are merely symbols. Consider, for example, a simple word like rock. The teenager immediately thinks of loud music; the geologist thinks of a hard object created millions of years ago; the burglar thinks of a diamond ring; the old person thinks of sitting in a favorite chair, and so on. The point is that a word can have almost as many meanings as there are people who use it.
- Language is learned. Thus, in a sense we are programmed, and the meaning of words stays within us for future reference. This programming is extremely helpful because, once we learn a word, it usually remains ours for a lifetime. However, this programming can also serve as an impediment to open communication with others in that we often refer to our original conceptions of words without thinking how others might interpret them. For example, the word girl, once used to refer to any female, is now clearly inappropriate in referring to an adult woman.
- No two people are programmed alike. Therefore, no symbol can always be interpreted the same way. We differ in the nature and degree of our understanding. We perceive our environment differently according to our own frame of reference; consequently, meanings differ.
- It is impossible for any individual to encode or process all parts of a message. Besides the fact that words are often inadequate to describe accurately what we are feeling or thinking, there is the problem of distortion—that is, altering the event to suit our own purposes. But even if we have the precise word and communicate it without distortion, we still are faced with the problem of whether or not the receiver receives it in the same way in which it was intended.

- Some experts claim that the single greatest problem with communication is the assumption of it. We assume that our messages are clearly understood. We also sometimes assume that our perceptions are more accurate than the perceptions of another. Where human communication is concerned, no assumptions can or should be made.
- We are constantly communicating. Anything we say or do can be interpreted in a meaningful way as a message. Even during periods of silence, communication takes place. Nonverbal behaviors (which will be discussed shortly), such as eye contact, facial expressions, gestures, body posture, voice inflections, hesitations, and the like, all speak volumes. In fact, most sociological research claims that approximately two-thirds of the total message is communicated via nonverbal channels, especially where human emotions are concerned.
- Listening is communication too. Unfortunately, not everyone is a good listener. However, that should not be too surprising because listening as a communication skill is rarely, if ever, formally taught. To speak precisely and to listen carefully present a real challenge to all of us. The way in which we listen and respond to another person is crucial for building a fulfilling relationship. When we listen carefully—with understanding and without evaluation—and when we respond relevantly, we implicitly communicate to the speaker, "I care about what you are saying, and I'd like to understand it."
- The most effective communication occurs when the receiver of a message gives understanding responses, sometimes called paraphrases. A client might say, "I don't know . . . I doubt that we can afford to send both of our kids to college." Using an understanding response you would reply, "So you're just not sure you have the resources for college educations right now." While it might be tempting to try to convince the clients at this juncture that there is a way to finance their children's college educations, the understanding response communicates a desire to understand the clients without evaluating these statements as right or wrong. It also helps you to see clients' ideas and feelings from their point of view.
- Personalizing messages enhances the communication process and the advisor-client relationship. The hallmark of personal statements is the use of the personal pronouns—I, me, and my. Using generalized pronouns such as everyone, anyone, or somebody to refer to our own ideas only tends to confuse clients and, hence, results in ambiguity and faulty understanding. Personal statements, like "I can appreciate your concern over not having adequate resources," reveal your own feelings to clients and build rapport by increasing the personal quality of the relationship.

Elements of Nonverbal Behaviors

nonverbal behaviors

As mentioned above, clients communicate many feelings and attitudes to you through nonverbal behaviors including (but not limited to) fear, anxiety, sincerity, confusion, anger, aggression, happiness, hostility, interest, boredom, and concern. In the counseling context, *nonverbal behaviors* refer to those aspects of communication other than the words themselves. The two main sources of nonverbal behaviors are the body and the voice. From these two sources come seven types of nonverbal signs of meaning: body positions, body movements, gestures, facial expressions, eye contact, voice tone, and voice pitch. Each of these types of non-linguistic signs conveys a wealth of information if you are observant. Note that you must check out your first impressions of the meaning or significance of any body language against other clues the client gives.

Elements of Nonverbal Behaviors

- Body
  - Body positions
  - Body movements
  - Gestures
  - Facial expressions
  - Eye contact
- Voice
  - Voice tone
  - Voice pitch

The Body

When learning to improve your ability to observe clients' nonverbal behaviors, it is important to notice the various ways by which the body actually communicates, either in agreement or in disagreement with what is actually said. In particular, you should notice and learn to interpret the communications that are transmitted by your client's body positions and movements, hand and arm gestures, facial expressions, and eye contact.

The Voice

You can observe nonverbal voice clues in the tone and pitch of your client's voice. Tone and pitch are qualities of the voice that may indicate the speaker's feelings, quite apart from what is actually said. You should observe them closely.

Interpreting the Meaning of Nonverbal Behaviors

Nonverbal behaviors are clues that you must clearly observe and compare with what your client says to determine whether they are appropriate or compatible. For example, if a client blurts out, "I am furious with the broker who sold me that bunch of junk last year!" and strikes the desk, the gesture is compatible with the verbal message—it agrees with what the client says. If the client makes the same statement and sits smiling calmly, however, there is incompatible behavior—the body language does not jibe with the verbal message. When you observe incompatible behavior in a client, you should mention it in order to clarify the element of the communication that is correct.

Nonverbal behaviors are clues or indicators. Although they signify something, their meanings can be clouded by incompatibility, distortion, or vagueness. Premature assumptions about what they really mean would be as unprofessional as failing to notice them altogether. For example, a client's trembling hands might be due to one or more of the following causes: nervousness, fear, Parkinson's disease, too much coffee, chemical poisoning, and/or alcoholism. The client who always talks loudly may be angry or hearing impaired, or merely overbearing. The client who shows no interest in a financial planning session may be worn out from worrying whether recent commodities futures trading is going to wipe him or her out with margin calls, whether he or she should buy term or whole life for estate liquidity, or whether he or she will have an estate. The client may be taking tranquilizers due to anxiety about a son and heir who abuses drugs. For any number of reasons, the client may need psychological counseling or therapy before he or she can undertake financial planning. In short, not all the problems that clients may bring to financial planning sessions are financial in origin or nature. When present, these nonfinancial problems will distort client messages and add to the difficulties of clarifying them.

Observant advisors need to be astute enough to discern from among all the verbal and nonverbal clues the client presents and be aware that in most cases there will be a mixture of compatible and incompatible clues. In other words, as an advisor, you should understand who your clients are, where they are, where they want to go, and then suggest optimal ways to help each client get there. You should not assume that you know what a given behavior means. You should examine it and clarify your perceptions of that behavior with each client.

In addition, you should not forget that you communicate in both verbal and nonverbal ways, just as the clients do, and that your communication behaviors very much affect clients. This is particularly true of nonverbal messages. Therefore, any of the communication and psychological considerations that apply to clients also apply to you. As a financial planning advisor, you will want to remove from your own behaviors those elements that present obstacles to successful communication with clients and with other professionals. Clients are then more likely to accept you as a financial advisor and, ultimately, to accept the financial plans that you develop to meet their financial needs and goals. Similarly, other professionals whose expertise you may need in developing and implementing your clients' financial plans will also respect you as a financial advisor.

ATTENDING AND LISTENING SKILLS

Paying attention to clients is the first necessary component in good communication. No matter how expert your other communication skills are, if you are inattentive to clients' verbal and nonverbal behaviors, you are apt to lose the clients at the outset. How often have you been in the company of another person who shies away from looking at you, who glances nervously at his or her wristwatch, who interrupts you, and who, literally and figuratively, turns his or her back to you? Surely, if you have had this kind of experience, you can recall just how uncomfortable and ill at ease you were with this inattentive behavior.

If your goal is to understand clients, you must first pay close attention to and focus on their verbal and nonverbal messages. Poor attending and poor listening lead to poor understanding.

Physical Attending

physical attending

Gerard Egan, a renowned counselor-educator, categorizes attending behavior into (1) *physical attending,* or using the body to communicate, and (2) psychological attending, or listening actively. He identifies five basic attributes associated with physical attending.[11] These attributes are as follows:

- Face the other person squarely.
- Adopt an open posture.
- Lean toward the other person.
- Maintain good eye contact.
- Be relaxed while attending.

As has been mentioned previously, communication is constantly taking place, so you should use your body—gestures, posture, eyes—to communicate whatever message you wish to communicate. Otherwise, the body may communicate something you do not wish to communicate. In other words, you should try to make your body work in behalf of the advisor-client relationship.

Active Listening

active listening

So far, attending has been described as a physical activity; *active listening* brings in the psychological activity involved in attending. Many advisors take listening for granted, but there is a distinct difference between simply hearing and actively listening. Hearing means receiving auditory signals. A person says, "I have a bad headache," and we hear that message and respond, "That's too bad," or "Here, have a couple of aspirin." An active listener, on the other hand, might respond, "You look as though it's really getting you down." In

11. Gerard Egan, *The Skilled Helper: A Model for Systematic Helping and Interpersonal Relating* (Monterey, CA: Brooks/Cole, 1975): chapter 3, pp. 64-70

short, the active listener responds not only to the verbal message received through the auditory channel, but also to the unspoken, or nonverbal message, communicated by the sender's body, facial expression, and/or tone of voice.

Active listening, then, means putting the nonverbal behavior, the voice, and words together—all the cues sent out by the other person—to get the essence of the communication being sent. An active listener is an understanding listener, one who attempts to see the world from the other's frame of reference. If you can state in your own words what a client said, and the client accepts your statement as an accurate reflection of what he or she said, then it is safe to say that you listened actively and understood with accuracy.

Active listening is not merely parroting another's words—a toy can be programmed to do that. Active listening means involving yourself in the inner world of another person while, at the same time, maintaining your own identity and being able to respond with meaningfulness to the messages of that other person.

Understanding Responses

As indicated above, active listening is hard work and requires intense focusing and concentration. Years of not listening have made most of us poor listeners. We are distracted easily. We tend to evaluate and judge what is being said while it is being said so that we are framing our own responses to the speaker's statement before the speaker is finished talking. Thus, we miss the message.

There are several simple ways of responding to people so that they feel accepted and understood. Let us look at some of these understanding responses.

continuing response

Perhaps the simplest type of understanding response is a *continuing response.*[12] Nonverbally, if you want a client to continue talking, you might smile or nod your head to communicate agreement and/or understanding. Equally as effective in communicating understanding is a minimal encourager like "uh-huh," "mmmm," "then?" or "and . . . ?" These relatively unobtrusive responses encourage the speaker to continue talking. They communicate to the speaker, "Go on, I'm with you."

restatement-of-content response

Another type of understanding response is the *restatement-of-content response.* The rationale for restatement is to let speakers hear what they have said on the assumption that this may encourage them to go on speaking, examining, and looking deeper. Restatement communicates to a client, "I am listening to you very carefully, so much so that I can repeat what you have said." The most effective restatements are those that you phrase in your own words, a paraphrase of what the speaker has stated.

Just as you manifest understanding for your client by responding to the content of the client's message, so may you also show understanding of the client's experience by responding in a way that reflects the feelings expressed.

12. Allen Ivey and M. Ivey, *Intentional Interviewing and Counseling* (Pacific Grove, CA: Brooks/Cole, 2003).

Sometimes feelings are expressed directly; at other times they are implied or stated indirectly. To respond to a person's feelings, we must observe the behavioral cues like tone of voice, body posture, gestures, and facial expression, as well as listen to the speaker's words.

reflection-of-feeling response

Consider this client statement: "Within the next few months, we need to buy a new refrigerator and another car. [Sigh] I just don't know where the money is going to come from." A *reflection-of-feeling response* might be, "You sound pretty hopeless about your financial state. It sure is hard to break even, let alone get ahead, these days." Again, by responding in an empathetic way to your client's statement, you communicate an understanding of your client's experience; in addition, you progress one step further by addressing the non-verbalized feelings. This illustrates to your client that you understand so well what your client is stating that you can paraphrase both words and feelings.

It is helpful to both your client and you to struggle to capture in words the uniqueness of your client's experience. The most effective types of understanding responses capsulize both the feeling and the content of your client's message. The basic format for this type of response is "You feel __________ [feeling] because __________ [content]." This response enables your client to get in closer touch with the feelings that are an outgrowth of his or her situation. That, in turn, facilitates working through the problem, because you involve your client in exploring himself or herself in the problem. Because you have accurately understood and responded to your client, your client will go on to share other personal experiences that bear upon the presented problem.

clarifying response

Two other types of understanding responses should be mentioned. Each is related to the restatement-of-content and the reflection-of-feeling responses. Yet there is a subtle shade of difference. The first is the *clarifying response;* it tends to amplify the speaker's statement. The clarifying response does not add anything new to what your client has said; it simply expands what he or she has already stated. You attempt to restate or clarify for your client what your client has had some difficulty in expressing clearly. It is akin to a translation of your client's words into language that is more familiar and understandable to both your client and you. To the extent that your response is on target, the puzzle becomes clear and more readily solved.

Two Clarifying responses are helpful for your client because they

- facilitate client self-understanding
- attend especially to your client's feelings
- communicate your understanding to your client
- move your client toward a clearer definition of the problem

Another side to the clarifying response concerns your need to have communication made clear. When you are puzzled, it is certainly legitimate to ask for clarification such as, "I'm sorry. I don't follow what you're saying. Can you make that clearer for me?"

summarization response

The second type of understanding response is the *summarization response.* Summaries are especially helpful toward the end of a meeting, because they concentrate on and capsulize a series of scattered ideas to present a clear perspective. The summary has the effect of reassuring clients that you have been tuned in to their many messages. Sometimes, however, it is better to have your client do the summarizing. In this way, your client maintains the responsibility for bringing the messages together into a meaningful conclusion.

In the last section we covered some basic principles of communication with the emphasis on nonverbal behaviors. In this section, we directed our attention to the skills of physical attending and active listening plus five types of understanding responses associated with active listening (that is, continuing, restatement of content, reflection of feeling, clarifying, and summarization). The element common to all five of these understanding responses is that you as the advisor follow, or track, your client's lead. These types of responses communicate a high level of understanding that enable your client not only to experience what it feels like to be understood, but also to progress further toward an ultimate resolution of the situation.

Types of Understanding Responses Associated with Active Listening

- Continuing
- Restatement of content
- Reflection of feeling
- Clarifying
- Summarization

LEADING RESPONSES

leading response

Now the focus turns to a *leading response* in which the advisor, to a certain extent, takes the lead and deviates somewhat from the client's preceding responses. When the financial advisor decides to make a leading response, it is the advisor's frame of reference that comes into focus. Up to this point, the advisor's responses have followed from the client's statements. Here, the emphasis shifts. An obvious danger of this shift is that you may move in a direction in which your client is not yet ready or willing to move. Despite this danger, if you have followed your client closely so far, and if a good relationship has been established, then this different kind of response should not threaten your client as long as it is used carefully and tentatively.

explanatory response

The first type of leading response is the *explanatory response.* An explanation is a relatively neutral description of the way things are. It deals in logical, practical, and factual information. It is often offered at the client's request, although there are instances when you will offer an explanation without its being requested. Your explanation should be simple, concise, and comprehensible. Long-winded explanations tend to become vague and hard to follow. You should also guard against using a condescending, patronizing, or pedantic tone. The best explanations are those that are exchanged between equal partners (not superior-subordinate) in a relationship.

interpretive response

Another type of leading response is the *interpretive response.* Interpretations can be particularly risky when you go too deep too soon, or when the interpretation is off base. Interpretations often come across as sounding overly clinical, diagnostic, and authoritarian. Despite these drawbacks, interpretations can be extremely effective responses because they often cut to the heart of the matter. The client, moreover, is free to accept, modify, or deny your interpretation, and this is very important. If your interpretation is inaccurate, it is far better to discover that early than to proceed indefinitely along the wrong path.

reassuring response

A third type of leading response that advisors frequently employ is reassurance, or encouragement. A *reassuring response* is designed with the intention of making the client feel better, to bolster his or her spirits, and to offer support in a time of need. It communicates clearly to the client that "I am here ready to help you in any way that I can." As a means of helping, however, the reassuring response tends to be merely a temporary measure. The reflection-of-feeling type of understanding response discussed in the previous section on active listening is far more effective when emotions surface. The reflection-of-feeling response communicates accurate empathy, while the reassuring response offers only sympathy, and very few people like to feel pitied. Reassurance, while not a harmful response, promises pie in the sky and delivers nothing.

suggestive response

The final type of leading response involves giving advice and is called a *suggestive response*. Many people actively seek the advice of others, possibly hoping that the advice giver will make the difficult decisions for them or solve their problems for them. And, as chance or human nature would have it, there is certainly no dearth of people in this world willing to dole out free advice. In an advisor-client relationship, however, the best kind of advice is self-advice. Advisors who have been responding in an understanding fashion are already well on their way toward helping clients discover, in their own way and in their own time, what advice is best for them. There are times in an advisor-client relationship when proffering advice in acceptable, but these times are few. When advice is given, it should be offered tentatively in the form of a suggestion or recommendation about which the client has the final decision. Otherwise, the advisor not only leads, but he or she also takes over the ultimate responsibility for the client's financial plan. Each person has the right to form his or her own plan. Advice giving robs the client of this right.

Types of Leading Responses

- Explanatory
- Interpretive
- Reassuring
- Suggestive

The next section looks at another type of communication technique—perhaps the most commonly used communication technique—the question. Questions come in many varieties, some much more effective in communication than others.

THE QUESTION

The question is surely one of the most timeworn communication techniques. It is appropriate when used sparingly to gather information from the client in order to develop a plan or to devise strategies. Unfortunately, the question is not always used in this fashion because many advisors see their main role, however inappropriate, as an interviewer or even an interrogator. Moreover, a lengthy question-answer dialogue sets up a pattern of communication that is difficult for the participants to break: the client waits for the inevitable question; the question comes, followed by the answer (and not much more); then comes the wait for the next question. Questioning almost always casts you in the role of the authority figure and the client in the role of a somewhat passive subordinate—certainly not the type of interpersonal, advisor-client relationship conducive to effective financial counseling.

Despite the disadvantages of using questions, there are times when only a well-phrased question will suffice, particularly when you are seeking data from the client (step 4 of the selling/planning process). Even here, though, there is a qualitative difference between the various types of questions that you might ask. With this in mind, we will discuss several categories of questions in this final section of the chapter.

Open-Ended versus Closed-Ended Question

open-ended question

closed-ended question

Ideally, the questions you pose should be open-ended and require more than just a yes or no response; otherwise, they tend to stifle interaction. The *open-ended question* allows the client to select a response from a full repertory. The *closed-ended question* limits the client to a specific, narrow response, often either a yes or a no. The open-ended question solicits opinions, thoughts, ideas, values, and feelings. The closed-ended question typically solicits singular facts or one-word replies. However, despite the drawbacks of closed-ended questions, there are times when they can be effectively used to gather certain types of information.

Leading Question

leading question

A type of closed-ended question that is not only ineffective but also manipulative is a *leading question*. A leading question usually begins with, "Don't you think . . . ," or "Do you really feel . . ." More often than not it leads the client toward a conclusion that you (not the client) have already formulated, so that there is an element of dishonesty in even asking the question. It is far more effective and honest to rephrase the leading question into a declarative statement that shares a perception or opinion. Declarative statements, generally speaking, communicate far more clearly and are more respectful than manipulative leading questions. A good rule to follow is to make as many statements as possible and save the questions for honest information seeking.

Either/Or or True/False Question

either/or question

true/false question

Another type of relatively ineffective question is the *either/or question* or the *true/false question*. While this type of question is not quite as closed-ended as the leading question, it is only slightly less closed, since it limits the client to only two options. Although the client might consider both options, he or she might also consider neither option or a third or fourth option. So when you phrase the question as an either/or question, the client is forced to choose from the two options offered. The world is not simply black or white; there are various shades of gray. By opening up the question, you allow the client to respond freely from the client's own frame of reference and not from yours. And for most purposes, this is what information gathering in the selling/planning process requires.

Why Question

why question

Even though a *why question* can be classified as an open-ended question and thus theoretically appear sound, this is not the case. On the surface, questions beginning with why appear to be legitimate enough, signifying the inquiry of casual relationships as in, "Why are you planning to retire at age 62?" Unfortunately, when you ask why questions in your role as an advisor, they carry a connotation of implied disapproval, thus forcing the client to justify or defend his or her thoughts, ideas, or actions. Even when that is not the meaning you intend, that is generally how the client receives why questions. The why question tends to question the client's motivation (or lack of motivation) and thus creates a certain defensiveness. Consequently, it is generally better to avoid why questions unless there is a valid reason for asking one and no other type of question will suffice.

Question Bombardment

question bombardment

Still another kind of faulty questioning technique, called *question bombardment*, occurs when the advisor asks double, triple, or even quadruple questions without waiting for a response. This is frequently referred to as question bombardment. As absurd as this type of questioning may sound, it occurs far too frequently in interviews and planning meetings. If you need to ask more than one question, it is better to form separate questions, waiting for a full response to each question before going on to the next one.

Categories of Questions

- Open-ended questions
- Closed-ended questions
- Leading questions
- Either/or and true/false questions
- Why questions
- Question bombardment

Concluding Remarks

Questioning is a technique in the communications repertory of most financial advisors. However, if you wish to become a better communicator, you need to convert some of your questions (especially closed-ended, leading, either/or, and why questions) into declarative statements. By using statements, you assume responsibility for what you say. By asking questions, you shift the responsibility to your clients; this may sometimes be necessary. Nonetheless, far too often, advisors simply shirk their responsibility for and involvement in the interaction with clients when they revert to questioning. As stated earlier in this chapter, counseling is not the same as interviewing. If you hope to make counseling your primary means of structured communication in the selling/planning process, you need to do far more than simply ask one question after another.

CHAPTER REVIEW

Key Terms and Concepts are explained in the Glossary. Answers to the Review Questions and Self-Test Questions are found in the back of the textbook in the Answers to Questions section.

Key Terms and Concepts

interviewing
directive interview
nondirective interview
counseling
advising
social styles
financial life planning
resistance
disclosure statement
unconditional positive regard
accurate empathy
genuineness
self-awareness
nonverbal behaviors
physical attending
active listening
continuing response
restatement-of-content response
reflection-of-feeling response
clarifying response
summarization response
leading response
explanatory response
interpretive response
reassuring response
suggestive response

open-ended question
closed-ended question
leading question
either/or question
true/false question
why question
question bombardment

Review Questions

2-1. Describe the three types of structured communication used in the selling/planning process.

2-2. Describe the importance of structuring communication with clients.

2-3. Identify the four social styles and explain the characteristics of each.

2-4. Identify several sources of client resistance behavior in the selling/planning process.

2-5. What types of information do clients want to know about their advisors?

2-6. Identify the attributes of an effective advisor.

2-7. What is the importance of self-awareness in the advisor-client relationship, especially as it relates to value orientations and differences?

2-8. Describe several basic principles of communication.

2-9. Identify the ways in which nonverbal behaviors are communicated by the body and the voice.

2-10. Why is it important to assess the meaning of both verbal and nonverbal behaviors?

2-11. Identify the five basic attributes associated with physical attending.

2-12. What type of understanding response made during active listening does each of the following examples illustrate?
a. "Well, let's see what we've concluded then. You want to set aside about $3,000 per year to save for a down payment on a vacation house at the shore, and safety is your prime consideration in the investment of that money."
b. "I'm not sure I'm following you. Tell me again what your plan is for disposing of your interest in the partnership."
c. "From what you just told me, then, I gather that you want to stay away from the limited partnership and put the money into the stock market instead."

2-13. Describe four types of leading responses.

2-14. What type of question or questioning technique does each of the following examples illustrate? (Each example may illustrate more than one type of question or questioning technique.)
a. "Why haven't you started converting some of that term insurance to whole life?"
b. "Don't you think your present portfolio of investments is pretty illiquid?"
c. "What goals do you have with respect to the education of your children?"
d. "Do you plan to hold on to your mutual fund?"
e. "Don't you think you should put $4,000 into an IRA this year? That isn't much money for you, is it? After all, don't you have at least that much in your passbook savings account right now? Or am I mistaken on that point?"
f. "You were born in 1946, right?"

Self-Test Questions

Instructions: Read the chapter first, then answer the following questions to test your knowledge. There are 10 questions; circle the correct answer, then check your answers with the answer key in the back of the book.

15. Which of the following best describes the advisor attribute of unconditional positive regard?

(A) The advisor expresses appreciation of the client as a unique and worthwhile person.
(B) The advisor is open and willing to listen to the client.
(C) The advisor has an awareness of his or her own value system.
(D) The advisor gives the client the feeling that he or she is in touch with the client.

16. Which of the following statements concerning client resistance in the selling/planning process is correct?

(A) The advisor typically does not encounter client resistance in the selling/planning process.
(B) The advisor should deal with covert hostility directly by focusing on the client's behavior.
(C) The advisor should set himself or herself above the client in a critical and judgmental manner.
(D) The advisor should avoid discussing the client's marital problems.

17. It is important for the advisor to personalize communications to the client for which of the following reasons?

(A) It helps the client to better understand the advisor's values.
(B) It helps the client to move directly toward the necessary decisions.
(C) It enhances the quality of the relationship with the client.
(D) It is consistent with the fiduciary status of the advisor.

18. Which of the following best describes a client with the social style of analytical?

    (A) The client is forceful, direct, and wants power.
    (B) The client is outgoing, enthusiastic, and wants recognition.
    (C) The client is easygoing, dependent, and wants approval.
    (D) The client is logical, quiet, and wants respect.

19. Which of the following statements concerning basic communication principles is (are) correct?

    I. It is impossible for any individual to encode or process all parts of a message.
    II. Some experts claim that the single greatest problem with communication is the assumption of it.

    (A) I only
    (B) II only
    (C) Both I and II
    (D) Neither I nor II

20. Which of the following statements concerning the types of structured communication used in the selling/planning process is (are) correct?

    I. Counseling and advising are synonymous and interchangeable with each other.
    II. Interviewing is a process of communication with a predetermined and specific purpose.

    (A) I only
    (B) II only
    (C) Both I and II
    (D) Neither I nor II

21. Which of the following statements concerning interviews is (are) correct?

    I. They typically take place in a formal and structured setting.
    II. Digressions from the subject are encouraged.

    (A) I only
    (B) II only
    (C) Both I and II
    (D) Neither I nor II

READ THE FOLLOWING DIRECTIONS BEFORE CONTINUING

The questions below differ from the preceding questions in that they all contain the word EXCEPT. So you understand fully the basis used in selecting each answer, be sure to read each question carefully.

---

22. All the following are types of understanding responses associated with active listening EXCEPT

    (A) restatement of content
    (B) summarization
    (C) reflection of feeling
    (D) suggestive

23. Clarifying responses by the advisor are helpful for the client because they do all the following EXCEPT

    (A) facilitate client self-understanding
    (B) attend especially to the client's feelings
    (C) move the client toward a clearer definition of the problem
    (D) communicate the client's understanding to the advisor

24. Elements of nonverbal behavior include all the following EXCEPT

    (A) facial expressions
    (B) word selection
    (C) eye contact
    (D) voice pitch

3

Gathering Information and Establishing Goals

Learning Objectives

An understanding of the material in this chapter should enable the student to

3-1. Describe the relevance of the initial financial planning meeting to the information gathering process.

3-2. Explain the importance of using fact finders.

3-3. Identify the major sections of the Personal Financial Planning Fact Finder, and describe the types of information contained in each of the sections.

3-4. Describe the importance of goal setting in the financial planning process.

3-5. Identify the major topic areas for determining client personal and financial planning goals.

3-6. Explain the purpose and content of the agreement letter.

The development of either a multiple-purpose or comprehensive financial plan covering some or all of the major planning areas is neither a quick nor an easy task. The diversity and complexity of needed information require a systematic method to effectively gather, organize, and process that information. Although there are many possible ways to systematize the gathering of information, one way that has proven helpful is to use a structured fact-finder form. A well-designed fact-finder form helps to organize both the quantitative and the qualitative information that must be processed and used in counseling clients regarding their financial goals. By gathering personal and financial information with the aid of a fact finder (the topic of discussion in the first half of the chapter), you are able to determine a client's current financial position and cash flow status. You are also able to thoroughly explore and record the client's financial attitudes, values, goals, and priorities. Without this type of personal and financial information about the client, it would be impossible for you to develop a worthwhile financial plan and/or formulate strategies to achieve the client's financial goals.

Although it is true that few people begin a vacation without a specific destination in mind, it is also true that millions of people make significant financial decisions without a specific financial destination in mind. Determining a specific financial destination—that is, goal setting—is as critical to creating a successful financial plan as information gathering with the aid of a fact finder. Few people, however, actually set clearly defined goals. By leading the client through the goal-setting exercise (the focus of the second half of the chapter), you can help the client establish SMART[13] goals (that is goals that are Specific, Measurable, Achievable, Relevant, and have a Target date) reasonable, achievable goals.

THE INITIAL MEETING

To ensure that fact-finding and planning meetings with the client will be productive and efficient, the selling/planning process usually begins with an initial meeting to determine whether the client is interested in your services. The initial meeting typically begins with you in your advisor role explaining the format and subject matter of the interaction that is to follow. Your task here is to make the purpose of the selling/planning process clear to clients at the outset. You should clearly explain the products and/or services that you have at your disposal to facilitate the process. In addition, you need to agree on exactly what the client's and your responsibilities are and on how decisions will be made. If you do not live up to your client's expectations during the initial meeting, there will be no second or follow-up meeting. The initial meeting with your client sets the stage for future meetings.

If you hope to establish an advisor-client relationship with a client at the initial meeting, you must clarify certain ground rules. Foremost among them is the understanding that meaningful financial planning for the client can be done only if complete information about the client's personal and financial situation is revealed. The client should understand the need to furnish financial records and documents and to participate in fact-finding and planning meetings with you, during which time his or her financial situation, problems, and goals will be thoroughly discussed.

However, before you begin the information-gathering process, you should discuss a few concerns with the client. First, the client should be made aware that he or she will have to invest time, perhaps a significant amount of time, in the information-gathering stage of financial planning. Even though part of your responsibility as an advisor is to avoid consuming the client's time unnecessarily, this commitment of the client's time is essential. The magnitude of the needed time commitment will depend on the scope and complexity of the client's goals and circumstances, but the proper development of even a narrowly focused and fairly uncomplicated plan requires information that only the client can furnish.

Second, the client should be made aware that he or she probably will have to provide you with some information that is highly confidential, perhaps even sensitive or painful to reveal. Again, the scope and complexity of the client's goals will influence this matter. The creation of even relatively simple financial plans, however, may require clients to disclose such things as their income and

13. See www.extension.org/pages/SMART_Financial_Goal-Setting.

spending patterns, their attitudes toward other family members, or their opinions as to the extent of their own financial responsibilities to others.

THE IMPORTANCE OF FACT FINDERS

fact finder form

If the initial meeting is successful and your client wants to continue the process, schedule the second meeting for the near future and tell your client that you will be sending him or her a letter confirming the time and location. In addition, at this time you should either hand your client a *fact-finder form* or enclose one with the letter so your client can begin to gather and organize his or her personal and financial information. Included as part of The American College's Personal Financial Planning Fact Finder (hereinafter referred to simply as Fact Finder) is a checklist of the various documents that should be made available to you. This appears on page 25 of the Fact Finder (reproduced in appendix A) and is also shown in the figure below. Your client should provide this preliminary information well in advance of the information-gathering meeting to give you ample time to

- review the information
- form preliminary impressions of the client's financial condition
- determine those areas in which more detailed information and insight into the client's condition is needed

During this preliminary review of financial records and documents, you should record important information from the appropriate sections of the Fact Finder, which will save valuable time in the fact-finding meeting. Some of the information must be obtained from other sources, such as the client's employer, attorney, or CPA. To authorize you to obtain this information from the client's other advisors or employer, he or she must sign an Authorization for Information, which can be found on page 25 of the Fact Finder. You may also need to do some research for the client to verify that certain information is correct.

Figure 3–1 Checklist of Documents

Insurance Policies: Life, Long-Term Care, Medical/Dental, Disability Income, and Property/Liability

Company	Policy Number	☑	Company	Policy Number	☑
______	______	☐	______	______	☐
______	______	☐	______	______	☐
______	______	☐	______	______	☐
______	______	☐	______	______	☐

Annuities, Mutual Funds, Stocks, Other Securities

______	☐	______	☐
______	☐	______	☐
______	☐	______	☐

Personal/Family Documents (copies)

- ☐ Tax returns (3–5 years)
- ☐ Wills (client and spouse)
- ☐ Living wills (client and spouse)
- ☐ Healthcare power(s) of attorney
- ☐ Power(s) of attorney/appointment
- ☐ Trust instruments
- ☐ Financial statements
- ☐ Personal/family budgets
- ☐ Sale/purchase contract
- ☐ Current insurance offers
- ☐ Current investment offers
- ☐ Deeds, mortgages, land contracts
- ☐ Guardian nominations
- ☐ Leases (as lessor or lessee)
- ☐ Notices of awards, elections
- ☐ Separation/divorce/nuptial
- ☐ Patents/copyrights/royalties
- ☐ Other (specify)
- ☐ Other (specify)

Employment/Business Documents (copies)

- ☐ Employee benefits booklet
- ☐ Employee benefits statement
- ☐ Deferred-compensation plan
- ☐ HR-10 plan (Keogh)
- ☐ IRAs (Roth/traditional)
- ☐ Simplified employee pension (SEP)
- ☐ Pension/profit-sharing plan
- ☐ §401(k) or §403(b) plan
- ☐ Stock-option/purchase agreement
- ☐ Employment agreement
- ☐ Other (specify)
- ☐ Other (specify)

Assembling complete, accurate, and up-to-date information about the client is the single most important task in financial planning. Some fact-finder forms, however, are only thin pamphlets that ask for basic information; the forms most useful for financial planning purposes generally are thick booklets that seek very detailed information. It is therefore imperative that the fact finder used to gather information for financial planning purposes be sufficiently comprehensive to enable the advisor to

- evaluate the client's total financial condition
- identify what type of person the client really is
- determine where the client wants to be
- formulate the most appropriate strategies for getting there

If the client is married, his or her spouse should be fully involved in providing information, and both the client and spouse should be present during fact-finding and planning meetings with you, unless there are compelling personal reasons to the contrary (such as an impending divorce). Indeed, in households in which both spouses have income and assets, you should counsel both spouses and develop a plan that reflects their mutual as well as their individual concerns and goals. In such cases, appropriate sections of the fact finder should be duplicated and filled out by both the client and spouse.

Because every financial advisor operates in a complex marketplace of varying services, products, and clients, no single fact-finder form can serve the needs of everyone. If you are not required to use your company's designated fact finder, the experienced advisor typically will modify an existing fact finder or develop a new one that can be used to meet the needs of his or her practice. The type of information requested by personal financial planning fact finders includes not only quantitative data about the client's current financial position but also qualitative information about the client's personal circumstances. Armed with complete information about the client, you are then able to analyze and evaluate the client's financial condition and make appropriate recommendations in the form of a multiple-purpose or comprehensive plan tailored exclusively for the client.

In cases where your services are engaged to provide solutions for single- or multiple-purpose planning objectives and you do not need all the information elicited by a comprehensive fact finder, have the client fill out only those sections of the Fact Finder that are relevant to analyzing and evaluating the specified planning objective(s). To help determine exactly what information is needed in each case, you must ask yourself the following questions:

- What information do I need from my client for a particular area (or areas) of planning?
- How do I evaluate this information and discuss it with my client?
- What information on products, services, and taxes do I need to address this area (or areas) of planning? (That is, what information do I need from the marketplace?)
- How do I apply this information to my client's planning objective(s) to develop recommendations that the client will adopt and implement?

Because many clients do not understand how multiple-purpose or comprehensive financial planning can benefit them, they seek help only in a planning area (or areas) in which they have a financial problem or goal that needs immediate attention. For these clients to understand and embrace financial planning, they must be exposed to its principles and procedures through the selling/planning process. You can accomplish this when you present your recommendations for the planning area (or areas) in which the clients are seeking help. At this time, you must show these clients how your recommendations affect other planning areas and explain to them how a personal financial plan can thoroughly integrate and coordinate all the planning areas.

PERSONAL FINANCIAL PLANNING FACT FINDER

The variety of clients and potential planning areas requires a fact finder that is both flexible and adaptable. It should be divided into several sections and subsections that can be used individually or in various combinations. The American College's Fact Finder (reproduced in appendix A) was designed with these requirements in mind.

Together, all sections of the Fact Finder elicit the information necessary to design and implement a personal financial plan customized exclusively for the client. In cases where the whole Fact Finder elicits more information than is necessary, you can select the relevant sections for the client to fill out. In those rare cases where you need more extensive and detailed information than the whole Fact Finder can provide, you can supplement the Fact Finder with special analysis forms and computer software programs specifically designed for more complex planning situations.

objective information

You will need to gather two broad types of information: objective and subjective. A financial plan that is customized to address the goals, needs, and objectives of an individual client requires gathering information on a wide range of planning areas. A few examples of *objective information* (factual) that you might need from the client include

- personal and family information
- a list of securities holdings
- an inventory of assets and liabilities
- the current estate plan
- a list of annual income and expenditures
- a summary of present insurance coverages
- the current financial plan

subjective information

Of at least equal importance is the *subjective information* about the client. You often will need to gather information about the client's (and his or her spouse's, if applicable) hopes, fears, values, preferences, attitudes, financial goals, and nonfinancial goals. This type of subjective information may include

- getting to know something about the client's personal life and relationships
- assessing the client's level of risk tolerance
- identifying the client's nonfinancial goals
- establishing the client's personal financial planning goals and priorities

The primary advantage of the Fact Finder is that it provides a systematic method for gathering client information to

- support the specific planning strategies, techniques, and methods for the client's case (and therefore valuable compliance and errors-and-omissions documentation)
- diagnose and review the client's total personal, financial, and tax position based on financial statements
- administer and periodically report on the client's case
- share information with other financial or legal advisors who are serving the client's needs

The Fact Finder is also designed to support your roles as information manager, fiduciary, and trusted advisor. To perform these roles well, you need to know far more than the numbers required for software processing. The Fact Finder includes many personal questions that elicit responses to a wide range of typical issues. These questions, asked from a counseling perspective, should be used to determine as clearly as possible how well each client understands financial planning and what each client wants to do with his or her financial resources.

The information assembled about the client's personal financial transactions can also fulfill these important needs:

- getting the client involved in the thought processes and procedural methods (the delivery system) of financial planning
- creating a professional language for financial planning that guides both you and the client
- determining the client's need for services and/or products based on your knowledge of their availability
- establishing the trusted advisor relationship with the client

The Fact Finder is a powerful information-management tool that enables you and each client to communicate about real issues and problems, both personal and financial. The Fact Finder can motivate both you and the client to become involved in planning by systematically addressing the first requirement—complete and accurate information.

You must also take time to humanize the process by developing much of the qualitative information in the Fact Finder such as the client's personal financial planning priorities, financial risk tolerance, and retirement planning assumptions. Most financial planning software programs are not designed to record all of the personal information that the client might share with you in the information-gathering meeting. Nevertheless, you should make notes on all items that relate to the client's financial concerns and planning objectives and retain these notes as part of the client's permanent hard copy file. There is ample white space in the Fact Finder for this purpose.

Although The American College's Fact Finder can be used by financial advisors, its purpose in being included in this book is to demonstrate how important a fact finder is to multiple-purpose financial planning. Most advisors choose fact finders that are designed to be used with specific financial planning software to simplify data entry. Moreover, many large financial services companies have developed their own fact-finder forms to satisfy their compliance departments, and they fully expect their advisor-representatives to use them. However, The American College's Fact Finder is an example of the types of client information needed in personal financial planning. To this end, a section-by-section discussion follows that describes the Fact Finder and how the information it gathers relates to multiple-purpose financial planning.

Personal Data

To involve clients in the planning process and diminish the time spent in fact-finding meetings, you need to provide your clients with at least a portion (if not all) of the fact-finder form. As noted earlier in this chapter, you can either hand it to your client at the end of the initial meeting or mail it to him or her in conjunction with the follow-up letter discussed in chapter 2. You should instruct clients to fill out as much of the fact-finder form as possible (that is, as much of the Fact Finder that you actually gave them), but you must make it clear that at a minimum they need to provide you with the insurance policies, personal/family documents, and employment/business documents listed on the checklist on page 25. Preferably these items should be in your possession prior to the fact-finding meeting so that you will have had ample time to review them.

The Fact Finder begins the accumulation of client information with the Personal Data section. This section includes general personal information about your client and his or her family. It begins on page 2 by requesting the street addresses, phone numbers, and e-mail addresses of the client (and spouse if the client is married). The unmarried client should ignore spaces requesting information about a spouse unless he or she has a domestic partner, in which case these spaces can accommodate this type of arrangement.

Also on page 2, this section asks for information about the client's other advisors. One of these advisors may become a resource for clarifying the client's financial history. These other advisors may also become members of the professional team whose expertise, services, and products will implement the financial plan ultimately developed for the client. Moreover, it is important for you to know who holds your client's confidence and trust and who (if anyone) is already considered your client's primary financial advisor. Knowing who your client's other advisors are helps to avoid alienating them, infringing on their territory, or giving them cause to thwart the planning process.

On page 3of the Fact Finder, the Personal Data section requests relevant information about the client's entire family. Support obligations are vital in determining the client's income needs while working, in retirement, or in the event of disability. They also help determine the income needs of survivors in the event of the client's (or spouse's) death. In addition, the section requests information about any health problems and/or special needs of the client and family members.

It is important for you to pay particular attention to the number and ages of your client's children, as this information will give you some indication of your client's current and future support obligations to all family members. This will affect decisions about the disposition of income-producing and appreciating assets to fund those needs as well as decisions about the purchase of appropriate life and disability income insurance coverage.

The personal information sought on the top half of page 4 of the Fact Finder is designed mostly to uncover potential complications in the client's (or spouse's) situation, such as previous marriages and alimony or child-support obligations, the anticipated assumption of future financial responsibility for a family member other than children, the existence (or lack) of prenuptial or postnuptial agreements, and the existence of benefits resulting from military or government service. It also requests the client's and spouse's level of education. These items may provide insight into what kind of person the client is and the level of sophistication and complexity of the client's current financial program. You should tactfully explore all client concerns here in order to anticipate later planning considerations. If there are problems, both the client and spouse may want to make some financial arrangement to equalize a particular family member's situation. For example, quite often the client will want to provide partial or full support for parents or for the spouse's parents.

Future Goals and Objectives

The Future Goals and Financial Objectives section on page 5 of the Fact Finder consists of two subsections. The first one asks the client (and spouse, if applicable) to circle the listed life events within the occupational, personal, and financial categories that he or she expects to occur in the near future. This helps you gain insight into financial and nonfinancial factors that may affect your client's planning decisions based on his or her respective stage of the financial life cycle.

The second subsection asks the client to rank his or her financial planning priorities regarding nine potential financial objectives. Be aware, however, that both the rankings and the objectives are subject to change. Subsequent analysis of your client's actual financial position and expectations may require revising priorities and objectives, or at least deferring the target dates for achieving some of the objectives. Often, your client will establish different priorities and objectives as a result of going through the planning process. Nevertheless, these preliminary rankings of objectives will give you an insight into your client's thinking. Insight into your client's priorities and objectives will help you and your client articulate the client's financial planning goals.

The final question in this section—"What do you think financial planning should do for you?"—may bring to a head a range of client concerns. Your client's response to this question will have an impact on what direction the selling/planning process should take.

Factors Affecting Your Financial Plan

In this section of the Fact Finder, the questions on page 5 are focused on the client's personality and willingness to implement subsequent recommendations. The first question asks whether the client or spouse has ever made gifts.

The next question asks whether the client is dissatisfied with the results of previous savings/investments. It is followed by a question that asks whether the client feels committed to any of his or her savings/investments. If the answer to either of these questions is yes, you should explore the client's thoughts. The Risk/Return Profile on page 22 of the Fact Finder may offer some insight into the source of the client's dissatisfaction and/or commitment.

The remaining questions in this section ask attitudinal-type questions regarding the client's (and spouse's, if applicable) knowledge of and ability to handle and manage personal financial affairs. Answers to these questions, which are extremely personal, may be difficult for the client to articulate. It is not easy for a client to divulge truthful feelings about a spouse and other family members. Yet the client's feelings and perceptions about these matters affect the selling/planning process, which must accommodate them to be successful.

If the client and spouse are not of like mind, they must resolve their differences. Finally, the last several questions ask about special problems or circumstances that may have an unusual impact on the client's financial plan.

The questions in this section are not meant to be exhaustive but rather to indicate the types of questions that yield important information about how the client (and spouse, if applicable) feels regarding sensitive personal and family issues. The client's answers usually lead to further discussion and to a clearer sense of what he or she hopes to achieve. They frequently disclose problem areas that may be difficult for the client to make clear, especially in the spouse's presence. You may need to use your most tactful counseling skills to find out how your client really feels about these issues. Your client's responses also provide clues about how to integrate factual and quantitative details with what your client wants to do and is willing to implement.

Having adequate factual and personal information early in the planning process makes the process more effective by enabling you to review the information, get to know your client, observe and evaluate verbal and nonverbal messages and communication styles, and complete sections in the Fact Finder that your client has not completed. The more information you secure initially, the better you can focus on your client's real needs.

One final comment is necessary. It concerns the relevance of the types of personal information sought on pages 2 through 5 of the Fact Finder. It is in these areas that the client's most sensitive feelings and thoughts are likely to emerge and that profound human and relational concerns are likely to be discovered. Therefore, these areas demand sensitivity in exercising the communication skills and techniques you learned in chapter 2. Even though the client may provide extensive and accurate data before and during the information-gathering meeting, you should thoroughly evaluate the client's responses for clues regarding personal, family, and economic problem areas. You should ask appropriate clarifying questions in a nonjudgmental way. The client's responses should be compared with information and facts provided in other sections of the Fact Finder to ascertain consistency.

Objectives Requiring Additional Income/Capital

The section titled Objectives Requiring Additional Income/Capital is on page 6 of the Fact Finder; it gathers details about specific client financial objectives that may require income and/or capital beyond what is needed for retirement and estate planning purposes. The most common objective that requires additional income/capital is the client's desire to send his or her children to college. Because of the importance of education funding to a large number of people, the topic is specifically listed on page 6 of the Fact Finder and is covered in greater depth in chapter 8.

College Education Funding

If the client wants help in developing a funding plan for specific objectives such as children's college educations, it is important to have a quantifiable determination of his or her financial risk tolerance. This can be provided by a questionnaire such as the Survey of Financial Tolerance located in appendix B. (The topic of financial risk tolerance is discussed at length in chapter 4.) This specific objective may require either funding that is separate from the funding allocated to long-range objectives, such as capital accumulation for retirement, or temporary allocations of all or part of the client's financial resources.

Clients often delay funding college expenses because they have no idea what those expenses will be in the future. Without precise information, you can estimate these expenses from existing studies, such as those conducted by The College Board (collegeboard.com), which publishes estimates of the average college costs for 2-year and 4-year public and private colleges. College cost estimates will enable you to project the total education expenses for each child. Therefore, you should use them with clients whenever possible. Although no one knows with precision what future rates will be, any meaningful estimates of future college costs must assume an inflation rate.

Along with the estimated tuition cost in today's dollars and the tuition inflation rate, the child's name and age, the number of years until the child begins college, and the number of years the child is expected to attend college once he or she begins should all be listed. All existing capital and monthly income allocated for the specific purpose of college funding should also be listed. The growth rate of these earmarked funds should also be recorded.

In addition, you may want to ask your client some questions regarding education funding such as

- How do you plan to pay for your children's college educations?
- Have you made any contingency plans for funding your children's college educations if you become disabled or die before they reach college age?
- Have you considered all the potential resources available for college funding?

As a financial advisor, you should determine whether your client's financial resources can be supplemented by other help, such as scholarships; part-time work; loans from federal, state, or family sources; and wills, trusts, and other gift programs by grandparents or other relatives. Help may be expected from a previous spouse. You should explore all possible sources in an effort to reduce or even eliminate the client's share of anticipated costs. This will free investment capital and cash flows for allocation to other financial objectives. Be sure that the name of each child for whom a client expects to provide full or partial funding of college expenses (or other education expenses) is entered in the table.

Other Income/Capital Objectives

Besides education funding, the client may have other objectives that require either long- or short-term planning and allocation. These objectives could include a desire to take care of a handicapped child, to provide support for a parent or other relative, or to accumulate funds for a future charitable bequest. You should explore the client's situation and uncover all funding objectives beyond the need to provide for personal economic well-being.

Retirement Planning

Most clients should complete the Retirement Planning section of the Fact Finder. It consists largely of questions designed to clarify just how the client wants to live during retirement and what financial resources will be available to support the desired lifestyle. Moreover, there are several questions dealing with retirement planning assumptions. They ask what the client expects the inflation rate and investment rate of return will be both before and after retirement begins, and the age when the client and spouse expect to retire. Keep in mind that you may have to educate and guide clients in choosing acceptable and realistic assumptions because they may have no idea of what assumptions are reasonable for retirement planning.

Retirement, or the achievement of economic independence, is a threshold that clients often cross with a changed outlook on life, certain postretirement lifestyle assumptions, and modified financial planning objectives. For this area of planning, you need to determine from the client's answers to the personal questions on the lower half of page 7 exactly what changes he or she may want to make. These changes must be recorded in the Retirement Planning Objectives and Concerns subsection on the bottom half of page 6. Some financial planning software systems calculate estimated Social Security benefits based on information about a person's work and income history. The client may use one of these software systems to estimate his or her Social Security benefits to answer the questions in the Social Security Benefits subsection at the bottom of page 21 of the Fact Finder. More than likely, however, you will have to estimate the client's Social Security benefits from stand-alone software programs.

Estate and Gift Planning

Estate planning involves both conservation planning and distribution planning. This entails structuring the assets in the client's estate for lifetime and testamentary transfers of property in ways that best achieve the client's overall estate distribution objectives. Lifetime financial planning creates the estate, and what it actually consists of must be inventoried through the use of other sections of the Fact Finder. These include sections dealing with insurance coverages, assets and liabilities, and all cash and capital items associated with employment.

The specific questions in the Estate Planning section on page 29 of the Fact Finder are designed to provide information regarding how the estate is to be conserved and distributed at the client's death and beyond. These questions focus primarily on what the client wants to do after considering informed possibilities. The questions may raise issues that will need to be clarified and resolved through further counseling and the exchange of tax and technical information and options.

The questions asked in this section involve the existence of wills, trusts, or custodial accounts for children or others; guardian nominations for the children; trusts in which the client (or spouse) is the beneficiary; and gifts or inheritances pending or anticipated. In spite of their importance, however, the Fact Finder does not attempt to gather detailed information about existing estate planning documents. If these items exist, you need to examine them to determine if they are in line with the client's expressed wishes and goals. The client's perception of problems in his or her personal affairs should also be explored at this time so you will have the benefit of the client's current thoughts and feelings about these sensitive matters.

Clients may want to consider specific lifetime strategies to minimize potential federal and state death taxes in developing their financial plans. These strategies will be discussed in the goal-setting section of this chapter as well as in chapter 5, which deals with analyzing information.

Sources and Uses of Cash

Page 7 of the Fact Finder is a survey of the client's (and spouse's, if applicable) sources and uses of cash. The first several questions deal with the existence of a liquid emergency fund and a formal household budget. The next several questions ask about savings and investments, sources and uses of income, and employment stability. Then there is a question about increases or decreases in earned income over the next 3 years. Finally, there is a subsection in which the client lists the amount of federal, state, and local income taxes that he or she paid last year along with the estimated quarterly income taxes that he or she will have to pay this year.

Cash Flow Statement

It is critically important that the figures for all items in the Cash Flow Statement on page 8 are complete and correct. Most individuals and families do not follow a realistic and exacting budget; indeed, many are averse to doing so. Therefore, the completion of the Cash Flow Statement, detailing all items of income and expense, will be an uncomfortable task for which most will not have kept adequate records. Nevertheless, completing this statement, analyzing and evaluating total income and expenses, and seeing their relationship to both short- and long-term financial objectives are extremely important in the selling/planning process. Clients must have a positive net cash flow in the long run if they want the flexibility to fund additional financial objectives that may arise. Clients who experience a negative net cash flow will either have to borrow or liquidate assets in order to balance income and expenses. No financial plan can work, let alone be formulated, if net cash flow is consistently negative.

After the client has provided all of the income information, you should check tax returns to verify the amounts reported. The information gathered in this section must be complete and correct because cash flow management is a pivotal area for all other areas of planning. Many recommendations you may make for family budgeting, savings and investments, funding for specific objectives, additional insurance coverages, tax planning, retirement planning, and estate planning will be related to the current and continuing income sources inventoried on page 7.

Because of their importance to financial planning, cash flow statements (along with financial position statements) are discussed and analyzed in greater depth in chapter 5.

Inventory of Assets and Liabilities

Two Fact Finder sections, the Inventory of Assets and the Inventory of Liabilities, are essential in financial planning. Transferring information about a client's assets and liabilities to the Financial Position Statement (discussed in chapter 5) reflects the client's total financial position and net worth. Moreover, this inventory of assets and liabilities will enable you to understand how your client uses financial resources and debt, what your client's preferences and aversions are, what your client's liquidity position is, what problems exist, and whether all your client's assets (including any business interest) are being used efficiently to meet financial objectives. In addition, the inventory will allow you to determine how diversified your client's assets are, whether your client is aware of his or her total financial condition (or even wants to be), and how your client thinks and feels about his or her present assets and financial resources.

Many clients have an inexact and often sketchy idea of what their total assets are. Even more have a poor grasp of whether their assets are working efficiently toward their objectives or whether their investment risk exposures are really consistent with their risk tolerances. No other area of the client's financial posture is more crucial for achieving realistic financial objectives than his or her total asset and liability positions and their tax implications, particularly if the client's business interest represents a substantial portion of his or her total assets.

Inventory of Assets

In the Inventory of Assets on pages 9–12 of the Fact Finder, it is of the utmost importance to not only list and substantiate all the client's currently held cash and near-cash equivalents, other financial assets, and property, but also to characterize each asset according to the information called for in the column headings. This information will be crucial in assessing how well the client's assets are performing in relation to personal objectives and in evaluating the relative proportions of each type of asset in the client's total portfolio—that is, the client's asset-allocation mix. These column headings will also aid in later decisions as to how the client could liquidate some or all of these assets, if desirable, so that he or she could redeploy the capital freed in other investment vehicles whose performances may be more consistent with client-established needs and objectives.

The specific columns on pages 9 and 10 require listing the number of units or shares of each asset, the date acquired, the amount, cost or other basis, the ownership, the current market value, the annual yield, any indebtedness, and the location and/or reason for holding the asset if applicable. Of course, not every column will be applicable to each type of asset owned; nor will complete information about each type be ascertainable. However, the extent to which you obtain details regarding the inventory of assets will directly contribute to your ability to analyze the information in the context of the client's overall financial plan.

The "Titled Owner(s)" columns on pages 9 and 10 refer to the abbreviations C, S, JT, TC, TE, CP, and O, which represent the most common forms of ownership. The abbreviation that corresponds to how the property is owned should be written in the column. Briefly listed below are descriptions of these forms of ownership:

- Client (C)—Fee simple title and ownership are held in the name of the client.
- Spouse (S)—Fee simple title and ownership are held in the name of the spouse.
- Joint tenancy (with rights of survivorship) (JT)—Title and ownership are held jointly by two or more parties; on the death of one of the joint tenants, the deceased's entire interest passes to the survivor(s) by operation of law.
- Tenancy in common (TC)—Title and ownership are held by two or more parties, but each tenant may sell, donate, or dispose of his or her proportionate interest by will. Upon the death of a tenant, there is no provision of law that passes the tenant's property to other cotenants.
- Tenancy by the entireties (TE)—Title and ownership are held jointly by spouses in common-law states; on the death of one of the spouses, the deceased's entire interest passes to the surviving spouse by operation of law.
- Community property (CP)—Ownership of all property acquired by husband and wife during their marriage, while domiciled in a community-property state, may be deemed to be owned equally by each.
- Other (O)—Assets and property designated as other are either held by the client (or the client's spouse) as a life estate, leasehold or term interest, future interest, or general power of appointment; or they are owned by the client's children, a trust, or a custodial account (such as Uniform Gifts to Minors Act account). While some of these assets

and property may not be owned by the client, strictly speaking, the client may nevertheless have sufficient control over them to incur income or estate taxation.

In completing and discussing the inventory of assets, you can discover existing problems in your client's total asset picture and get a sense of your client's feelings regarding currently held assets.

Cash and Near-Cash Equivalents

The Inventory of Assets section of the Fact Finder begins with a subsection on cash and near-cash equivalents. If your client seems strongly disposed toward holding cash and/or near-cash equivalents, you should probe to ascertain whether he or she is satisfying psychological needs that may obscure unexamined risk attitudes.

Bonds, Bond Funds, and Preferred Stock

Two subsections on page 9 of the Fact Finder ask for the issuer, maturity, and call dates of various types of U.S. government, municipal, and corporate bonds as well as bond funds and preferred stock. Bonds (except U.S. government bonds) and preferred stock are frequently issued with call dates prior to maturity at which time the issuer may redeem the bonds or preferred stock at specified prices relative to their face or par values. (In this respect, call dates are merely alternative—and shorter—potential maturity dates for the securities in question.) This flexibility enables the issuer to take advantage of the right to redeem these securities when current interest rates are favorable. To compensate the holders of these bonds or preferred stock for this inconvenience, the issuer usually will pay a small premium over the face or par values of these securities for the right to call them.

Bond funds are often unit investment trust funds of a one-time selection of either corporate or municipal bonds of several issuers with similar maturities. The yield of unit investment trust funds is a composite yield of all the bonds, minus the management fees. As the separate bonds mature and are redeemed or called before maturity, proportionate shares of principal plus accrued interest are returned to the holders of unit investment trust interests. Bond unit investment trust funds should be listed in the asset inventory by their fund names. If bond funds are technically mutual funds rather than unit investment trusts, they should be listed under mutual funds.

Common Stock

The next Inventory of Assets subsection on page 9 of the Fact Finder is Common Stock. Common stock is either listed (traded on a national and/or regional securities exchange), unlisted (traded on the over-the-counter market), or nonmarketable (restricted stock held by the officers of listed or unlisted companies or shares of closely held corporations for which there is no active market). To enable you to evaluate the marketability of the client's holdings of common stock, each stock in the inventory should be marked with an L for listed, U for unlisted, or NM for nonmarketable.

There are several important points to note about a client's common stock. If most of the client's holdings are in listed stocks, there generally will be an active market for those stocks although their prices can fluctuate. The same is true for most over-the-counter stocks. If the client holds restricted stock of publicly traded companies or stock of closely held corporations, there may be problems either in liquidating it or in providing for its redemption upon the client's disability, retirement, or death. In the Financial Position Statement, which will be discussed in chapter 5, under the column heading "Other Financial Assets," client holdings of nonmarketable stocks are listed separately from other common stock holdings. This distinction indicates their relative lack of liquidity.

Warrants and Options

The Warrants and Options subsection of the client's Inventory of Assets on page 9 should include the issuer and expiration date of warrants held to buy common stock, options to buy stock in the company for which the client works or has worked, and options bought or sold on a national or regional stock options exchange. Although only a few clients trade in warrants, many are involved in options contracts—usually the writing of call options to sell underlying shares of common stock at a specified price within a designated time period. Because these contracts can involve sizable blocks of stock that move in and out of the client's portfolio, you and the client's investment advisor (if not you) need to know the full details of the client's positions at all times. In addition, the client's preferences about trading in stock options provide additional information about his or her risk profile.

You should discuss the stock options with your clients to determine how they relate to their total financial positions and future plans.

Mutual Funds

Mutual funds are typically very liquid (with each share being redeemable at net asset value) but are usually acquired for long-term purposes. Another common reason for clients to hold mutual fund shares is that they are managed (for a fee) by the investment companies that issue them, thus relieving the client (or financial advisor) of that responsibility. Mutual funds are classified as to the type of investment objective or underlying securities characteristic. The most common classifications and their respective abbreviations should be indicated in this subsection on page 9 of the Fact Finder as follows: growth (G), income (I), balanced for growth and income (B), indexed, that is, made up of the shares included on a common stock market index (IX), and speculative (S). (Although money-market funds are a type of mutual fund, they are included in the Cash and Near-Cash Equivalents subsection of the Inventory of Assets because they are composed of highly liquid, frequently traded, short-term investments.) Income, balanced, and speculative mutual funds typically have varying proportions of both stocks and bonds; growth and indexed funds are usually composed of common stocks.

Real Estate

The inventory of the client's assets covers real estate holdings on page 11, which includes real property held as a personal residence and seasonal or vacation homes, residential property held for investment, and commercial property held for appreciation purposes (such as undeveloped commercial property). Clients with extensive real estate holdings may need supplementary pages.

Long-Term, Nonmarketable Assets

The next category of assets listed on page 11 of the Fact Finder consists of long-term assets. These assets are generally illiquid and nonmarketable with benefits the client cannot realize directly until some future date (for example, vested retirement benefits). Some of the assets in this category are those for which the client will incur an IRS penalty and/or institutional surrender charge if they are liquidated. Examples of these are long-term CDs, deferred annuities, Keogh plans, and IRAs. Also listed in this subsection are unit interests in limited partnership investments that generally have no ready market; these ordinarily cannot be liquidated until the general partners decide to sell or a foreclosure of mortgages or loans occurs. However, because they are assets and sometimes constitute a significant part of the client's total net worth, it is important for you to have complete and accurate information about them.

Personal Assets

The next subsection of assets on page 11 is Personal Assets. This category can vary enormously among individual clients in its extensiveness and worth of assets. Some clients own relatively few personal assets apart from household furnishings and automobiles—and even these holdings can be minimal in number and value or extremely costly and extensive. Other clients acquire a whole range of personal items, often with investment as well as personal-use motives. Such clients may have large holdings of jewelry, gems and precious metals, antiques, art, and other collectibles that represent a substantial percentage of their total assets. The typical relatively affluent client may simply have no idea how large this category of assets is until there is a complete inventory. All personal property items of any significant value should be listed.

Regardless of whether your client's motivation for acquiring and holding personal assets is for personal use and enjoyment, for investment purposes, or for some combination of the two, the inventory of these assets should be complete so that you can transfer the information to a property-liability insurance coverage worksheet to determine whether your client has appropriate types and amounts of insurance protection.

Miscellaneous Assets

The last Inventory of Assets subsection provides a place to record information about miscellaneous assets such as interests in trusts; accounts or notes receivable; or patents, copyrights, and royalties.

When you and your client have completed the Inventory of Assets section, the appropriate figures for the assets should be transferred to the client's Financial Position Statement.

Inventory of Liabilities

The Inventory of Liabilities is not an exhaustive list; it includes only typical liabilities that a client will likely incur. Other liabilities that a client has incurred should be noted on the inventory under the category of Other.

The purpose of the information requested about each liability item is not only to determine its amount, length, and term, but also to note when current financial commitments will be fulfilled so that the resources now committed to fulfilling them can be reallocated and used elsewhere. This section also discloses how much credit your client can command. The maximum credit available, present balance, and monthly/annual repayment columns can provide useful information about your client's current and potential use of debt and leverage to achieve financial objectives. How much your client is paying in interest on current debt indicates the cost efficiency of his or her debt service.

The list of liability items begins with the most current: revolving credit such as retail charge accounts and credit cards. Large outstanding balances in these items may mean that your client is using credit unwisely and is paying exorbitant carrying charges. The other types of outstanding loans can also reveal how your client uses debt and for what purposes. You will want to know whether your client has too much or too little debt in relation to his or her total financial position and objectives, shops prudently for low-cost debt, overutilizes credit cards and installment buying, has an affluent lifestyle funded with high-interest credit and repayment drains on cash flow, possesses credit and installment balances that are insured or secured by collateralizing capital assets or other property, and/or has plans that will require the assumption of additional debt.

The remaining items in the Inventory of Liabilities may or may not be as indicative of the client's attitudes and practices regarding debt financing. Income tax liabilities are fixed by your client's level and kind of income, although these liabilities can almost always be reduced through planning. (It is important to know, however, whether your client is meeting them currently through withholding and cash flow or through borrowing.) Property taxes are also fixed if they are due and payable. If they are not included in mortgage payments, however, you should determine whether your client is setting funds aside for this obligation; if he or she is setting funds aside, you should ascertain whether they are in interest-bearing short-term investments.

Although the remaining items in the liability inventory allow little margin for choice if they are applicable to a particular client's situation, it is nevertheless important to gather complete information about them. Answers to the two questions at the end of the inventory about potential liabilities against the client's estate and liabilities planned for the future are also necessary for a complete picture of the client's liability position.

In conjunction with information from the Inventory of Assets, information from the Inventory of Liabilities should also be transferred to the Financial Position Statement, which will be discussed in chapter 5. The completed Financial Position Statement will provide you with a summary of the client's current total asset/liability/and net worth positions.

Individually Owned Insurance

The Fact Finder asks for information about any life, long-term care, medical/dental, disability income, and property/liability insurance policies the client currently holds. Complete information about these coverages is crucial for developing a personal financial plan. For example, the coverage amounts provided by the client's personal life and disability income policies should also be listed on the Fact Finder, where they will constitute important elements of the client's current resources available for death, disability, and retirement needs. Personal life insurance coverage amounts will also be a factor in the value of the client's estate and its liquidity position. Moreover, personal property and liability insurance coverages should be analyzed to see if they give adequate protection against potential property and liability losses.

People typically do not know how to read and interpret the provisions of their insurance policies, so your client probably cannot provide this type of information accurately to you. You will most likely have to record this information directly from the client's insurance policies.

Once you have reviewed the policies and filled out the appropriate spaces of the Fact Finder, you should review the amounts, types of coverages, and other relevant policy provisions with your client and analyze them in light of areas of risk in your client's personal and financial situation. By the end of the information-gathering phase (step 4, gather information and establish goals) of the selling/planning process, you should have enough information about your client's (and his or her family's) current insurance coverages to determine whether he or she has adequate protection relative to his or her overall financial position and degree of exposure to risk.

The financial advisor who is not an insurance specialist should include appropriate specialists on the financial planning team who can thoroughly analyze all of the client's business and personal risk exposures and recommend appropriate coverages if needed.

Note

This Fact Finder purposely has no section that pertains to the client's business interest. Financial planning for business owners and professionals is a highly specialized area of financial planning that merits its own fact finder. Because the focus of this book and Fact Finder is on personal financial planning, there are only occasional and incidental references to a client's business ownership interests or self-employment activities.

Employment-Related Benefits

The Employment-Related Benefits Checklist on page 20 and the Employment-Related Retirement Benefits/Deferred Compensation section of the Fact Finder have several important uses in financial planning. If a client or spouse owns a controlling interest in a business, these sections provide a convenient place to record existing employee benefits and to identify additional benefits that might be implemented to put the business ownership to more effective use (and to greater tax advantage) in planning for personal financial objectives. If a client and spouse have no business ownership interest, or have no control over the kinds of benefits their business interest can provide, then those pages should be used as a checklist for the benefits they actually derive from their employment. The client and spouse should each furnish the name and title of the person in their companies who can provide detailed information and documents they may not have in their own possession. The documents relating to these benefits are listed on Receipt for Documents, which is also a checklist of information and documents that the client and spouse, or their companies, will need to make available for your use.

The column titled "Information/Comments" on the Employment-Related Benefits Checklist can be used either to describe a benefit or to indicate your or the client's feelings about the benefit. Besides listing the amounts of employment-related retirement and/or deferred-compensation benefits, along with anticipated Social Security retirement, survivor, and disability income benefits, these amounts should also be listed in the Income and Lump-Sum Resources for Disability, Retirement, and Death section.

Risk/Return Profile

The Risk/Return Profile on the Fact Finder is designed to provide a quick assessment of the client's psychological tendency for risk taking— that is, his or her financial risk tolerance. (A detailed treatment of financial risk tolerance is presented in chapter 4, and a sample risk tolerance questionnaire titled Survey of Financial Risk Tolerance is presented in appendix B.)

A note about how the Risk/Return Profile is used: On the top part of the page, the client is asked to evaluate on a scale of 1 to 5 (with 5 representing a strong preference and 1 representing an aversion) his or her preference for a range of savings and investment instruments, from a savings account (conservative, virtually no risk) to commodities (speculative, extremely high risk). In the middle part of the page, the client is asked to rate personal financial concerns, also on a scale of 1 to 5 (5 indicates a strong concern, and 1 indicates little or no concern). The results of the two rankings should correlate with each other, giving an indication of the client's financial risk tolerance. However, if the rankings are inconsistent and do not correlate well with each other, you should question the client about the inconsistencies and, if necessary, make changes. When both you and the client are satisfied with the rankings, you should note the results on the bottom part of the page and indicate the types of investments that are consistent with the client's level of risk tolerance and most likely to achieve his or her goals and objectives.

Income and Lump-Sum Needs for Disability, Retirement, and Death

The client should record the monthly amounts of income needed if the client or his or her spouse becomes disabled, retires, and/or dies. These estimates of monthly income needs should be expressed in current dollars—that is, in amounts needed now. However, in formulating a retirement plan for the client, you will have to adjust the client's estimate of these monthly needs by an agreed-on inflation factor.

Survivors' monthly income needs in the event of the client's or spouse's death are assessed for three periods: (1) an adjustment period when a continuing and unreduced income flow is needed, (2) a period of reduced income after the adjustment period until the youngest child is self-supporting, and (3) the period after the youngest child is self-supporting.

In addition, the survivors may need certain lump sums—to establish an emergency fund, to pay postmortem expenses, to pay off any outstanding mortgage balance on a personal residence, to pay off the deceased's notes and loans, to pay accrued taxes, and to fund college educations for surviving children. These lump-sum needs can be substantial and very real, but often there is not enough ready cash or other assets to meet them.

Close consultation with your client in establishing both income and lump-sum needs upon disability, retirement, and/or death is always called for. But there is little purpose in establishing the precise amounts needed unless there is also a concerted planning effort to assure that the resources are available when necessary.

Income and Lump-Sum Resources for Disability, Retirement, and Death

Your client should record the lump-sum and monthly amounts of income resources available to the client or his or her spouse for disability, retirement, and/or death. (Income and lump-sum resources are not to be confused with the income and lump-sum needs asked about on the Fact Finder.) These estimates of monthly income resources for disability and death, as with monthly income needs, are also to be expressed in current dollars—that is, in amounts available now. However, in estimating retirement income resources for your client, you will have to assist your client in calculating the future dollar amounts of monthly income and lump-sum resources available when he or she expects to retire. This will require adjusting your client's estimate of the lump-sum resources that exist today by an agreed-on inflation factor. Also, future projections will have to be made for contributions to qualified and nonqualified retirement programs. These projections must take into account both current and future contribution amounts, as well as the compound interest rates at which those amounts will grow.

All potential sources of funds are to be considered for each applicable category of need, including

- continuing income sources for both the client and spouse (taken from the cash flow statement)
- Social Security benefits and employer-related retirement benefits/deferred-compensation benefits
- life and disability income insurance proceeds (estimated from the Fact Finder)
- immediate annuities or deferred annuities
- any personal or business assets that may be liquidated or sold

Observations and Goals from Planning Meetings

Before you begin to develop your client's financial plan, you should sum up your observations and impressions about the client on the Fact Finder in the section titled Observations and Goals from Planning Meetings. These observations and impressions are vital to the planning process and to the acceptability and ultimate success of your client's plan, which will incorporate some of the most profound and far-reaching decisions your client will have made about life and relationships. The plan, however, will not be implemented unless it reflects the kind of person your client is; or, if it is implemented, it will not be updated. The selling/planning process will have been wasted and a client relationship lost.

Also, as you ascertain your client's goals financial goals, needs, and priorities, be sure to note them. Some of the goals may be quantitative, while others may be qualitative in nature. These goals will not all emerge at once, so in the course of the initial meeting and the fact-finding meeting that follows, it is important that you list each client goal as soon as it surfaces. This will assist you in maintaining an ongoing inventory of these goals as well as an understanding of the motivational factors that will eventually push the client to take action.

Case Management Checklist

The Case Management Checklist is exclusively for your use as a financial advisor. The items listed in the Scope of Planning Agreement subsection at the top of the Checklist represent a complete list of the different subject areas for which you perform personal financial planning. For each client, depending on your planning agreement, you circle only those subject areas that apply. The items listed in the Planning Tasks Completed subsection in the middle of the Checklist allow you to keep track of when you sent and received certain documents as well as when each remaining step of the selling/planning process was completed. The items listed in the Confidential Client Summary Information subsection at the bottom of the Checklist provide a quick summary of the client's current financial position.

Authorization for Information

The Authorization for Information section contains two different authorization forms you can use to send to your client's financial services companies and other advisors to request documents and information you need in the financial planning process. The form on the top half of the page is generic in nature and nonspecific as to whom it can be sent. It asks the provider to send you any information you ask for in connection with your client's financial affairs. The form on the bottom half of the page asks a specific company to provide you with information on any policies, contracts, securities, or certificates that your client owns. Your client must sign both forms before you send them.

Receipt for Documents and Checklist for Documents

The Receipt for Documents and Checklist for, respectively, in the Fact Finder look identical at first glance. However, the major difference is that the Receipt for Documents has lines on which you and your client sign your names and the date when copies of documents relevant to planning are received from and returned to the client. The Checklist for Documents is to be used by your client as a list of policies, contracts, and other important papers that need to be assembled and delivered to you either before or at the beginning of the fact-finding interview.

Conclusion

A major function of the Fact Finder is to gather enough information about the client so that you can develop his or her financial position and cash flow statements. Together, these two statements provide a profile of the client's total financial condition as of a particular date, which relates to what has occurred in the past. In addition, you must verify all relevant information from the respective sections of the Fact Finder so that you can use it to assess the client's current financial condition. After this assessment, you can develop recommendations that will help the client achieve his or her financial goals while also improving his or her financial condition. However, to help clients achieve their goals through application of the selling/planning process, those goals must first be established and articulated. With this in mind, let us look more closely at how a client's financial goals are established.

ESTABLISHING GOALS

Because personal financial planning is concerned primarily with helping clients meet their financial goals, identifying those goals and exploring financial products and strategies to meet them are of critical importance in the planning process. A goal or objective defined and broken down into its component parts is frequently half met simply by doing so. In this section, we will categorize and outline the financial goals and objectives common to most people involved in multiple-purpose financial planning. In chapter 6, where development of the financial plan is discussed, we will examine the possible resources available to help meet these goals and objectives.

Purpose of Determining Client Goals

Before you can proceed with analyzing the information obtained in the fact finder and developing the client's financial plan, you must help the client to establish and prioritize his or her personal and financial goals. The client's personal values and attitudes shape his or her goals and the priority placed on them. Accordingly, the client's goals and priority placed on them must be consistent with his or her values and attitudes in order for him or her to make the commitment necessary to accomplish them.

Prioritized goals give focus, purpose, vision, and direction to the planning process. It is important, therefore, to establish SMART goals. Your role as a financial advisor is to facilitate the goal-setting process by making sure that your client's goals are SMART. When necessary, you must explain to your client the implications of trying to adopt unrealistic goals.

Importance of Goal Setting in Financial Planning

goal setting

Goal setting in financial planning is the process of establishing SMART financial goals and personal aspirations toward which to target a client's effort, resources, plans, and actions. Goal setting is critical to creating a successful financial plan, but few people actually set SMART goals. By leading the client through the goal-setting process, you not only help the client establish SMART goals, but you also set the tone for the entire planning process.

Clients typically express concern about such topics as retirement income, education funding, premature death, disability, taxation, qualified plan distribution, and a myriad of others. Sometimes, clients enumerate specific prioritized goals, but they are more likely to present a vague list of worries that suggest anxiety and frustration rather than direction. Your responsibility as an advisor is to help clients transform these feelings into goals.

goal prioritization

Another important service of the financial advisor is *goal prioritization.* Goal prioritization is the process of ranking goals according to their importance for the purpose of deciding the order for their achievement. Clients usually mention competing goals such as saving for retirement and saving for education. As an advisor, you should help clients rank the importance of these competing goals.

Once established, a person's financial goals do not remain static. What may be entirely appropriate for a young married man with small children may prove quite inappropriate for an executive with college-age children or for a husband and wife approaching retirement.

Organizing Client Goals and Objectives

Although the emphasis on particular goals and objectives will change over a family's financial life cycle, the following classification of topics provides a systematic way to identify clients' specific personal financial goals and objectives. The order in which these topics are discussed is as follows:

- life planning
- insurance planning and risk management
- employee benefits planning
- specialized financial planning goals
- investment planning
- income tax planning
- retirement planning
- estate planning

With the exception of life planning and specialized goals, these topics are viewed as the major planning areas that fall under the financial planning umbrella. Even though each one of these planning areas is a specialty unto itself, together they make up the totality of what is known as comprehensive financial planning.

Life Planning

A Comprehensive Approach

life planning

Life planning is a comprehensive approach to planning that is appropriate and useful for all ages—young adults as well as those nearing retirement. It is based on the philosophy that the most successful and satisfying experiences are based on a series of thoughtful, future-focused decisions made throughout one's adult life. Skills, values, attitudes, resources and relationships that are developed and honed during one stage of life all contribute to meeting the challenges and recognizing the opportunities of the next stage of life." Life planning explores and honors past knowledge and experience; assesses and confirms present reality; and, finally, visualizes and designs future possibilities. In a practical sense, life planning is an ongoing exercise in "what if?" scenarios that can help people sort out the possibilities and use creative solutions to shape the lifestyle they desire.[14]

Life planning adds a holistic element to the process of financial planning by considering nonfinancial decisions that are made throughout the individual's life. It focuses on personal goals and then assigns a financial cost to satisfying needs and wants.

Relevance in Financial Planning

Because of the holistic nature of life planning, it helps individuals to place financial planning activities in a context that is personally meaningful and, therefore, more motivating. As a result, financial planning activities are directed to achieving the client's personal and specific goals rather than to the more nebulous target of "building wealth and security for the future."

Financial planning starts where life planning leaves off—you do not start with the financial plan and then work the life plan into it. Life planning is a dynamic educational process that allows people to visualize their personal goals and then model the financial consequences of those choices.

The Financial Life-Planning Approach

Today, financial advisors increasingly understand the need to take a more holistic approach with their clients. However, most are not comfortable with exploring and advising in nonfiscal matters. They are concerned that they will be called upon to be all things to all clients and to step outside their areas of expertise. Therefore, in the financial life-planning approach, the advisor conversationally explores life issues as they relate to money, and facilitates a dialogue in a way that communicates his or her interest in the client as a whole person. This can be accomplished without taking the advisor too far out into the psychological tide.

The financial life-planning approach is client centered. Intuitively, your clients will see the wisdom in developing a plan to use their money to make a life rather than using their life to make money. Most individuals are receptive to the professional who has the skill to draw out their vision for their lives and help that vision materialize. Your clients' money has powerful meaning to them as individuals. To make the life connection, you need to ascertain the intended purpose of the money, the values that created the assets, and the legacy the clients intend to leave.

Financial life planning is not about having all the right answers; it is about asking the right questions. It involves broadening the conversation from asset

---

14. Carol A. Anderson and Joyce Cohen, Life Planning: An Effective Model for Retirement Planning Education, Unconventional Wisdom.

management to money as it relates to each aspect of a client's life. Financial life planning involves

- exploring what money represents to your clients
- defining both the tangibles and intangibles that clients expect their assets to provide them
- anticipating life events and transitions and making financial preparations for those transitions
- assisting clients in the process of establishing financial goals that facilitate their life goals
- developing a network of professionals to whom you can confidently refer your clients

The concept of life planning is the starting point for clients in the formulation of financial goals that relate to the more traditional components of financial planning. The formulation and articulation of client financial goals will be discussed below.

Insurance Planning and Risk Management

insurance planning and risk management

This category of financial planning goals, *insurance planning and risk management*, recognizes most people's desire to protect themselves and their families against the risks they face in everyday life. These risks can arise from the possibility of

- premature death losses
- disability income losses
- medical care expenses
- long-term care expenses
- property and liability losses
- unemployment

These risks, the consequences of which can be adequately insured against occurring or managed, represent the primary focus of financial planning that should typically be addressed before capital accumulation and investment goals are pursued. Each of these risks will be discussed separately, along with their potential ramifications for clients.

Premature Death Losses

Commonly, a major planning objective is to protect dependents from the financial consequences of death. Some people also are concerned with the impact of their deaths on their business affairs. At this point, let us briefly note the various financial losses that may result from a person's death. These are the

- loss of the deceased's future earning power that would have been available for the benefit of his or her surviving dependents
- costs and other obligations arising at death
- increased expenses for the family

- loss of tax advantages
- loss of business values because of an owner's or key person's death

Disability Income Losses

Another major planning objective of most people should be to protect themselves and their dependents from financial losses arising out of their disability, whether that be total (either temporary or permanent) or partial. Disability, particularly total and permanent disability, is a serious risk almost everyone faces. Yet, surprisingly, it is often neglected in financial planning.

Actually, the statistics shown in Table 3-1 clearly indicate that the odds of death during an individual's working years are much less than the odds of a significant long-term disability (one lasting more than 90 days). This is something for the young family man and woman to think about.

Table 3-1
Probability of Disability vs. Death

Age	Ratio of Disability to Death
30	2.31 to 1
35	2.21 to 1
40	1.95 to 1
45	1.69 to 1
50	1.53 to 1
55	1.33 to 1
Source: 1985 Commissioners' Disability Individual Table A and 1980 CSO Mortality	

The financial losses from disability generally parallel those resulting from death. An important difference from the consumer's viewpoint, however, is that there is a wide range of possible durations of total disability—from only a week or so to the ultimate personal catastrophe of total and permanent disability. Thus, a person must recognize in personal financial planning that he or she could become disabled for a variety of durations—from a few days to the rest of his or her life. Virtually all experts agree, however, that clients should pay the greatest planning attention to protecting themselves against long-term total and permanent disability rather than being unduly concerned with disabilities that last only a few weeks. For example, depending on individual circumstances and resources, it is often much more economical for a family to rely on their emergency investment fund for shorter-term disabilities than to buy disability income insurance to cover such disabilities.

The total and permanent disability of a family breadwinner is actually a much greater financial catastrophe than the breadwinner's premature death. This is because as a disabled person, the breadwinner remains a consumer, whose consumption needs may even increase because of the disability, and because other family members, especially a spouse, must devote at least some time to caring for the disabled breadwinner as long as he or she is alive. In fact, total and permanent disability has been graphically described as a "living death."

One final point about the risk of disability is in order. The disability of someone who owns real property and/or investments may give rise to particular property and investment management problems because the disabled person might be in such a physical or mental state that he or she is unable to manage his or her affairs effectively. Advance planning to take care of handling this unhappy contingency is desirable.

Medical Care Expenses

There is little need to convince most people of the need to protect themselves and their families against medical care costs. Mounting medical care costs have become a national problem. Health care costs have escalated so rapidly in the last 20 years that even a minor medical problem could threaten a person's financial security indefinitely. Medical expense coverage is a necessity. The unexpected nature of both illnesses and accidents fosters in many individuals the need to know that if either should strike, financial ruin will not be added to their family's problems. For personal financial planning, it may be helpful to divide family medical care costs into three categories, as follows:

- "normal" or budgetable expenses. These are the medical expenses the family more or less expects to pay out of its regular monthly budget such as the annual out-of-pocket deductibles and copayments associated with routine visits to physicians, expenses of minor illnesses, and small drug purchases.

  Just what expenses are "normal" or budgetable depends a great deal on the needs, other resources, and desires of the individual or family. But as a general rule, the larger the amount of annual expenses a family can afford to assume, the lower its overall costs will be. This is true because buying insurance against relatively small potential losses results in what is called "trading dollars with the insurance company," which usually is an uneconomical practice for the insured. Also, to the extent an emergency fund is established to meet unexpected expenses and losses (of all kinds), the investment earnings on this fund would be available to the client.
- "larger than normal" expenses. These are medical expenses that exceed those that are expected or budgetable. If they occur, they probably cannot be met out of the family's regular income. To meet such expenses, most people need insurance. The cutoff point between "normal" and "larger than normal" expenses depends on the family's circumstances.
- "catastrophic" medical expenses. These are expenses so large that they cause severe financial strain on a family. They are important to plan for because they are potentially so damaging. Again, the dividing line between "larger than normal losses" and "catastrophic losses" depends on individual circumstances. One family, for example, may feel that

uninsured medical expenses of over $1,000 in a year would be a severe financial strain. Another family, however, with a larger income and an emergency fund, may feel that it could tolerate uninsured medical expenses of several thousand dollars, provided the annual cost savings were significant enough for the family to assume this much risk. The significance of the dividing line lies in the fact that insurance generally is necessary to protect the family against truly catastrophic medical expenses, while the family may elect to assume at least some of the larger than normal expenses. In many cases, however, this decision is, in effect, taken away from the individual because his or her employer provides group medical expense insurance. There really is no way for you to know in advance just how large catastrophic medical expenses might be. Because they could be very large, clients should plan for that possibility and insure themselves accordingly.

Long-Term Care Expenses

People are living longer because advances in medicine, nutrition, and so forth have developed preventions, cures, and treatments for diseases and conditions that were once fatal. Thus, there are more people reaching advanced ages in which dependency on others is more prevalent. As life spans increase, the length of time people will need long-term care (LTC) due to this dependency will almost certainly increase as well. An often quoted statistic indicates that over 40 percent of all 65-year-olds will spend some time in a nursing home.

The out-of-pocket payments for LTC by people who must pay for their care from personal resources can be astronomical. In 2006, average annual nursing home costs were approximately $69,000 for a semi-private room.[15] The average nursing home stay is 2.5 years.

Long-term care insurance (LTCI) is a form of insurance that usually provides coverage for personal or custodial care, intermediate care, and skilled care in various settings that may include nursing homes and at-home care, as well as adult day care and assisted-living facilities. The financial reason for purchasing LTCI is to protect a person's assets from being depleted by having to pay for LTC.

Property and Liability Losses

All families are exposed to the risk of property and/or liability losses. For planning purposes, it is helpful to consider property exposures and liability exposures separately because somewhat different approaches may be used for each.

---

15. *The MetLife Market Survey of Nursing Home & Assisted Living Costs,* October 2007, The MetLife Mature Market Institute, p. 4.

Property Losses. Ownership of property brings with it the risk of loss to the property itself, called direct losses, and the risk of indirect losses arising out of loss or damage to the property, called consequential losses.

Direct and consequential losses to property can result from a wide variety of perils, some of which, such as fire, theft, windstorm, and automobile collision, are common, while others, such as earthquake and flood, are rare except in certain geographical areas.

Some of the kinds of property individuals and families own that may be exposed to direct loss are as follows:

- primary residence
- summer home
- investment real estate
- furniture, clothing, and other personal property
- automobiles
- boats (and aircraft)
- furs, jewelry, silverware, and fine art works
- securities, credit cards, cash, and the like
- professional equipment
- assets held as an executor, trustee, or guardian
- assets in which the person has a beneficial interest

Some of the consequential losses that may arise out of a direct loss to such property are the

- loss of use of the damaged property (including additional living expenses while a residence is being rebuilt, rental of a substitute automobile while a car is being repaired, and so on)
- loss of rental income from damaged property
- depreciation losses (or the difference between the cost to replace damaged property with new property and the depreciated value, called "actual cash value," of the damaged property)
- cost of debris removal

Many property losses are comparatively small in size, but some are of major importance. As with disability income losses and medical care expenses, what constitutes a "small" loss depends on the resources and attitudes of those involved. Also, like disability income and medical expense exposures, a financial planning decision needs to be made as to how much property loss exposure your client should assume and how much he or she should insure. Another decision is what property to insure against what perils.

Liability Losses. By virtue of almost everything clients do, they are exposed to possible liability claims made by others. These liability claims can arise out of their own negligent acts, the negligent acts of others for whom they may be held legally responsible, liability they may have assumed under contract (such as a lease), and the liability imposed on them by statute (such as workers' compensation laws).

Some of the exposures that may result in a liability claim are

- ownership of property (for example, residence premises or a vacation home)
- rental of property (for example, a vacation home)
- ownership, rental, or use of automobiles, boats, aircraft, snowmobiles, and so on
- hiring of employees (for example, domestic and casual employees)
- other personal activities
- professional and business activities (including officerships and directorships)
- any contractual or contingent liability

Most people realize the financial consequences that could occur as a result of liability claims against them. However, they may not recognize all the liability exposures they have and may not protect themselves against the possibility of very large claims. Like medical expenses, there really is no way a person can know in advance just how large a liability loss he or she may suffer. Judgments and settlements for $1 million and more are not unusual by any means.

Therefore, prudent financial planning calls for the assumption that the worst can happen and providing for it through the purchase of additional liability coverage with an umbrella liability insurance policy.

Unemployment

Unemployment has received greater attention in recent years as many capable persons have lost their jobs because of various economic uncertainties. However, a reasonable emergency fund can help prevent the problem of temporary unemployment from becoming a crisis by giving the family time to adjust before disturbing their other investments.

Employee Benefits Planning

employee benefits planning

Many of the financial needs of individuals and their families are met—or at least partially met—with benefits provided and/or available to them because of their employment. Employee benefits include a wide variety of benefits and services. They represent a major portion—and a growing percentage—of total employee compensation. Because employee benefits form the basis of almost all financial plans advisors develop for their clients, the need for proper benefit planning is a crucial component of the financial planning goal-setting process.

As indicated, employee benefits form the basis on which any sound financial plan is designed. For example, if an employee's goal is to have a retirement income of $70,000, it is important to know the extent to which Social Security and the employee's employer-provided retirement plan are already meeting this goal. As another example, an employee who should have $500,000 in life insurance may have Social Security and an employer-provided group life insurance program that meets a substantial portion of this need. Moreover, many employees are able to purchase additional life insurance and/or retirement benefits from their employer-sponsored plans. In addition, some executive-level employees are able to negotiate their own compensation packages, including employee benefits.

Financial advisors need to understand and quantify employee benefits so they can incorporate them into the financial plans they are developing for their clients. Furthermore, the advisor should recommend coordinating the employee benefits of the client and his or her spouse and integrating those benefits with insurance and investment planning goals.

Specialized Financial Planning Goals

specialized financial planning goals

In addition to the major planning areas that pertain to almost every client, there are a number of more *specialized financial planning goals*. These specialized goals are, for the most part, subsets of, and typically involve several of, the major planning areas. However, because all of these specialized goals are unique, they merit separate treatment. They should be part of a client's personal financial plan only if he or she is affected by them. Typically, a single-purpose or multiple-purpose financial plan that is focused on the particular planning need deals with these specialized areas.

The most important of these specialized goals in terms of the number of people it affects is education funding, a topic discussed briefly below and covered in greater depth in chapter 8. The other specialized areas worthy of mention are those that can be categorized as financial planning for special circumstances. These areas typically include planning for

- divorce
- terminal illness
- nontraditional families
- job or career change
- job loss, including severance packages
- dependent parents who need long-term care
- other dependents with special needs
- the purchase of a first home
- the purchase of a vacation or second home

As previously mentioned, all of these specialized financial planning goals are subsets of one or more of the major planning areas. For example, divorce planning could affect every single one of the major planning areas but nevertheless should not be part of a comprehensive financial plan unless the client is contemplating divorce. Even then, divorce planning would be better handled under a single-purpose or multiple-purpose financial plan because of its unique aspects and shorter planning horizon than the major planning areas.

Capital Accumulation

Many people and families do not spend all their disposable income, and thus they have an investable surplus. Many also have various semiautomatic accumulation plans, such as profit-sharing plans, that help them build up capital. Some receive gifts and/or inheritances that must be invested. Thus, in one way or another, an important and desirable financial objective for many is to accumulate and invest capital.

There are a number of reasons why people want to accumulate capital. Some of the more important are for an emergency fund, for the education of their children, for retirement purposes, and for a general investment fund to provide them with capital and additional income for their own financial security. In other words, people want to accumulate capital to promote their own personal financial freedom. People also save with certain consumption goals in mind, such as the purchase of a new house, new car, or taking an extended trip or vacation.

The relative importance of these reasons naturally varies with individual circumstances and attitudes. A woman in her 50s may be primarily interested in preparing for retirement, while a younger family man or woman may be concerned with educating his or her children or the capital growth of a general investment fund.

Education Needs

consumer price index (CPI)

Most clients with children understand the need to save for college and are aware that college costs have risen at a faster pace than the *consumer price index (CPI)*. Still, the vast majority of families accumulate far too little money for college by the matriculation date. They usually have to cut back on living expenses, borrow money, tap into retirement assets, or seek additional employment to meet the funding need. Often, they lower their sights and target schools that are less expensive rather than the ones best suited to their children's needs. Consequently, planning to meet the costs of higher education has become a necessity for most parents.

The cost of higher education has increased dramatically, particularly at private colleges and universities. For example, it may cost $30,000 to $40,000 or more per year in tuition, fees, and room and board for a student to attend some private colleges. This can result in a tremendous financial drain for a family with college-age children, and yet it is a predictable drain that can be prepared for by setting up an education fund.

The size of the fund obviously depends on the number of children, their ages, their educational plans, any scholarships and student loans that may be available to them, and the size of the family income. It also depends on the attitude of the family toward education. Some people feel they should provide their children with all the education they can profit from and want. Others, however, feel that children should help earn at least a part of their educational expenses themselves. What types of schools the children plan to attend also has a considerable bearing on the costs involved.

An investment fund for educational needs is often a relatively long-term objective, and the hope is that the fund will not be needed in the meantime. Thus, wider investment latitude to secure a more attractive investment yield seems more justified than in the case of the emergency fund. All that is really necessary is for the funds to be there by the time each child is ready for school.

Investment Planning

General Investment Fund

People often accumulate capital for general investment purposes. They may want a better standard of living in the future, a second income in addition to the earnings from their employment or profession, greater financial security or a sense of personal financial freedom, the ability to retire early or to take it easier in their work in the future, or a capital fund to pass on to their children or grandchildren. Or they may simply enjoy the investment process. In any event, people normally invest money for the purpose of maximizing their after-tax returns, consistent with their objectives and the investment constraints under which they must operate.

The size of a person's investment fund depends on how much capital there originally was to invest, how much the person can save each year, what other sources of capital there are, and how successful the person or his or her advisors are. There are, of course, wide variations in how much different people have to invest.

investment planning

There are many ways people can accumulate capital and many possible investment planning strategies they might follow. In terms of the objective of capital accumulation, however, an individual basically has these factors to consider:

- an estimate of how much capital the individual will need at various times in the future (perhaps including an estimate for future inflation or deflation)
- the amount of funds available to invest
- an estimate of how much he or she will save each year in the future
- the amount of time left to meet objectives
- the general investment constraints, such as safety of principal, stability of income, liquidity, marketability, diversification, tax status, and the like
- the adoption of an investment program that will give the best chance of achieving as many financial objectives as possible within the limitations of the investment constraints

Investment and Property Management

The need and desire to obtain outside investment management and/or property management vary greatly among individuals and families. Some people have a keen interest in investments and property management and hence seek little, if any, help in managing their affairs. Others who may be knowledgeable enough to handle their own investment and property management nevertheless prefer to devote their full time and energies to their business or profession and leave managing their personal financial affairs to professionals in that field. Then, of course, there are those who by temperament or training simply are not equipped to manage their own financial affairs.

The growing complexity of dealing with investments, tax problems, insurance, and the like generally has increased the need for investment and property management. Also, these complexities tend to increase as personal incomes and wealth increase in our society.

Questioning clients regarding their attitudes about the costs involved relative to the benefits received for investment and property management will reveal whether these services should be a component of your clients' investment planning strategies. If your clients do desire these services, you should be prepared to refer them to the proper experts.

Income Tax Planning

income tax planning

Income tax planning involves the analysis, evaluation, and client acceptance of the income tax consequences of every capital and financial transaction—before the transaction is made. In other words, it is a delineation and analysis of primary tax considerations in determining when, whether, and how to conduct various personal and business transactions to effect the desired economic end and to minimize the income tax impact of achieving that end.

People are subject to many different income taxes. These include Social Security taxes, federal income taxes, and state and/or local income taxes. The relative importance of these taxes varies considerably among families, depending on their circumstances and income levels. When engaging in income tax planning, however, most people's planning objectives are concerned primarily with minimizing and managing the amount of federal income taxes they will pay.

In many ways, we have a tax-oriented economy in the United States. Most people have the legitimate objective of reducing their income tax burden as much as is legally possible consistent with their nontax objectives. Also, they must at least consider the tax implications of most financial transactions, and they should enter into some transactions because of their tax advantages. Thus, income tax planning has an important role in personal financial planning.

As an advisor, it is common sense for you to secure the greatest possible income tax advantage for your clients consistent with their financial objectives and basic motivations. Careful and diligent tax planning can hold to a minimum the tax liability resulting from many transactions; often, it can affect either immediate or long-term benefits, whichever the clients choose. As clients reach higher tax brackets and the level and complexity of their financial affairs increase, it becomes more critical that clients seek and you provide sound income tax planning as a central part of personal financial planning.

Thus, the impact of taxation on nearly all types of income and assets is usually one of the primary concerns of clients engaged in personal financial planning.

Retirement Planning

retirement planning

Retirement planning begins with advisors listening to their clients' objectives and expectations for retirement. This requires exploring and understanding the clients' goals, attitudes, and personal preferences. Clients have a variety of goals that range from never having to work again to working full-time during retirement. Clearly, as an advisor you have your work cut out for you as you deal with a plethora of expectations and, in some cases, help to frame your clients' retirement planning objectives. Because of the importance and unique characteristics of retirement planning, it is dealt with separately from other capital accumulation goals.

Within the process of establishing your clients' goals and expectations for retirement, you must gather a considerable amount of information about your clients. You must conduct a financial inventory of retirement assets and assess the strategies that clients have available to them. For example, as an advisor you must determine what resources clients have allocated to retirement, and you must note all opportunities that clients have available to them such as being able to contribute to a Roth IRA or to participate in a 401(k) plan at their place of work.

Furthermore, you should be prepared to help clients meet goals that are important to them such as

- maintaining their preretirement standard of living during retirement
- becoming economically self-sufficient
- minimizing taxes on retirement distributions
- adapting to the retirement lifestyle
- taking care of a dependent parent
- handling their own special health needs

In addition, you should be prepared to deal with a variety of attitudes on how long clients want to work, what their probabilities are for health and longevity, whether the clients can be disciplined enough to save for retirement, and to what extent they accept investment risk.

An important responsibility for you as an advisor in planning for your clients' retirement is to make them aware that they are making lifestyle choices that can affect their retirement security every day. For example, should the client take an expensive vacation or take a moderately priced vacation and save the difference for retirement? You cannot force the client to make lifestyle choices that will provide an adequate source of retirement funds. You can, however, make the client aware of the large amount of funds needed for retirement and point out that a spendthrift lifestyle during the client's active working years hurts his or her chances of adequately funding for retirement.

A client's basic personal financial planning goal is to provide a sufficient retirement income for the client and for his or her spouse, if applicable. Clients want to make sure they can live independently and comfortably during their retirement years.

This objective has become increasingly important in modern times because of changes in our socioeconomic institutions and because most people now can anticipate living to enjoy their retirement years. As Table 3-2 shows, the life expectancy at all the specified ages far exceeds the average retirement age in the United States, which is age 62.

Estate Planning

An estate plan has been defined as "an arrangement for the distribution of one's wealth." For a great many people, such an arrangement can be relatively simple and inexpensive to establish. But for larger estates or estates with special problems, estate plans can become quite complex.

estate planning

Unfortunately, the impression has developed over the years that *estate planning* is only for the wealthy. However, many persons who would not regard themselves as wealthy actually do have potential estates large enough to justify the use of estate planning techniques.

Table 3-2
Life Expectancy in Years

Age	Male (Rounded to Nearest Year)	Female (Rounded to Nearest Year)
25	52	55
30	47	51
35	42	46
40	37	41
45	33	36
50	28	32
55	24	27
60	20	23
65	16	19

Source: 2001 Commissioners Standard Ordinary Mortality Table.

Estate planning issues are specific to each client and depend largely on the client's personal concerns and the composition of the estate. How the client feels about these issues is often more important than their estate tax implications.

Generally, if the estate includes relevant asset items, the following issues are typical of the client's personal goals, concerns, and wishes related to estate planning:

- whether there are sufficient assets to support a surviving spouse
- whether a valid current will and other relevant estate planning documents such as a living will, power of attorney, and/or a trust exist or are needed
- whether personal goals, concerns, and wishes have been given equal weight with planning strategies designed to minimize estate taxes
- whether the possibility of physical disability or mental incompetence can be planned for
- whether bequests to charity under the will are suitable

- whether lifetime gifting programs are suitable
- whether asset management for the education of grandchildren is advisable
- whether the estate has sufficient liquidity to fund postmortem expenses and estate/inheritance tax liabilities

Many of these issues probe beyond the factual type of information in the Fact Finder. They explore clients' knowledge of estate planning concepts and uncover their feelings about what they want to happen both before and after their deaths to expedite their estate distribution wishes in a tax-efficient manner. The discussion of these topics will help clients to articulate their feelings and crystallize their personal estate planning objectives. As their advisor, you will then be able to formulate appropriate recommendations and act as a resource to facilitate the implementation of your clients' wishes.

Estate planning is a technical and specialized field where such diverse areas of knowledge as wills, trusts, tax law, insurance, investments, and accounting are important. Thus, it frequently is desirable to bring together several professionals or specialists into an estate planning team to develop a well-rounded plan. This concept will be explored further in chapter 6 in the section on developing the plan.

THE AGREEMENT LETTER

The information-gathering process is often a very complex one. More than one meeting may be necessary before the process is complete. Prior to the beginning of each meeting, you need to review and confirm the information you gathered in the fact-finding meetings. Always be sure that you and the client are thinking along the same lines.

agreement letter

To get a preliminary commitment from your client regarding the results of fact-finding meetings, you must send an agreement letter. An *agreement letter* is a written acknowledgment and confirmation of the facts, feelings, values, and attitudes uncovered in the selling/planning process to this point. It states your client's present situation and what he or she wants to accomplish financially, and it outlines the commitment to continue to work together cooperatively to achieve these objectives. The agreement letter is an acknowledgement and confirmation that you and your client understand his or her financial problems and goals. It is also the basis for proceeding to the next step of the selling/planning process where you will analyze your client's current situation and, in conjunction with his her goals, develop several appropriate recommendations.

The contents of this letter should

- specify the purpose of the letter along with introductory remarks
- indicate the client's current status, including facts, observations, and understandings about his or her situation, attitudes, values and major areas of concern.
- state the client's goals and desired situation, as well as any major areas of concern

- specify the client's assessed level of risk tolerance
- disclose the available capital and/or income resources that may be allocated toward reaching the client's financial goals
- indicate specific areas of financial planning your recommendations will address such as insurance planning and risk management, income tax planning, retirement planning, and college education planning
- acknowledge the areas you will not address in your recommendations because you are not qualified or licensed to do so such as legal or tax advice (You may discuss alternative resources you can make available to the client to provide these services.)
- specify the fees you will charge for your services, if any apply, and/or other types of compensation you will receive such as commissions on financial products you may sell
- request that the client correct and/or clarify any statements made in the letter
- specify what the next step is and how it will be conducted, and schedule the next client/advisor meeting

When your client reads the agreement letter, he or she should know whether to proceed with the process, reconsider his or her goals and priorities, or offer additional fact or other relevant information. The letter is designed to help clarify the advisor/client relationship and define the commitment necessary to complete the planning process. It helps both the advisor and client come to a mutual understanding of the current situation and what the client wants to accomplish.

The agreement letter lays the groundwork and provides a blueprint for proceeding through the next step(s) in the selling/planning process, which are the analysis of the information and development of recommendations. It is an essential ingredient for establishing the foundation of a true client/advisor relationship. This agreement to work together toward mutually acceptable solutions to the client's financial goals and concerns establishes a climate of trust and partnership as the process continues.

When your client signs and returns the letter, with or without any corrections and/or clarifications, he or she is confirming that the information gathered accurately reflects his or her current financial status, planning goals, and concerns. There is now a written and signed commitment by your client to continue the process.

CHAPTER REVIEW

Key Terms and Concepts are explained in the Glossary. Answers to the Review Questions and Self-Test Questions are found in the back of the book in the Answers to Questions section.

Key Terms and Concepts

fact finder form
objective information
subjective information
goal setting
goal prioritization
life planning
insurance planning and risk management
employee benefits planning
specialized financial planning goals
consumer price index (CPI)
investment planning
income tax planning
retirement planning
estate planning
agreement letter

Review Questions

3-1. During the initial meeting, what should a client understand and become aware of regarding the information-gathering process?

3-2. Describe the relative importance of information gathering for the advisor in the financial planning process.

3-3. What are the major information-gathering sections in the Personal Financial Planning Fact Finder?

3-4. Describe the contents and use of the Case Management Checklist section of the Personal Financial Planning Fact Finder.

3-5. Explain why goal setting is important to the financial planning process.

3-6. Identify the topic areas for determining client personal and financial planning goals.

3-7. What items should the agreement letter address?

Self-Test Questions

Instructions: Read the chapter first, then answer the following questions to test your knowledge. There are 10 questions; circle the correct answer, then check your answers with the answer key in the back of the book.

8. Information from the two Fact Finder sections, Inventory of Assets and Inventory of Liabilities, will form the basis for which of the following documents that will be included in the personal financial plan?

   (A) cash flow statement
   (B) financial position statement
   (C) budget analysis statement
   (D) disclosure statement

9. In which of the following forms of ownership do spouses in common-law states hold property title and ownership jointly?

   (A) joint tenancy (with rights of survivorship)
   (B) tenancy in common
   (C) tenancy by the entireties
   (D) community property

10. Which of the following is the most important of the specialized financial planning goals in terms of the number of people it affects?

    (A) education planning
    (B) nontraditional families
    (C) job or career change
    (D) dependent parents who need long-term care

11. Which of the following statements concerning the agreement letter is correct?

    (A) It should be sent to the client before the information-gathering meeting takes place.
    (B) It confirms that the client will purchase any needed financial products from you.
    (C) It is an essential ingredient for establishing the foundation of a true client/advisor relationship.
    (D) Its purpose is to get a final commitment from the client to work together with the advisor.

12. Which of the following statements concerning fact finding in financial planning is (are) correct?

    I. Assembling complete, accurate, and up-to-date information about the client is the single most important task in financial planning.
    II. The type of information requested includes both quantitative data about the client's current financial position and qualitative information about his or her personal circumstances.

    (A) I only
    (B) II only
    (C) Both I and II
    (D) Neither I nor II

13. Which of the following statements concerning life planning is (are) correct?

    I. It adds a holistic element to the process of financial planning by considering nonfinancial decisions that an individual makes throughout his or her life.
    II. It is a dynamic educational process that allows a person to visualize personal goals and then model the financial consequences of those choices.

    (A) I only
    (B) II only
    (C) Both I and II
    (D) Neither I nor II

14. Which of the following statements concerning the goals of retirement planning is (are) correct?

    I. Retirement planning has become less important today because of changes in our socioeconomic institutions and because most people now anticipate working at least part-time during their retirement years.
    II. An important responsibility for you as an advisor in planning for your clients' retirement is to make them aware that they are making lifestyle choices about their retirement every day.

    (A) I only
    (B) II only
    (C) Both I and II
    (D) Neither I nor II

READ THE FOLLOWING DIRECTIONS BEFORE CONTINUING

The questions below differ from the preceding questions in that they all contain the word EXCEPT. So you understand fully the basis used in selecting each answer, be sure to read each question carefully.

---

15. All the following statements concerning income tax planning are correct EXCEPT

    (A) Most people have the legitimate objective of reducing their tax burden as much as is legally possible, consistent with their nontax objectives.
    (B) As an advisor, it is common sense for you to secure the greatest possible income tax advantage for your clients, consistent with their financial objectives and basic motivations.
    (C) The relative importance of the different types of income taxes varies considerably among families, depending on their circumstances and income levels.
    (D) It involves the analysis, evaluation, and client acceptance of the tax consequences of every capital and financial transaction—after the transaction is made.

16. All the following statements concerning the gathering of subjective information about the client are correct EXCEPT

    (A) It involves the client's hopes, fears, values, preferences, attitudes, financial goals, and nonfinancial goals.
    (B) It includes a summary of present insurance coverages.
    (C) It involves getting to know something about the client's personal life and relationship.
    (D) It assesses the client's level of risk tolerance.

17. The client should provide the financial advisor with preliminary information well in advance of the information-gathering meeting to give the advisor ample time to do all the following EXCEPT

    (A) review the information
    (B) form preliminary impressions of the client's financial condition
    (C) determine which financial products might best serve the client's needs
    (D) determine those areas in which more detailed information is needed

4

Financial Planning Tools and Techniques

Learning Objectives

An understanding of the material in this chapter should enable the student to

4-1. Describe several basic concepts underlying the time value of money.

4-2. Calculate the future value of a single sum using time-value-of-money tables.

4-3. Calculate the present value of a single sum using time-value-of-money tables.

4-4. Calculate the future value of an annuity and an annuity due using time-value-of-money tables.

4-5. Calculate the present value of an annuity and an annuity due using time-value-of-money tables.

4-6. Explain the basic concepts of risk, risk/return trade-off, and risk tolerance.

4-7. Describe several reasons why it is difficult to assess a client's risk tolerance.

4-8. Describe and evaluate several techniques for assessing a client's risk tolerance.

4-9. Identify some guidelines that a financial advisor should follow when assessing a client's risk tolerance.

4-10. Explain the portfolio management techniques for asset allocation, diversification, and rebalancing.

This chapter begins with a discussion of several basic concepts that are essential to understanding the time value of money and its application to financial planning. These concepts are divided into those dealing with present values and those dealing with future values. The second topic covered in the chapter is financial risk tolerance. Understanding a client's risk tolerance is critically important to proper financial planning. Financial plans frequently are developed in conjunction with investment portfolios that are uniquely tailored to fit the client's level of risk tolerance. The management of these portfolios is the final topic in the chapter.

TIME-VALUE-OF-MONEY BASICS

opportunity cost

Money now versus money later is an easy choice when it is the same dollar amount. Offer someone a choice between receiving $1,000 today or $1,000 a year from now and he or she will invariably take the money today. To get the person to wait for the money there needs to be an incentive to wait. That incentive is the return he or she can expect to receive by waiting. Investors want to be compensated for the use of their money by others over time. If they wait for the money, they incur what economists call an *opportunity cost.* The opportunity cost of an activity (in this case waiting to receive the money) is the value of the lost opportunity to engage in the best alternative activity (spending or investing the money now) with the same resource (the specified sum of money). The opportunity cost is typically expressed as a percentage rate of return.

time value of money (TVM)

Conversely, most people would intuitively conclude that if they must pay out a specified sum of money, they would prefer to pay it later rather than sooner. Why? Because the longer they can delay the payment, the longer they can use the money either by spending it or investing it for their own benefit. If they pay the money early, they also incur an opportunity cost. These differences in value over time, due to opportunity costs, relate to the *time value of money (TVM).* The time value of money reflects the idea that a dollar received today is worth more than a dollar received in the future.

The Role of Interest

A given sum of money due in different time periods does not have the same values, so a tool is needed to make the different values comparable. That tool is interest. Interest is a way of quantifying the opportunity cost incurred by waiting to receive money or by giving up the opportunity to delay payment.

Example

If you deposit $1,000 in a savings account and leave those funds there for one year, you expect to have more than $1,000 in the account at the end of the year. You expect the account to earn interest. By postponing your use of the money and allowing the bank to use it, you incur an opportunity cost. The bank pays interest as compensation for that loss of use.

To reverse the situation, assume a loan you took out at your bank matures in one year, at which time you are obligated to pay $10,000. If you repay the loan today, a year early, you should be required to pay less than the full $10,000. If you forgo the opportunity to delay the repayment, you should be compensated by a reduction in the amount of the repayment due.

---

risk-free rate

risk premium

The specific interest rate used to quantify opportunity cost consists of two components: a *risk-free rate* and a *risk premium.* At a minimum, the opportunity cost of letting someone use your money is the rate of return you could have earned by investing it in a perfectly safe instrument. A reasonable measure of this minimum opportunity cost is the rate of interest available on 3-month U.S.

Treasury bills. These bills are always available and, for all practical purposes, risk free.

In contrast, most situations in which you allow someone else to use your money entail some risk. For example, the market value of your investment instrument may decline. Inflation may erode the purchasing power of your principal sum. The person or organization using your funds may default on scheduled interest and principal payments. Tax laws may be changed to lower the after-tax return on your investment. These and other types of risk associated with letting someone else use your funds should be reflected in a risk premium, in addition to the risk-free opportunity cost of money. Theoretically, the higher the degree of risk, the greater the risk premium and, therefore, the higher the interest rate you should require.

Simple Interest versus Compound Interest

simple interest

compound interest

There are two ways to compute interest. *Simple interest* is computed by applying an interest rate to only the original principal sum. *Compound interest* is computed by applying an interest rate to the sum of the original principal and the interest credited to it in previous periods.

The difference between simple and compound interest can be demonstrated with an example.

Example

Assume $1,000 is deposited in an account that earns 6 percent simple interest per year. At the end of each year, the account will be credited with $60 of interest. At the end of 5 years, there will be $1,300 in the account (if no withdrawals have been made), as shown in the table below.

If, instead, the account earns 6 percent compound interest per year, the deposit will grow to a larger amount than $1,300, as shown below. The extra $38.23 in the account at the end of 5 years is the result of interest earned on previous interest earnings.

Table 4-1
Accumulation of $1,000 in 5 Years at 6 Percent Simple and Compound Interest per Year

	Simple Interest			Compound Interest		
Year	Principal Sum	Interest	Ending Balance	Principal Sum	Interest	Ending Balance
1	$1,000	$60	$1,060	$1,000.00	$60.00	$1,060.00
2	$1,000	$60	$1,120	$1,060.00	$63.60	$1,123.60
3	$1,000	$60	$1,180	$1,123.60	$67.42	$1,191.02
4	$1,000	$60	$1,240	$1,191.02	$71.46	$1,262.48
5	$1,000	$60	$1,300	$1,262.48	$75.75	$1,338.23

Notice the difference in the annual amount by which the account grows when compound rather than simple interest is credited. The balance grows by a constant amount, $60 per year, when simple interest is credited. In the case of compound interest, the account balance grows by an increasing amount each year because the interest is paid on the principal plus interest already earned. However, the rate of growth in the compound interest case remains the same 6 percent as in the simple interest case.

Compound interest can have a powerful impact on future value, especially when a high interest rate or a long period of time is involved. For example, in the year 1980, the consumer price index (CPI), a commonly used measure of the inflation rate, rose by 13.5 percent over the preceding year. If that rate of inflation had continued, the same bag of groceries that cost $100 at the beginning of 1980 would have cost about $355 at the beginning of 1990 and would have risen to over $3,900 by the beginning of 2009.

Most of the day-to-day situations requiring time-value-of-money calculations involve compound interest rather than simple interest. Hence, our discussion will deal only with compound interest.

Compounding versus Discounting

compounding

discounting

The process by which a dollar today, a present value, grows over time to a larger amount, a future value, is called *compounding*. The process by which a dollar due in the future, a future value, is reduced over time to a smaller amount today, a present value, is called *discounting*.

The following figure shows the difference between present and future value with compound interest as the link between the two. Compounding can be viewed as a movement up the curve, while discounting can be viewed as a movement down the curve. Note also that the link between present and future value in Figure 4-1 is shown as a curve (and not a straight line) to reflect the application of compound interest rather than simple interest. When compound interest is used, the future value rises each year by an increasing amount as shown by moving up the curve (or the present value declines by a decreasing amount as shown by moving down the curve).

Figure 4–1 Compound Interest as the Link between Present Value and Future Value

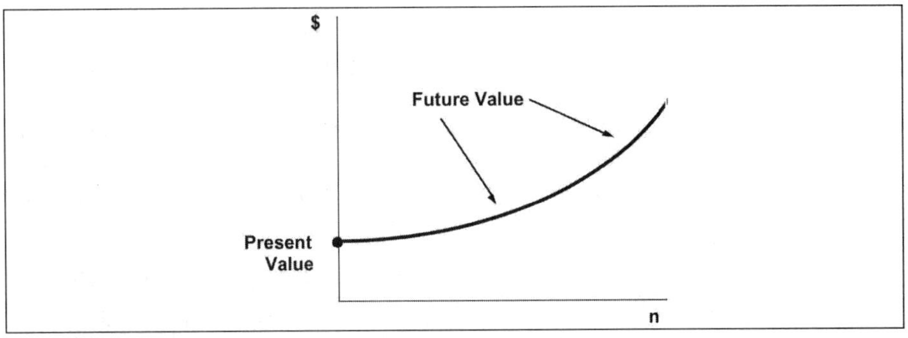

This figure depicts compound interest as the link between the two values. Dollar amounts are reflected by the vertical axis, and the number of years (periods) during which compounding or discounting occurs (n) is reflected on the horizontal axis. As you move up the curve (compounding), the future value grows by increasing amounts. As you move down the curve (discounting), the present value declines by decreasing amounts.

Two major factors influence the shape of the curve in the preceding figure. These are (1) the number of periods over which compounding or discounting occurs and (2) the interest rate used in the compounding or discounting process. Consequently, as the number of periods increases, the difference between the present value and the future value also increases. Similarly, all other things being equal, the higher the interest rate, the steeper the slope of the curve. Thus, as the interest rate increases, the difference between the present value and the future value also increases.

These relationships among the number of periods (n), the interest rate (i), the future value of money (FV), and the present value of money (PV) can be summarized as follows: In compounding, FV moves in the same direction as n and i (it increases as they increase); in discounting, PV moves in the opposite direction from n and i (it decreases as they increase).

Note that there are four key values in the most basic problems involving the time value of money. These values are the number of periods, the interest rate, the present value, and the future value. In these problems, you will be given three of the values and be called on to solve for the fourth.

Values in Basic TVM Problems

1. Number of periods (n)
2. Interest rate (i)
3. Present value (PV)
4. Future value (FV)

Effect of Income Taxes

Financial advisors must consider the impact of income taxes—federal, state, and local—on their time-value analyses. For example, the nominal rate of return realized on most investments should be adjusted downward to an after-tax basis. Similarly, a borrower should adjust the nominal payment or interest rate on a loan downward to an effective payment or rate if the payments are deductible for income tax purposes. Therefore, for the purpose of realism, we will assume that all values in the problems discussed are after-tax values.

Frequency of Compounding or Discounting

There is another factor in addition to the interest rate and the number of years that affects the size of the present and future values of money. That factor is the frequency with which the interest rate is applied in the compounding or discounting process.

FOCUS ON ETHICS
Ethics and the Time Value of Money

At first glance, a discussion of ethics may seem ill-suited to the topic of the time value of money. After all, does time value of money not rely strictly on mathematical formulas without regard to ethical values? Although it is true that mathematical formulas are neither moral nor immoral in and of themselves, it is also true that these formulas, improperly used, can lead to some extremely misleading results. These errant results can lead to decisions that are not in the client's best interests.

TVM formulas depend on interest rate assumptions. Higher rates of return provide more optimistic results. In a competitive marketplace, it is not uncommon for projected yields to be a determining factor as the client weighs alternative courses of action. Time-value-of-money formulas do not know one yield from another. If an advisor offers an exaggerated yield, the formula will provide an exaggerated result. It may be the decisive factor in leading the client into an inappropriate purchase.

A $10,000 tax-deferred investment that earns 8 percent per year will grow to $46,610 in 20 years. What if a financial advisor exaggerates the rate of return to 10 percent per year? The mathematical result is $67,275—a 44 percent increase in future value. Would this projection "close the sale"?

There is an old saying: "Figures don't lie, but liars figure." The ethical financial advisor uses projected rates of return that are fully justified in terms of historical experience and analysis of future economic conditions.

Throughout the time-value-of-money discussion in this chapter we will apply the interest rate only once per year, which is called annual compounding or discounting. However, you should recognize that in many cases, interest rates are applied several times within a year—semiannually (2 times a year), monthly (12 times a year), weekly (52 times a year), or daily (usually computed in commercial transactions by applying the interest rate 360 times per year). In fact, all other things being equal, the greater the frequency with which compounding or discounting occurs, the greater the effect on the growth in future values or the decline in present values. Nevertheless, for our purposes in this chapter, you should assume that compounding or discounting occurs on an annual basis.

Measuring the Number of Years (Periods)

Before moving on, you should keep in mind one other factor regarding the compounding or discounting process—the importance of accuracy regarding the timing of payments. Drawing time lines, such as those in the following figure, can be helpful. The timing of known dollar values can be noted on the line with unknown dollar values denoted with question marks. In the figure, the upper time line depicts a case in which you are to calculate the future value as of the beginning of year 6 (which is the same as the end of year 5) of a deposit made at the beginning of year 1. The lower time line depicts a situation in which you are to compute the present value as of today (the beginning of year 1) of a series of payments that will occur at the end of each of the next 4 years. Time lines can be constructed for all types of time-value-of-money problems, as will be shown throughout our time-value-of-money discussion.

Figure 4–2 Time Lines as a Help in Counting the Number of Years (Periods) of Compounding or Discounting

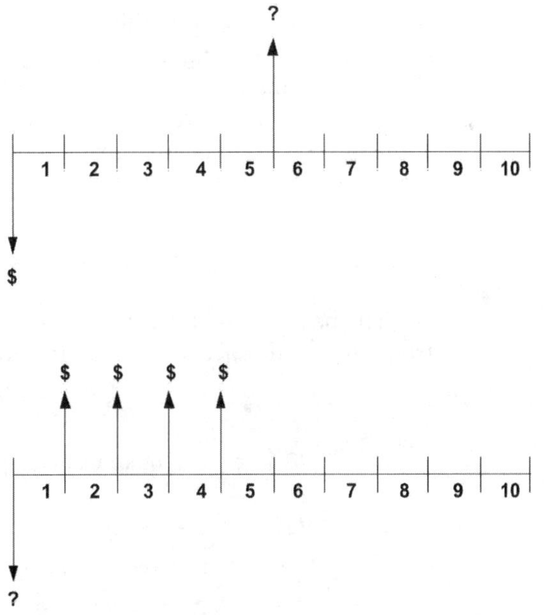

The top time line reflects a problem where a present value is deposited at the beginning of year 1 and you are asked to solve for the future value at the beginning of year 6, or the end of year 5. The lower time line depicts a problem where a sum of money is paid at the end of each of the next 4 years and you are asked to solve for the present value as of the beginning of year 1.

Plan of the Time-Value Discussion

Although several time-value-of-money formulas are presented in this chapter, you should avoid becoming bogged down with memorizing them. All the problems presented can be solved using simple multiplication and TVM tables that provide values for the portions of the formulas that are too difficult to remember and calculate. What is important is for you to be able to recognize the different types of TVM problems and to learn the approach for solving each of them using the values presented in the appropriate TVM table(s).

The balance of our TVM discussion utilizes and builds on the basic concepts presented thus far. It focuses on the future value and present value of a single sum of money and on the future value and present value of an annuity or an annuity due. Therefore, let us continue our TVM discussion by looking next at the future value of a single sum.

FUTURE VALUE OF A SINGLE SUM

future value of a single sum (FVSS)

The most frequently encountered and easiest to understand application of the time-value-of-money concept involves the *future value of a single sum* (FVSS). As explained earlier, determining the future value of a sum of money requires compounding, or increasing, the present value at some interest rate for a specified number of years. The most common example is the growth of a sum placed in an interest-bearing savings account. Recall, for example, that in Table 4-1 a \$1,000 deposit made today (present value) will grow to \$1,338.23 (future value) at the end of 5 years at 6 percent compound interest.

Future Value of a Single Sum Formula

FVSS formula

FVSS factor

The basic formula for computing the future value of a single sum of money, from which all other time-value formulas are derived, is the following:

$$\text{FVSS} = \text{PVSS} \times (1 + i)^n$$

where FVSS = the future value of a single sum

PVSS = the present value of a single sum

i = the compound annual interest rate, expressed as a decimal

n = the number of years during which compounding occurs

$(1 + i)^n$ = *FVSS factor*

When expressed in words, the FVSS formula requires you to add the interest rate (expressed as a decimal) to 1 and raise the sum to a power equal to the number of years over which compounding occurs. Then multiply the result by the present value of the single sum or deposit in question.

Because the term $(1 + i)^n$ in the FVSS formula is the FVSS factor, the FVSS formula can be simplified and written as follows:

FVSS = PVSS x FVSS factor

For example, assume that $500 is placed on deposit today in an account that will earn 9 percent compound annual interest. To what amount will this sum of money grow by the end of year 7? This problem is depicted on a time line in the following figure and, as shown in the next section, can be solved using the FVSS formula.

Figure 4–3 Time Line Depiction of FVSS Problem

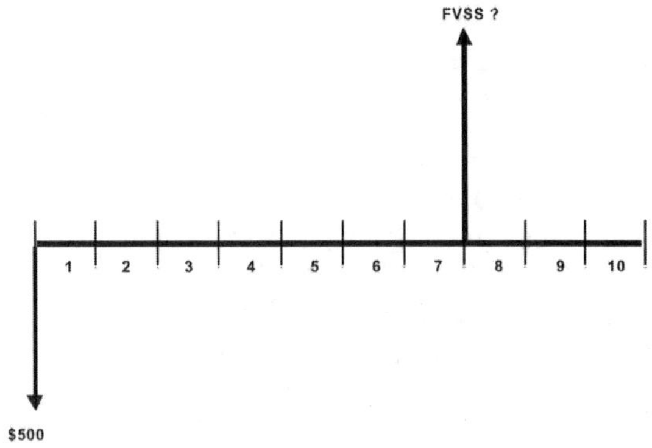

This time line depicts a problem in which a known single sum, $500, is deposited today, at the beginning of year 1, and you are to calculate its future value as of the end of year 7. The time line also illustrates the basic trade-off in all time-value-of-money problems. Here, the trade-off is a cash outflow today (the deposit shown below the time line) for a larger cash inflow later (the account balance shown above the time line at the end of the 7th year).

It is important, both conceptually and mathematically, to recognize that in every time-value-of-money problem there is an implicit trade-off over time of a sacrifice for a gain or a cost for a benefit. For instance, you may be willing to loan money to a friend today (a cost or cash outflow in the present) in order to be repaid a larger amount later (a benefit or larger cash inflow in the future). You need to understand the nature of this trade-off to fully grasp the time value of money. For purposes of consistency when using the time lines to depict various types of TVM problems, future values and periodic cash inflows will be shown above the line; present values and periodic cash outflows will be shown below the line.

Using the FVSS Formula

Returning to the problem at hand, the $500 that is placed on deposit today represents a present value. The future value to which it will grow at 9 percent compound annual interest by the end of the 7th year can be computed using the FVSS formula with the appropriate FVSS factor as follows:

FVSS = PVSS × FVSS factor

substituting the $500 present value and appropriate FVSS factor from the table

FVSS = $500 × 1.8280
= $914.00

Impact of a Change in Compound Interest Rate or Number of Years (Periods)

To emphasize a point made earlier in this chapter, the higher the compound interest rate (i) or the greater the number of years (n), the larger the FVSS. Conversely, the lower the interest rate or the fewer the number of years, the smaller the FVSS. So keeping money invested longer increases its future value, as does earning a higher return on the money. Lowering the return or shortening the investment horizon has the opposite effect on money; it decreases its future value.

Rule of 72 Approximation

So far we have calculated the future value of a single sum. Occasionally, you may want to approximate the impact of interest on a single sum. In this situation, the Rule of 72 can be useful.

Rule of 72

The *Rule of 72* is a quick method to estimate how long it will take for a sum to double at some interest rate. The formula is

$$72 \div i = n$$

where i = the interest rate expressed as a whole number—that is, 7 percent is stated as 7

n = the number of years it will take a single sum earning i to double

For example, at a compound annual interest rate of 9 percent, a single sum of $1 will double in value and reach $2 in approximately 8 years (72 ÷ 9). This value will double again and reach $4 in approximately another 8 years and double still again, reaching $8, at the end of approximately 8 more years. On the other hand, at a compound annual interest rate of 4 percent, the growth of the single sum will be slower; it will take about 18 years (72 ÷ 4) for each doubling to occur.

Remember that the Rule of 72 provides only an approximation and that for most purposes, you will want to be more precise. The higher the interest rate, the less precise the result using the Rule of 72.

PRESENT VALUE OF A SINGLE SUM

present value of a single sum (PVSS)

So far we have discussed compounding—that is, accumulating a known single sum of money at a compound annual interest rate over a specified number of years to determine a future value. Now, rather than moving forward in time and compounding, we will move back in time by discounting a future value to a present value. We will use an interest or discount rate to calculate the *present value of a single sum (PVSS)*. A single sum is an individual cash flow and not an annuity or series of cash flows.

Example 1 Assume that in 4 years you will spend $100,000 to replace a piece of manufacturing equipment. How much should you set aside today to pay for that equipment if the account is expected to earn 10 percent compound annual interest?

Example 2 Assume that 5 years from now, you will receive a $95,000 single-sum distribution from a trust. How much is that distribution worth in today's dollars if the appropriate discount rate is 7 percent per year?

Both of these problems are depicted on time lines in the figure below.

Present Value of a Single Sum Formula

We learned earlier that the FVSS can be solved using the formula

$$\text{FVSS} = \text{PVSS} \times (1 + i)^n$$

By multiplying both sides of this equation by

$$1 \div (1 + i)^n$$

the formula can be written as

$$\text{FVSS} \times [1 \div (1 + i)^n] = \text{PVSS}$$

or alternatively

$$\text{PVSS} = \text{FVSS} \times [1 \div (1 + i)^n]$$

PVSS factor

PVSS formula

where PVSS	=	the present value of a single sum
FVSS	=	the future value of a single sum
i	=	the compound annual interest or discount rate expressed as a decimal
n	=	the number of years over which discounting occurs
$1 \div (1 + i)^n$	=	*PVSS factor*

Figure 4–4 Time Line Depiction of PVSS Problems

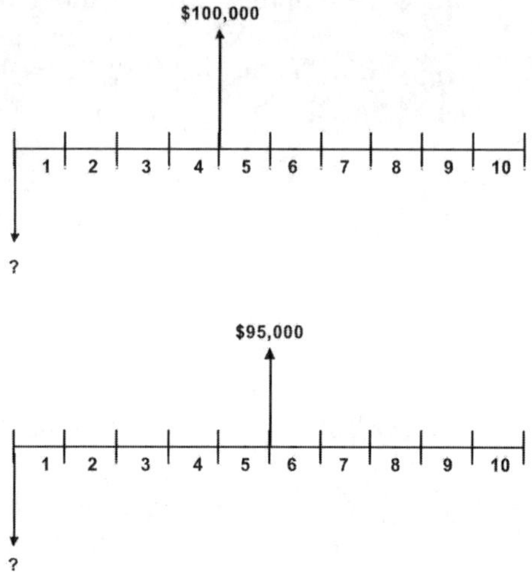

The time line on the top represents a problem in which you are asked to determine the present value of a $100,000 single sum due 4 years hence. In the time line on the bottom, the problem is to compute the present value when the future value is $95,000 due in 5 years.

When expressed in words, the PVSS formula requires you to divide into 1 the sum of the interest rate (expressed as a decimal) and 1 raised to a power equal to the number of years over which discounting occurs. You then multiply the result of this division by the future value of the single sum or amount specified.

Because the term $[1 \div (1 + i)^n]$ in the PVSS formula is the PVSS factor, the PVSS formula can be simplified and written as follows:

$$\text{PVSS} = \text{FVSS} \times \text{PVSS factor}$$

Using the PVSS Formula

Using the time line depiction in the figure above, the top illustrates the problem where you need $100,000 in 4 years to replace some manufacturing equipment. If the funds are expected to earn 10 percent compound annual interest, you will need to set aside $68,300 today to have the $100,000 you need in 4 years.

Using the PVSS formula with the appropriate PVSS factor to solve for the present value is as follows:

PVSS = FVSS × PVSS factor

substituting the $100,000 future value and appropriate PVSS factor from the table

PVSS = $100,000 × .6830
= $68,300.00

That is, $68,300 accumulating at 10 percent compound annual interest will grow to the $100,000 needed in 4 years.

The bottom of the figure illustrates the second problem where there is a $95,000 trust fund distribution due in 5 years. If the fund is discounted at a compound annual interest rate of 7 percent, its present value is $67,735. That is, using the PVSS formula with the appropriate PVSS factor to solve for the present value is as follows:

PVSS = FVSS × PVSS factor

substituting the $95,000 future value and appropriate PVSS factor from the table

PVSS = $95,000 × .7130
= $67,735.00

Impact of a Change in Discount (Interest) Rate or Number of Years (Periods)

You should understand the impact on the PVSS resulting from a change in the discount rate (i) or the number of years (n). The higher the discount rate, the lower the PVSS. The greater the number of years, the lower the PVSS. Discounting is stripping away interest to arrive at the value in today's dollars. A higher discount rate or a longer investment horizon means there is more interest to be stripped away, which lowers the present value. Conversely, a lower discount rate or a shorter investment horizon means there is less interest to be stripped away, which raises the present value.

FUTURE VALUE OF AN ANNUITY OR AN ANNUITY DUE

Earlier in this chapter, we explained how to compute the future value of a single sum credited with compound interest. Now we will build on and expand that case to deal with the calculation of the future value of a series of equal deposits or payments. For example, if $3,000 is deposited or paid into an account each year and is credited with 11 percent compound annual interest, how much will be in the account at the end of 6 years? The income stream is called an annuity. An annuity is a finite stream of equal periodic payments.

future value of an annuity (FVA)
future value of an annuity due (FVAD)
annuity
annuity dues

The above example describes either a *future value of an annuity (FVA)* or a *future value of an annuity due (FVAD)* problem. An *annuity* is a series of equal payments made at the end of each year (or period) for a specified number of years (periods). An *annuity due* is a series of equal payments made at the beginning of each year (or period) for a specified number of years (or periods).[16]

There are many personal and business situations where money is invested periodically. Some businesses, for instance, enable their employees to invest deductions from each paycheck in U.S. government savings bonds. Many individuals deposit predetermined amounts each week or month in Christmas club or vacation club accounts at banks or credit unions. Many individuals deposit funds each year in individual retirement accounts (IRAs) at banks, thrift institutions, brokerage firms, insurance companies, or mutual funds. Tax-advantaged employee retirement programs, like 401(k) plans or 403(b) tax-deferred annuity plans, enable employees to make periodic deposits that may also have matching employer contributions. Businesses may contribute sinking fund payments to accumulate money to purchase fixed assets.

Assumptions

To simplify the solution of FVA and FVAD problems, we will assume that the deposits or payments are made annually. Also, we will assume that the deposits or payments all earn the same rate of compound annual interest.

It is particularly important in annuity problems to accurately measure the length of time during which each deposit or payment earns compound interest. One possible assumption is that all deposits or payments are made at the beginning of each year (an annuity due); the other is that they are all made at the end of each year (an annuity).

Example Assume that five annual deposits of $1,000 each earn 7 percent compound annual interest. At the end of the 5th year, the future value of these equal annual deposits will be $6,153.29 if they are made at the beginning of each year versus only $5,750.74 if they are made at the end of each year. The $402.55 difference between the two future values occurs because each deposit earns one more year of interest under the FVAD than under the FVA. That is, when deposits are made at the start of each year, the

---

16. In some fields, such as insurance, the terms annuity and annuity due are used to refer to a series of payments, the value of which includes both compound interest and mortality factors. Such annuities are more accurately referred to as life annuities or life annuities due.

first deposit earns interest for 5 years rather than 4; the second deposit earns interest for 4 years rather than 3, and so on. The last deposit earns interest for one year rather than none.

Using Formulas to Compute the FVA and the FVAD

A problem that requires the calculation of the future value of an annuity or annuity due can be viewed as a collection of FVSS problems. Each annuity deposit or payment can be viewed as a single sum, each of which earns compound annual interest for a different number of years. Hence, the FVA or FVAD is really the sum of a series of FVSS calculations.

To illustrate, assume that $100 is deposited at the end of each of 4 years and earns 5 percent compound annual interest. What is the total future value of these annual $100 deposits at the end of the 4th year? The first $100 deposit earns interest for 3 years (that is, from the end of year 1 until the end of year 4). The future value of this $100 deposit using the FVSS formula with the appropriate FVSS factor is

$$\begin{aligned} \text{1st FVSS} &= \text{PVSS} \times \text{FVSS factor} \\ &= \$100 \times (1.05)^3 \\ &= \$100 \times 1.1576 \\ &= \$115.76 \end{aligned}$$

Figure 4–5 Time Line Depiction of FVAD and FVA Problems

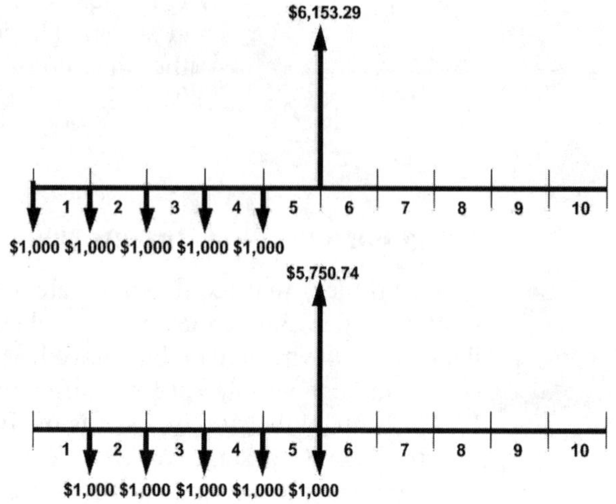

The top line depicts a problem in which $1,000 deposits are made at the beginning of each of 5 years (an annuity due) and invested at 7 percent compound annual interest. The problem is to determine the future value as of the end of the 5th year. In the lower time line, the problem is the same in all respects except that all deposits are made at the end of each of the 5 years (an annuity).

The future value of the second $100 deposit, which earns interest for 2 years, is

$$\begin{aligned} \text{2d FVSS} &= \text{PVSS} \times \text{FVSS factor} \\ &= \$100 \times (1.05)^2 \\ &= \$100 \times 1.1025 \\ &= \$110.25 \end{aligned}$$

The future value of the third $100 deposit, which earns interest for 1 year, is

$$\begin{aligned} \text{3d FVSS} &= \text{PVSS} \times \text{FVSS factor} \\ &= \$100 \times (1.05)^1 \\ &= \$100 \times 1.0500 \\ &= \$105.00 \end{aligned}$$

And the future value of the fourth $100 deposit is the same as its present value because it earns no interest. Thus, the FVA in this problem is $431.01 (that is, $115.76 + $110.25 + $105.00 + $100.00).

If, on the other hand, the deposits had been made at the beginning of each year, their future values (using the appropriate FVSS factors from the table) would have been calculated as follows:

1st FVSS	=	$\$100 \times (1.05)^4$	=	$100 × 1.2155	=	$121.55
2d FVSS	=	$\$100 \times (1.05)^3$	=	$100 × 1.1576	=	115.76
3d FVSS	=	$\$100 \times (1.05)^2$	=	$100 × 1.1025	=	110.25
4th FVSS	=	$\$100 \times (1.05)^1$	=	$100 × 1.0500	=	105.00
FVAD					=	$452.56

FVA formula

For cases where the deposits are made at the end of each year, there is an alternative to the approach of adding the future values of each of the separate deposits. Using the FVA formula with the appropriate FVA factor achieves the same result in one step, as follows:

$$FVA = \text{annual deposit} \times [(1 + i)^n - 1 \div i]$$

where the bracketed portion is the *FVA factor*

FVA factor

Because the bracketed portion of the equation is the FVA factor, the FVA formula can be simplified and written as follows:

FVA = annual deposit × FVA factor

Using the FVA formula with the appropriate FVA factor to determine the future value of the deposits made at the end of each year,

FVA = annual deposit × FVA factor

substituting the $100 annual deposit and appropriate FVA factor from the table

= $100 × 4.3101

= $431.01

Cases in which the deposits are made at the beginning of each year use a modified version of the FVA formula (that is, a FVAD formula). Because each deposit will be credited with one extra year of interest, it is necessary to multiply the result of the FVA formula by (1 + i). That is, if deposits are made at the beginning of each year, the simplified version of the FVA formula is transformed into

FVAD formula

FVAD = FVA formula × (1 + i)

which is the same as

FVAD = (annual deposit × FVA factor) × (1 + i)

substituting the $100 annual deposit, appropriate FVA factor from the table, and the interest rate

FVAD = ($100 × 4.3101) × 1.0500

= $431.01 × 1.0500

= $452.56

In other words, a simple way to determine the FVAD is to calculate the FVA and then multiply the result by 1 plus the interest rate (1 + i).

PRESENT VALUE OF AN ANNUITY OR AN ANNUITY DUE

present value of an annuity (PVA)
present value of an annuity due (PVAD)

An earlier section of this chapter contained an explanation of how to calculate the present value of a single sum that is due or needed at some time in the future. This section deals with the question of how to compute the present value of a series of level future payments. This type of problem is a *present value of an annuity (PVA)* problem if the payments are made at the end of each year or a *present value of an annuity due (PVAD)* problem if the payments are made at the beginning of each year.

To illustrate this type of problem, assume that you have lent money to a business associate and expect to be repaid in eight annual payments of $1,000 each, starting 1 year from now. How much would you be willing to sell the promissory note for today if you believe you can earn 6 percent compound annual interest on the money in an alternative investment? What is the present value of this 8-year annuity discounted at 6 percent?

Assumptions

As discussed earlier in the chapter, each payment is assumed to be made annually. In addition, we need to specify whether the annuity payments are to be made at the end or at the beginning of each year. For example, an 8-year, $1,000 annuity discounted at 6 percent interest has a PVA of $6,209.79 versus a PVAD of $6,582.38. (See the time line depiction of these two types of problems below.)

Figure 4–6 Time Line Depiction of PVA and PVAD Problems

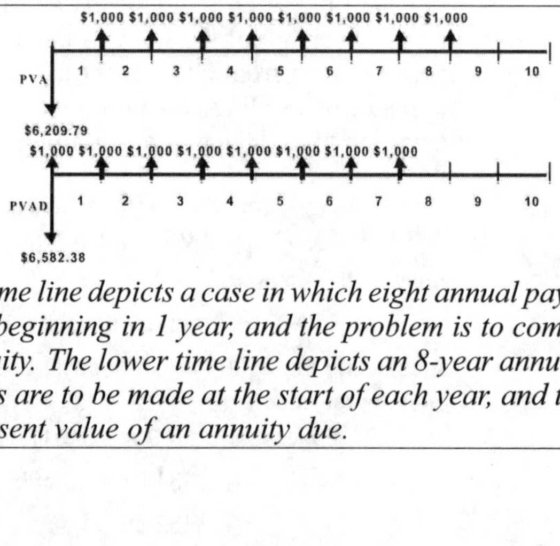

The upper time line depicts a case in which eight annual payments of $1,000 are to be made beginning in 1 year, and the problem is to compute the present value of an annuity. The lower time line depicts an 8-year annuity due, in which $1,000 payments are to be made at the start of each year, and the problem is to compute the present value of an annuity due.

Using Formulas to Compute the PVA and the PVAD

The basic formula for computing the present value of a single sum can also be used to compute the present value of an annuity or an annuity due. All that is needed is to calculate the PVSS for each annuity payment separately and total the results.

For example, assume that as part of a divorce settlement, a father has been ordered to deposit a lump sum in a trust account sufficient to provide child support payments for his son. The child support payments are to be $5,000 per year for 4 years, beginning 1 year from today. If the amount placed in the trust account is assumed to earn 7 percent compound annual interest, how much should the father place in the trust account today?

Using the formula for the PVSS described earlier in the chapter, you can find the present value of each separate payment. Once you have calculated the present value of each separate payment, you can easily determine the present value of the sum of all four payments.

Specifically, you can calculate the present value of the first $5,000 child support payment to be made 1 year from now using the PVSS formula with the appropriate PVSS factor as follows:

$$\begin{aligned} \text{1st PVSS} &= \text{FVSS} \times \text{PVSS factor} \\ &= \$5{,}000 \times [1 \div (1.07)^1] \\ &= \$5{,}000 \times .9346 \\ &= \$4{,}673.00 \end{aligned}$$

The PVSS of the second, third, and fourth $5,000 child support payments are calculated as follows:

2d PVSS	= $\$5{,}000 \times [1 \div (1.07)^2]$	= $5,000 × .8734	= $4,367.00
3d PVSS	= $\$5{,}000 \times [1 \div (1.07)^3]$	= $5,000 × .8163	= $4,081.50
4th PVSS	= $\$5{,}000 \times [1 \div (1.07)^4]$	= $5,000 × .7629	= $3,814.50

The sum of these present values, the PVA, is $16,936.00 (that is, $4,673.00 + $4,367.00 + $4,081.50 + $3,814.50). This amount deposited today at 7 percent compound annual interest will be just enough to provide four annual child support payments of $5,000 each beginning 1 year from now. To verify this, examine what would happen to the account each year as that year's payment is made.

Year	Beginning Balance	Interest Earnings	Amount Withdrawn	Ending Balance
1	$16,936.00	$1,185.52	$5,000.00	$13,121.52
2	$13,121.52	$ 918.51	$5,000.00	$9,040.03
3	$ 9,040.03	$ 632.80	$5,000.00	$ 4,672.83
4	$ 4,672.83	$ 327.10	$5,000.00	($0.07)

If, on the other hand, the four annual child support payments were to be made at the beginning of each year rather than at the end, the PVAD would be calculated by adding the four separate PVSSs.

1st PVSS	= $5,000 × [1 ÷ $(1.07)^0$]	= $5,000 × 1.0000	=	$ 5,000.00
2d PVSS	= $5,000 × [1 ÷ $(1.07)^1$]	= $5,000 × .9346	=	$ 4,673.00
3d PVSS	= $5,000 × [1 ÷ $(1.07)^2$]	= $5,000 × .8734	=	$ 4,367.00
4th PVSS	= $5,000 × [1 ÷ $(1.07)^3$]	= $5,000 × .8163	=	$ 4,081.50
PVAD	=			$18,121.50

Note that a larger amount ($18,121.50 compared with $16,936.00) would have to be deposited in the trust account if the child support payments were to be made at the beginning of each year rather than at the end. This is because when payments are made at the beginning of each year, total interest earnings are lower. Each withdrawal to make a child support payment occurs a year earlier under a beginning-of-year assumption compared with an end-of-year assumption.

As an alternative to the approach of adding the present values of each of the separate payments, you can achieve the same result in one step by using the PVA formula with the appropriate PVA factor for cases where the payments are made at the end of each year:

PVA formula

$$PVA = \text{annual payment} \times [1 - [1 \div (1 + i)^n] \div i]$$

where the bracketed portion is the *PVA factor*

PVA factor

Because the bracketed portion of the equation is the PVA factor, the PVA formula can be simplified and written as follows:

PVA = annual payment × PVA factor

Using the PVA formula with the appropriate PVA factor to determine the amount that must be deposited in the trust account to make the child support payments at the end of each year,

PVA = annual payment × PVA factor

substituting the annual $5,000 child support payment and appropriate PVA factor from the table

= $5,000 × 3.3872

= $16,936.00

Cases in which the child support payments are made at the beginning of each year use a modified version of the PVA formula (that is, a PVAD formula). To reflect the fact that each child support payment will earn one less year of interest before being distributed, it is necessary to multiply the result of the PVA formula by (1 + i). That is, if the child support payments are made at the beginning of each year, the simplified version of the PVA formula is transformed into

PVA formula

PVAD = PVA formula × (1 + i)

which is the same as

PVAD = (annual payment × PVA factor) × (1 + i)

substituting the annual $5,000 child support payment, appropriate PVA factor from the table, and the interest rate

PVAD = $5,000 × 3.3872 × 1.0700

= $16,936.00 × 1.0700

= $18,121.52

The slightly higher result of $18,121.52 compared with $18,121.50 (derived by adding the present values of each of the separate payments) is due to rounding. Do not dwell on this difference as it is not important.

UNDERSTANDING FINANCIAL RISK TOLERANCE

As a financial advisor, you are under a legal and an ethical obligation to help clients determine a suitable asset allocation for their investment portfolio. Suitability is based on an analysis of a client's particular circumstances with respect to his or her financial goals, financial ability to sustain a loss, and psychological attitudes toward financial risk taking. The purpose of this section of Chapter 4 is to introduce you to the approaches that can be used to assess the last item noted—financial risk tolerance.

Recommending a suitable asset allocation for a client's portfolio should lead to a lasting relationship that can be profitable to both the client and you. Not only will the client be happy, but you will also come away with a sense of personal satisfaction and professional pride from having fulfilled the client's expectations. Conversely, extreme client dissatisfaction with an incorrect asset allocation can result in an unsuitability lawsuit. In such disputes, the charge is that a financial advisor knew—or should have known—that the asset allocation was inappropriate for the client. Knowing and understanding the client helps to determine whether an asset allocation is appropriate.

The need for information about the client's ability to tolerate financial risk is especially critical when you are using a computerized asset-allocation program based on portfolio theory. Proper allocation of assets is predicated on a determination of the client's level of acceptable risk. All other calculations are a function of this initial determination.

You may not find asset-allocation computer packages necessary to perform your duties competently. However, irrespective of the exact process you use, your role as a financial advisor is to recommend an asset allocation that delivers the maximum returns possible, given the client's ability to tolerate risks. Other factors being equal, you should guide the client toward selecting the asset allocation with the higher potential return when he or she faces alternative allocations that provide equally tolerable levels of risk. On the other hand, when the choice is between asset allocations with equal expected returns, you should advise the client to select the one with the lower risk.

Consequently, both you and your client need to seriously consider the concepts of risk, risk/return trade-off, and risk tolerance during the development of your client's financial plan. What follows is a brief explanation of these concepts.

Basic Concepts in Risk

Risk

risk

In its broadest sense, the term *risk*, as used in an asset-allocation context, is the probability that the actual return on the investment portfolio will be lower than the expected return. This risk is measured by the volatility or variability in returns. An investment portfolio that has low variability in returns (or value) from month to month, quarter to quarter, and year to year is less risky in this sense than an investment portfolio that goes up and down during this same period. It is less risky because it is more predictable. In other words, there are fewer surprises.

Risk/Return Trade-off

risk/return trade-off

In general, the investment portfolio that, on average, produces higher rates of return also has greater variability in its returns. This relationship is called the *risk/return trade-off*. To stand the possibility of relatively high returns, the client must also take the chance that the returns may be relatively low. Sometimes the value of the investment portfolio can drop below the amount the client initially placed into it (the principal). In some cases, the loss of principal is permanent, while in other cases, there is a chance for a recovery.

As you may infer from the above, a negative outcome from a risky investment portfolio can take two forms: (1) not getting as much of a return as desired (for example, a 4 percent rather than a 20 percent return), and (2) paying a penalty for trying to get the higher return (loss of principal). Most people's intuitive understanding of the term risk revolves primarily around the notion of loss of principal, although once the concept is explained, most are also able to understand how variability in returns, even when only positive outcomes are considered, also defines risk.

Risk Tolerance

risk tolerance

risk seeker

risk averter

risk aversion

Differences in clients' psychological makeups produce differences in their *risk tolerance*—that is, their willingness to expose themselves to greater losses for the chance of getting greater earnings. The term *risk seeker* describes the client who is willing to take the chance. The client who is unwilling to take the chance is called a *risk averter*.

Of course, there are different degrees of risk tolerance and *risk aversion*. Although it may be easier to lump people into just two categories, this conceptualization is an oversimplification of the state of nature. With most characteristics, including risk taking, people vary from each other to a degree. In other words, the differences are relative rather than absolute. Therefore, it is more appropriate to conceptualize risk aversion/risk tolerance as a continuous characteristic rather than one with just two discrete categories (such as gender).

However, the distribution of people on this dimension is such that more people are on the risk-averse end than on the risk-tolerant end of the continuum. This type of distribution is expected on theoretical grounds, and various empirical investigations, including surveys of the public, tend to confirm it.

Difficulties in Assessing Risk Tolerance

Assessing the client's level of risk tolerance is a difficult process for a number of reasons. First, risk tolerance is an elusive, ambiguous concept to most people. If they have no previous investment experience, it is especially hard for clients to specify how risk tolerant they are. Under such circumstances, the client is likely to resort to an analysis of his or her behaviors in other types of risky situations, be they physical, social, or ethical. In other words, people often tend to base their level of financial risk tolerance on their willingness to take a risk in physical situations (which involve risks that could result in bodily harm, such as mountain climbing or skydiving), social situations (which involve risks that could lead to loss of self-esteem or another person's respect), or ethical situations (which involve risks that could compromise moral or religious standards or society's legal standards). However, research on risk taking demonstrates that a person's level of risk tolerance for other types of risky situations is not a good gauge of risk taking in situations involving the potential loss of money, such as in investment decisions. It would not be unusual, for example, to find a trapeze artist who is extremely conservative in investment matters.

Second, while numerous approaches to assessing risk tolerance for financial matters have been proposed (which we will discuss shortly), the results of these procedures are often discrepant. A client may seem risk averse using one procedure and appear risk tolerant using another technique. This is because each technique is subject to different sources of error.

Third, risk tolerance is not a fixed characteristic of the individual. The particulars of a given situation are as strong an influence on the person's willingness to accept a risk as are his or her natural predispositions to be risk taking or risk averse. For example, most people are more willing to take risks with money acquired through a windfall than with money they had to work hard to earn.

Moreover, certain demographic characteristics also offer clues to a person's risk tolerance. For example, it has been found that risk aversion increases with age and number of dependents and decreases with wealth. However, you should never rely solely on demographic characteristics as the means for assigning a level of risk tolerance to a given client. Allocation of assets on the basis of a demographic profile, without any further assessment of the client's actual tolerance, is unacceptable. An analysis of demographic factors should serve primarily as a means for developing some hunches about a client, which you must confirm or disconfirm through additional and more direct means of assessment.

Finally, many clients find it difficult to open up to their financial advisors and provide the information needed to help them. These clients fail to see you as a professional confidant.

ASSESSMENT OF THE CLIENT'S RISK TOLERANCE

Purpose of Assessment

So far, we have examined some of the factors that exert an influence on a person's willingness to undertake a risky course of action. Now comes the issue of assessment. How do you measure a client's typical level of risk tolerance? By typical, we mean the level at which the aforementioned distortions do not cause the client to make decisions that are either riskier or safer than would generally be characteristic of that individual.

One way is to observe the client repeatedly over an extended time period in situations that are likely to reveal his or her characteristic risk-tolerance level. Of course, this approach is not really feasible because it is unreasonably time-consuming for you and constitutes an unwarranted intrusion for the client. Some observations may even be misleading because the individual may not even be aware of the risks he or she is incurring. Consequently, there is a need to estimate the client's risk tolerance within a relatively short time period.

The sections that follow review some of the available options for estimating the client's risk tolerance within a relatively short time period. All of these options call for sensitivity to appropriate cues and an ability to integrate them into a total impression of the client.

Whatever method you use, you should realize that the assessment process is meant to help clients understand their own level of risk tolerance. Quite frequently, as already noted, clients are not aware of how risk tolerant or risk averse they are. To them, risk tolerance is a vague concept that requires both explanation and exploration. The purpose of assessment is not for you to impose your perceptions on the client. For example, it is inappropriate to advise the client that the choice is between "eating" (risky investments) and "sleeping" (non-risky investments). In the end, clients must determine what constitutes an acceptable level of risk. Your role is to help them learn enough about themselves to be able to make that determination.

Assessment Methods

Many financial advisors fail to appreciate the complexity of the task facing them in trying to determine a client's risk tolerance accurately. Considerable time and effort are required to do it correctly. As already noted, a major problem is that frequently the various techniques do not give the same picture of a particular person's level of risk tolerance. Often, the individual may appear to be a risk taker when assessed with one technique and risk averse when assessed with another. Practically, this means that you should employ more than one approach for an accurate assessment of a client's risk-taking propensity.

Contrasts between Qualitative and Quantitative Assessment

The assessment process can be either qualitative or quantitative. When you rely on a qualitative approach, you typically collect the necessary information primarily through conversations with your clients, without assigning numbers to the information gathered. The information is collected in an unstructured format and intuitively evaluated based on your training and experience. A quantitative approach, in contrast, relies on the use of a structured format—questionnaires, for example—that allows you to translate observations into some type of numerical score. These scores are then used to interpret the client's risk-taking propensities. Most advisors do not rely on one approach to the exclusion of the other. Even so, few quantitatively oriented advisors are willing to surrender their professional judgment to the results of a questionnaire. It is really a matter of degree as to how qualitative or quantitative one advisor is compared with another.

Often, when you use a questionnaire or similar device to assess a client's risk tolerance, it can facilitate the beginning of a dialogue between you and the client. The content of the questionnaire highlights issues that the client may not have thought about. Another advantage is that a quantitative approach allows you to standardize the assessment process.

A number of limitations are inherent in a strictly qualitative approach—that is, one in which you rely solely on the verbal comments a client makes. Financial advisors (like all people) are often overconfident about their ability to make intuitive judgments. Ambiguous client statements are subject to a wide range of interpretation. Even with more straightforward statements, there is often a lack of consensus about their meaning. "Rubber yardsticks" of this sort can be minimized in a quantitative-assessment approach.

When using a qualitative approach to the assessment of risk tolerance, you should be familiar with good interviewing skills, as discussed in chapter 2. There are standards for quantitative assessment procedures as well. For example, a quantitative measurement device, such as a test or even a questionnaire, needs to be constructed carefully. The questions should be written so that they do not lead or bias the individual to answer them in a certain way. Moreover, evidence must be provided to demonstrate that the test or questionnaire does, in fact, assess the attributes it is meant to measure and that it measures them accurately on a consistent basis.

norms

Provided that they are accurate, the best quantitative measurement devices have *norms*, standards of measurement, such as averages, that allow you to compare a particular individual with a representative group. Through the use of these norms, you can compare the individual to the public at large or to some subgroup. For instance, using a normed measure of risk tolerance, it is possible to see whether your client is more or less risk tolerant than people in general or with other people of the same age and sex.

Unfortunately, many assessment devices financial advisors now employ to measure client risk tolerance have not been developed under such strict standards. Many of these devices were created for in-house use by individual advisors, brokerage houses, or mutual funds, and many of the developers of these devices are probably unaware of such requirements. There is a critical need for well-constructed questionnaires that provide some evidence to support their use as measures of risk tolerance.

Most of the available assessment devices suffer from the same problems. In some, the wrong questions are asked or they are presented in an incorrect format. Many devices are too short, thereby failing to contain an adequate representation of questions. It has been demonstrated repeatedly that answers to similar questions about risk tolerance may not concur. To avoid being misled by the answer to any one question, you need to ask a series of questions. Some answers may underestimate the client's true level of risk tolerance, whereas others may overestimate it. Other things being equal, the more questions that are used to measure a psychological characteristic, the more precise are the results.

thrill seeker

Some questionnaires do not separate the different contexts of risk taking, so a high score on such a questionnaire is probably better at identifying a *thrill seeker* than someone who has a high risk tolerance for investment or financial matters. For all these reasons, you must exercise caution. It is strongly recommended that you examine the content of the questionnaire. A questionnaire purporting to assess risk tolerance may, in fact, be measuring some other attribute.

There are many techniques to assess a client's risk tolerance. Some lend themselves more to a qualitative approach, whereas others call for a more quantitative approach. The material that follows takes a pragmatic look at the various approaches to assessing risk tolerance and considers their relative merits and drawbacks.

Aspects Considered in the Most Common Approaches Used to Measure Client Risk Tolerance

- Investment objectives
- Preferences for various investment products
- Real-life choices involving risk
- Self-classification of risk-taking propensity
- Preferences for different probabilities and payoff levels

Investment Objectives

Frequently, clients are asked to identify their financial objectives. For example, the client may be asked to indicate how important the following are to him or her: liquidity, safety of principal, appreciation, protection from inflation, current income, and tax reduction.

The client's level of risk tolerance is inferred from the answers. If the client's primary concerns are safety of principal and/or liquidity, then risk aversion is assumed. If, however, the main objectives are protection from inflation or tax relief, then the inference is that the client is risk tolerant.

Objectives, however, must not be confused with risk tolerance. There are many individuals who desire tax relief, yet are quite risk averse. A client's stated objectives may, in fact, be quite incompatible with his or her level of risk tolerance. In many cases, the client may be unaware of this incongruity. In a sense, the client's level of risk tolerance should be the basis for evaluating how reasonable the client's objectives are. However, using objectives for the purpose of gauging risk tolerance, without any further attempts to assess actual risk tolerance, is a mistake. To do so is to have "the tail wag the dog."

Example Rank the following investment objectives from 1 to 6, with 1 being the most important:

_____ liquidity

_____ safety of principal

_____ protection from inflation

_____ growth

_____ current income

_____ reduced taxation

Preferences for Various Investment Products

This is the most direct approach to measuring a client's risk tolerance. With this method, the client indicates the products that he or she prefers as investments. There are several variations of this procedure. In its simplest form, the client is presented with the available alternatives and is then asked how he or she wishes to distribute available assets among these options. The products are usually presented in some rank order, ranging from very safe investments to very risky investments.

Example

If you received a large windfall, how would you allocate it among the following? (Percentages must total 100.)

_____% U.S. government securities

_____% certificates of deposit

_____% corporate bonds and bond mutual funds

_____% stock and stock mutual funds

_____% options

_____% futures contracts

The accuracy of this procedure (in all its variants) rests on the client's knowledge of the actual risk-return potential of the various investments. Preferably, you have taken the time to explain and specify these differences to the client, because many clients may lack even basic knowledge. You should never assume that clients are highly knowledgeable about financial matters.

FOCUS ON ETHICS
When Risk Attitude and Risk Capacity Collide

Consider the case of client John Doe who views himself to be highly risk tolerant in financial matters. His existing portfolio consists of common stock investments in small, highly risky companies. A third-party evaluation of this client's risk tolerance confirms that he is among the top 5 percent in terms of his attitude toward risk. The client asks about specific aggressive stocks. Should you as the advisor feel free to recommend or sell high-risk investments to this client?

Now consider some additional information. The client is a 30-year-old widower with three small children. He is an aeronautical engineer employed by a defense contractor that relies entirely on the government for revenues. His total savings including his investment portfolio are less than one month's earnings, and he is not vested in his pension plan. He has no life or disability income insurance. Both his father and grandfather died of heart attacks in their mid-40s.

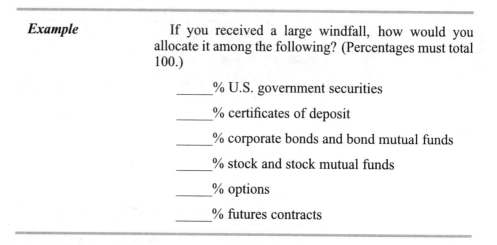

FOCUS ON ETHICS **When Risk Attitude and Risk Capacity Collide**
Ask the question again: Should you as the advisor feel free to recommend or sell high-risk investments to this client? Clearly, this client has an attitude toward risk tolerance that is at odds with his economic and family situation. Selling the client what he wants will generate a commission—but is it ethical?

Real-Life Choices Involving Risks

Although a person's past performance is no guarantee of future performance, it has been observed that the best predictor of future behavior is typically past behavior. This notion underlies the real-life choices approach to risk-tolerance assessment—that is, gathering and evaluating factual information about the client's life. The following lifestyle characteristics can be used to gauge a client's disposition toward financial risk:

- composition of present investment portfolio. How risky is it? What percentage of total assets are in passbook savings accounts, Treasury notes, mutual funds, stocks, options, commodities, and so on? If the client owns stocks, does he or she use short selling and margin buying? If the client owns an annuity, is it of the fixed or variable type? How satisfied or dissatisfied is the client with this type of portfolio? If changes were made to a previous portfolio, were these changes in a more conservative or more aggressive direction?
- debt ratio. The ratio of the client's liabilities to his or her gross assets has been used as a measure of risk tolerance. Some have suggested that a debt ratio over 23 percent reflects risk taking, under 8 percent reflects risk aversion, and 8 percent to 23 percent reflects a risk-neutral attitude.
- ratio of life insurance to annual salary. The assumption is that the larger the resulting ratio, the higher the client's level of risk aversion.
- size of deductibles on property-liability coverage. It has been observed that as the amount of wealth allocated to risky securities rises, so does the size of the deductible on the client's insurance coverages. Risk-tolerant individuals elect larger deductibles.
- percentage of net wealth used for recreational gambling. The larger the ratio, the more risk-seeking the individual is considered to be.
- job tenure. The willingness to make a voluntary job change is considered an indicator of a willingness to take financial risks. Therefore, clients can be asked how many job changes they have made during the last 15 years. More than three changes is considered by some as a sign of a risk-taking attitude. Quitting a job before finding a replacement job is particularly significant. Job changes at middle age may also be especially noteworthy.

- variations in income. Risk-taking individuals may show greater variations in their annual income from year to year, and not always in an upward direction. You should also look at the duration of unemployment if the client was ever unemployed. Did the individual take the first job offer received during this period of unemployment, or did the client wait until finding a job to his or her liking? What was the salary of the new job the client took after the period of unemployment? If it was lower than that of the previous job, it could indicate risk aversion.
- type of mortgage. A willingness to undertake a variable rather than a fixed mortgage could be a sign of financial risk taking. If the client has chosen a fixed mortgage, did he or she lock in on a guaranteed rate before settlement? Locking in is a sign of risk aversion.

Self-Classification of Risk-Taking Propensity

Another approach to assessing risk tolerance involves asking clients to classify themselves with respect to the amount of risk that they can tolerate. An extremely popular question is something like: "Where would you place yourself on a 10-point scale on which 1 equals extreme risk aversion and 10 equals extreme risk tolerance?"

This type of question requires clients to think about their past behaviors and current attitudes and to somehow subjectively weight these experiences and combine them into a single impression of themselves. Clients vary in their ability to perform this type of self-analysis. Some are much more introspective and self-aware than others. If a client has not gone through the necessary introspection, the overall self-evaluation may be biased by one or two events, perhaps recent ones that may be atypical incidents but that, because of their recency, the client overemphasizes. You have no way of knowing what biases are operating because a given individual does not explain the criteria he or she uses to make the self-rating, so its accuracy rests with whatever procedure the client used to arrive at the number.

Research indicates that on questions of this type, clients tend to overestimate rather than underestimate their actual level of risk tolerance because of a desire to appear socially acceptable. Risk taking is valued in our culture, and quite naturally most people desire to impress others. Therefore, the accuracy of this procedure depends on the degree to which clients have insight into their typical behavior and the extent to which they are willing to accept their advisors as professional confidants. It is usually best to ask a question of this type only after the client is asked to consider his or her attitudes toward more specific issues.

Because you can never hope to eliminate completely the subjectivity involved in self-ratings, asking your clients more specific questions about how they react to risky situations may reduce some of the subjectivity. First of all, bringing up specific issues forces clients to think about their behaviors. In a sense, it imposes introspection on clients who may not be introspective by nature. It forces them to deal with issues they may never have thought about before. The following list is a sample of more detailed questions:

- After making an important financial decision, how often do you regret your choice?
- Do you experience anxiety or thrill when awaiting the outcome of an important investment decision?
- How do you react to unexpected financial news?
- How easily do you adapt to unfavorable financial changes in your life?
- How long does it take you to make an important financial decision?
- Are you generally pessimistic or optimistic about your financial decisions?
- What is the worst investment decision you have made?
- Do you view risk as an opportunity or danger?
- How afraid are you of losing what you have?

When you ask these questions, there is a choice of either allowing for open-ended answers or asking the client to select a response from a preselected set of answers. The latter approach, which limits the client's range of possible answers, is much more amenable to quantification. That is, the answers can easily be assigned numerical values and aggregated into some score. However, in contrast to open-ended answers, these answers do not permit clients to use their own words in the reply. Open-ended answers, therefore, have the advantage of eliciting responses that offer relatively greater depth and detail. They may reveal some of the nuances in the client's perceptions.

Realize, too, that with either approach subtle variations in the wording of a question can produce markedly different answers. Consequently, it is prudent to ask the same questions in a number of different ways. Pose several similar, though not identical, questions. For instance, inquire about how the client sees himself or herself compared with how others see him or her. Be careful with closed-ended questions where the answer can be given in a yes-no fashion. Questions of a yes-no nature do not allow you to evaluate the intensity of the client's feelings.

As noted earlier, risk-averse clients are more likely to overreact. Therefore, clients who overreact frequently are likely to be more risk averse than those who overreact only occasionally. So whenever possible try to get clients to respond with answers that reveal the degree to which they behave in a certain area. On questionnaires, for example, a greater range of options permits you to make more specific distinctions among different clients. The use of adjectives and adverbs on questionnaires can create gradations in response options. Even a yes-no type of question can be put on a gradient by using terms such as definitely and probably (for example, definitely yes, probably yes, probably not, definitely not).

The number of options you should provide in a questionnaire depends on how many distinctions clients can really make. Generally speaking, when you are measuring the strength of attitudes, five options suffice in most situations, although it is sometimes advantageous to have as many as 10 response categories. If the questionnaire is extremely long, or if a client with a low level of education is completing it, a smaller number of response categories may be advisable. It is also necessary to be sensitive to the client's nonverbal communication. (For example, does the mere question make him or her fidget?)

Example Do you experience anxiety or thrill when awaiting the outcome of an important investment decision?

____ always experience anxiety

____ most frequently experience anxiety

____ experience neither anxiety nor thrill

____ most frequently experience thrill

____ always experience thrill

Preferences for Different Probabilities and Payoff Levels

A variety of assessment techniques fall under this classification. Three types will be considered:

- preferences for certain versus probable gambles
- minimum required probability of success
- minimum required return

All of these methods rely on a manipulation of at least one of the four elements found in any gamble: probability of loss, probability of gain, amount to be lost, and amount to be gained. Consequently, the techniques falling under this classification are best used in a quantitative approach to assessment.

framing

Advisors who use the probability-and-payoff-preferences approach to measuring a client's risk tolerance need to be aware of how framing a question affects the answer, lest they be misled by the results. *Framing* refers to the way in which a question is structured with regard to the issue being evaluated. For example, the same objective facts can be described either in terms of the probability of gaining or the probability of losing. Although it may not seem that—to use an analogy—describing a bottle as half empty or half full should have any marked consequences on a person's choices in a risky situation, the evidence shows otherwise. When a risk is described (framed) in terms of the probability of success, more people are willing to take it than when the same risk is described in terms of the chances of failure. Likewise, describing ground beef in terms of how lean versus how fat it is makes a big difference.

To shoppers, ground beef described as 90 percent lean is seen as a better buy than the same ground beef described as 10 percent fat.

unpacking effect

Another consideration is the *unpacking effect.* This principle refers to the finding that the perceived likelihood of an event is influenced by how specifically it is described. The more specific the description becomes, the more the situation is judged as likely to occur.

Preferences for Certain versus Probable Gambles. Gambles are abstract representations of real-life situations. One common technique is to present the client with two alternatives. One choice is a certain win, whereas the other choice offers only some probability of winning.

Example 1

You are asked to indicate whether you would choose

1. a sure gain of $1,000
2. a 50 percent chance of gaining $2,000

Persons who are risk averse chose options similar to A, whereas risk-taking individuals chose options similar to B.

Example 2

On some questionnaires, these choices are woven around a story line. An item of this type may be to imagine you are a winning contestant on a game show. Which of the following actions would you take?

1. Stop playing with a certain cash prize of $8,000.
2. Go another round with a 50 percent chance of winning $16,000 and a 50 percent chance of winning nothing.

Minimum Probability of Success Required before Undertaking a Risky Venture. In questions of this type, individuals are asked to specify the lowest level of probability they require to undertake a risky course of action. The higher the minimal odds of success required, the more risk averse the individuals are likely to be. The following is an example of this type of question.

Example

Assume you are a contestant on a TV game show. After winning a prize that is equivalent to 1 year's salary, you are offered the option of walking away with the prize money or taking a chance on either doubling it or losing it all. What are the odds of success that you would require before agreeing to accept this gamble?

- would not take the bet no matter what the odds
- 9 in 10 (90 percent probability of success)
- 8 in 10 (80 percent probability of success)
- 7 in 10 (70 percent probability of success)
- 6 in 10 (60 percent probability of success)
- 5 in 10 (50 percent probability of success)
- 4 in 10 (40 percent probability of success)
- 3 in 10 (30 percent probability of success)
- 2 in 10 (20 percent probability of success)
- 1 in 10 (10 percent probability of success)

Minimum Return Required before Undertaking a Risky Venture. In this type of question, the individual is presented with a hypothetical situation in which the odds of success or failure are specified. The individual has to specify how much of a return the risky venture would have to pay out in order for the risk to be acceptable. An example of this type of question is, "You are offered an investment in which you stand an even chance of either losing half of your personal net worth or making a certain amount of money. What's the lowest return you would need to make such an investment?" As should be obvious, the higher the return required, the more risk averse the individual is likely to be.

When using this type of question, it is important to realize that people react differently when the same odds are presented in terms of the probability of success compared with the probability of failure. When the question is phrased in terms of the probability of success, more people agree to take the risk than when the probability of failure is pointed out in the question. To draw on the "bottle half full versus bottle half empty" analogy, it does make a difference how you describe the situation. Describing it in terms of the probability of success makes the client more willing to undertake the risk than if you describe the same situation in terms of the probability of failure.

The following figure provides a sample question for each of the risk-tolerance estimation approaches discussed above. (Appendix B presents The American College's Survey of Financial Risk Tolerance, which is a 40-item questionnaire that also utilizes each of the risk-tolerance estimation approaches discussed above.)

Figure 4–7 Sample Questions for Estimating Risk Tolerance

1. Investment Objectives
   Rank the following investment objectives from 1 to 6, with 1 being the most important:
   ___liquidity
   ___safety of principal
   ___protection from inflation
   ___growth
   ___current income
   ___reduced taxation

2. Preferences for Various Investment Products
   If you received a large windfall, how would you allocate it among the following (percentages must add to 100)?
   ___% Certificates of deposit
   ___% U.S. government securities
   ___% Corporate bonds and bond mutual funds
   ___% Stock and stock mutual funds
   ___% Options
   ___% Futures contracts
   Total 100%

3. Real-Life Choices Involving Risks
   How often have you used "short selling" or "margin buying" in stock market investments?
   ___ Never ___ Seldom ___ Frequently ___ Very Frequently

4. Self-Classification of Risk-Taking Propensity
   Do you experience anxiety or thrill when awaiting the outcome of an important investment decision?
   ___Always experience anxiety
   ___Most frequently experience anxiety
   ___Experience neither anxiety nor thrill
   ___Most frequently experience thrill
   ___Always experience thrill

5. Probability/Payoff Preferences: Certain versus Probable Gambles
   In some instances you are faced with a choice between (a) earning a certain amount of money for sure and (b) taking a risk and earning either a larger amount of money or nothing at all.
   For example, consider an investment choice between a certain gain of $50 and an 80 percent chance of earning $100. If you take the certain choice, you will get $50 for sure (no more, no less). On the other hand, if you take the 80 percent probability of earning $100, you also stand a 20 percent chance of earning nothing at all.
   For the choices shown below, please indicate whether you would take the sure gain or some probability of earning twice as much (or nothing at all). Be sure to select one option for each pair, A through F.

   Pair A: 1. Certain gain of $10,000
   2. 80 percent probability of gaining $20,000 (with a corresponding 20 percent chance of earning nothing)

   Pair B: 1. Certain gain of $10,000
   2. 50 percent probability of gaining $20,000 (with a corresponding 50 percent chance of earning nothing)

   Pair C: 1. Certain gain of $30,000
   2. 80 percent probability of gaining $60,000 (with a corresponding 20 percent chance of earning nothing)

   Pair D: 1. Certain gain of $30,000
   2. 50 percent probability of gaining $60,000 (with a corresponding 50 percent chance of earning nothing)

   Pair E: 1. Certain gain of $50,000
   2. 80 percent probability of gaining $100,000 (with a corresponding 50 percent chance of earning nothing)

   Pair F: 1. A certain gain of $50,000
   2. 50 percent probability of gaining $100,000 (with a corresponding 50 percent chance of earning nothing)

6. Probability/Payoff Preferences: Required Probability of Success
   Assume you are a contestant on a TV game show. After winning a prize that is equivalent to 1 year's salary, you are offered the option of walking away with this prize money or taking a chance on either doubling it or losing it all. What are the odds of success that you would require before agreeing to accept this gamble?
   1. Would not take the bet no matter what the odds
   2. 9 in 10
   3. 8 in 10
   4. 7 in 10
   5. 6 in 10
   6. 5 in 10
   7. 4 in 10
   8. 3 in 10
   9. 2 in 10
   10. 1 in 10

7. Probability/Payoff Preferences: Minimum Required Return
   You are faced with an investment opportunity in which you have a 50 percent chance of losing half of your personal net worth and a 50 percent chance of making a certain amount of money. What percentage of expected return would you require to take this risk? ______%

Guidelines on Assessment

It is possible to analyze a client's risk tolerance through a variety of procedures ranging from preferences for different gambles to choices the individual has made in real life. Some techniques deal with a client's feelings about risk; others consider more public behavior. As you may have deduced from the preceding discussion of the available approaches to assessment, there is no ideal method for completing this task. Each techniques has its pitfalls.

In collecting the information on risk tolerance, you can best understand a client by diversifying the approaches you use and compare the impression of the client that emerges from one approach with the impression from another approach. If all indicators point to the same conclusion, the job of assessment is easy. Frequently, however, you will obtain discrepant images of the client. You should pay attention not only to the client's answer on each type of task, but also to the potential reasons why a client may be inconsistent in his or her answers from one approach to another. You should discuss with the client why he or she answered a given question a certain way, because the client's stated rationale can provide valuable insights into which type of measurement approach may be the best indicator of the client's level of risk tolerance. Probe and clarify until you are satisfied that you have identified causes for the discrepancies.

A major cause for inaccurate results when assessing a client's financial risk-taking propensity is asking an insufficient number of questions. Frequently, financial advisors believe that all they need to ask is whether the client "can sleep" if a given investment were to be made. In order to obtain a stable estimate of financial risk tolerance, however, you must consider more than just a few questions. A client's reasons for answering a given question a certain way are manifold. Only by presenting the client with a sufficiently large number of questions can you hope to get a representative sample of past behaviors, current attitudes, and intentions regarding the future. The greater the number of questions asked, the more accurate the results of the assessment are likely to be. Given the importance of this task, you should not be willing to settle for a second-rate assessment.

In the absence of any information regarding which approach is most effective with a particular client, averaging the answers from the different approaches will probably provide the best estimate of the client's risk tolerance. Some approaches may overestimate the true level of risk tolerance, whereas others may underestimate it. By averaging the results, you may be able to cancel out these two errors and arrive at the most accurate impression possible, given the circumstances.

Even under ideal circumstances, though, it is impossible to truly peg the client's financial risk tolerance. Some authorities contend that it may not be possible to obtain a single number that represents the client's risk-tolerance level. At best, the results of the assessment are an approximation of the client's actual level of financial risk tolerance. The more inconsistent the client's answers to different questions that attempt to gauge risk tolerance, the less likely it is that a single score will predict how a client will react when faced with a decision involving financial risk. Unless you have information to the contrary, consider the results of the assessment to be an overestimate of the client's true level of financial risk tolerance, because most people tend to overstate rather than understate their risk-taking proclivity (especially on the 1-to-10 self-classification scale). Always assume that the client is risk averse and then see if you can find substantial evidence to the contrary. If not, suggest a risk-averse asset allocation for the client's investment portfolio.

In most instances, the assessment, as with fact finding in general, should not be a one-shot effort. With some clients, it may take time for you to establish the credibility necessary for honest answers. Moreover, frequently a client's actual level of financial risk tolerance becomes evident only after the client has experienced a loss. It is only at this point that some clients come to grips with their actual feelings. Finding the proper asset mix for the client may have to be somewhat of a trial-and-error procedure, although the results of the assessment of the client's financial risk tolerance definitely give you a place to start. Remember, too, that risk tolerance is a dynamic characteristic of the individual that can alter with changing client circumstances such as age, income, number of dependents, and wealth. Therefore, it is sensible to reevaluate the client's financial risk tolerance on a periodic basis. Any significant change in the client's life warrants a reexamination.

Information about the client's financial risk tolerance can be captured through the use of both formal and informal procedures. Formal procedures, such as questionnaires, have merit in that they permit you to standardize the assessment process. Moreover, such questionnaires can serve as teaching tools almost to the same extent as they are assessment devices. By going through the questions/exercises in a questionnaire, the client is forced to deal with the issue of financial risk and how he or she reacts to it. The questionnaire also allows the client to convert his or her subjective experiences into more public language, so that he or she can communicate it to you. Often, it is possible to quantify the answers to a questionnaire and to develop some index of risk tolerance. In no case, however, should either the client or you accept such an index blindly as the "final say" regarding the client's level of financial risk tolerance. The questionnaire can serve only to create the framework for collecting the information and trying to understand how the client reacts to risk. Although a score may be provided to help in the process, in the final analysis, it is the client who must determine what level of financial risk he or she is willing to bear.

PORTFOLIO MANAGEMENT TECHNIQUES

In today's changing financial landscape, it is important that clients become actively involved in managing their portfolios. To do this they need to have a working knowledge of three portfolio management techniques: asset allocation, diversification, and rebalancing. Together these techniques operate to protect a portfolio from wild swings in the value of any one type of investment.

Asset Allocation

asset allocation

The maxim "Don't put all your eggs in one basket" is an excellent rationale for *asset allocation* because smart clients who have investment portfolios do not put all their money in one type of security or asset category. Instead, they spread or diversify their risk by investing in different types of securities. When one asset category is performing poorly, another may be doing well and compensating for the poor performance of the other. In fact, research has shown that more than 90 percent of the time, the most important factor in determining the investment results for a portfolio is the way its assets are allocated among stocks, bonds, and cash equivalents.[17]

Asset allocation involves determining the optimal allocation for broad categories of assets in an investor's portfolio. What exactly is an optimal allocation for a specific client depends, of course, on what asset categories are being allocated as well as on the client's financial goals and return objectives, time horizon and stage of the financial life cycle, and level of risk tolerance.

The consensus among most financial advisors is that asset allocation is one of the most important decisions that clients with portfolios make. To help them make the decision, many investment firms publish recommended asset allocations for investors of different age ranges and risk-tolerance levels. Yet, we must emphasize that there is no simple formula that can find the right or optimal asset allocation for every investor. Even in situations where you have full knowledge of your client's goals and return objectives, time horizon and stage of the financial life cycle, and level of risk tolerance, professional judgment still plays a large part in determining the optimal allocation.

The asset-allocation decision normally is made among three broad asset categories and specifies the percentage of total portfolio assets to be invested in each category. These broad asset categories are stocks, bonds, and cash equivalents. Each of these broad categories can be subdivided into several smaller categories with different risk and return profiles. In addition, real estate, precious metals, and "alternative investments," such as hedge funds and commodities, are sometimes set up as asset categories.

Although decades of history have conclusively proved that it is more profitable to be a stockholder than a bondholder, there are times when stock ownership is less attractive than bond ownership or when stocks do not fit with the particular goals or needs of the client. A retiree, for example, with a large portfolio and no other source of income is going to want to invest a significant portion of that portfolio in fixed-income securities that generate a steady source of retirement income. His or her need is not necessarily to increase net worth, but to preserve principal while living on the earnings.

On the other hand, a young corporate executive in the early career phase of his or her financial life cycle is going to be more interested in building wealth. He or she can ignore market fluctuations because he or she does not depend on

---

17. Gary P. Brinson, Brian D. Singer, and Gilbert L. Beebower, *Financial Analysts Journal*, July/August, 1986. Updated in *Financial Analysts Journal*, May/June, 1991.

investments to meet everyday living expenses. A portfolio heavily concentrated in stocks, under reasonable market conditions, would be a good allocation for this client.

As already indicated, each broad asset category could be subdivided into several smaller categories with different risk and return profiles. Risk refers to the possibility that an investment or security will experience variations in its returns over time. This variation of return is often referred to as volatility. Return refers to the increase or decrease in the value of the investment or security. Return is usually expressed as a percentage. In general, the greater the return an investment or asset category has generated in the past, the greater the risk that its value will fluctuate in the future. This means that to earn the highest potential returns, clients have to invest their money in those securities or asset categories with the highest risk. The broad stock and bond categories can be subdivided into the following smaller categories, many of which are designed for higher risk investments. Possible subdivided stock categories include

- large cap stocks (stocks of large, well-established and usually well-known companies)
- small cap stocks (stocks of small, less well-known companies)
- international stocks (stocks of foreign companies)

Each of these smaller stock categories can be further subdivided into

- value stocks (stocks whose prices are below their true values for temporary reasons)
- growth stocks (stocks of companies that are growing at a rapid rate)

Possible subdivided bond categories include

- different maturities (long-term of 10 years or more, intermediate-term of 3 to 10 years, and short-term of less than 3 years)
- different issuers (corporate, municipal, government and agencies, and foreign)
- different types (inflation-protected bonds, zero-coupon bonds, callable bonds, high-yield bonds, and so on)

As we have seen, the purpose of asset allocation is to protect a client's portfolio from wild swings in the value of any one type of asset. By spreading investments over a variety of asset categories, the client ensures that he or she will benefit, no matter what category is performing best during any given period. If the client does not have an asset-allocation strategy, he or she needs to develop one with your guidance. An asset-allocation strategy is a prerequisite for a successful investment program.

Diversification

diversification

After formulating an asset-allocation strategy, the next step in the investment planning process is asset selection, whereby specific investments or securities are recommended and purchased. Asset selection, however, should be carried out only in conjunction with a diversification plan. By selecting the "right" investments or securities, the client will not only be diversifying his or her portfolio but will also be reducing its risk. *Diversification* is a portfolio-management technique that is designed to minimize the impact of any one security, investment, or asset category on overall portfolio performance.

Establishing several asset categories and selecting investments for those categories is not diversification if each one of the categories is designed for investments that have similar risk and return profiles as the investments in other categories. True investment diversification occurs only when a portfolio is composed of several asset categories, each one of which is designed for investments with risk and return profiles that are dissimilar to the profiles of investments in other categories. Thus, a downward movement of investments in one asset category is, ideally, offset by an upward movement of investments in another asset category.

In reality, it is difficult to establish asset categories whose performance will be exactly opposite but in the same proportion all the time. With most diversified portfolios, clients select investments for several asset categories that, while not perfectly dissimilar in terms of the risk and return profiles of the investments, offer better protection than if the portfolios consisted of several asset categories whose investments have fairly similar risk and return profiles.

Diversification is necessary not only among asset categories but also within each category. A portfolio with a large-cap-stocks category should not hold both General Motors and Ford. Diversification requires avoiding excessive concentration in an industry. Similarly, it requires avoiding concentration across asset categories. If the client holds stock in General Motors, he or she should not also hold General Motors bonds. The diversification requirement cannot be stated in terms of fixed allocation percentages but instead depends on the facts and circumstances of each asset category as well as the individual investments within each category. It also depends on such factors as the purposes of the portfolio, the amount of portfolio assets, and financial and economic conditions. Finally, the client should be cautious about investing too heavily in investments that are closely aligned with his or her occupation. The reason is that if the industry collapses, then not only would there be a drop in the value of the client's portfolio, but he or she also might be out of a job. It is tempting for clients to want to invest in industries with which they are familiar, but they should do so with caution. They should always adhere to the principle of diversification, no matter how strong the temptation to do otherwise.

Rebalancing

rebalancing

Once a client establishes an optimal asset allocation and properly diversifies both within and across asset categories, the client, in conjunction with his or her advisor, needs to periodically review the portfolio to make sure that its composition still matches the original allocation plan and that the plan is still right for his or her financial goals, return objectives, time horizon, phase of the financial life cycle, and level of risk tolerance. However, even if the client's circumstances have not changed, an optimal asset allocation can become "unbalanced" over time because some asset categories will outperform others, throwing off the carefully planned allocation percentages.

Even though the client's portfolio starts with his or her optimal asset allocation, such as 60 percent stocks, 30 percent bonds, and 10 percent cash equivalents, these percentages will tend to change over time because of fluctuations in and movements of security prices. Thus, to maintain the planned allocation percentages, the portfolio should be reviewed periodically to see if it has become unbalanced. Just how often this review should be undertaken is difficult to say because it depends on each client's unique situation as well as on economic and market conditions. In any event, a portfolio review should be conducted no less frequently than annually, and in turbulent economic times, it should be conducted more often than annually.

rebalancing

An unbalanced portfolio can be brought back in line by *rebalancing*. This involves selling assets from any asset category whose percentage of the portfolio has increased relative to its planned allocation percentage and buying assets for any asset category whose percentage has decreased relative to its planned allocation percentage. For example, if the client starts with a planned allocation of 60 percent stocks, 30 percent bonds, and 10 percent cash equivalents, and over the course of the year a number of stocks do spectacularly well, then the portfolio could suddenly have percentages of 70, 22.5, and 7.5, respectively. The percentage decline in the bond and cash equivalent holdings is not because their market values have gone down but because the market value of the stocks has gone up, making it a larger percentage of the portfolio. To balance this portfolio and get back to the planned allocation percentages, the advisor must sell a sizable portion of the portfolio's stock holdings and invest the proceeds in bonds and cash equivalents.

Having determined that stocks must be sold to rebalance the portfolio, the question then becomes, "Which stocks should be sold?" Some advisors believe the answer to this question is to sell the very stocks that appreciated in value and caused the portfolio to become unbalanced in the first place. Selling these stocks, however, will create several problems for the advisor. First, the client will have to pay taxes on the gains from the sale of the appreciated stocks. Second. the advisor will have to explain to the client why he or she is selling off the best performing stocks. Finally, if the advisor sells only the best performing stocks each time he or she rebalances the client's portfolio, eventually the client's portfolio will contain only stocks that can best be described as dogs, not exactly the kind of stocks the client wants to hold in his or her portfolio.

The better answer to the question is to sell the poorest performing stocks. Stocks that have performed poorly in the past, and for which there is no credible evidence that they will perform any better in the future, should be the first ones sold when rebalancing the portfolio. Obviously, if there is some evidence to indicate that a poor performing stock will perform much better in the future, the stock should probably be retained. However, without such evidence, poor performing stocks should be sold when rebalancing requires that the percentage of stocks in the portfolio be reduced. In addition, if there is evidence that some of the portfolio's better performing stocks might suffer a significant price decline in the not too distant future, they also should be candidates for sale. In other words, when rebalancing requires that some stocks be sold, those that are candidates include stocks currently performing poorly and expected to continue performing poorly plus stocks currently performing well but expected to decline soon. In any event, the key to keeping the client's portfolio in balance is a periodic review to determine if any asset category has strayed outside of its range of variance.

When a client first implements an asset allocation plan, he or she needs to work with the advisor to establish an acceptable range of variance for each asset category. For example, if the planned allocation for stocks is a range of 57 to 60 percent, then as long as the stock holdings are within the range, rebalancing is not necessary. However, if, during a bullish move, stocks increase to 61 percent of the portfolio, then some stocks will have to be sold to keep the portfolio in balance. This way, when the client and advisor periodically review the portfolio—whether that be quarterly, semiannually, or annually—it will be easier for them to keep the portfolio in balance if they have ranges to work within.

Even if the portfolio has not become unbalanced because of security performance variations, a change in the client's goals, return objectives, time horizons, phase of the financial life cycle, and/or level of risk tolerance could warrant a change in his or her planned asset allocation percentages. This will require the client to rethink and adjust his or her asset allocation percentages to suit the changed circumstances. For example, young clients typically will want to allocate their longer-term retirement assets to riskier investments because they have time to ride out the ups and downs of the market. However, as these young clients grow older, their planned asset allocations will slowly shift toward safer investments because retirement is moving ever closer and older clients should be more concerned about keeping what they have already accumulated in order to be ready for retirement.

Although an asset-allocation strategy is designed to eliminate a lot of the day-to-day decisions involved in investing, it obviously does not mean that a client should establish a strategy and then forget it. Clients should periodically review their portfolios with their advisors so that they can keep their financial plans on track by rebalancing their portfolios if necessary.

CHAPTER REVIEW

Key Terms and Concepts are explained in the Glossary. Answers to the Review Questions and Self-Test Questions are found in the back of the textbook in the Answers to Questions section.

Key Terms and Concepts

opportunity cost
time value of money (TVM)
risk-free rate
risk premium

simple interest
compound interest
compounding
discounting
future value of a single sum (FVSS)
FVSS formula
FVSS factor
Rule of 72
present value of a single sum (PVSS)
PVSS factor
PVSS formula
future value of an annuity (FVA)
future value of an annuity due (FVAD)
annuity
annuity dues
FVA formula
FVA factor
FVAD formula
present value of an annuity (PVA)
present value of an annuity due (PVAD)
PVA formula
PVA factor
PVA formula
risk
risk/return trade-off
risk tolerance
risk seeker
risk averter
risk aversion
norms
thrill seeker
framing
unpacking effect
asset allocation
diversification
rebalancing
rebalancing

Review Questions

4-1. You have received a bill for services rendered, and the invoice requests that you pay within 30 days. Should you pay the bill immediately on receipt or wait until the end of the 30 days? Explain.

4-2. Draw a time line depicting each of the following problems:
a. To what amount will a deposit of $X made at the end of year 1 grow by the beginning of year 7?
b. What is the present value at the beginning of year 1 of a sum of $Y due to be received at the end of year 4?

4-3. The FVSS formula for calculating the future value of a $5,000 single sum for a particular number of years and a particular interest rate can be represented as $5,000 x $(1.07)^6$. What compound annual interest rate is being used, and how many years of compounding are involved?

4-4. How is the future value of a single sum (FVSS) affected by the
a. interest rate used in the calculation
b. number of years used in the calculation

4-5. According to the Rule of 72, approximately how long will it take for a sum of money to double in value if it earns a compound annual interest rate of 4 percent?

4-6. The factor for calculating the present value of a single sum for a particular number of years and discount rate can be represented as $1 \div (1.11)^7$. What discount rate is being used, and how many years of discounting are involved?

4-7. How is the present value of a single sum (PVSS) affected by the
a. discount rate used in the calculation
b. number of years used in the calculation

4-8. Draw a time line depicting a problem in which you are to calculate the future value of
a. an annuity of $100 per year for 5 years
b. an annuity due of $200 per year for 4 years

4-9. Draw a time line depicting a problem in which you are to calculate the present value of
a. an annuity of $100 per year for 5 years
b. an annuity due of $200 per year for 4 years

4-10. Explain what is meant by the risk/return trade-off.

4-11. a. a. Identify the four major types of life situations that involve risk taking.
b. Can a financial advisor assume that a person who is a risk taker in one of these life situations is also a risk taker in his or her investment decisions? Explain.

4-12. Identify several reasons why it is difficult to assess an individual's level of financial risk tolerance.

4-13. Identify the major problems associated with quantitative approaches to the assessment of clients' risk tolerances.

4-14. Briefly describe each of the following techniques for assessing a client's risk tolerance:
a. examining investment objectives
b. identifying preferences for different investment products
c. reviewing past real-life choices involving risk
d. requesting a self-classification of risk-taking propensity
e. assessing preferences for different probabilities and payoffs

4-15. Describe several guidelines that the financial advisor should observe when attempting to assess clients' risk tolerances.

4-16. Briefly describe several smaller asset categories that can be created by subdividing the broad categories of
a. stocks
b. bonds

Self-Test Questions

Instructions: Read chapter 4 first, then answer the following questions to test your knowledge. There are 10 questions; circle the correct answer, then check your answers with the answer key in the back of the book.

The first two questions below are based on the following tables:

Table 4-2
Time-Value-of-Money Factors for 3%

Years	FVSS Factors	PVSS Factors	FVA Factors	PVA Factors
6	1.1941	0.8375	6.4684	5.4172
7	1.2299	0.8131	7.6625	6.2303
8	1.2668	0.7894	8.8923	7.0197
9	1.3048	0.7664	10.1591	7.7861
10	1.3439	0.7441	11.4639	8.5302

Time-Value-of-Money Formulas

- FVSS = PVSS × FVSS factor
- PVSS = FVSS × PVSS factor
- FVA = annual deposit × FVA factor
- PVA = annual payment × PVA factor

17. If you invest $1,000 today and earn 3 percent compounded annually, what will it be worth in 6 years?

    (A) $837.50
    (B) $1,194.10
    (C) $5,417.20
    (D) $6,468.40

18. If you can afford to make a $1,000 loan payment at the end of each of the next 8 years, how much can you borrow today if the interest rate is 3 percent?

    (A) $789.40
    (B) $1,266.80
    (C) $7,019.70
    (D) $8,892.30

19. The unpacking effect refers to the

    (A) finding that the perceived likelihood of an event is influenced by how specifically it is described
    (B) way in which a question is structured with regard to the issue being evaluated
    (C) standards of measurement that allow an individual to be compared with a representative group
    (D) fact that choices are shaped not only by knowledge and rational thinking but also by values and emotions

20. At a compound annual interest rate of 3 percent, a single sum of $1 will double in value and reach $2 in approximately how many years?

    (A) 3 years
    (B) 9 years
    (C) 18 years
    (D) 24 years

21. Other things being equal, which of the following changes will increase the future value of a present sum of money?

    I. an increase in the interest rate used in the compounding process
    II. a decrease in the number of years over which compounding occurs

    (A) I only
    (B) II only
    (C) Both I and II
    (D) Neither I nor II

22. Which of the following statements concerning portfolio rebalancing is (are) correct?

    I. It requires investors to sell the best performing assets that have appreciated in value and purchase assets that have declined in value.
    II. It requires investors to periodically review their portfolios so that adjustments can be made if necessary.

    (A) I only
    (B) II only
    (C) Both I and II
    (D) Neither I nor II

23. Other things being equal, which of the following changes will increase the present value of a future sum of money?

    I. an increase in the interest rate used in the discounting process
    II. an increase in the number of years over which discounting occurs

    (A) I only
    (B) II only
    (C) Both I and II
    (D) Neither I nor II

24. The major types of life situations that involve risk taking include all the following

    (A) monetary situations
    (B) physical situations
    (C) gender situations
    (D) social situations

READ THE FOLLOWING DIRECTIONS BEFORE CONTINUING

The questions below differ from the preceding questions in that they all contain the word EXCEPT. So you understand fully the basis used in selecting each answer, be sure to read each question carefully.

---

25. All the following lifestyle characteristics would seem to indicate that a client is disposed toward financial risk tolerance when the EXCEPT

    (A) composition of his or her investment portfolio is considered aggressive
    (B) ratio of his or her liabilities to gross assets is very low or nonexistent
    (C) percentage of his or her net wealth used for recreational gambling is very high
    (D) size of the deductibles selected for his or her property-liability coverages is very high

26. The broad asset-allocation category for stocks may be subdivided into several smaller categories that include all the following EXCEPT

    (A) small cap
    (B) international
    (C) large cap
    (D) inflation protected

5

Preparing Personal Financial Statements and Analyzing Information

Learning Objectives

An understanding of the material in this chapter should enable the student to

5-1. Explain the importance of personal financial statements in financial planning.

5-2. Explain what a financial position statement indicates to a financial advisor, and describe its key components.

5-3. Explain the steps involved in the preparation of a financial position statement.

5-4. Explain how financial position statements are used in the financial planning process.

5-5. Explain what a cash flow statement indicates to a financial advisor, and describe its key components.

5-6. Explain the purpose of cash flow management, and describe its key components.

5-7. Explain the steps involved in the preparation of a cash flow statement.

5-8. Explain how cash flow statements are used in the financial planning process.

5-9. Identify the 13 components of a personal financial plan.

5-10. Explain how the analysis of the client's information can be used to

  a. identify the client's goals and objectives

  b. identify concerns and problems

  c. work with the client's personal and financial planning assumptions

  d. develop recommendations

5-11. Explain the process for analysis of the client's existing plan information in the main areas of financial planning.

This chapter covers the preparation of personal financial statements for your client. These statements are used in the analysis of your client's existing financial situation and in the development of a personal financial plan to improve that situation. This chapter identifies the components of a financial plan and explains how they can be used as guidelines to analyze, construct, present, implement, and monitor a plan. In addition, this chapter lays the groundwork for the next chapter, which discusses the development of personal financial plans.

PERSONAL FINANCIAL STATEMENTS

The preparation of organized financial information is an important but often ignored aspect of personal financial planning. Like businesses, individuals must often prepare financial information for external use. Banks and other lending institutions rarely make loans to individuals without first analyzing their current financial situations and their future ability to repay the loans. However, the primary use of financial information in personal financial planning is for you in your role as a financial advisor and for your clients.

Financial analysis, planning, and control are important planning techniques, whether performed by the client alone or the client assisted by you. Personal financial statements that summarize your client's current financial situation as well as those that project future results are both useful for planning purposes. In fact, it is difficult to develop a financial plan and/or formulate strategies to achieve your client's financial goals without first knowing his or her current financial situation and resources. Moreover, the ongoing analysis of your client's personal financial information is crucial in monitoring whether or not he or she is achieving his or her financial goals.

financial position statement (balance sheet)
cash flow statement (income statement)

In personal financial planning, the primary financial statements that you would use to develop a financial plan for your client are the *financial position statement* (or *balance sheet*) and the *cash flow statement* (or *income statement*). Before each is discussed, a few general comments about the timing of their preparation and use are in order.

pro forma

Personal financial statements are not prepared at arbitrary times but rather when the information is needed for the planning process. Moreover, while your client's current financial position and cash flow statements relate to what has occurred in the past, it is also necessary to prepare *pro forma* (or projected) financial position and cash flow statements. Pro forma statements illustrate what future financial statements are expected to show if certain activities are implemented under specified assumptions. Finally, current financial statements can be compared with past pro forma statements to see if your client's financial goals are being realized. (Although pro forma statements will be discussed in this chapter, they are not illustrated in any of the tables).

What Is a Financial Position Statement?

The financial position statement shows your client's (or his or her family's) wealth at a point in time and reflects the results of his or her past financial activities. It contains three basic classifications—assets, liabilities, and net worth—that make up the basic accounting equation:

Assets = Liabilities + Net worth

As a financial advisor, you can choose from many different formats for the financial position statement since there is no standard. However, statements usually group the items that make up assets and liabilities into subclassifications that better enable you to analyze the components of your client's total financial situation and to evaluate the mix of assets and liabilities in relation to the client's objectives. The following table shows a typical financial position statement prepared for Jack and Jill Klient.

Obviously, a financial statement should be in a format that is understandable, and uniformity is desirable. The actual format, however, is really secondary to the quality of the information. Note that the format of a financial position statement (and a cash flow statement) is often determined by the software system the financial advisor uses to analyze data and produce reports.

As illustrated in the table, financial position statements have traditionally been presented in two columns—one containing assets, the other containing liabilities and net worth. The term balance sheet is derived from the fact that the two side-by-side columns must balance according to the accounting equation (total assets = total liabilities + net worth).

Assets

Assets are items your client owns. It is immaterial whether the items were purchased for cash, financed by borrowing, or received as gifts or inheritances. Items that your client possesses but does not own, such as rented apartments or leased automobiles, are not shown as assets.

It is common practice for personal financial position statements to show assets at their current fair market values. These values may vary considerably from the original purchase prices. In contrast, business balance sheets list many assets on the basis of adjusted historical costs, net of depreciation.

At a minimum, assets should be subdivided into two categories: financial assets and nonfinancial (or personal) assets. Many statement formats include other categories such as use assets, nonuse assets, personal assets, investment assets, and retirement assets. The financial position statement presented in the table for Jack and Jill Klient separates total assets into three broad categories as follows:

- cash and cash equivalents
- other financial assets
- personal assets

Other financial assets are sometimes further subdivided according to their relative liquidity, income characteristics, tax status, or growth characteristics.

Liabilities

Liabilities are your client's debts. Although the financial position statement in the following table does not separate liabilities into categories, it is not unusual to see liabilities grouped by the time period in which they must be repaid. For example, the statement might show subtotals for short-term liabilities (due in one year or less), intermediate-term liabilities (due in more than 1 year but no more than 5 years), and long-term liabilities (due in more than 5 years).

The liabilities section of the financial position statement should show all liabilities as of the date of the statement. This process may require your client to make estimates for such items as taxes due, utility charges owed, and credit card obligations. For personal financial planning purposes, you and your client may choose to ignore accruals that are relatively small.

Your client's total liabilities, taken from the Inventory of Liabilities on page 14 of the Fact Finder (presented in appendix A), are subtracted from total assets to determine his or her net worth.

Net Worth

Net worth measures your client's wealth or equity at the date of the financial position statement. To increase this bottom-line figure is one of the primary objectives of financial planning. It is calculated by restating the basic accounting equation as follows:

$$\text{Net worth} = \text{Total assets} - \text{Total liabilities}$$

or

$$\text{Ours} = \text{Own} - \text{Owe}$$

In other words, net worth is what remains if all your client's assets are sold at their fair market values and all debts are paid. If your client has a negative net worth, he or she is considered to be bankrupt. However, clients with a negative net worth can avoid formal bankruptcy proceedings if they have a cash flow that is sufficient to service all financial obligations.

By itself, net worth reveals little about the nature of the assets or liabilities. If your client has a considerable net worth, he or she may have all his or her assets tied up in non-income-producing assets such as homes, automobiles, and other personal possessions. Conversely, if your client has a modest net worth, he or she may hold most assets in the form of financial assets that may be generating income, capital appreciation, or both. Further, it is possible for your client to have a positive cash balance with a negative net worth or to have a zero cash balance with a very high net worth. The key to understanding net worth is to realize that it is simply the difference between total assets and total liabilities.

Table 5-1
Financial Position Statement for Jack and Jill Klient: September 30, 2009

Assets		**Liabilities and Net Worth**	
Cash and Cash Equivalents		Liabilities	
Cash	$12,000	Credit card balances	$2,000
Money market fund	50,000	Consumer loans	4,000
Life insurance cash value	18,000	Automobile loans	12,000
	$80,000	Mortgage loans	220,000
Other Financial Assets			
Stocks	$150,000	**Total Liabilities**	**$238,000**
Bonds, taxable	90,000		
Bonds, tax exempt	80,000		
Vested pension and 401(k)	120,000	**Net Worth**	**$692,000**
	$440,000		
Personal Assets			
Residence	$300,000		
Automobiles	30,000		
Household furnishings, possessions, jewelry, art	80,000		
	$410,000		
Total Assets	**$930,000**	**Total Liabilities and Net Worth**	**$930,000**

Your client's net worth may increase or decrease during a period of time. Other things being equal, it will increase as a result of any one of the following:

- appreciation in the value of assets
- addition to assets through retaining income
- addition of assets through gifts or inheritances
- decrease in liabilities through forgiveness

The following are examples of actions that have no effect on net worth:

- paying off a debt. The cash account declines by the same amount that the liability declines, leaving the difference between total assets and total liabilities unchanged.
- buying an asset with cash. Total assets remain unchanged because cash declines by the same amount that the other asset category increases. However, commissions and other transaction costs cause net worth to decline because the cash that pays these costs is not reflected in the value of the purchased asset.

Preparing a Financial Position Statement

Because net worth is determined by subtracting total liabilities from total assets, preparing your client's financial position statement involves

- identifying each of his or her assets and liabilities
- valuing each asset and liability as of the date of the statement
- recording the values of assets and liabilities in an appropriate format that shows net worth as the difference between total assets and total liabilities

Identifying the Client's Assets and Liabilities

Assets. Assets (items your client owns) can be categorized in a number of ways. One commonly used approach is to divide your client's assets into two groups—financial assets and nonfinancial (personal) assets.

financial assets

Financial Assets . *Financial assets* consist of cash and cash equivalents (or liquid assets) and other financial (or investment) assets. Cash and cash equivalents are liquid in the sense that they are either already cash or can be converted into cash relatively quickly with little, if any, loss in value. In addition to cash on hand, cash and cash equivalents include various transactions accounts such as checking, savings and money market deposit accounts, money market mutual funds, and certificates of deposit that mature in the near future (generally, within one year). Your clients require cash and liquid cash equivalents to

- pay daily expenses
- provide funds to cover unanticipated emergencies that may arise
- provide funds to take advantage of unforeseen investment opportunities that may arise

Assets classified as "investment assets" for financial position statement purposes represent a variety of assets in which clients may invest to earn a return. Investment assets include

- savings bonds
- other bonds—corporate and mortgage-backed bonds; federal, state and local government bonds; and foreign bonds
- stocks (direct ownership of publicly traded stocks is more widespread than it is for bonds)

- mutual funds (excluding money market funds)—directly held stock funds, taxable funds of government-backed bonds, tax-exempt bond funds, other bond funds, and combination funds
- tax-advantaged retirement accounts—IRAs and employer-sponsored accounts such as 401(k) plan accounts, 403(b) plan accounts, profit-sharing plan accounts, stock bonus plan accounts, and ESOP accounts
- life insurance cash values
- other managed assets—personal annuities, trusts with an equity interest, and managed investment accounts
- other—assets generally acquired or held for investment purposes such as futures contracts, stock options, oil and gas leases, commodities, royalties, loans made to others, and proceeds from estates in settlement

nonfinancial (personal) assets

Nonfinancial (Personal) Assets. *Nonfinancial (personal) assets* include your client's

- primary residence
- other residential real estate
- net equity in nonresidential real estate such as commercial property, rental property, farm land, and undeveloped land
- net equity in privately held businesses such as sole proprietorships, various types of partnerships, subchapter S corporations, and other types of corporations that are not publicly traded
- vehicles such as cars, vans, sport utility vehicles, trucks, motor homes, recreational vehicles, motorcycles, boats, airplanes, and helicopters
- other tangible personal assets such as clothes, household furnishings, appliances, artwork, jewelry, antiques, hobby equipment, and collectibles

Financial Assets. *Financial assets* consist of cash and cash equivalents (or liquid assets) and other financial (or investment) assets. Cash and cash equivalents are liquid in the sense that they are either already cash or can be converted into cash relatively quickly with little, if any, loss in value. In addition to cash on hand, cash and cash equivalents include various transactions accounts such as checking, savings and money market deposit accounts, money market mutual funds, and certificates of deposit that mature in the near future (generally, within one year). Your clients require cash and liquid cash equivalents to

- pay daily expenses
- provide funds to cover unanticipated emergencies that may arise
- provide funds to take advantage of unforeseen investment opportunities that may arise

Assets classified as "investment assets" for financial position statement purposes represent a variety of assets in which clients may invest to earn a return. Investment assets include

- savings bonds
- other bonds—corporate and mortgage-backed bonds; federal, state and local government bonds; and foreign bonds
- stocks (direct ownership of publicly traded stocks is more widespread than it is for bonds)
- mutual funds (excluding money market funds)—directly held stock funds, taxable funds of government-backed bonds, tax-exempt bond funds, other bond funds, and combination funds
- tax-advantaged retirement accounts—IRAs and employer-sponsored accounts such as 401(k) plan accounts, 403(b) plan accounts, profit-sharing plan accounts, stock bonus plan accounts, and ESOP accounts
- life insurance cash values
- other managed assets—personal annuities, trusts with an equity interest, and managed investment accounts
- other—assets generally acquired or held for investment purposes such as futures contracts, stock options, oil and gas leases, commodities, royalties, loans made to others, and proceeds from estates in settlement

Nonfinancial Assets. Nonfinancial (personal) assets include your client's

- primary residence
- other residential real estate
- net equity in nonresidential real estate such as commercial property, rental property, farm land, and undeveloped land
- net equity in privately held businesses such as sole proprietorships, various types of partnerships, subchapter S corporations, and other types of corporations that are not publicly traded
- vehicles such as cars, vans, sport utility vehicles, trucks, motor homes, recreational vehicles, motorcycles, boats, airplanes, and helicopters
- other tangible personal assets such as clothes, household furnishings, appliances, artwork, jewelry, antiques, hobby equipment, and collectibles

Liabilities. Liabilities are debts your client has incurred by borrowing. Individuals and families borrow for a variety of reasons. Borrowing to purchase a home accounts for the bulk of a typical family's borrowing.

When your clients borrow, they incur debts that must be repaid in the future—that is, they incur liabilities. Liabilities are generally identified by the type of debt incurred. The most common types of liabilities clients incur are

- charges for the purchase of consumable goods and services such as rent, appliance repairs, utilities, and medical expenses
- balances for credit cards and other lines of credit
- mortgages and other loans secured by residential property
- installment loans to finance the purchase of items such as automobiles, furniture, and appliances

- other forms of borrowing such as loans from life insurance policies and retirement accounts

Valuing Each Asset and Liability as of the Date of the Statement

Once you have identified your client's assets and liabilities, you must determine a value for each. Assets should be listed on your client's personal financial position statement at their fair market values as of the date the statement is being prepared. Values for most financial assets can be determined from checking account, savings account, investment account, and tax-advantaged retirement account statements. For traditional whole life insurance policies with fixed level premiums and guaranteed cash values, the amount of the policy's cash value can be determined from a table of lapse (nonforfeiture) option values contained in the policy or from the insurance company. For other policies whose cash values reflect actual or anticipated investment, mortality, and/or expense experience, statements sent periodically to the policyowner can be used to determine cash value amounts.

A variety of techniques may be used to estimate the fair market values of different types of personal assets. For example, you can estimate the current market value of your client's home using information gathered from local newspapers and/or the Internet regarding the prices of similar houses in the area that are being advertised for sale or have recently been sold. On the other hand, the value of quality pieces of art and jewelry may best be estimated by an appraisal. Today the values of many types of personal assets can be estimated using Internet websites.

Values must be determined for each of your client's liabilities. Liabilities are valued by using the amount your client owes as of the date the financial position statement is prepared. Likewise, liabilities resulting from mortgages and other types of loans are valued at the outstanding loan balance—that is, the amount of the unpaid principal—as of the date the financial position statement is prepared.

Recording the Values of Assets, Liabilities, and Net Worth in an Appropriate Format

The final step in the preparation of a financial position statement is to record the values of your client's assets and liabilities in an appropriate format that shows his or her net worth as the difference between total assets and total liabilities. Although financial position statements have traditionally been presented in a two-column balance sheet format as illustrated in Table 5-1, it is also quite common to present them in a single-column format.

What Is a Cash Flow Statement?

The cash flow statement summarizes your client's financial activities over a specified period of time by comparing cash inflows and cash outflows, and indicating whether the net cash flow for the period is positive or negative. The cash flow statement has three basic components—income, expenses, and net cash flow—that are related as follows:

Income – Expenses = Net cash flow

which can also be stated as

Sources of funds – Uses of funds = Change in cash position

or

Money in – Money out = Change in cash

The cash flow statement for a given year indicates how your client's financial activities changed his or her wealth (net worth) position from that depicted in the financial position statement at the beginning of the year (the end of the previous year) to that depicted in the financial position statement at the end of the year.

When based on your client's past income and expenses, the cash flow statement (or income statement) gives you a summary of your client's financial activities for a specified period prior to the start of your professional relationship with the client. This information can be used to analyze your client's present financial situation. On the other hand, a pro forma cash flow statement based on projections of future income and expenses for a specified planning period gives you a means to assess the anticipated impact of various alternative planning strategies on the achievement of your client's goals. As such, the cash flow statement plays a central role in carrying out the various cash flow management activities in providing financial planning services to clients.

What Is Cash Flow Management?

cash flow management

Cash flow management is another name for the budgetary planning and control process. Financial advisors adopted the change in terminology partly because cash flow management is more inclusive than budgeting. More important, the word budget carries negative connotations for many clients, making them less likely to participate in the process.

Cash flow management consists of three basic components: cash flow analysis, cash flow planning, and budgeting. In practice, you may decide to combine the three and consider them a single process.

cash flow analysis

Cash Flow Analysis. *Cash flow analysis*, or income and expense analysis, is the process of gathering data concerning your client's cash flow situation, presenting the data in an organized format (the cash flow statement), and identifying strengths, weaknesses, and important patterns. Cash flow analysis is also a good starting point for you to assist your client in developing goals and objectives. In addition, it reveals inefficient, ineffective, or unusual utilization of resources, highlights alternative courses of action, motivates your client, and makes family members aware of the need to conserve resources.

cash flow planning

net cash flow

Cash Flow Planning. *Cash flow planning* identifies courses of action that will help optimize net cash flow. *Net cash flow* is defined as the difference between income and expenses. A positive net cash flow is available for any use, whether for consumption, investment, or gifting, although in most financial planning situations, the primary benefit of a positive net cash flow is to provide a source of investable funds.

Note that the goal is to optimize rather than to maximize cash flow. Maximizing net cash flow means to make it as large as possible and in any way possible. Presumably, this includes working longer hours, finding a second job, or seeking employment for the non-earning spouse. On the expense side, maximization implies having a less expensive home and automobile, quitting the club, and discontinuing vacations and eating out. Clearly, these approaches represent changes in lifestyle and standard of living, not to mention family relationships. In contrast, optimization means seeking the best, not necessarily the largest, net cash flow. Optimal net cash flow implies a balance between investing for the future and maintaining and/or improving the current lifestyle. Optimization holds greater appeal for your clients because it puts wealth accumulation in perspective. It also gives your clients greater control because they ultimately decide their own funds allocation according to their personal preferences.

Cash flow planning, which is interwoven through almost all aspects of financial planning, can be used as an extension of cash flow analysis in a sequential process that involves the major planning areas. For example, cash flow analysis reveals opportunities for increasing net cash flow by addressing income and expense factors. Cash flow planning then considers what to do with the increase in net cash flow. The result may include an insurance or investment alternative that represents a financial commitment. Typically, the commitment raises expenses, thus lowering cash flow calculated in the cash flow analysis. Based on this new level, your client may consider another alternative for the remaining net cash flow.

budgeting

Budgeting. *Budgeting* is the process of creating and following an explicit plan for spending and investing the resources available to your client. The process works through the establishment of a working budget model followed by a comparison of actual and expected results. By regularly monitoring the budget, you and your client can recognize problems as they occur and even anticipate them. Budgeting provides both a means of financial self-evaluation and a guideline to measure actual performance.

The following are some guidelines for establishing a budget:

- Make the budget flexible enough to deal with emergencies, unexpected opportunities, or other unforeseen circumstances.
- Keep the budget period long enough to utilize an investment strategy and a workable series of investment procedures—typically one calendar year.
- Make the budget simple and brief.
- Follow the form and content of the budget consistently.

- Eliminate extraneous information.
- Estimate insignificant items.
- Tailor the budget to specific goals and objectives.
- Remember that a budget is also a guideline to measure actual results. Unforeseen results should be analyzed for possible inclusion in a revised budget.
- Pinpoint, in advance, variables that may influence the amounts of income and expenses. Income may vary because of expected annual raises and increases or decreases in interest or dividend rates. Expenses may vary because of fluctuating living costs, changing tastes or preferences, or changing family circumstances.

Role of Cash Flow Management

Cash flow management is one of the most basic tools in financial planning. Ironically, however, you may find that your clients resist the cash flow management process more than any other technique even though it is critical to reaching a goal. Communicating the importance of cash flow management and talking your clients through the process are among your greatest services as an advisor.

The advantages of cash flow management cut across all income levels. Cash flow management is always beneficial; it is especially useful when your clients need to accomplish any of the following objectives:

- measure periodic progress toward the achievement of specific goals (1) within a defined time frame and (2) within the confines of limited resources
- monitor especially complex elements of economic activity
- provide guidelines for evaluating the economic performance of elements constituting cash flow
- communicate a planning strategy to those affected by a budget
- provide incentives (goals) for the performance of others involved
- control household expenses
- achieve desired wealth accumulation/savings goals such as retirement or children's educations
- monitor the performance of a specific investment such as a securities portfolio, rental property, or a closely held business
- reposition assets to improve the likelihood of accomplishing goals

Preparing a Cash Flow Statement

Although budgeting requires looking to the future, you must first gather past income and expense data from your client to determine his or her present cash flow situation. It is your client's present cash flow situation that provides the starting point for carrying out the three activities of the cash flow management process mentioned earlier: analysis, planning, and budgeting.

Financial advisors generally use a cash flow worksheet to gather income and expense data and input it into a computer program that creates the cash flow statement.

Because net cash flow is determined by subtracting total expenses from total income, preparing a cash flow statement for your client involves

- identifying the sources and amounts of gross income your client receives
- identifying the types and amounts of expenses your client incurs
- recording the amounts of income and expense in an appropriate format that shows net cash flow as the difference between total income and total expenses

For a cash flow statement, most financial advisors use a 12-month period. This period is comparable in length to the 12-month period that most advisors use for budgeting. The one-year period commonly used for a cash flow statement can be broken down on a month-by-month basis to show cash flows that occur only in specific months and to permit more frequent monitoring of the performance of your client's cash flow plan.

Constructing a cash flow statement is largely a mechanical process involving very specific steps. The items to include typically are those shown in the Cash Flow Statement on page 11 of the Fact Finder (presented in appendix A). The majority of your clients fit into the following framework.

Identifying the Sources and Amounts of Gross Income Received by the Client

Identify the amount of gross (before-tax) income from each of the following:

- salary
- bonus(es)
- commissions
- self-employment
- real estate
- dividends—publicly traded and closely held corporations
- interest—savings accounts, taxable bonds, and tax-free bonds
- trust income
- other fixed-payment income
- variable sources of income

Basic sources of information regarding items of income include, among others, check stubs from work, bank and investment account statements, prior years' income tax returns, and personal financial position statements that show income-generating assets as well as previously owned assets that your client has sold. Clients who use Microsoft Money®, Quicken®, or other personal finance software packages have the ability to develop personal financial statements with that software. Even if your client is using the software only to facilitate electronic bill payments, it still provides a cash flow history that can help you prepare a cash flow statement.

Identifying the Types and Amounts of Expenses Incurred by the Client

Annual expenses can be classified as either fixed or discretionary. Fixed expenses involve payments your client makes for products and services essential to meet basic needs (for example, food and clothing) and/or to meet obligations established by contract or law (for example, mortgage payments or rent and income tax payments). Some fixed expenses involve equal periodic payments over time. Monthly mortgage or rental payments, installment loan payments, contributions to retirement plans, and insurance premiums are examples of this type of fixed expense. Other fixed expenses, such as payments for food, clothes, household furnishings, medical needs, and utilities, involve payments that vary from one time period to another.

Your client has considerable choice whether or not to incur discretionary expenses. Examples include payments for vacations, charitable contributions, and education.

Identify the amount of expense from each of the following:

- fixed expenses
  - housing costs (mortgage or rental payments)
  - utilities
  - food, groceries, and so on
  - clothing and cleaning
  - federal, state, and local income taxes
  - Social Security and Medicare taxes
  - property taxes
  - transportation costs
  - medical and dental expenses
  - debt repayments
  - household supplies and maintenance costs
  - life and disability income insurance premiums
  - property and liability insurance premiums
  - current school expenses
- discretionary expenses
  - vacations, travel, and so on
  - gifts and contributions
  - household furnishings
  - education fund
  - savings
  - investments
  - other

Basic sources of information regarding items of expense include checking account statements, credit card statements, investment account statements, and prior years' income tax returns. Usually, you must estimate expenses incurred for items your client purchased with cash.

Note that your client's expenses can vary generally in the upward direction as a result of increased costs of living, unexpected business expenses, financial catastrophes (such as uninsured theft or fire losses), changes in tastes or preferences, and large-scale expenses (such as college or retirement).

Recording the Amounts of the Client's Income and Expenses to Show the Client's Net Cash Flow

The following table illustrates a cash flow statement for Jack and Jill Klient for the year prior to the beginning of their financial planning process. Subtracting total expenses from total income reveals the Klients' net cash flow. The table indicates that with their present pattern of consumption, investment, and gifting/contribution activities, the Klients' net cash flow is negative. They experienced a cash shortfall of $4,500 during the period from October 1, 2008, to September 30, 2009. They met this shortfall by a reduction of their cash and cash equivalents (a reduction of assets) and/or by borrowing (an increase in liabilities). In either case, their net worth was reduced by $4,500.

Suppose another client experienced a positive net cash flow (that is, an excess of income over expenses) for a given year and that, as with the Klients, his or her discretionary expenses included amounts for savings, investments, and an education fund. Because the net cash flow is positive, this client can allocate even more to these categories. A positive net cash flow for a given period can be used to increase assets and/or reduce liabilities, the net result of which is an increase in the client's net worth.

Individual clients, like businesses, commonly experience some months with positive net cash flows and others with negative. In practice, cash or cash-equivalent balances simply grow in positive months and shrink in negative months. A vacation or holiday spending can reduce cash balances in the months surrounding these events.

ANALYZING INFORMATION

Once you have gathered information about your client; organized it; checked it for accuracy, consistency, and completeness; and assisted the client in determining his or her goals, your next task is to analyze and evaluate the information to determine the client's present financial status. Analysis and evaluation are critical to the selling/planning process because they help you establish the foundation from which you can make recommendations that are specific to your client's goals and priorities. The objective here is to gain an understanding of the strengths and weaknesses of your client's current financial situation and then to evaluate the extent to which your client can satisfy these goals and priorities with available resources.

Table 5-2
Cash Flow Statement for Jack and Jill Klient for the Period October 1, 2008, to September 30, 2009

Annual Income	**Amount**	**% of Total Income**
Salary/bonus—Jack	$110,000	71.9%
Salary/bonus—Jill	30,000	19.6
Dividends—investments	3,000	2.0
Interest on savings accounts	2,000	1.3
Interest on bonds, taxable	5,000	3.3
Interest on bonds, exempt	3,000	2.0
Total Annual Income	**$153,000**	**100.1%***
Fixed Expenses		
Housing (mortgage/rent)	$ 15,500	10.1%
Utilities and telephone	7,000	4.6
Food, groceries, etc.	10,500	6.9
Clothing and cleaning	7,000	4.6
Income taxes	23,500	15.4
Social Security and Medicare taxes	7,500	4.9
Real estate taxes	5,000	3.3
Transportation	8,000	5.2
Medical/dental expenses	8,000	5.2
Debt repayment	5,000	3.3
Housing supplies/maintenance	6,000	3.9
Life insurance	8,000	5.2
Property and liability insurance	5,000	3.3
Current school expenses	4,500	2.9
Total Fixed Expenses	**$120,500**	**78.8%**
Discretionary Expenses		
Vacations, travel, etc.	$ 4,000	2.6%
Recreation/entertainment	5,000	3.3
Contributions, gifts	7,500	4.9
Household furnishings	5,000	3.3
Education fund	5,000	3.3
Savings	3,000	2.0
Investments	2,500	1.6
Other	5,000	3.3
Total Discretionary Expenses	**$37,000**	**24.3%**
Total Annual Expenses	**$157,500**	**103.1%**
Net Cash Flow	**– $ 4,500**	**–3.0%**

*Discrepancies in totals are due to rounding.

This analysis may reveal certain strengths in your client's present financial position relative to his or her goals. For example, your client may be living well within his or her means, thus freeing up resources to meet some near-term wealth accumulation goal. Maybe your client has a liberal health insurance plan through his or her employer that adequately covers the risks associated with disability. Perhaps your client's attorney has recently reviewed the client's will and brought it up-to-date.

More than likely, however, the analysis of your client's present financial position will disclose a number of weaknesses or conditions that are hindering the achievement of his or her goals. For example, your client may be paying unnecessarily high federal income taxes or using debt unwisely. Maybe your client's portfolio of investments is inconsistent with his or her financial risk tolerance. Perhaps your client has overlooked critical loss-causing possibilities such as exposure to a huge lawsuit arising out of the possible negligent use of an automobile by someone other than your client.

One conclusion from your analysis may be that your client cannot attain some of the goals established in step 4. For example, your client's resources and investment returns may prevent reaching a specified retirement income goal. In this case, you can help your client revise the goal or show him or her changes that can be made to achieve the goal. Postponing retirement, saving more money, seeking higher investment returns, and using up principal during retirement are four ways to help your client realize the goal. Presented with these alternatives, your client can then restate the original goal to make it achievable.

Your analysis of your client's present financial situation may uncover other planning issues that you should address. If this is the case, you may want to redefine the scope of your relationship with your client and obtain additional information. Once you and your client agree on the scope of the relationship, you should take charge of your client's information and begin to analyze it. By this time you should have some idea of what the components of the financial plan will be and which components will require significant work, possibly beyond your expertise. To facilitate the analysis of information and the review of documents, you should organize your client's file and develop an outline of the planning process. Although there are many approaches you can use, we recommend a format that encompasses all the major planning areas, whether or not they all pertain to your client at this time. This format will be the approach followed in this book.

Content of a Personal Financial Plan

When it comes to the task of financial planning, most clients prefer to concentrate on only one or a few related issues at any one time. In cases where your client wants a plan that is multiple-purpose or comprehensive in nature, developed incrementally over a period of time or all at one meeting, what should the plan contain? Clearly, financial planning is such an ambitious and complex undertaking that it must cover numerous elements.

Overview of Plan Components

A personal financial plan should at least touch upon 13 components, whether or not they all relate to the client. The order, depth, and style in which these components are discussed in the plan document may vary considerably. The components are

- client goals

- identification of concerns and problems
- planning assumptions
- financial position statement
- cash flow statement
- insurance planning and risk management
- employee benefits planning
- specialized financial planning goals
- investment planning
- income tax planning
- retirement planning
- estate planning
- recommendations

When analyzing and developing a multiple-purpose or comprehensive financial plan, you as the advisor are responsible for all of its components. Although most advisors are highly trained in one or several disciplines, clients often seek assurance that their advisors will be able to provide well-rounded plans that span all the important aspects of their financial situations. If you are unable personally to address each of the component areas in the development of a plan (and not many advisors are), you should involve other experts and coordinate their activities in developing the plan. When you do not personally perform technical areas such as legal and trust services, the financial plan or plan supplement should include supporting documentation that you have or will coordinate these areas.

components of a personal financial plan

The 13 *components of a personal financial plan* can serve as guidelines that you can use to analyze, develop, present, implement, and monitor your client's plan. The following sections of this chapter focus on using these components to analyze your client's information. The next chapter focuses on using them to develop the plan itself. Each of the 13 components is listed and briefly described below. This is followed by a separate discussion of each component as it relates to analyzing your client's information.

Using the Components of a Personal Financial Plan As Guidelines

1. Client Goals. First, your client's financial plan should list his or her stated goals and objectives, indicating the priority of each one and the time frame for achieving it. This statement of goals provides the framework around which the plan is to be developed.

The goals should be expressed in as specific and precise language as possible. For example, a statement of a goal should read "Retire at age 62 in present home and maintain current standard of living" rather than "a comfortable retirement."

2. Identification of Concerns and Problems. The plan should identify and discuss all the relevant concerns and problems that you, other advisors, and/or your client may have as they relate to the development of the plan. It should list personal and financial concerns and problems that could affect your client such as possible catastrophic medical costs, unplanned high costs of educating children, and high current tax burdens. Although your client may be aware of many, if not all, of the concerns, you in your role as an advisor may discover other areas that are or could develop into problems.

The client's concerns and problems, when combined with his or her goals and objectives, provide direction for the plan. Because style and order are not the primary considerations, the analysis of recommendations section of the plan may be a more appropriate place to address concerns and problems.

3. Planning Assumptions. The assumptions that you are planning to use to prepare your recommended strategies should be identified. All assumptions should be explicitly spelled out in plan documents and should at least include future inflation rates, investment yields, level of risk tolerance, and life expectancy.

4. Financial Position Statement. This statement lists your client's assets and liabilities in itemized schedules when appropriate. Net worth is what is left over after liabilities are subtracted from assets. In addition to the schedules, footnotes should be included when needed.

5. Cash Flow Statement. This statement includes the client's sources and uses of funds for the current year and other relevant years, both past and future. It subtracts the client's uses of funds (living expenses, debt service, acquisition of assets, taxes paid, and so forth) from his or her sources (earned income, investment income, sale proceeds, gifts, and so on) to determine net cash flow, which can be both positive and negative.

6. Insurance Planning and Risk Management. This involves an analysis of your client's financial exposure because of mortality, morbidity, legal liability, and property ownership. Business is included to the extent that it affects your client's personal financial situation. The analysis encompasses the following:

- mortality—survivor income and capital needs analysis
- morbidity—impact of ill health
- property—loss of value
- liability—legal exposure
- business—loss due to business involvement

All current insurance policies should be listed and analyzed to make sure they cover the financial exposures they are supposed to cover. If any coverage gaps exist, they should be promptly closed if the exposures cannot be budgeted for or handled with some other risk management technique.

Existing insurance coverage and/or risk exposures should be analyzed to determine their possible impact on your client's needs, goals, and objectives. If any area of insurance is not within your expertise to handle, you have the responsibility to coordinate the development of this part of the plan with other professionals and document this coordination in the plan. Documentation should include the other professional's summary review, if completed, or his or her name and time frame for when the review will be completed.

*7. **Employee Benefits Planning.*** The plan should contain a statement regarding the current status, use, and cost of your client's employee benefits. The statement should also address the likelihood that these benefits will be modified or even terminated in the future. The analysis and discussion should include the types of benefits available and their relationship to other plan components such as insurance coverages, retirement planning, and estate planning.

8. Specialized Financial Planning Goals. The plan should analyze any future capital needs that your client might have for special purposes such as funding college educations for his or her children. The analysis should include a projection of resources expected to be available to meet these needs as well as the time horizon required for funding each goal.

9. Investment Planning. All securities in your client's investment portfolio should be listed. The portfolio should then be analyzed with respect to its marketability, liquidity, degree of diversification, overall performance, and so on. The suitability of the investments in relation to your client's goals, financial ability to sustain a loss, level of financial risk tolerance, and personal management efforts should also be addressed. Some evaluative criteria used in investment planning are briefly defined below:

- risk tolerance— your client's willingness to accept financial risk
- suitability—appropriateness of the investment for your client
- liquidity—availability of assets that can quickly be converted into cash without loss
- diversification—appropriate mix of assets to meet your client's needs, goals, and objectives
- personal management efforts—degree to which your client wants to manage and is capable of managing his or her portfolio

10. Income Tax Planning. This includes an analysis of your client's income tax returns for the current year and for recent past years. It should also include projections for several years into the future. Projections should show the nature of the income and deductions in sufficient detail to permit calculation of the tax liability. The analysis should identify the marginal tax rate for each year and any special situations, such as the alternative minimum tax, passive loss limitations, and so on, that may affect your client's tax liability. The plan should also indicate if any taxes (for example, state or city) have not been addressed.

11. Retirement Planning. This involves an analysis of the capital needed at some future time to provide for the goals of financial independence and/or a desirable retirement lifestyle. This analysis should include a projection of resources expected to be available to meet these goals. To achieve the goals of financial independence and/or a desirable retirement lifestyle, inflation, growth of assets, and company benefits should be considered where applicable.

Some retirement planning topics may require special treatment in the financial plan. For example, company benefits may require an analysis of the types of benefits available, pre- and post-tax contributions needed, tax treatment of plans, and investment of benefit plan assets.

*12. **Estate Planning.*** This entails addressing your client's estate plan. This typically involves the identification of assets to be included in the estate and an analysis of the control, disposition, and taxation of those assets, as follows:

- control—authority to manage or direct the use of assets by means of title, trusteeship, power of attorney, and so on
- disposition—transfer of ownership by will, trust, beneficiary designation, or operation of the law
- taxation—the tax treatment of your client's estate and the income and estate tax consequences to the beneficiaries

*13. **Recommendations.*** The plan should list your client's concerns and problems previously identified in the plan and your written recommendations that specify how to achieve the client's goals and objectives. All recommendations should be clearly identified and stated and should include any actions that would be required to compensate for shortfalls.

1. Client Goals

As a general principle, it is desirable for your clients to formulate and state their financial goals and objectives as explicitly as possible. This has several advantages:

- It forces your clients to think through their financial goals.
- By doing this, your clients are less likely to overlook some goals while concentrating unduly on others.
- When your clients carefully define their goals, they may see solutions that they had overlooked before.
- Your clients are less likely to be sidetracked into short-term actions that run counter to their long-range planning goals.
- The explicit determination of their financial goals establishes a rational basis for clients to take appropriate action to realize them.

Your clients goals can be collected from two locations within the Fact Finder. The first set of goals comes from the Future Goals and Objectives section. The remainder of the goals comes from the Personal and Financial Goals, Needs, and Priorities subsection.

After organizing and analyzing your client's goals and information and noting any conflicts, you should summarize and consolidate your client's goals into a concise list of personal and financial goals, noting your client's time horizons and priority preferences for achieving them. This list of goals is the framework around which your client's plan will be built. In addition to the specific goals that the client may have identified, you may be able to determine ones from the subjective information you collected about the client. These additional goals should be confirmed with the client to assure that they are, in fact, the client's goals and not yours.

2. Identification of Concerns and Problems

Closely related to, but somewhat different from, clients' goals are their personal/financial concerns and problems. These are items that may keep your clients from accomplishing their goals between today and the time specified for achieving them. For example, one of your client's goals may be to send his or her children to college. A concern in this regard would be your client's ability to afford the high cost of a college education.

Concerns and problems can be either personal or financial. They are usually issues that revolve around maintaining a manageable financial status quo while working toward accomplishing specific goals. However, your client's personal concerns may cause him or her to be anxious about the impact they may have on his or her overall financial planning goals. Nonetheless, these personal concerns are usually financially related. Problems, on the other hand, are indications of challenges or obstacles your client may face in successfully completing his or her desired plans. An example might be a client with a severely handicapped child who has special medical or educational needs.

You should assemble a list of your client's concerns and problems to use throughout the analysis and development phases of the selling/planning process. You should keep this list as a backdrop throughout your formulation of recommendations for the client. Your client's concerns and problems, when combined with his or her goals, complete the framework and direction for the financial plan.

Furthermore, throughout the analysis of your client's existing plan, you should evaluate his or her financial concerns to determine how problematic they have been up to now. If there are imbalances between your client's specific financial concerns and his or her financial accomplishments, you should note and include them in the presentation of the new plan.

The following are some common client concerns, along with a brief description of their relevance:

- liquidity—maintaining some investments that can be quickly converted to cash without loss of value
- safety of principal—being sure that original investments do not lose value
- capital appreciation—maintaining some investments that increase in value over time
- current income—maintaining an income level associated with a comfortable lifestyle
- inflation protection—preserving purchasing power by having savings and investment dollars keep pace with the rate of inflation

- future income—having a level of income in the future that eliminates worry about finances
- tax reduction/deferral—obtaining all the tax benefits that are available
- others—a catch-all category for personal concerns and problems such as possible future unemployment, disability, or the disability of a family member

3. Planning Assumptions

In analyzing your client's information, you have to utilize client-specified, mutually agreed upon, and/or other reasonable assumptions. You must consider both personal and financial/economic assumptions in this step of the process. Personal assumptions may include such factors as

- retirement age(s)
- life expectancy(ies)
- risk tolerance level(s)
- time horizons
- special needs

Financial/economic assumptions may include such factors as

- cash and income needs
- inflation rates
- tax rates
- investment returns

With each of your clients, you will make and use assumptions that help determine the appropriateness of short-term and long-term planning alternatives. You can use these assumptions as guidelines to assist you in processing and analyzing the wealth of information you collected about your client's personal and financial situation. However, before you prepare even a preliminary financial profile of your client, these assumptions need to be formally stated to help focus all the client information you gathered. The Personal Financial Planning Fact Finder) is the place to do this as it includes several information fields in table form where you can enter assumptions about various planning areas.

The first table of assumptions in the Fact Finder is in the Retirement Planning section. Notice that there are fields here in which to make the specific types of changes to the planning assumptions that normally take place as your client moves into retirement. Entries in all these fields provide the basis for clarifying the client's retirement planning objectives.

The second table of assumptions in the Fact Finder involves employment-related retirement and deferred-compensation benefits. Projections of lump-sum and anticipated monthly income benefits payable from these plans to your client and his or her survivors affect other planning areas such as insurance planning, retirement planning, and estate planning. Also the third table of assumptions, a table of Social Security benefit assumptions, can be used in life and disability income insurance planning as well as retirement planning.

The fourth table of assumptions is in the Income and Lump-Sum Needs for Disability, Retirement, and Death section of the Fact Finder. The items in this table represent typical financial planning assumptions about your client's (and his or her spouse's, if applicable) dollar amounts of monthly disability, retirement, and survivors' income needs. Also, survivors' lump-sum needs should be itemized and totaled. These assumptions must then be compared to the income and lump-sum resources for disability, retirement, and death listed on the Fact Finder, so that adequate amounts of life and disability income insurance can be recommended. Strategies for filling the retirement income gap can then be developed if shortages exist in the present plan.

4. Financial Position Statement

Using a Financial Position Statement

In addition to providing a format for summarizing the asset and liability data gathered in step 4 (gather information and establish goals) of the selling/planning process, your client's financial position statement is an important source of information you can use to help the client achieve his or her goals. The information provided by this statement is especially useful in steps 5 and 6 of the selling/planning process.

In step 5 (analyze the information) of the process, your client's current financial position statement gives you a picture of his or her financial position at the beginning of the planning process. Information about your client's present financial position enables you to answer a number of key questions:

- What types and amounts of assets does your client currently hold?
- What are the types and amounts of the various liabilities your client has?
- What is the amount of your client's wealth—net worth—at the beginning of the planning process?
- Given this picture of your client's present financial position, will further discussion be required to help your client revise and/or prioritize his or her goals stated in step 4 of the selling/planning process?

Although a look at your client's current financial position statement may be sufficient to answer these questions, further analysis of the data is necessary for you to identify the various obstacles that your client's current financial position presents to achieving his or her goals. For example, obstacles may arise from the current distribution of assets and/or liabilities. Analysis of the distribution of assets in the current financial position statement may reveal that achieving your client's goals will be hampered because he or she

- holds too high a percentage of total assets in non-income-producing personal assets rather than in financial assets that provide income and/or appreciation
- holds too high a percentage of financial assets in cash and cash equivalents rather than in other financial assets that provide an opportunity to earn a higher return
- fails to take appropriate advantage of tax-advantaged retirement plans

Analyzing the Use of Assets and Liabilities

Inventory of Assets and Liabilities. You will need an inventory of your client's assets and liabilities for the analysis step of the selling/planning process. The inventory is essential to produce an accurate financial position statement. It is also vital for the analysis of investment planning and management, planning for economic independence and retirement (including wealth liquidation), estate and gift tax planning, and insurance planning.

The inventory of assets and liabilities reveals much useful information for analysis and planning purposes. For example, it helps answer the following questions:

- How does your client use financial resources?
- What are your client's preferences for and aversions to different types of investments?
- How liquid is your client's current financial position?
- How diversified are your client's assets?
- How consistent with your client's financial objectives are the types of assets he or she holds?
- What is your client's basis in investment assets for income tax purposes?
- Are any of your client's assets earmarked for specific purposes?
- Does your client have emotional (or sentimental) reasons for holding certain assets?
- What pure risk exposures does your client's current asset/liability position create?
- Are the risk characteristics of your client's investment assets consistent with his or her financial risk tolerance as determined by the Survey of Financial Risk Tolerance (located in appendix B) or some other method?
- Does your client use debt (leverage) to finance the acquisition of investment assets?
- Is your client aware of the increase in risk that comes with leveraged investments?
- Does your client have a clear investment policy or strategy?
- Which of your client's assets should be flagged for possible liquidation and reinvestment of capital?
- Which of your client's assets are best suited for
  - giving to family members

- meeting short-term or estate liquidity needs
- donating to charities or other tax-exempt organizations
- funding a trust
- being held in the estate under a specified form of ownership

Inventory of Assets. A detailed evaluation of your client's assets may disclose which assets are most suitable for repositioning to accomplish your client's personal and financial goals. Some potential uses of assets to look out for in analyzing the information are giving to family members, meeting short-term liquidity needs, donating to charities or other tax-exempt organizations, funding trusts established to meet specific objectives, increasing the growth rate of funds earmarked for retirement, or simply retaining the assets in the estate your client is building. Only a thorough assessment of each asset's features will permit a wise choice of which assets to use for these purposes.

Cash and Near-Cash Equivalents. As you are gathering and evaluating this information, you should consider several critical issues. For instance, how much ready cash is available in checking and savings accounts to meet emergency needs? If more than the equivalent of 3 to 6 months' income is held in low-yielding savings instruments, your client's need for the highest yield on cash equivalents consistent with safety may not be met. Excess cash beyond emergency needs may be more advantageously placed in money-market funds. In fact, even cash for emergency reserves may be held in money-market funds, particularly when yields are high. If your client has large accumulated cash values and dividends in life insurance policies, he or she could free some cash currently held in savings deposits for emergency needs, and reposition it in higher-yielding instruments.

You need to raise several questions to evaluate your client's cash-management program:

- Does your client currently have a systematic savings program that maintains both a minimum cash reserve and a savings pool from which investments can be made? Is too much of your client's savings locked into CDs at fixed below-market interest rates?
- Is your client's cash position large enough to suggest direct investment in high-yielding, short-maturity Treasury bills or commercial paper?
- In general, does your client have an efficient cash-management system that places discretionary cash and short-term funds to work at optimum yields consistent with his or her risk profile?

It is important to observe how much of your client's current income is held in cash and near-cash vehicles in anticipation of future investment opportunities. Evaluating your client in this area is a way to diagnose his or her tendency for investing and, ultimately, for getting involved in goal-oriented personal financial planning.

Bonds, Bond Funds, and Preferred Stock. Individuals typically own these types of fixed-income securities because they provide a reliable stream of income. The interest rate percentage they pay and their inherent market value are both a function of changes in the relative rates of interest, the general economy, and the interest rates being paid on similar types of securities offered currently. The advisability of holding, selling, or purchasing more of these fixed-income securities depends on your client's investment objectives and level of risk tolerance within the context of his or her goals.

Common Stock. You must consider what your client holds—and why—when recommending appropriate strategies for retaining, liquidating, or redeeming stock as part of his or her overall financial plan. You should also determine from the composition of your client's stock holdings and their total value in relation to other financial assets whether they are consistent with his or her risk profile and with the short- and long-term objectives of the financial plan. If you uncover inconsistencies, restructuring the stock holdings and/or repositioning capital out of stocks and into other forms of investment may be called for.

However, the liquidity and marketability of any common stock your client holds require careful consideration. Stock of publicly held companies traded on recognized exchanges is easily sold with the proceeds being repositioned. However, unlisted or nonmarketable stock requires more careful disposition planning.

Options. If your client holds options to buy stock at specified prices in the company where he or she works or has worked, any intentions to exercise those options should be determined. Exercising these options will frequently involve sizable cash outlays that must be funded either from current income, from repositioning capital tied up in other assets, or from bank loans or loans from your client's company. Because your client may know this company better than outsiders do, his or her assessment of the feasibility and desirability of exercising such stock options is a crucial factor for you to know. Motivations that are not purely financial are frequently involved; tax-planning implications always are. In any case, you should discuss with your client any stock options that he or she holds and determine how they relate to his or her total financial position and future plans.

Mutual Funds. In the inventory of your client's mutual fund holdings, the type of fund or funds held is another important indicator of both his or her risk profile and degree of direct involvement in the investment program. These may be important considerations in the evaluation of your client's current position and future planning alternatives and should be carefully studied. If your client has substantial holdings in growth mutual funds whose performance is both satisfactory and consistent with his or her longer-term objectives, those funds are probably a good index of what suits your client, and alternative investment possibilities should be evaluated accordingly.

Real Estate. Real estate is generally considered one of the least liquid types of assets and is usually bought for investment purposes and for its tax benefits. It can also be used for donating to charity or giving to a family member. Or it may be placed in a trust to lower the tax liability on the income produced and to take advantage of the gift tax exclusion. However, some investors hold real property for long-term income-producing purposes. You should determine your client's reasons for holding real property and his or her intentions for it. If your client is an aggressive investor, he or she may want to leverage some real estate to generate capital for further investments, either in more real estate or in other assets.

Long-Term Nonmarketable Securities. Long-term nonmarketable securities are not very flexible investments for financial planning purposes. They generally cannot be used to restructure your client's assets due to their restricted or future availability. Consequently, their use as an investment vehicle for financial planning purposes is very limited.

Personal Assets. In reviewing your client's personal property inventory, you should be looking for several important clues about how he or she spends money. Are personal property items acquired for personal and/or family use and enjoyment, for investment purposes, or for some combination of these motives? If such items are acquired for investment purposes, you should evaluate them with respect to their inherent investment characteristics. You should also view them in relation to your client's risk profile, financial goals and objectives, and need for tax relief. Furthermore, if your client's acquisition of personal property is significantly reducing the options available for achieving his or her overall financial objectives, you should tactfully point this out and allow him or her to decide whether to allocate less money to consumption and more to savings.

Inventory of Liabilities. One thing to watch for in analyzing liabilities is how your client manages short- and long-term debt. The total amount of credit in retail and revolving charge accounts is frequently rolled over into consolidating long-term loans, with the result that items such as groceries and personal assets are purchased through debt rather than through a controlled budget of balanced income and expenditures. As the debt burden mounts, payments and interest due increase making fewer dollars available for savings and investments.

Using Personal Financial Ratios to Analyze Information in the Financial Position Statement

liquidity ratio

Comparison of the holdings of various types of assets and liabilities may also reveal possible obstacles to the achievement of your client's goals. For example, comparing the amount of your client's liquid assets with the amount of total current debts by calculating a *liquidity ratio* (described below) may indicate either that your client could face serious difficulty in paying current debts if income were unexpectedly reduced or that he or she could be holding an excessive amount of funds in liquid assets. The liquidity ratio is calculated as follows:

Liquidity Ratio = Liquid Assets ÷ Total Current Debts = Liquid Assets ÷ (Current Liabilities + Annual Loan Payments)

A high liquidity ratio, such as 2.00 or higher, indicates that your client holds enough liquid assets to cover two times the amount of his or her existing total current (one year) debt. This excessive current debt coverage suggests that you recommend some reallocation of your client's total assets from cash and low-yielding cash equivalents to other financial assets with higher potential rates of return.

In contrast, if your client has a low liquidity ratio, such as .20, or 20 percent, this indicates that he or she can cover only 20 percent of present one-year debt obligations with existing liquid assets. Thus, if your client were to lose his or her job, current liquid assets would cover existing total current debt for only a little over 2 months. In this case, you should recommend some reallocation of your client's total assets to build up his or her liquid reserves to provide a longer period of protection. The amount of liquid assets required would depend on such factors as the state of the relevant job market, other potential sources of income to help meet current debts, and the period of time with which your client is comfortable.

solvency ratio

Another ratio, the *solvency ratio*, provides an estimate of the extent to which the market value of your client's total assets could decline before wiping out all of his or her wealth as measured by net worth. The solvency ratio is calculated as follows:

Solvency Ratio = Net Worth ÷ Total Assets

Referring to the table , the Klients' solvency ratio is .74 ($692,000/$930,000). As with the high liquidity ratio, this high solvency ratio suggests that the Klients have room to reallocate some of their present financial assets to higher-risk assets that also provide the potential to earn a higher rate of return.

Another use of the financial position statement in step 5 of the selling/planning process is using pro forma statements to project your client's future wealth position This projection of net worth can be used to determine whether your client is likely to achieve his or her financial goals at various key points in the future, assuming no changes in cash flow and asset and liability management.

5. Cash Flow Statement

Sources and Uses of Cash

The Fact Finder includes a survey of your client's income from all sources, including the income of a spouse and anticipated salary increases for 1, 2, and even 3 years in the future. You and your clients will find it useful to trace their tax liabilities to the income sources. Clients who suffer from excessive tax burdens usually have not considered the tax consequences of their income. You should be able to analyze these sources and point out to your clients why they are paying too much in taxes.

The Sources and Uses of Cash section of the Fact Finder also contains questions about your client's current monthly budgeting, annual savings, and annual investments. If your client has no cash or financial management program, yet strongly believes in them, there is clearly a disconnect between what your client believes and what he or she actually does. If your client does not have a program but wants to save and invest more, you should ask your client why he or she does not have a program. By asking the right questions, you can help your client realize exactly what is preventing him or her from effectively managing money. Sometimes the problem is your client's lifestyle or lack of self-discipline; often, however, it is the demands of others (spouse, children, dependents) on your client's resources or the rising tax burden on your client's income combined with inflation. Your client's inability to overcome these and perhaps other obstacles often gives rise to frustrations, which themselves become additional obstacles to achieving goals.

If your client is already doing all that he or she wants to do in managing personal and family finances, then planning based on the need for tighter financial controls and more savings and investment will probably be unacceptable. On the other hand, if your client wants to save and/or invest more, a leaner budget, cutbacks in discretionary spending, and other controls you may suggest will probably be well received.

Using a Cash Flow Statement

Your client's cash flow statement for the prior year (prepared from data you gathered) provides a picture of his or her cash flow situation. You can use the income and expense data in this statement to help analyze your client's cash flow situation and achieve his or her financial goals. This data is especially useful in steps 5 and 6 of the selling/planning process.

In step 5 (analyze the information) of the process, your analysis of your client's present cash flow situation—referred to earlier as cash flow analysis—enables you to identify various opportunities, as well as obstacles, for achieving his or her goals based on the way he or she currently manages cash flow. You should identify and discuss these cash flow management opportunities and/or obstacles with your client before plan development (step 6 of the selling/planning process) begins. In analyzing your client's cash flow, you will need answers to the following questions:

- Is your client's current rate of saving adequate enough to enable him or her to achieve stated financial goals? If not,
    - To what level must your client's rate of saving increase to achieve those goals?

  - Is your client both willing and financially able to make the changes required to achieve this increased rate of saving?
  - Is your client willing to modify either the timing of his or her goals and/or the factors influencing the amount of resources required to achieve them?

- If your client's net cash flow is negative, what alternative courses of action are available for either increasing income or reducing expenses? Some possibilities include

  - reallocating some assets from low-yielding cash and cash equivalents to other financial assets with higher potential returns
  - reducing the amount of spending for discretionary expenses
  - reducing the amount of certain fixed expenses to the extent possible
  - refinancing the home mortgage at a lower interest rate
  - reducing income taxes through greater use of tax-advantaged retirement accounts and tax-exempt bonds
  - revising and/or prioritizing the goals stated in step 4 of the selling/planning process
  - modifying the timing of some goals requiring the accumulation of savings

- If your client's net cash flow is positive, what opportunities exist for increasing savings and investment and/or tax-advantaged gifts and contributions (instead of spending the entire amount of positive net cash flow on nonfinancial assets)?

Whether responding to opportunities or obstacles found during cash flow analysis, your clients should be realistic in identifying revisions they need to make to their management of cash flows. In any event, you should encourage your clients to avoid lowering savings, investment, and education funding amounts unless there is no alternative.

Using Personal Financial Ratios to Analyze Information in the Cash Flow Statement

Saving is essential for achieving many, if not most, of your client's goals. The percentage of after-tax income your client saves is a critical factor in determining if and when he or she achieves those goals.

savings ratio

The percentage of after-tax income your client saves, or savings ratio, can be computed as follows:

Saving Ratio = (Net Cash Flow + Amounts Already Being Saved or Invested) ÷ Annual After-tax Income

Using the data from the table, the Klients' savings ratio is calculated as follows:

Savings Ratio = (-$4,500 + $10,500) ÷ ($153,000 – $23,500) = $6,000 ÷ $129,500 = .046

The numerator of the ratio includes the $4,500 negative net cash flow and the $10,500 currently being saved as indicated by the amounts listed for savings, investments, and the education fund in the table above. The denominator shows the $23,500 expense for income taxes subtracted from the Klients' total annual income of $153,000.

The savings ratio indicates that the Klients are saving slightly less than 5 percent of their total after-tax income. Whether or not this is sufficient for your client is his or her prerogative. It is achieving your client's specific financial goals that should, along with other personal considerations, determine the increased percentage of after-tax income that he or she is willing to attempt to save. For example, the Klients might want to increase their rate of saving to reach a goal requiring the accumulation of funds at a quicker pace than would be possible with their present 5 percent savings ratio. Given the negative net cash flow associated with their current income and spending pattern, the Klients would have to increase their income and/or reduce their expenses even further than would be necessary to merely eliminate the existing income shortfall if they wished to increase their future rate of saving above 5 percent.

debt service ratio

Although adequate personal saving is important to financial planning, even more important is your client's ability to pay his or her debts promptly. Personal debt burden has traditionally been measured by a *debt service ratio* that compares debt payments to gross (before-tax) income but does not include liquid assets in the denominator as a source of debt repayment. Your client's debt service ratio is calculated as follows:

Debt Service Ratio = Total Debt Payments ÷ Gross Income

Using the values of Jack and Jill Klients' debt payments and gross income shown in the table , their debt service ratio is calculated as follows:

Debt Service Ratio = (Mortgage Payment + Debt Repayment) ÷ Gross Income

Debt Service Ratio = ($15,500 + $5,000) ÷ $153,000 = $20,500 ÷ $153,000 = .134

The Klients' debt service ratio indicates that their annual debt payments account for only 13.4 percent of their annual income. Although their debt service ratio is slightly higher than that for typical families with similar incomes (11.1 percent) and net worths (10.9 percent), the Klients should have little, if any, difficulty repaying their current debts with their income.

6. Insurance Planning and Risk Management

Once you have inventoried and totaled all of your client's income and lump-sum resources you should compare them to the income and lump-sum dollars that your client needs (and spouse, if applicable) in the event of disability, retirement, or death. You should quantify and note any shortfalls in each of the respective categories of need as either insurance or retirement planning goals. Subsequently, you must analyze these needs within the context of all the major planning areas to formulate appropriate recommendations that are consistent with your client's planning goals and priorities, level of risk tolerance, and investment objectives.

Use of Insurance in the Financial Planning Process

You must analyze your client's current insurance holdings to determine exposure to potential loss of income or assets. There are three basic ways to deal with such exposures:

- Your client bears the risk of the entire loss himself or herself (self-insurance or retention).
- Your client pays another to assume the risk for him or her (shifting the risk through insurance).
- Your client utilizes some combination of these strategies.

The following section reviews the factors to consider in analyzing and calculating your client's needs in the major areas of personal insurance. It also addresses the concept of an emergency fund.

Premature Death Losses/Survivor Needs. Calculate the extent of the existing potential losses in terms of survivor cash needs today and income needs for each of the remaining years of your client's (and spouse's, if applicable) life expectancy.

Cash Needs. Total the lump-sum cash needed to pay for such items as final expenses, a readjustment fund, mortgage and debt cancellation, children's education, and estate settlement costs for the deceased, and subtract that amount from existing capital resources available from the government, your client's employer, savings, and existing insurance. If there is a shortage of capital to cover cash needs at death, you should note it accordingly.

Income Needs. Indicate the annual income the surviving spouse needs in the event of the other spouse's death, and subtract the projected total income available from all resources from this amount. Note any shortage of annual income needed for survivors today, as well as for years projected into the future, based on agreed upon interest earnings and inflation assumptions. Add the income need shortage to any cash need that may exist to determine the total amount of capital required to solve the deficit funding of survivor needs.

Disability Income (DI) Losses. List the total household monthly income objective at the level needed today and at the inflation-adjusted income levels that are anticipated until at least your client's (and spouse's, if applicable) retirement age. From this amount, you need to subtract the spouse's income available, if any, and group DI insurance in force, any personally owned DI insurance, any assets that can be used to provide income, and any government benefits to be factored in if so desired. If a shortage exists today, you should address it by recommending the appropriate amount of monthly DI insurance benefit.

Medical Care Expenses. Your client needs to be insured against the possibility of catastrophic medical care expenses. You should analyze the extent and cost of your client's coverage and the amount of self-insurance in conjunction with his or her budget constraints, capital resources, and financial goals. If coverage is provided to your client by his or her employer, you should examine your client's options regarding the types of coverage and the amount of out-of-pocket costs to make sure that your client's risk exposure is consistent with his or her cash management goals. If your client has individual medical expense insurance, analyze it for cost saving opportunities and to see that the internal policy limits provide adequate coverage. If no coverage exists, you should work with your client to budget the acquisition of adequate medical expense insurance.

Long-Term Care (LTC) Expenses. To cover this risk adequately, you should estimate the cost in today's dollars based on the LTC facilities and home health care average price ranges in the geographic area in which your client lives. From this amount, subtract an estimate of all possible resources the client would want to use to pay LTC expenses such as personal savings, existing LTC insurance, and government funding. This will give your client an idea of how to structure the LTC insurance policy he or she may need to purchase, as well as what additional benefits to consider.

Property and Liability Losses. Analyze your client's exposures to the types of direct and consequential property losses discussed in chapter 3, seeking to minimize your client's loss exposures in a manner that is consistent with his or her budget, risk tolerance, and financial goals. You should note any changes in existing insurance coverage that are necessary to enhance your client's protection against property and liability risk exposures, and consider these changes when you are developing your plan recommendations.

Emergency Fund. As discussed previously in the financial position statement, your client should maintain an emergency fund to pay for the "smaller" disability income losses, medical expenses, and property losses, and to provide a financial cushion against prolonged unemployment. If your client does not have this risk management fund in place, you should make a note of this and, in the recommendations section of the finished plan, suggest that he or she create an emergency fund.

7. Employee Benefits Planning

You need to analyze your client's employee benefits in relation to his or her life and health insurance needs, and to the extent that they affect retirement planning.

In the area of insurance, you should determine the existence and amounts of employer-provided medical expense, life, disability income, long-term care, and any other types of insurance your client (and spouse if applicable) is provided. You should also determine the probability of these benefits continuing at existing levels. Then factor them into the appropriate rows and columns of the Income and Lump-Sum Resources for Disability, Retirement, and Death section on page 22 of the Fact Finder. As with personally owned types of insurance, they should be aggregated and totaled for the purpose of determining any shortfalls that may exist in terms of lump-sum or income needs. If your client has supplementary purchase options at his or her workplace for the types of insurance benefits he or she needs, you should investigate them when making your plan recommendations.

In the area of employment-related retirement benefits and deferred compensation, again you should determine the existence and projections of any lump-sum or monthly income benefits available to your client (and spouse, if applicable). You should factor these, too, into the appropriate rows and columns of the Income and Lump-Sum Resources for Disability, Retirement, and Death section on page 22 of the Fact Finder. Then you should compare them to the retirement planning needs your client established in the fact-finding meeting to determine if a shortfall exists. If it does, part of a possible solution may be to begin or to increase your client's contributions to available employer-sponsored qualified defined-contribution retirement plans. You can test the impact of various contribution amounts and interest earnings assumptions by factoring them into financial planning software or by using a financial calculator.

In those cases where it is apparent that your client is overutilizing employment-related benefits, paying too much for them, or would be better served by owning individual insurance products because they provide more comprehensive coverage, you should consider what alternatives to recommend when developing your client's plan. You should evaluate any cost-saving opportunity or benefit enhancement for its possible inclusion in the plan. Because employee benefits have such a far-reaching effect on virtually all the other areas of financial planning, you need to carefully analyze them to see how they fit into the financial plan you are developing for your client.

It is also a good practice to periodically review the status of these employee benefits with your client. Employment-related benefits are subject to revision based on changes in employer or career, employee contractual renewals, economic trends, government benefit changes, changes in marital/dependency status, and job promotion, to name just a few.

Finally, you should also consider the amount of Social Security benefits that will be available to your client to provide for his or her survivors, and for his or her retirement or disability. Government-provided benefits have a direct bearing on the amount of life insurance, disability income insurance, and retirement income funding needed, as well as on employee benefit planning.

8. Specialized Financial Planning Goals

Quantitative information for analyzing your client's specialized financial planning goals comes from the Objectives Requiring Additional Income/Capital section of the Fact Finder. Qualitative information about your client comes from the sections called Future Goals and Objectives, and Factors Affecting Your Financial Plan in the Fact Finder, and from your discussions with the client regarding his or her personal and family goals. When planning for your client's specialized goals, your primary task is to help him or her develop a plan for funding them.

The steps for calculating the funds needed for any type of specialized financial planning goal are as follows:

1. Estimate the annual or total cost of the goal in today's dollars.
2. Determine the date in the future when the funds will be needed.
3. Apply an inflation rate to the dollar estimate from step 1 and project it to the date in the future determined in step 2.
4. Determine the amounts of capital and/or income currently available for funding the goal, assign a compound growth rate to those amounts, and project them to the date in the future determined in step 2.
5. Compare the projected amounts currently available from step 4 to the inflation-adjusted estimated cost from step 3. To the extent that the estimated cost from step 3 exceeds the projected amounts currently available from step 4, a shortfall of funds is indicated.

As a component part of your client's financial plan, you should develop and include strategies for funding the shortfall.

In analyzing specialized financial planning goals, however, keep in mind that the choices your client makes regarding one component of a financial plan will often affect other components. For example, if both retirement planning and education funding are priorities, you need to help your client balance the two. After fact finding, you should have a clear picture of the assets and/or discretionary income your client has available to fund both of these goals. If your client's assets and/or income are insufficient for this purpose, he or she may have to tighten the budget, earn more income, or modify one or both goals. If goal modification is the choice, your client may have to forego plans to retire at age 60 if he or she wants to send the children to college. This may require that he or she postpone retirement to age 65 or even 70. Moreover, your client may also have to compromise on his or her children's choice of colleges or their lifestyle while attending college. This may mean that the children have to attend the less expensive state university instead of the elite private university, or that they have to live at home and commute to a junior college for the first 2 years before transferring to a 4-year university. These are some of the compromise choices your client may have to make to achieve a balance between two priority goals.

9. Investment Planning

There are two components to analyzing your client's investment portfolio. The first one is easy. It involves listing all of your client's current investment assets. That is, what are the accounts in which investment assets are held? What are the investments in each account? What are their current market values? Much of this type of information can be found in the Inventory of Assets, beginning on page 12 of the Fact Finder. Equally important to your analysis is your client's projected contributions. That is, just how much does he or she plan to invest each year? If projected contributions are inadequate, this may require your client to redirect some of his or her cash flows from spending for consumption to saving for investment.

The second component to analyzing your client's portfolio is to identify any potential constraints. Of primary concern is evaluating your client's risk tolerance. (Risk tolerance is discussed in chapter 4.) This is very important because it affects the types of investments you can recommend for your client's portfolio. For example, if your client is extremely risk averse, he or she may not be willing to hold enough equity investments to earn a high enough rate of return to reach his or her accumulation goal.

Another possible constraint is your client's phase in his or her financial life cycle. If your client is older, attaining the accumulation goal may not be possible without devoting a higher percentage of the portfolio to riskier assets than is usually recommended. The management of the portfolio is less flexible because the stock market's cycle of peaks and valleys may not cooperate with your client's plan. On the other hand, if your client is younger and has more time to reach his or her accumulation goal, he or she might be willing to ride out a decline in the stock market.

Determining Your Client's Risk Tolerance

As mentioned earlier, it is critical in analyzing your client's portfolio that you determine his or her risk tolerance. Unfortunately, no one has figured out how to truly measure investment risk aversion in a client and how to translate this into a portfolio prescription. However, the fact that the perfect method of measuring risk tolerance has not yet been developed does not excuse you from trying to determine how much financial risk your client is willing to tolerate. In this regard, a risk tolerance questionnaire like the College's 40-question Survey of Financial Risk Tolerance will generate some sort of score. Low scores usually indicate a high degree of risk aversion, while high scores indicate a high degree of risk tolerance. The College's Survey of Financial Risk Tolerance is similarly designed. The higher the total score on all Survey questions, except question 32, the more risk tolerant your client is likely to be. The range of possible total scores on the Survey is from 44 (very risk averse) to 213 (very risk tolerant).

Question 32 is excluded from the scoring because it needs to be assessed apart from the other questions.

Determining Your Client's Asset Allocations

Clients with low Survey scores will be directed to highly conservative asset-allocation strategies, while those with high scores will be directed to aggressive asset allocations. Keep in mind, however, that there is no precision to this process. A risk tolerance score is at best only a guideline and is not intended to substitute for your professional judgment of your client's level of risk tolerance and of the asset-allocation strategy that he or she should follow.

Based on the investment accumulation goal agreed to with your client, you can establish the approximate rate of return needed to attain that goal. You must then look at various asset-allocation combinations to see which ones will achieve the desired rate. Finally, given your client's level of risk tolerance, you must determine which asset-allocation combination is optimal for him or her.

Having analyzed your client's current investment portfolio, assessed his or her level of risk tolerance, and determined an asset-allocation strategy consistent with that level of risk tolerance, you are now ready to develop a financial plan that will enable your client to reach his or her accumulation goal.

10. Income Tax Planning

Income tax planning involves analysis, evaluation, and client acceptance of the tax consequences of every financial transaction—before the transaction is made. It is one thing for you to determine the income tax consequences of your client's economic activity during the past year; it is quite another thing for you to determine the income tax consequences of your client's future economic activity. In other words, income tax planning requires you to analyze all your client's transactions beforehand to make sure they are carried out in the most tax-advantaged way, consistent with his or her financial goals.

Regardless of how complicated your client's financial situation is, there is almost always an alternative transaction that you can recommend he or she take. Financial strategies and products each have their own inherent advantages and disadvantages and therefore are rarely appropriate for every client situation. When you consider income tax consequences as well, there is even more divergence—some transactions result in greater, some in lesser, income tax liability. Keep in mind, however, that the transaction you recommend for an immediate (or even long-term) income tax saving may not, in the final analysis, be the most advantageous one. Income tax and economic advantages and disadvantages must be consistent with the client's goals and level of risk tolerance. What works well for one client may not work at all for another client in virtually the same situation. What works well this year may be a disaster next year or several years down the road.

A client who is able to control the timing, form of ownership, and type of investment vehicle used to carry out a financial transaction can generally control its income tax results. Control is the key consideration. Once a transaction is complete, the income tax consequences will flow from the tax code sections that govern how the transaction works. Any strategy to control the income tax consequences of a transaction after the fact is merely reactive and diverts energy and resources better used elsewhere. Therefore, you should plan each transaction beforehand to achieve the desired tax consequences for your client in light of his or her cash flow situation, stated financial goals, and level of risk tolerance.

Although income tax planning is a highly complex area of financial planning, not all financial advisors are tax experts. Few advisors feel comfortable about undertaking the responsibilities of thorough income tax planning on their own. Therefore, its more technical features are best handled by legal counsel or accounting professionals who are thoroughly conversant with tax law. As a financial advisor, you should be able to draw upon the expertise of these specialists when needed. At a minimum, however, you should know enough about tax law to be able to explain the income tax consequences of every financial transaction you recommend that your client take. To make sure that all your recommendations are carried out in the most tax-efficient manner that is consistent with your client's stated financial goals, level of risk tolerance, and cash flow situation, you must determine as much as possible about your client's income tax position. To this end, either you or a qualified tax professional should perform an analysis of your client's recent years' income tax return(s). Copies of these returns should already be in your possession after the fact-finding process.

11. Retirement Planning

Steps in Calculating the Retirement Income Need

How much money will your client want or need during retirement? The answer to this question varies as much as your clients and is a function of the following factors:

- your client's target retirement age
- the number of years your client will spend in retirement
- a target income based on your client's lifestyle expectations for retirement
- an assumed inflation rate
- the total financial resources available to your client
- the amount of interest earnings on savings and assets earmarked for retirement
- your client's projected amount of savings by his or her retirement age
- how long your client will live

Most of this information is found in the Retirement Planning section on page 8 of the Fact Finder. Some will come from the cash flow statement, financial position statement, and the Employment-Related Retirement Benefits/Deferred Compensation section on page 19 of the Fact Finder.

Performing a retirement need analysis for your client will answer the question, "How much is enough?" But first you must also refer to the Retirement Planning Objectives and Concerns subsection on the Fact Finder to determine what your client envisions his or her retirement lifestyle should be like. Will your client stay in his or her current home or downsize at or during retirement? Does your client plan to travel or take up an expensive hobby once he or she has more leisure time? Once your client has expressed his or her retirement expectations and you have determined the planning assumptions, the amount of money the client has now, and the amount of money he or she is expected to accumulate, you can help the client develop a plan for reaching the retirement income goal.

Target Retirement Age. Generally, people think that retirement should begin at age 65. The truth, however, is that the average retirement age has declined to age 62. Meanwhile, Social Security's full retirement age is increasing from age 65 to age 67. Therefore, people who plan to retire earlier than age 67 will have to rely on other sources of retirement income until they reach age 67 or take a reduced Social Security benefit. The key to choosing a retirement age, like the key to choosing an inflation or earnings rate, is to be realistic.

Number of Years in Retirement. With the Social Security age for full retirement increasing from age 65 to age 67, you and your clients need to consider that longevity is increasing. For younger clients, it may be better to be on the safe side and assume a longer life expectancy than currently anticipated. This conservative approach allows for the trend of increasing longevity to continue.

Setting a Target Income. There are basically two methods for setting a target income for your client. One is to assume that a certain percentage of your client's current income will be needed in retirement. The other is to project the specific expenses your client will have at retirement.

For most advisors using the percentage of income method, it is advisable to assume that during retirement, clients will continue to need 80 to 100 percent of what they currently spend for basic living expenses. This is because if your clients have a mortgage, monthly payments will continue, as will other types of periodic expenses such as those for home repairs, travel and vacations, and vehicle replacement. In addition, your clients may want to increase the amounts they are giving to charities and/or their grandchildren. The costs of health insurance, long-term care insurance, and general health care usually increase during retirement compared to what they were at younger ages. Therefore, it may be wishful thinking to assume that the cost of living decreases significantly during retirement.

Although it is more time consuming, it is often better to use the projection-of-expenses method to set a target retirement income. Whether you use a worksheet or retirement planning software, the steps in the process are similar. They include

- listing your client's current expenses
- estimating the changes in expenses that will occur based on your client's retirement expectations and an inflation assumption
- estimating the average income that your client will need to cover those expenses
- determining the resources that your client can convert to retirement income
- setting a target for savings

An Assumed Inflation Rate

We suggest that you estimate inflation conservatively. Based on historical trends, an estimate of between 3 percent and 4 percent per year, both before and after retirement, appears to be realistic. Be aware that the financial plan is extremely sensitive to the inflation rate assumption. An estimate that is too low will underestimate the income required through the clients' retirement years.

Total Financial Resources Available to Clients

A retiree's income generally comes from a combination of three sources: Social Security, pensions, and personal savings. Because you are trying to determine the amount of personal savings necessary to supplement Social Security and pensions, you must first estimate the benefits your client expects to receive from these two sources. After you estimate the benefits from Social Security and pensions, you should then look at what your client has personally saved. Seeing what your client has personally saved for retirement will not only tell you how much is currently available, but it will also help you determine the annual rate at which he or she is saving. Is this rate high enough, or does your client need to save more to reach the projected savings target?

Most of your client's personal retirement savings will be in savings accounts, CDs, deferred annuities, mutual funds, and stocks and bonds. The amount of savings your client has invested in each of these vehicles depends on such factors as his or her age and level of risk tolerance. Also, do not overlook home equity. Your client may be able to convert this source of personal savings into a reverse mortgage, or alternatively, he or she may be able to cash out some of the equity by moving to a less expensive residence.

Interest Earnings on Savings and Assets Earmarked for Retirement

As long as your client agrees, the long-term rate assumed for retirement assets should be no more than 4 percent above the average inflation rate. With any investment or savings vehicle, it is better to err on the conservative side and underestimate the rate. Although trends from the recent past may give you an idea of what rate to assume, there is no guarantee that a vehicle will continue to perform in the future as it has in the past. The assumption used must be realistic if you plan to rely on it to develop a plan for your client.

Projected Amount of Savings by Retirement Age

Projections of retirement savings using different assumptions can be generated by a financial calculator or financial planning software. The goal is to have a projection that reaches the target amount of savings using realistic assumptions. Once you determine the amount of savings your client can realistically accumulate, you will be in a better position to help him or her develop a plan for reaching (eliminating) the retirement income goal (gap). If your client cannot reach a retirement income goal, then you need to help him or her adjust the goal downward.

Reconciling the Retirement Income Gap

The difference between the amount of money your client must accumulate to reach his or her retirement income goal and the amount he or she expects to have from all sources is the retirement income gap. Everyone's situation involves different variables, but at a minimum, your client should seek a savings target that would eliminate the retirement income gap.

As discussed earlier in this chapter, most clients have to accept some compromises in their financial planning goals. Virtually no client can achieve all of his or her goals, regardless of wealth. Therefore, your clients must decide what is most important to them.

In the next chapter we will discuss preretirement planning strategies, techniques, and financial products that can be implemented to help your clients eliminate the retirement income gap.

12. Estate Planning

Ten Key Steps in Estate Planning

Estate planning for your clients is often best approached by following 10 key steps:

1. Take an inventory of assets and liabilities.
2. Estimate asset valuation and estate complexity.
3. Calculate current net worth and potential estate taxes.
4. Determine goals.
5. Consider various legal tools.
6. Consider different types of property ownership.
7. Investigate tax minimization strategies.
8. Provide for estate liquidity.

9. Execute legal documents and planned actions.
10. Perform periodic reviews.

We will briefly review each of these steps as part of a systematic and organized approach to analyzing your clients' personal estate planning needs.

1. Take an Inventory of Assets and Liabilities

Your clients need to know what they own, how they own it, and what it is worth to properly plan their estates. Often, the current fair market values of assets differs substantially from the amount paid for them. Also, your clients need to have an understanding of their liabilities. This information about your client's assets and liabilities serves as a starting point from which they can determine what is available for their heirs, how it will be distributed, and how estate taxes will be computed.

You can help your clients assemble this information by using the Fact Finder. They may be surprised to learn that they face potential estate tax liabilities. Educating them about these liabilities enhances your status as their financial advisor.

2. Estimate Asset Valuation and Estate Complexity

Once your client's assets and liabilities have been inventoried, you can use the information in the Inventory of Assets section of the Fact Finder to gauge the estate's complexity and whether an estate tax return must be filed. An unusual mix of assets or a mix of assets that is located in several jurisdictions may indicate a need for more sophisticated planning. For example, clients who own real estate in several states may face duplicate estate settlement costs.

3. Calculate Current Net Worth and Potential Estate Taxes

The next step is to determine your client's net worth, which is calculated in the financial position statement. You should also estimate the amount of your client's probate estate. Your client's current net worth provides insight into the value of the taxable estate and the potential for an estate tax bill. If your client's net worth is in excess of this year's estate tax exemption equivalent, there is a potential for federal estate tax liability. Current net worth also provides insight into how much money will eventually be expended for costs associated with death, including funeral and estate administration costs. Once again, consideration must be given as to how these costs will be paid. Will liquidity be provided by selling assets, or will it be provided by savings or life insurance proceeds?

4. Determine Goals

What your clients want to do with their property determines the ultimate direction of their estate plans. Estate planning goals should have been clearly articulated in the fact-finding process. Your clients will act on plans that are aimed at accomplishing their goals. They will purchase financial products that facilitate goal achievement. Plans that fail to meet client goals tend not to be implemented.

5. Consider Various Legal Tools

It is often easier to work with legal tools if they are divided among those that facilitate lifetime care and property management, those that are used during life to transfer property and save estate settlement costs, and those that focus on the disposition of property at death. Tools that facilitate lifetime care and property management include living trusts, powers of attorney, living wills, and health care proxies. Tools used during life to transfer property and save estate settlement costs include lifetime gifts and irrevocable trusts. Finally, the primary tool used for the disposition of property at death is the will. When a person dies without a will, assets are distributed according to the intestacy laws of his or her resident state.

6. Consider Different Types of Property Ownership

Property can be owned in several ways. Each way has its own estate planning implications. For example, property that is individually owned by your client passes through his or her estate at death. This subjects the property to the administrative delays of probate. On the other hand, joint ownership of property with the right of survivorship can simplify estate administration, but it can also provide unintended estate distribution results. Your clients need to be alert to both the opportunities and pitfalls of joint ownership of property.

7. Investigate Tax Minimization Strategies

Although reducing taxes usually is not the primary estate planning concern of most clients, they nonetheless are grateful when you can help them plan their estates in a tax-efficient manner. There are many ways to lower gift and estate taxation. Three of the most useful techniques are the

- marital deduction
- credit exclusion/equivalent bypass trust (CEBT)
- annual gift tax exclusion

Appropriate use of these techniques allows your clients to give more of their estates to heirs and less to the government.

8. Provide for Estate Liquidity

The costs associated with dying typically include final illness expenses, funeral costs, estate administration costs, executor allowances, attorney fees, and estate taxes. When these costs occur, they must be paid to settle the estate. To avoid the forced sale of estate assets to raise the funds with which to pay estate costs, the estate must have sufficient liquidity. Some typical sources of estate liquidity include the following:

- life insurance proceeds
- savings and investments
- sale of assets

In all likelihood, your client will choose to provide estate liquidity from more than one source. The key to having the right amount of liquidity in the estate is to realistically estimate the estate's costs and then develop a plan for providing the liquidity to cover those costs.

9. Execute Legal Documents and Planned Actions

Clients sometimes take the initiative to meet with their legal advisors, discuss their options, and have necessary legal documents drafted—but then fail to execute the documents and take the steps to implement their plans. Clients need to take care of legal necessities, such as the execution of a will, or suffer the consequences of having others plan for them.

10. Perform Periodic Reviews

As in other major areas under the financial planning umbrella, estate plans should not be developed in isolation; nor should they be considered static. Life changes trigger the need to revise plans so they need to be flexible enough to meet changing circumstances. Major events influence the way your clients live and should be reflected in the way they plan their financial affairs, including their estates. Some of the more prominent events that can affect your clients' plans include

- death of a spouse
- remarriage
- serious illness
- marriage of an adult child
- divorce of an adult child
- birth of a grandchild
- a grandchild's college education
- receipt of an inheritance
- sale of the family home
- change in tax laws

The Advisor's Role in Estate Tax Analysis and Planning

The degree to which you can reduce the potential estate tax liability your clients will pay greatly depends on your estate planning expertise. As with other financial planning areas, if you do not have the requisite estate planning knowledge, you should serve as a resource person or team coordinator and enlist the help of other advisors who have the necessary expertise. Regardless of your estate planning expertise, however, you should develop relationships with attorneys who specialize in estate planning and planning for seniors, who can execute the necessary legal documents to put a plan into effect. Even if you are a knowledgeable estate planner, you no doubt will find it helpful to use software to calculate your client's potential estate tax liability under each alternative plan. The software can do the number crunching while you focus on developing the alternative plans. The best alternative plan is the one that is able to accomplish your client's goals with the smallest potential tax liability.

13. Recommendations

The analysis of each component of the financial plan should consist of a review of pertinent facts, a consideration of the advantages and disadvantages of the current situation, and a determination of what, if any, further action is required. The recommendations developed for each component should then be tested for consistency to make sure they do not conflict with or cause problems in another component of the plan. All recommendations should also improve the client's current financial situation and address each of his or her goals and concerns. A more detailed discussion of plan recommendations will be covered in the next chapter.

CHAPTER REVIEW

Key Terms and Concepts are explained in the Glossary. Answers to the Review Questions and Self-Test Questions are found in the back of the book in the Answers to Questions section.

Key Terms and Concepts

- financial position statement (balance sheet)
- cash flow statement (income statement)
- pro forma
- financial assets
- nonfinancial (personal) assets
- cash flow management
- cash flow analysis
- cash flow planning
- net cash flow
- budgeting
- components of a personal financial plan
- liquidity ratio
- solvency ratio
- savings ratio
- debt service ratio

Review Questions

5-1. Briefly describe how a financial position statement is used.

5-2. Identify the key components of a financial position statement and briefly explain what each component represents.

5-3. Identify the various ways in which a client's net worth can increase during a period of time.

5-4. Explain why the following actions have no effect on a client's net worth:
a. paying off a debt
b. buying an asset with cash

5-5. Distinguish financial assets from nonfinancial (personal) assets.

5-6. Briefly describe how a cash flow statement is used, and identify its three basic components.

5-7. Explain the purpose for each of the following components of cash flow management:
a. cash flow analysis
b. cash flow planning
c. budgeting

5-8. With regard to the preparation of a cash flow statement, describe and give examples of
a. fixed expenses
b. discretionary expenses

5-9. Explain the impact that a positive net cash flow for a given period has on a client's assets, liabilities, and net worth.

5-10. Identify the 13 components of a personal financial plan.

5-11. List and briefly describe the 13 guidelines for analyzing and developing a personal financial plan.

5-12. If a client's net cash flow is negative, what alternative courses of action are available either to increase income or reduce expenses?

Self-Test Questions

Instructions: Read the chapter first, then answer the following questions to test your knowledge. There are 10 questions; circle the correct answer, then check your answers with the answer key in the back of the book.

13. Which of the following statements concerning a personal financial position statement is correct?

    (A) Assets should be listed at their historical cost, adjusted for depreciation.
    (B) The current values of many types of assets can be estimated using Internet websites.
    (C) The final step in its preparation is to identify each of the client's assets and liabilities.
    (D) It reflects the results of a client's past financial activities over a specified period of time such as one year.

14. Which of the following is considered a personal assumption in the analysis of information step of the selling/planning process?

    (A) cash and income needs of the client
    (B) federal income tax rates
    (C) level of the client's risk tolerance
    (D) investment returns

15. Which of the following statements concerning the cash flow statement is correct?

    (A) It reflects a client's net worth at a specified time.
    (B) It has three basic components—assets, liabilities, and net cash flow.
    (C) It classifies annual expenses as either fixed or discretionary.
    (D) It reflects a client's wealth as of the date it is prepared.

16. Which of the following statements concerning estate planning is correct?

    (A) Estate plans typically are static and require a review only when the client requests one.
    (B) Reduction of estate taxes and settlement costs is usually the primary estate planning concern.
    (C) Estate liquidity should be exclusively provided from life insurance proceeds.
    (D) Clients need to know how their assets are owned and what they are worth to properly plan their estates.

17. Which of the following statements concerning the analysis of information is (are) correct?

    I. It is critical to the selling/planning process because it helps to establish the foundation from which recommendations can be made that are specific to the client's goals and priorities.
    II. The objective is to gain an understanding of the strengths and weaknesses of the client's current financial situation and to evaluate the extent to which the client can reach his or her goals with available resources.

    (A) I only
    (B) II only
    (C) Both I and II
    (D) Neither I nor II

18. Which of the following statements concerning liquidity or solvency ratios is (are) correct?

    I. Liquidity ratios compare the amount of a client's liquid assets with the amount of his or her total assets.
    II. Solvency ratios compare the value of a client's net worth with the amount of his or her total current debt.

    (A) I only
    (B) II only
    (C) Both I and II
    (D) Neither I nor II

19. Which of the following statements concerning income tax planning is (are) correct?

    I. A client who can control the timing, form of ownership, and type of investment vehicle used to carry out a financial transaction can generally control its income tax results.
    II. Financial advisors should know enough about income tax planning to be able to explain and evaluate the tax consequences of every move they recommend for clients.

    (A) I only
    (B) II only
    (C) Both I and II
    (D) Neither I nor II

READ THE FOLLOWING DIRECTIONS BEFORE CONTINUING

The questions below differ from the preceding questions in that they all contain the word EXCEPT. So you understand fully the basis used in selecting each answer, be sure to read each question carefully.

---

20. All the following statements concerning cash flow planning and/or budgeting are correct EXCEPT

    (A) Cash flow planning is identifying courses of action that will help maximize net cash flow.
    (B) Cash flow planning is interwoven through almost all aspects of financial planning.
    (C) Budgeting is the process of creating and following an explicit plan for spending and investing the resources available to the client.
    (D) Budgeting provides both a means of financial self-evaluation and a guideline to measure actual performance.

21. All the following are common concerns of clients that may affect their accumulation goals EXCEPT

    (A) liquidity of investments
    (B) marketability of investments
    (C) safety of principal
    (D) inflation protection

22. All the following statements concerning retirement planning are correct EXCEPT

    (A) The retirement income gap is the difference between the client's retirement income goal and the amount he or she expects to have.
    (B) Retirement income generally comes from a combination of three sources: Social Security, pensions, and personal savings.
    (C) The long-term rates of return on retirement assets should be no more than 4 percent in order to plan safely and conservatively.
    (D) Projections of the total savings available at retirement should be generated by using either a financial calculator or financial planning software.

6

Developing and Presenting the Plan

Learning Objectives

An understanding of the material in this chapter should enable the student to

6-1. List factors that are involved in developing the financial plan.

6-2. Describe the format and the content areas of the financial plan.

6-3. Explain the preparation for the financial plan presentation.

6-4. Explain the organization of the financial plan presentation.

6-5. Describe key aspects of presenting the financial plan.

6-6. Explain the differences between features and benefits and why this is important to the presentation.

This chapter covers the development and presentation of the financial plan and its recommendations, which are based on the previous fact-finding and analyzing steps of the selling/planning process. The chapter will first review considerations in developing the plan and then look into the key components of presenting the plan to your client.

DEVELOPING THE PLAN

In the last chapter, we reviewed the process of analyzing your client's current plan information. It is now time to develop a plan to meet your client's specific needs and goals.

Developing and presenting the plan represents the very heart of the financial planning process. It is at this point that you, using your knowledge, intuition, judgment, and experience, artfully and systematically formulate the recommendations designed to achieve your client's goals, needs, and priorities. Some financial advisors may view this process as one action or task. In reality, however, it is a series of distinct but interrelated tasks.

Financial advisors can use the following three questions to differentiate among the several tasks that are part of this process:

- What is possible?
- What is recommended?
- How is it presented?

The first two questions involve your creative thought, analysis, and professional judgment, and they are typically asked and answered outside the presence of your client. First, you must identify and consider the various alternatives, including continuing the present course of action. Second, you must develop the recommendations from among the potential alternatives. Once you have determined what to recommend, the final task is how to communicate those recommendations to your client.

The first two tasks will be considered in this section; the task of presenting the plan will be discussed in the next section.

Identifying and Evaluating Financial Planning Alternatives

After analyzing the client's current situation (step 5 of the selling/planning process), and prior to developing and presenting the recommendation(s) (step 6 of the selling/planning process), you must identify alternative actions, and in doing so, evaluate the effectiveness of these actions in their ability to meet your client's goals, needs, and priorities.

This evaluation may involve, but is not limited to, considering multiple planning assumptions, conducting appropriate research, and consulting with other professional advisors. This process may result in a single alternative, multiple alternatives, or no alternative to your client's current course of action. In considering alternative actions, you also must recognize and take into account your legal, regulatory, and licensing limitations and your level of competency in properly addressing each of your client's financial planning issues.

More than one alternative may reasonably meet the client's goals, needs, and priorities. Also keep in mind that alternatives that you identify may differ from those of other practitioners or advisors, illustrating the subjective nature of exercising professional judgment and the broad range of possible acceptable solutions.

Developing Financial Planning Recommendations

After identifying and evaluating the alternatives, the next step in the process is to develop recommendations based on a comparison of the selected alternatives and the current course of action. Recommendations should be consistent with and driven by the following factors:

- your client's goals, needs, and priorities
- the qualitative and quantitative information your client provided
- agreed upon personal and financial planning assumptions
- your analysis and evaluation of your client's current situation

Sometimes your recommendation may be to change nothing at all. However, if you do recommend changes, they must be specific and sufficiently detailed to provide direction for your client. At other times, it may be necessary for you to recommend that the client modify a goal in order to help make it more attainable and realistic.

Designing the Plan

You should prepare a few alternative recommendations, if appropriate and available, to give your client choices based on the features and benefits of each option. Having choices is something that most clients appreciate. Your role as a financial advisor is to act as an expert, a counselor, and consultant, and to educate your client on the key advantages and differences among recommendation alternatives. Your client is then free to be involved in and to control the decisions that affect his or her financial future.

Plan design is a balancing act between your client's prioritized needs and the available resources to commit to your proposed recommendations. As you design the plan, it is better to limit your financial product alternative choices to just a few so that you do not confuse your client. You can always customize to those few basic designs further by introducing modifications (within cost limitations) that add or subtract certain features, or prioritize recommendations and implement them over a period of time as funds become available.

Format of a Personal Financial Plan

A personal financial plan, whether comprehensive or not, is essentially a report to your client of your findings and recommendations regarding the client's current and desired financial situation. This report results from the application of the planning/selling process to the client's present situation to assist the client in meeting his or her financial goals. Every personal financial plan should include certain types of information. For example, every financial plan should

- address the current status of all of the major planning areas, even if recommendations are not included for every one of them
- be based on SMART goals set by your client (that is, on goals that are Specific, Measurable, Achievable, Relevant, and have a Target date)
- be structured around strategies for achieving your client's goals
- be developed around information gathered during a fact-finding process. Much of this information, such as financial statements, should also be included in the plan.

In addition, the process for developing a personal financial plan should incorporate the strategy of building the plan from the ground up in three stages, using the components of the financial planning pyramid discussed in chapter one. This type of plan typically requires several meetings with the client over a period of years. At the first stage of plan development, the advisor should concentrate his or her efforts on protecting the client against unexpected occurrences that could cause financial hardship. At the second stage, the advisor should focus on the client's wealth accumulation objectives. At the third and final stage, the advisor should address retirement and estate concerns.

The format for discussing the development of the personal financial plan for clients on the following pages uses the same 13 components for analyzing and developing a personal financial plan introduced earlier. Depending on the extent of your client's current goals, needs, and capital resources, you may present recommendations that address some or all of the components in a multiple-purpose or comprehensive financial planning format.

Regardless of the format you adopt to organize a financial plan, it is important to remember that you should communicate the plan to your client in a written report. This report should be easy for the client to understand and evaluate what you are proposing. In general, the simpler the report, the simpler it will be for the client to understand and adopt. Careful organization, as well as the intelligent use of graphs, diagrams, and other visual aids, can help in this regard.

1. Client Goals

client goals

The financial plan you develop for your client should include a list of the client's stated goals and objectives, indicating the priority of each one and the time frame for achieving it, where applicable. *Client goals* can be displayed and listed in several ways. One approach is to list the client's personal goals that are financially oriented, and then to list the client's goals that are strictly financial.

Example

Personal objective: Devote myself full-time to my artwork during retirement

Financial objective: Accumulate $850,000 of retirement income capital to maintain my current inflation-adjusted income during retirement

---

Another approach is to list goals according to the broad category of planning into which they fall such as lifetime planning and disposition of assets at death.

Example

For lifetime planning:

1. Fund college education for children.
2. Assure comfortable retirement.
3. Reduce tax burden.
4. Build vacation home.

For dispositions at death:

1. Assure sufficient assets in estate to provide for spouse and minor children in the event of my premature death.
2. Use estate assets to provide first for spouse and any minor children; distribute assets remaining at spouse's death equally among children.

Yet another method is to list goals according to the specific area of financial planning into which they fall, along with the current and required percentages and dollar amounts necessary to achieve them.

Example

Life insurance and risk management:

survivorship income—56 percent of objective currently available if client dies; 41 percent of objective if spouse dies

disability income—requirements are 67 percent satisfied if client becomes disabled for 90 days or longer

Specialized financial planning goals:

education goal—currently 41 percent funded when needed

Retirement planning:

financial independence—currently 68 percent funded

Restating your client's goals, including any additions or modifications since the fact-finding meeting, will remind your client of the reasons he or she initially undertook the task of financial planning. These goals represent the foundation upon which the plan is built. The degree to which you can develop financial plans that adequately address client goals will determine your ultimate success as a financial advisor and your clients' satisfaction with the design of your plans.

2. Identification of Concerns and Problems

identification of concerns and problems

Software programs used to develop personal financial plans often include a section that focuses on the *identification of concerns and problems* as well as a system that can be used to rate the importance of each. The resulting financial plans that utilize this rating information can include a narrative statement that briefly describes the impact that each of these concerns and problems could have on a client's plan with respect to such things as:

- liquidity
- safety of principal
- capital appreciation
- current income
- inflation protection
- future income
- tax reduction/deferral
- others

It is also advisable to indicate the extent to which a client's existing financial plan has addressed each of his or her concerns and problems. The areas of discrepancies and the areas of consistencies between what the client wants to achieve and what he or she has achieved provide an important commentary on the strengths and weaknesses of the client's planning until now.

You should also cite personal concerns and problems within the applicable components of the plan and itemize them as necessary according to your client's individual situation. Explain to your client that you have factored these concerns and problems into your recommendations and that they can be mitigated or overcome by the actions and products you suggest for implementation now and in the future. The degree to which your recommendations directly address your client's concerns and problems will affect how willing your client is to accept the plan and begin to implement it.

3. Planning Assumptions

planning assumptions

The finished plan should include a list of assumptions that you used to define your client's personal and financial planning problems and challenges. These assumptions are also the restrictions within which you developed and prepared your planning strategies. They serve to remind your client of the obstacles and limitations that needed to be observed throughout the customization of his or her personalized financial plan. As stated previously, *planning assumptions* should include, but not be limited to, future inflation rates, investment yields, risk tolerance, and life expectancies, and they should be spelled out explicitly in the financial plan document.

4. Financial Position Statement

After you have analyzed the information about your client and, if necessary, refined or revised your client's goals, your next job is to devise a realistic financial plan to help your client attain those goals. To help in this effort, the client's financial position statement can be used in several ways.

As you consider alternative strategies you might include in a plan to achieve the client's goals, you can compare projected financial position statements—each reflecting a particular strategy—to determine the relative impact of the various strategies on your client's future wealth position under a given set of assumptions. This use is best illustrated by comparing pro forma financial position statements based on your client's current plan to one that incorporates your recommendations. A projection of your client's future financial position statement, assuming he or she adopts your recommended plan, compared to a financial position statement, assuming no change is made in cash flow and asset and liability management, will illustrate the extent to which your client's wealth position (and thus achievement of one or more goals) is expected to change.

5. Cash Flow Statement

You can use the cash flow statement to project cash flow and perform budget planning. After identifying the opportunities and obstacles in the analysis of your client's present cash flow situation in step 5 (analyze the information) of the selling/planning process, cash flow planning involves developing recommendations as to what your client should consider regarding

- the increase in your client's net cash flow that is expected to result from taking advantage of the opportunities
- your client's ability to deal with the obstacles to generating a net cash flow that is adequate to achieve his or her goals

You can prepare projected cash flow statements to show the expected impact of each of the alternative courses of action that take advantage of the existing opportunities or deal with the existing obstacles. As with the financial position statement, this is illustrated by using two pro forma cash flow statements. One should show the projected net cash flow for the upcoming year if your client makes no changes in cash management strategy. The second pro forma statement should show the expected net cash flow for the same period if your client undertakes an alternative strategy including recommended changes in asset allocation and cash flow management, along with any already planned changes such as an increase in your client's salary.

As with the financial position statement, you can compare a projection of the future cash flow statement, assuming the recommended plan is adopted, with the projected future cash flow statement, assuming no change is made in cash flow or asset management. This will indicate how much your client's net cash flow position (and thus the ability to achieve one or more goals) is likely to change.

Once the client approves the financial plan, the pro forma cash flow statement included in the plan becomes a budget—that is, an explicit plan for spending and investing the resources available if the financial plan is properly implemented.

6. Insurance Planning and Risk Management

In developing solutions to clients' exposure to insurable financial risks, it is important to consider all their existing insurance and personally owned assets that can be designated to cover those risks. To the extent that additional resource capital is needed, the four areas for developing solutions are insurance products, employer-provided benefits, supplementary employer-provided benefits that can be purchased, and government benefits (most of which cannot be purchased). In some cases, such as long-term care expenses, the use of personal resources and your client's reliance on family or friends who may act as caregivers, may reduce the capital needed to cover at least part of the cost. When developing specific recommendations in this area of planning, however, most financial advisors recommend the purchase of individual, group, or association insurance products. Therefore, the following sources will not be mentioned as we discuss developing recommendations within each category of need:

- Social Security disability income and medical benefits (Medicare)
- workers' compensation disability income and medical benefits
- other government benefits (veterans, civil service)
- Medicaid programs or state welfare programs
- medical payments coverage under liability and auto insurance policies
- railroad workers' benefits
- employer-provided fringe benefits

Although insurance planning is as personal as each individual client, the following general rules are worth keeping in mind when you are developing plan recommendations for your clients.

- Although life insurance is not the solution for all situations, current tax law does give permanent insurance products certain advantages that provide additional benefits to clients who need risk protection.
- Catastrophic risks should be insured against even when the probability of the occurrence of the loss is slight. Premium rates are usually low in these circumstances because rates are tied to the probability and magnitude of the loss.
- Small risks should generally not be insured against, especially when the probability of the occurrence of loss is high. Premium rates are usually relatively high and insurance is not cost effective.
- If your client has sufficient liquid assets to meet his or her stated objectives, it may be appropriate to fund these objectives from accumulated assets rather than from insurance proceeds.
- Insurance is a device for shifting the risks of loss from your client to an insurance company. Although many modern insurance products have substantial investment features, the primary function of insurance is still this risk-shifting function.
- Before you recommend additional (or replacement) insurance, you must be able to demonstrate to your client (1) that it meets one of his or her genuine needs or objectives and (2) that it is a more cost-effective means to achieve that need or objective than other planning techniques.
- Client objectives that will be met by the purchase of appropriate types and amounts of insurance coverage change over time. You must carefully review and monitor insurance planning along with the rest of your client's financial plan to assure that insurance coverage is adjusted as circumstances change.
- The need for insurance coverage does not always increase over time. Your implementation of effective financial and estate planning techniques may result in your client's having a decreased need for insurance.
- Insurance planning must always be coordinated with tax planning so that your client purchases coverage in a tax-efficient manner and takes into account the tax impact of ownership and beneficiary designations.

When insurance is properly used, it meets your client's need to minimize exposure to many types of serious losses as nothing else can. When insurance is improperly used, it decreases your client's positive cash flow and consequently prevents the achievement of other objectives. Unless the coverage is positioned properly, it may needlessly aggravate estate tax problems and cost your client's family thousands of dollars in unnecessary estate tax liabilities. Your judicious recommendations to purchase insurance contracts to insure against loss of income or assets can be a boon to your client. However, if your recommendations result only in your personal enrichment, the entire financial planning discipline suffers.

In developing insurance to protect your client against risk exposures and to meet his or her financial needs, you should apply the guidelines in the following sections, including the establishment of an emergency fund.

Premature Death Losses/Survivor Needs

The personal financial plan should contain a statement of the problems and solutions related to potential economic losses resulting from your client's and/or his or her spouse's premature death. List and express separately the extent of the existing potential losses in terms of survivor cash needs today and income needs for each of the remaining years of the client's (and spouse's, if applicable) life expectancy.

Cash Needs. If there is a shortage of capital to cover the client's cash needs at death, it should be clearly displayed (perhaps in red ink) and indicated based on today's dollar value.

Income Needs. Again, if the calculation of the client's income needs at death made during your analysis of the information results in a shortage, it should be clearly display (perhaps in red ink) and indicated for today, as well as projected into the future based on agreed upon interest earnings and inflation assumptions. Finally, you and your client should consider the insurance funding sources below to fill any cash and/or income needs that exist.

Potential Life Insurance Product Recommendations. Any life insurance product recommendations you propose should be compatible with your client's affordability, suitability, and planning priorities. Because life insurance protection is one of the fundamental building blocks in the financial planning pyramid that is of paramount importance in protecting the financial security of so many families today, you should make every effort to provide your clients with as much life insurance coverage as possible, given their financial resources. This involves experimenting with alternative product options for your clients to consider.

For example, if your client has a need for $1 million of life insurance and is in his or her early 30s, term insurance only or a combination of some permanent and mostly term insurance may be most appropriate. As with other components of the financial plan, you should develop several alternatives for your clients and let them choose the one they are most comfortable in purchasing.

Sources of Protection against Premature Death. Various kinds of death benefits may be available to a deceased client's family, as follows:

- individual life insurance purchased by the insured, his or her family, or others
  - privately through an advisor
  - through the insured's employer or business
  - through an association group plan provided through a professional or fraternal association, or similar group
- group life insurance
- credit life insurance payable to a creditor of the insured person to pay off a debt

Disability Income (DI) Losses

If your analysis of your client's income needs in the event of disability reveal a shortage in funding, you should recommend the appropriate amount of monthly DI insurance from among the sources of protection below.

Potential DI Insurance Product Recommendations. When considering DI insurance products to fill your clients' needs, you should design solutions that address the following factors:

- affordability
- length of elimination period
- duration of benefit period
- total, residual, and/or partial benefits
- appropriate definition of disability
- contract's renewability provision
- inclusion of riders regarding
  - future purchase options
  - inflation protection
  - social insurance supplements

Sources of Protection against DI Losses. The various sources of protection against DI losses are as follows:

- individual DI insurance purchased by the insured, his or her family, or others
  - privately through an advisor
  - through the insured's employer or business
  - through an association group plan
- group DI insurance

- credit DI insurance payable to a creditor of the insured person to pay off a debt
- DI benefits under existing individual and group life insurance policies
- DI benefits under private pension, profit-sharing, and nonqualified deferred-compensation plans
- employer salary-continuation (sick-pay) plans
- all other income, investments, or assets available to the family

As shown above, there often are more sources of protection available against premature death and disability than many people may think. The challenge is to recognize these sources and use them efficiently to meet your client's and your client's family's needs.

Medical Care Expenses

Medical care expenses represent a potential financial disaster to any individual or family if they are not insured. Most people have coverage provided to them by their employers. However, some have to rely on individually purchased plans or state or federally subsidized plans; many have no coverage at all. As a financial advisor, keep in mind the following general points regarding the acquisition of medical expense insurance coverage:

- Clients' medical expense coverage should protect against catastrophic expenses.
- Be sure that any internal policy limits are in line with customary hospital and medical expenses in the client's geographical area.

Potential Medical Expense Insurance Product Recommendations. To the extent that your clients' coverage is inadequate, your product recommendations should be based on their individual financial goals and/or family situation. When considering medical expense insurance products to fill your clients' needs, you should design solutions that address the following factors:

- affordability
- amount of annual deductibles
- amount of copayments for respective types of benefits
- amount of annual out-of-pocket limit for claims
- amount of aggregate policy limit payable on claims
- selection of benefits that are most relevant to the client's individual and family needs

Sources of Protection against Medical Care Expenses. The following are the major sources to which clients may look for coverage of medical care costs:

- health insurance
  - employer-provided medical expense coverage (including self-insured plans, Blue Cross–Blue Shield plans, insurance company comprehensive medical expense plans, health

maintenance organization plans, preferred provider organization plans, and point-of-service plans
  - individual medical expense insurance (including hospitalization/surgical expense insurance plans, and major medical plans such as stand-alone, supplementary, and comprehensive plans

- health savings accounts
- other assets available to the family

Long-Term Care (LTC) Expenses

If your analysis reveals that your client has a need for long-term care insurance, you should recommend the appropriate coverage from the sources below.

Potential LTC Insurance Product Recommendations. Product recommendations should be based on your client's needs, goals, and consideration of all LTC available resources. When evaluating LTC insurance products, you should address the following factors:

- affordability
- length of elimination period
- maximum daily benefit
  - reimbursement policy
  - indemnity (per diem) policy
- benefit period
- comprehensive or facility-only-type policy
- inflation protection—simple or compound interest adjustments
- tax-qualified or nonqualified policy

Sources of Protection against Long-Term Care Expenses. The following are the major nongovernmental sources to which you and your clients may look for coverage of long-term care costs:

- long-term care insurance purchased by the insured, his or her family, or others
  - privately through an advisor
  - through the insured's employer or business
  - through an association group plan
- group long-term care insurance
- long-term care insurance benefits in life insurance policies
- combination products—for example, life/LTC insurance and annuity/LTC insurance
- personal assets
- family caregivers

Property and Liability Losses

You should recommend to your clients that they have the most complete insurance against property and liability loss exposures that they can afford and educate them about the dangers of ignoring these risks.

Potential Property and Liability Insurance Product Recommendations. Below are some guidelines to keep in mind when you are developing product recommendations for your clients.

Auto insurance

- liability. At least $300,000 may be appropriate. This amount is frequently the base for an umbrella liability policy.
- deductibles. It may be practical for some clients to increase deductible amounts and reduce premiums. Many companies offer $500 and $1,000 deductibles.
- collision and comprehensive coverage. For older cars, clients may want to consider dropping this coverage if the cost is not worth the potential benefits.
- discounts. Determine whether clients have taken advantage of proper classifications, including multi-car discounts, good student driver discounts, safe driving programs, and so on.

Homeowners insurance

- dwellings. Coverage generally should be based on the estimated replacement cost of material for rebuilding, and you and your clients should review and update the coverage annually.
- personal property. All personal property should generally be insured for its replacement cost value. Also, you should determine if jewelry, art, silver, collectibles, and other personal property are insured for their actual replacement costs. Your client may want to have these items appraised and have them "scheduled" to insure them for their full value.

Umbrella liability

- Coverage should be coordinated with clients' homeowners and auto insurance to provide an additional layer of coverage over and above the base amounts in those policies.
- In view of substantial court judgments, this coverage may be essential, especially for high-income clients or those with significant net worth.

Sources of Protection against Property and Liability Losses. For most of your clients, the main source of protection against property and liability losses is insurance. This insurance generally is available under individually marketed property and liability policies, but it also may be available under "mass (or collective) merchandised" plans, usually through your client's employer. In some cases, it may be possible for individuals to protect themselves by not assuming liability under contract or by transferring a liability risk to others by contract. This really is not feasible, however, for most people.

Emergency Fund

You should recommend to your clients that they establish an emergency fund as a risk management tool to meet unexpected expenses not planned for in the family budget; to pay for the "smaller" disability income losses, medical expenses, and property losses that purposely are not covered by insurance; and to provide a financial cushion against such personal problems as prolonged unemployment.

The size of the emergency fund varies greatly and depends on such factors as the client's family income, number of income earners, stability of employment, assets, debts, insurance deductibles and uncovered health and property insurance exposures, and the family's general attitudes toward risk and security. The size of the emergency fund can be expressed as so many months of family income—typically 3 to 6 months.

By its very nature, the emergency fund should be invested conservatively. There should be almost complete security of principal, marketability, and liquidity. Within these investment constraints, the fund should be invested to secure a reasonable yield, given the primary investment objective of safety of principal. Logical investment outlets for the emergency fund include

- bank passbook savings accounts (regular accounts)
- bank and mutual fund money market accounts
- short-term United States Treasury securities
- United States savings bonds
- life insurance cash values

The careful client also may want to have some ready cash available for emergencies, even if it is non-interest earning.

7. Employee Benefits Planning

Employee benefits planning can have a direct effect on developing recommendations within all the other major areas of financial planning. Therefore, your client's existing benefits should be organized, categorized, and displayed to show the respective employer and employee contributions to benefits he or she currently has within each planning area. This gives your client a summary of what types of employee benefits he or she has, what contributions are being made to each type, what may be needed in additional employee benefits if available to purchase, and what other areas of planning are affected in reaching his or her planning goals. The following table is an abbreviated example.

Thus, in those areas of planning where your client can purchase additional benefits, such as life insurance, or can contribute additional amounts, such as 401(k) plans, you can recommend cost-efficient means to achieve your client's survivor needs or retirement planning goals. You can then present a summary of these suggested changes that reflects modifications in employee benefits— for example, additional contributions to the client's employer-sponsored qualified retirement plan.

Note the effect that this modification in employee benefits planning has on two other major areas of the client's personal financial plan—namely, income tax planning and retirement planning. The additional contributions to a defined-contribution plan, such as a 401(k) plan, will reduce the amount of income your client receives in the current year and thus reduce the amount of income tax paid on that income. The same contributions will also increase your client's accumulation of funds earmarked for retirement and thus further the realization of his or her retirement income goal.

Table 6-1
Current Employee Benefits Summary

Selective Benefits	Company Contribution	Employee Contribution
Deferred compensation	$0	$0
Executive bonus	$0	$0
Salary continuation	$0	$0
Standard Benefits	**Company Contribution**	**Employee Contribution**
Retirement plans	$4,500	$2,250
Group insurance	$3,600	$360
Paid time off	$4,350	$0
Government Benefits	**Company Contribution**	**Employee Contribution**
Social Security benefits	$5,738	$5,738

8. Specialized Financial Planning Goals

If your client has one or more specialized financial planning goals for which additional capital is needed, you should use a separate section of the personal financial plan to summarize these needs. It should include the total amount of dollars needed to fund the desired goal that you calculated during the analysis stage of the selling/planning process. This dollar amount should be compared to how much of that goal your client's current plan provides.

Example

Suppose that your clients have a goal to fund their children's college education, which requires that they accumulate an additional $200,000 over the next 15 years. You project that they will accumulate $95,000 at their current rate of saving. This shows a shortfall of $105,000 if your clients make no change in their current plan:

Total capital needed for college	$200,000
Current plan provides	95,000
Additional capital required	105,000

If there is a disparity between the amounts, you and your client can work together to develop solutions to meet the client's goal. In the example above, it is necessary to calculate the additional amount needed per year (shown in today's dollars) to fund this goal based on an assumed rate of return such as 6 percent interest. You should then summarize several funding alternatives for meeting the extra amount needed, in addition to having your clients continue their existing savings plan. The funding alternatives could include the following modes of payment and amounts:

• additional lump sum	$43,813
• additional monthly level savings	$359
• additional monthly inflated savings (amount shown is for the first year only; this amount must be increased annually by the assumed inflation rate of 3 percent)	$123

Bar graphs that depict how the increasing accumulations of cash will meet the needed cash accumulation goal for college funding are helpful in illustrating alternatives. Creating these bar graphs is simple, using the financial planning software available today.

Finally, you should assemble a list of all possible sources of funds that your client may not yet have considered. If, in the example above, all financial aid programs, student loans, scholarship sources, student employment income, and gifts from family members, such as grandparents, have already been factored into the calculation, along with all current education income tax credits and deductions, then the remaining amount needed to fill the funding deficit would have to come from financial vehicles and products. The following is a list that you can incorporate into your recommendations for college funding:

- Coverdell education savings account
- traditional IRA, Roth IRA, simplified employee pension plan (SEP), and SIMPLE plan distributions
- qualified plan loans and distributions
- qualified tuition programs (Sec. 529 plans)
- education savings bond programs
- home equity loans and lines of credit

Financial products could include

- savings accounts
- certificates of deposit
- mutual funds

- brokerage accounts (including stocks and bonds)
- annuities
- life insurance products

Legal instruments such as the following can also contain financial products used for education funding:

- Uniform Gifts to Minors Act accounts
- Uniform Transfers to Minors Act accounts
- Sec. 2503(b) trusts
- Sec. 2503(c) trusts

Your recommendations of financial products and funding vehicles will depend on your client's risk tolerance and time horizon, and they must be suitable for the specific situation. As with any component of the personal financial plan, you must present a choice of funding products and concepts that you think your client will find acceptable. Otherwise, your client may not implement the concepts you recommend, in which case everybody loses.

9. Investment Planning

The purpose of investing falls into two categories. The first category is prefunding anticipated expenses for major planning goals such as retirement and education. The second category is discretionary in the sense that investments are made with the more general goal of adding to the accumulation of your client's assets rather than funding a specific need. Because investments are usually made from cash available after paying for living expenses, the appropriate time to determine the amount to be invested is after you and your client have completed cash flow and insurance planning. By assuring there is no cash drain due to poor cash flow or inadequate insurance planning, the maximum dollar amount will be available for investment.

The choice of appropriate investment vehicles can vary widely from client to client. Recommendations on investments must be based on your careful assessment of your client's attitude toward risk and return. For example, it would not generally be appropriate to recommend trading in commodities futures to a risk-averse client whose previous investment choices have been federally insured savings deposits or CDs. Within the limits of a particular client's level of risk tolerance, however, there may be considerable leeway in the choice of investment vehicles. To a great extent, the choice among these vehicles will depend on your client's financial planning objectives.

As with insurance planning, you should carefully coordinate investment planning with the other aspects of your client's financial plan, and you should take care to ensure that your investment recommendations are suited to achieve your client's objectives.

Investment Portfolio Design

Investment planning typically is focused on selecting investments that will help a client achieve the specific financial goals set forth in his or her financial plan. Thus, before selecting any investments, you or your client's investment advisor should construct a recommended investment portfolio or asset-allocation model that is tailored to your client's level of risk tolerance. This asset-allocation model outlines your client's investment strategy within the context of his or her overall financial plan. The emphasis of an asset-allocation model is on the different categories of assets and the respective percentage to be placed in each category. Once your client has an asset-allocation model tailored to his or her unique circumstances, the next step is to select investments that fit within the boundaries of the model.

The asset-allocation models should range from conservative to aggressive, depending on the client's risk tolerance. A client with a low score on the Survey of Financial Risk Tolerance is assumed to be risk averse (conservative), and a client with a high score is assumed to be risk tolerant (aggressive). Clients with scores in the mid-range can be classified as moderately conservative, moderate, or moderately aggressive financial risk takers. These classifications are based somewhat on your subjective judgment, but they provide a working premise from which you can construct model investment portfolios for your clients.

You can begin with broad-based allocations between fixed-income and equity securities (see section titled "Investment Instruments for Capital Accumulation" for more information on these types of investment vehicles), and between foreign and domestic securities. You can further refine the model allocations between large and small capitalization securities, and between growth, blended, and value-type securities. For simplicity's sake, it is best to limit the model allocations to traditional, broad-based asset classes rather than sector funds and emerging market securities. (See the table below for a simplified illustration of how you can allocate assets to be consistent with a client's risk tolerance and investment objectives.)

The purpose in constructing an asset portfolio for clients is to achieve consistent, systematic returns over time on the entire portfolio to help them realize their financial planning objectives. Consequently, you must use assumptions in long-term projections that have a certain probability of achieving the client's desired outcome. You can use portfolio optimization software programs to accomplish this. These programs are a valuable resource for constructing a choice of asset-allocation portfolios that can give your clients a balance between risk and return consistent with their risk tolerance. Given a broad selection of investment inputs from which to choose, such as various classes of mutual funds, these programs will analyze the historical risk and returns of these securities over a selected recent time period, such as 5 or 10 years. Then the software will construct recommended asset allocations from among these securities that seek to optimize the client's rate of return within his or her risk tolerance level. Although they are not guarantees or even predictions of returns for the future, the data contain a certain degree of statistical probability for achieving the desired investment results.

Table 6-2
Model Asset-Allocation Portfolios Based on Client's Risk Tolerance

	Conservative	Moderately Conservative	Moderate	Moderately Aggressive	Aggressive
Equities	0%	25%	50%	75%	100%
Fixed income	100%	75%	50%	25%	0 %
Foreign/U.S.	0%/100 %	5%/95 %	10%/90 %	15%/85 %	20%/80 %

Because active investment strategies require continual monitoring and ongoing supervision, a passive investment strategy is generally best for most financial planning clients to implement portfolio allocations. This will usually (but not exclusively) involve the use of mutual funds and variable annuities, which consist of professionally managed accounts containing many similar securities, rather than individual securities that would require a money manager to buy and sell them when needed. A diversified portfolio of mutual funds and variable annuity accounts from the thousands that are available can be designed to meet most clients' investment goals without the need for frequent changes to their investment portfolios. There is ample research to support the assertion that once an appropriate asset allocation has been determined, a buy-and-hold approach works best over the long-term.

However, your client's asset allocations in conjunction with his or her financial goals will determine the performance standards by which to evaluate selected investments. If an investment is not meeting your client's standards, then it needs to be replaced.

Investment Instruments for Capital Accumulation

There are a wide variety of possible investment instruments that you can use to accumulate capital. The instruments are classified as fixed-dollar and variable-dollar (or equity) investments. Fixed-dollar investments are those where principal and/or income are contractually set in advance in terms of a specified or determinable number of dollars. Variable-dollar investments are those where neither the principal nor the income is contractually set in advance in terms of dollars. In other words, both the value and the income of variable-dollar investments can change in amount, either up or down, with changes in economic conditions.

Fixed-dollar investments include the following:

- savings accounts
- certificates of deposit, Treasury bills and notes, and other short-term debt investments
- money market funds
- fixed-interest annuities

- bonds
- preferred stock
- life insurance cash values (Note that the cash values of many currently available life insurance contracts are actually variable rather than fixed—for example, variable life and variable universal life, whose cash values are a function of investment performance rather than contractual determination.)

Variable-dollar investments are as follows:

- common stock
- mutual funds (stock and balanced funds)
- variable annuities
- options and futures
- commodities
- real estate
- limited partnership investments
- ownership of business interests
- fine arts, precious metals, and other miscellaneous assets

10. Income Tax Planning

After the analysis of information is complete, you must explore opportunities that would save your client income taxes (and other taxes, if applicable). If you are being paid a fee to deliver the financial plan, income tax planning is often a substantial portion of what you are being paid to do. Even when financial products are being offered for sale, it is your obligation to take a comprehensive and objective look at your client's situation and to save him or her from costly tax blunders whenever possible.

A major consideration in financial planning is the integrated and efficient use of financial resources and tax advantages to achieve your client's objectives. Therefore, you should consider all of your client's specific objectives that require additional income and/or capital in relation to your client's total financial condition and recommend funding them with the most appropriate tax-advantaged investment vehicles available.

Furthermore, when income tax savings can be combined with achieving a client's goals within other major areas of financial planning, you can compound the effect of those tax savings. For example, as mentioned earlier, clients who increase their contributions into an employer-sponsored 401(k) plan immediately reduce income taxation on those contributions, bolster the accumulation of money for use during retirement, defer taxation on the growth of the extra dollars within the plan, and make more efficient use of an employee benefit.

A wide variety of specific income tax saving concepts are being used or proposed today. In general, however, they fall under one or more of the following basic tax-saving techniques:

- reducing taxes, using adjustments to taxable income, income tax deductions, and income tax credits
- shifting the tax burden to others who are in lower brackets
- taking returns as long-term capital gains rather than ordinary income
- postponing or deferring income taxation

These tax-saving techniques should form the basis for the development of recommendations that address your client's income tax concerns within the broader context of his or her personalized financial plan.

11. Retirement Planning

Developing recommendations for funding your clients' retirement planning needs can be a difficult task for many reasons. First of all, calculating the amount of capital needed to fill a retirement income funding gap is based on assumptions that may prove to be inaccurate, or may change due to circumstances beyond your client's control. For instance, if you assume the rate of inflation to be 3 percent for the next 25 years and it turns out to be 4 percent, unless your client increases savings along the way, his or her retirement income goal will be underfunded. Or suppose the assumption for Social Security retirement benefits is $1,500 per month in today's dollars and due to legislative changes to the Social Security system, it turns out to actually be $750 per month. This can wreak havoc on the retirement planning process.

Furthermore, there are often conflicting goals or unexpected events that can present major obstacles to successful retirement planning. For instance, your clients could have children whom they plan to send to college. If the actual out-of-pocket cost to your clients turns out to be much higher than expected, this could postpone their retirement. Also, a family member's serious illness or disability could force your clients to deal with unforeseen financial responsibilities that can jeopardize successful retirement planning.

Thus, because retirement planning is a long and dynamic process, it requires periodic review of the actual progress compared to the plan, possible revisions to the assumptions that can affect it, and fine-tuning of factors that the client can control.

Developing the Retirement Funding Solution

Assuming your analysis of the information reveals there is a retirement income gap in the plan you are designing for your client, before you can select any financial products to fill that gap, you should keep in mind that there are basically only two ways (or a combination of the two) to solve the problem:

- increase the amount of money being saved and invested each month at the current assumed rate of return
- earn a higher effective rate of return based on the current contribution level of savings and investment

You can easily calculate the specific amounts of additional savings and/or earnings required using a financial calculator or financial planning software. After developing various options between what your client is presently saving and earning and the higher amount required, you should present them to your client in a straightforward and easily understood format.

Example

Assume your client's aggregate rate of return on retirement savings is 6 percent and that at the current level of savings, it will have to increase to 8 percent to achieve the capital required. Or assume that if the 6 percent rate of return does not change, your client will have to contribute an additional $400 per month to reach his or her goal. You can present these two options, along with some combinations of increased earnings and increased contributions, as shown below.

The presentation could also include one or several bar graphs showing the impact of each corresponding change.

Additional monthly savings needed	$400	$300	$200	$100	$0
Hypothetical rate of return needed	6.0%	6.5%	7.0%	7.5%	8.0%

Of course, any investment vehicles you recommend that would increase the overall rate of return for your client have to be consistent with his or her risk tolerance, investment objectives, and time horizon. Also, any additional contributions have to be affordable and consistent with your client's cash flow management strategy. After you and your client have considered these factors carefully, you must then choose the retirement programs and financial resources to use to achieve your client's retirement planning goal.

Sources for Providing Retirement Income

Today, there are many ways to plan for retirement. Some involve government programs while others rely primarily on private means; some involve tax advantages while others do not. Sources include the following:

- Social Security retirement benefits
- other government benefits

- employer-provided pension plans
- tax-advantaged retirement plans
  - (HR-10 plans) for the self-employed
  - individual retirement accounts and annuities (traditional and Roth IRA plans)
  - SEP plans
  - SIMPLE plans
  - tax-sheltered annuity (TSA) plans
- tax-deferred profit-sharing and other employee benefit plans (voluntary employee contributions to employer-sponsored plans)
- nonqualified deferred-compensation plans
- individually purchased annuities
- life insurance cash values
- other investment products and assets owned by the individual

Many of these instruments for providing retirement income offer substantial tax advantages if the plan meets the requirements of the tax laws. Because many of your clients will have a variety of retirement benefits available to them, coordination of these benefits becomes increasingly important.

12. Estate Planning

Deficiencies in the area of estate planning lead to the recommendation of nonfinancial vehicles and financial products that solve the problems uncovered in step 5 of the selling/planning process (analyze the information). The actions your clients may need to take must be customized to their specific qualitative and quantitative planning needs. In developing estate planning recommendations, you should help your client prioritize these needs so that they can be implemented according to their urgency or order of importance. You should factor the client's planning goals, along with conventional estate planning wisdom, into this exercise.

Example

If your client Albert Hall has only modest assets and his goal is to have sufficient assets in his estate to provide for his wife and minor children in the event of his premature death, he can achieve this with life insurance, which he should purchase immediately. If Albert also does not have a will, one should be drafted as soon as possible. However, the will may be completed after he obtains the life insurance because insurance itself addresses Albert's goal.

Although some advisors would recommend that basic estate planning documents, such as a will, be drafted before taking other actions, this would not accomplish Albert's objective, so it is less important in this situation.

If you do not have the knowledge to help your clients with estate planning, you should serve as a resource person and enlist the help of legal, estate tax, and trust planning experts who can facilitate this process.

Considerations in Developing Estate Planning Recommendations

For most of your clients, your judicious use of basic estate planning documents and diligence in avoiding common estate planning mistakes will address a majority of their goals and concerns in this area of financial planning.

Documents in Estate Plan. The basic documents to include in your client's estate plan are a

- will
- living will and advance medical directives
- durable power of attorney for health care
- durable power of attorney for property
- personal letter of instructions

Estate Planning Mistakes. The following are some common estate planning mistakes that you as a financial advisor must recognize and correct (if you do not have the expertise to do so, you must find someone who is qualified to rectify the problem):

- nonexistent, invalid, out-of-date, or poorly drafted will
- simple wills between spouses, which do not make proper use of both spouses' applicable credit amount
- improperly arranged or inadequate life insurance
- possible adverse consequences of jointly held property
- failure to utilize lifetime gifting and property transfers
- failure to protect assets from or properly use the probate process
- improper valuation of estate assets
- estate liquidity problems
- choice of the wrong executor or trustee

Finally, life insurance is the only product that can be used to simultaneously create and help to conserve an estate. Life insurance immediately increases the value of an individual's estate by the face amount of the policy when it is put in force. It can also provide an estate with liquidity to pay estate settlement costs. Furthermore, when a person or entity other than the insured owns the insurance, it can be used effectively to pay estate tax liability. Be sure not to overlook the possible uses for life insurance in estate planning.

13. Recommendations

recommendations

Once you have reviewed all information, techniques, and strategies in light of your client's circumstances and goals, you can formulate definitive *recommendations*. Written recommendations should specifically address the client's goals and objectives and all concerns and problems identified in the plan, as well as the actions necessary to compensate for any shortfalls. Recommendations should be clearly identified and stated straightforwardly.

In developing the formal plan document for presentation to the client, financial advisors may differ in the amount of documentation that they deliver with the plan. Some may choose to list only the recommendation of choice for a particular objective. Although this may be an economical way to develop plans, it is unlikely to meet your client's need to make an informed decision about his or her own life and affairs. If several alternatives are available, the better approach is to discuss each of them in the plan, identify the recommendation of choice for achieving your client's objective, and indicate any additional reasons why your client should adopt your recommendation.

Whenever possible, you should include in any planning recommendation citations to any authority or data (tax code sections, case names, numbers, assumptions, and so on) that you considered in formulating, explaining, or illustrating that recommendation. This information is particularly helpful to the client's other advisors when they review the financial plan because it allows them to follow your logic without spending unnecessary time in research. When references are included in the plan, it is much easier for other advisors to validate your recommendation. A well-documented plan is a work product that the client's attorney, accountant, or other advisor can use as a reliable blueprint in preparing documents or proposals in the implementation stage of the planning process.

PRESENTING THE PLAN

You reviewed the client's current situation and created recommendations to effect his or her desired situation. It is now time to present your recommendations to your client. This section of the chapter will discuss how to present the financial plan recommendations as solutions to your client's needs and goals.

Preparing for the Presentation

The key to an effective presentation is preparation. Take the time to create a standardized format for your presentation, and then practice and memorize it. Many advisors use financial planning software, and/or organize the presentation in a binder. The plan document should have a professional look, be in a binder of some kind, be printed on quality paper, and be neatly organized. Like in cooking, presentation is extremely important. The appearance and organization of your materials will go a long way toward the acceptance of your presentation and recommendations.

The amount of time you need to prepare will decrease as you gain experience, but initially you will want to create a detailed outline for each presentation meeting. Here are some ways for you to prepare for this meeting:

- Analyze your client. What were his or her attitudes toward insurance, investing, retirement planning, and so on? What are your client's probable motives for taking action? What are the barriers? What is his or her financial situation? What is the desired situation? What are his or her priorities?
- Create a summary of the fact-finding meeting that you can use as an outline to review with your client before you present your recommendations. Use a simple outline of the main points established from fact finding. Check the client information (name, age, and so forth) for accuracy.
- Create projections for all of your recommendations (where possible).
- Create comparisons for the probable outcome of current plans and those of the recommended alternatives.
- Check your suggested alternatives. How do they reflect your client's needs, priorities, and budget? What are the advantages and disadvantages of each alternative? Which do you feel is the best alternative and why?
- Create and organize a printed presentation document you will use with your client. Present this with as much detail and support material as appropriate to the case and the client.
- Collect any compliance-approved sales material you will use in the presentation. If you have a series of such items, include them in order in your sales presentation binder or portfolio.
- Confirm the appointment time and location with your client.

The better prepared you are, the more you can focus on your client and his or her reaction to your presentation, and the better you can respond to your client's objections or concerns. Furthermore, you will present a professional image to your client if everything you need is accurate, organized, and convincing.

The Mental Rehearsal

Before you meet with your client to make your presentation of recommendations, visualize what will happen in your presentation. How will your client respond to your recommendations? What documentation or sales aids will you need? How will you present this information? Where will you sit when making the presentation? How will your client answer your questions? How will you reply if your client asks a difficult question or voices an objection to your proposals?

This preparation is a mental rehearsal for the presentation meeting. Sit quietly and let your imagination take over the process. When you can see the presentation in progress and visualize your client saying yes, then you have the necessary confidence and are prepared for your meeting.

Delivering a presentation that will motivate your client requires both preparation and execution. Preparation begins with a vision of what a good presentation should cover. From this vision, you can develop an outline to ensure that critical points are covered. With the outline as your guide, you will be able to gather the necessary support materials and organize your presentation.

Organizing the Presentation

Although the specifics of an effective presentation will vary from advisor to advisor, there are a few simple ways to organize it. One method is to use financial planning software that organizes the material for you or enables you to present it in a manner compatible with your style. Whatever method you choose, your presentation of the printed financial plan should summarize for your client your analysis of the following:

- where your client is now (current situation)
- where your client wants to be (desired situation)
- your recommendations to get your client where the client wants to be

Client's Present Personal and Financial Situation

Some time will have elapsed between your initial and subsequent meetings with the client. Therefore, it is important to reestablish your client's goals and needs by summarizing the relevant points from prior meetings.

The plan should describe your client's present situation based on both personal and financial data. The summary of the personal situation should include basic information about your client and his or her family such as names, addresses, phone numbers, dates of birth, Social Security numbers, and so on. It should also include other relevant personal information that helps define your client's present situation and will consequently affect the financial plan. Other relevant information could include important attitudes and values, and special circumstances such as a child's serious health problem, a feeling of personal obligation to support aging parents, a desire to treat adopted or stepchildren differently from natural children, previous marriages and alimony or child-support obligations, and pending or anticipated gifts or inheritances.

Presentation Checklist
In preparing to deliver your presentation to your client, review the following *presentation checklist*: • Who is your client? • Have you determined your purpose? What are your client's financial goals and needs to which you will help find solutions? • What is your client's current situation? • What is your client's desired situation? • What specific factual and feeling-finding information have you collected? • How can you summarize your observations and key points from the fact-finding interview? • What are your client's buying motives? • What are the specific conditions for taking action such as a budget commitment, other available resources that can be committed, start date, time frame, and so on? • Does your client appear to agree with your assessment of his or her needs so far? • What solution and statements to support it have you developed? What are the alternative plans and their advantages and disadvantages? • What objections or concerns do you anticipate? What responses have you prepared? • Have you rehearsed your presentation and answers to objections or any other discussions? • Have you visualized a successful presentation as you would like it to proceed?

It is typical for the financial advisor to summarize a client's present financial situation by including a financial position statement on the plan date that lists the client's assets and liabilities and shows net worth, a cash-flow statement that identifies all income and expenses and indicates net cash flow for the latest period, and a copy and analysis of the client's most recent federal income tax return. There may also be projections of future financial position that are relevant to understanding the client's current position. In addition, this summary should include information about the client's current investment portfolio with an indication of its liquidity, diversification, and risk characteristics.

Client's Goals and Desired Situation

In presenting your plan, you should indicate the priority of each one of the client's goals and the time frame for achieving it. Every goal should be crafted to be as SMART as possible. Because there are likely to be a number of goals in the plan, it may be helpful to list them in relevant categories such as protection, accumulation, liquidation, and so forth. Keep in mind that the best way to meet a specific goal may involve a combination of strategies that embrace several of the major planning areas. For example, a strategy to reduce current income taxes could be tied into contributions to qualified retirement plans. Whatever approach you adopt to categorize goals, you should design the plan to avoid confusing your client. The format should be as simple as practical.

Essentially, you are summarizing your client's answers to these questions:

- What do you want to provide for your family?
- What do you want to leave to your heirs and to charity?
- What priorities do you have for your family's lifestyle?
- What specific financial goals do you have?
- What is your budget commitment to implementing the financial plan?

Planning Assumptions

In the process of formulating strategies, you must make assumptions and spell them out in the plan document. Typical assumptions include the interest rate to be earned on assets, risk-tolerance levels, time horizons, and the rate of inflation for a given time period. It is important to clarify these assumptions in the plan document and client presentation. Questions that you and your client are likely to discuss include the following:

- What assumptions were incorporated into planning?
- What has changed since the current planning decisions were made?
- Has anything changed since the fact-finding meeting?
- Would your client like to change any of the assumptions?

Summary of Your Observations

The best way to rekindle your client's interest in adopting the personal financial plan that you have developed is to emphasize the gap between his or her desired outcome and the projected outcome under current arrangements. As you summarize your observations about the client's financial picture and review the key points of the fact-finding meeting, you want your client not only to recognize this financial gap, but also to feel it on a personal level.

By pointing out the current plan's inability to accomplish your client's objectives, you can demonstrate just how important it is that your client implement the recommendations you are about to make if he or she wants to achieve his or her stated objectives. Be prepared to ask questions to make sure you understand what is important to your client and what he or she likes or dislikes about your recommendations.

Presenting Your Recommendations

For each goal, you should present at least three important areas of information:

- the problem(s) you have identified that your client will encounter in attempting to accomplish his or her goal

- the recommended financial services, products, and strategies to overcome the identified problem(s)
- the responsibilities of each party for implementing the plan and carrying it through to completion

You should have a recommendation and alternatives for each observation. As you review the recommendations with your client, remember that it is your responsibility to help him or her fully understand them and make informed decisions. Focus the discussion on the plan alternatives, highlighting the advantages and disadvantages of each one. Compare the expected outcomes of each alternative. Based on your recommendations, you want your client to select the alternative that best suits his or her needs, priorities, and budget. Your client must feel a sense of involvement and commitment, which will reinforce his or her confidence in the selected alternative's ability to meet the objectives.

It is important for you to explain fundamental concepts about how the plan works so your client can understand your recommendations. These underlying concepts include, but are not limited to, the

- personal and economic assumptions in the plan recommendations
- interdependence of recommendations
- advantages and disadvantages of each recommendation alternative
- risks your client faces if he or she does or does not implement the recommendation
- need to implement plan recommendations in a timely manner

It is also important to match your recommendations with your client's goals and priorities. In some cases, you can focus your presentation on a "hot button" priority if your client has a dominant concern or goal.

There are several ways to present your recommendations effectively:

- Begin with the solutions that are your client's top priorities and move down the list.
- Move from recommendations that are simplest to implement to those that are more complex.
- Follow the 13 guidelines for a comprehensive financial plan in order from beginning to end.

Regardless of the way you structure your presentation, make sure your client understands how difficult it will be to achieve his or her goals without adopting your plan recommendations. Review what may happen if he or she does not make changes in his or her financial plan. Give your client your professional assessment of the current plan's ability to realize his or her stated objectives, considering his or her current situation.

In communicating your recommendations, you must be clear when you are expressing an opinion and when you are explaining a fact. You must also make it clear that although your recommendations are designed to enable your client to attain his or her goals, needs, and priorities, changes in personal and economic conditions will inevitably alter the intended outcomes. Changes that will affect projected outcomes and that may require adjustments in plan recommendations include changes in legislation, family status, career events, investment performance, and health, to name but a few. Changes will be, in fact, inevitable. That is why monitoring the plan on a regular basis after it is implemented is critical.

If your client still has any reservations about taking action on the recommendations, review again the advantages and disadvantages of the relevant alternatives. To simplify this process, review only those alternatives that your client is considering.

Financial Planning Software

It is common to use financial planning software to develop and present financial plans. A sharp pencil and a yellow pad can only do so much. Planning software can create impressive-looking, attractive, easy-to-use and easy-to-understand packages for every aspect of financial planning.

Software also lends itself perfectly to the multiple-purpose approach to planning, because you can easily assemble modules for the areas of planning to address with a particular client based on his or her needs, goals, and priorities. The modules produced by these financial planning packages also offer a "track to run on" format that can systematize the presentation.

There are many software programs, and no program is right for everyone. Arriving at the proper fit for you requires a commitment to a lot of work and research. The more you put into the process, the more it will work for you. There are many philosophical differences among financial advisors, and there are real differences among clients. Therefore, you want to create a good match between your software presentation, your style, and your clients.

Implementing the Plan

The implementation phase of the process gives you and your client a plan and the steps to put the plan recommendations into action. It also identifies who is responsible for each step and establishes time lines for implementation.

A successful presentation enables your client to see how your recommendations clearly support his or her goals. You want to motivate (but not manipulate) your client to act on the recommendations he or she decides to implement. As you present and discuss your recommendations, keep in mind that your client must make the final decision about plan alternatives because the plan is his or hers, not yours. You should listen to the client's concerns and revise the recommendations as appropriate.

The following is an example of an implementation checklist that you can use for plan recommendations. You can fill in the specific recommendations as they apply to a particular client.

Implementation/Action Plan for Michael Client, October 2009 Prepared by Fred Advisor		
Action Date ______		Completion Date ______
	Insurance and Risk Management Planning	
____	Disability income insurance	____
____	Life insurance	____
____	Property and liability insurance	____
____	Long-term care insurance	____
____	Other ______________	____
	Income, Cash Flow, and Budget Planning	
____	1) ______________	____
____	2) ______________	____
	Investment Planning	
____	1) ______________	____
____	2) ______________	____
	Retirement Planning	
____	1) ______________	____
____	2) ______________	____
	Education Planning	
____	1) ______________	____
____	2) ______________	____
	Income Tax Planning	
____	1) ______________	____
____	2) ______________	____
	Estate Planning	
____	1) ______________	____
____	2) ______________	____

Multiple-Purpose Plan

The approach for delivering a financial plan to most clients is to build the plan in a modular or sequential manner. This type of planning usually requires several meetings with your client over a period of time, possibly even years. It is similar to the comprehensive model in that it addresses your client's priorities and concerns. It differs from the comprehensive model by concentrating on the highest-priority goal, then moving on to the next highest priority over time rather than being an all-inclusive one-time plan. The client may not have the time, money, or inclination to address all of his or her needs at once. Giving the client too many decisions to make will be tantamount to making no decision. Nevertheless, over time the ultimate outcome of the multiple-purpose approach should be a comprehensive financial plan.

Comprehensive Plan

As mentioned in previous sections, a comprehensive financial plan addresses the current status of all the major planning areas, even if recommendations are not included for every one of them. In developing the comprehensive plan document and presentation you may find it helpful to use the following outline, which is an example of how to organize a client's plan based on the areas of concern and your recommendations. Any multiple purpose or sequential plan will address only those selected areas of the comprehensive plan that correspond to the client's needs, situation, and preferences.

**Financial Plan for Michael Client: October 2009,
Prepared by Fred Advisor**

1. Your present situation
   - Personal situation
   - Financial position statement
     - Balance sheet
     - Cash flow analysis and management
     - Asset analysis
2. Goals and concerns
   - Increase disposable income for investment because saving has been difficult.
   - Improve investment liquidity to establish an emergency fund.
   - Reduce liability risk by obtaining additional insurance.
   - Increase survivor income at death, disability, or retirement.
   - Guarantee that children will be able to afford to attend college, if client lives or dies.
3. Planning assumptions
   - Inflation will continue at 3 percent indefinitely.
   - Investment assets will grow at a net aggregate rate of 6 percent.
4. Recommendations
   - Tax strategy (income, estate, and gift taxes)
     - Increase retirement plan contributions at work.

Financial Plan for Michael Client: October 2009, Prepared by Fred Advisor

  - Review and reduce income tax withholding because client receives a large refund annually.
- Investment strategy (investments and retirement)
  - Review budget to find additional discretionary dollars to invest.
  - Review asset allocation because risk exposure is high for a moderate risk taker.
- Risk management strategy (insurance)
  - Purchase additional life insurance to increase potential survivor income.
  - Purchase disability income insurance to protect income in the event of disability.
  - Purchase an umbrella liability policy to increase liability protection.
- Wealth transfer strategy (estate planning)
  - This area does not represent a high priority for the client currently.
  - Review will and other documents to determine that they reflect the client's intent.
- Summary and assignment of implementation responsibilities
  - Summarize observations and recommendations to determine what must be done, who must take action, timetable-action plan, and date of next review.

Presentation Techniques

No matter how well you have prepared or how good your recommendations are, presenting them is still the critical element in motivating your client to adopt them. There are four *presentation techniques* you can use to enhance the effectiveness of your presentation:

- Focus on relevant product features and benefits.
- Keep your client involved.
- Insist that all decision makers be present.
- Remember that presentations involve hypothetical projections.

Focus on Relevant Product Features and Benefits

One mistake advisors make is to think that the purpose of the presentation is to educate the client about the technical, legal, tax, and product aspects of financial planning. Although you should not overlook these areas and client education is important, you should discuss these aspects in a manner that matches your client's sophistication in that area. Take care not to confuse your client with technical information that is not important to the plan or is beyond your client's comprehension. Technical details should be discussed only in light of the features and corresponding benefits that are relevant to your client and form the basis of your recommendations.

feature

benefit

What are the differences between product features and benefits? A *feature* is a characteristic of the product itself—what it is. A feature is a fact about the product. Features are descriptive and are not given values. Conversely, a *benefit* is what the client gets as a result of the feature. It is what the product does for the client and why he or she wants it. Benefits are value laden and subjective. They are the solutions that a particular individual wants.

A feature may not be a benefit to one client, while it will be to another. If you are discussing health insurance with young single males, maternity and dependent coverage may not be a significant benefit, whereas to young married men with families, these features are an important benefit.

When presenting a recommendation, you want to explain what it is, how it solves the problem, and what it does for your client. The delivery of benefits is essential to your client's acceptance and purchase of the product or service. In considering a product or service, your client asks himself or herself questions such as: Is it worth the price? Is it the best option? Will it save money? How well will it work for me? You must address and answer these and other questions if you expect your client to act on your recommendation. Thus, you must always clearly communicate the benefits for your client.

An effective way to present features and benefits is as follows:

- State the feature.
- Follow it with the words, "What this means to you is. . . ."
- State the benefit as it relates to a need, value, or objective your client has expressed.

An example of presenting the features and benefits of a disability waiver-of-premium rider on a life insurance policy is shown below.

Example

Hugh, this policy contains the disability waiver-of-premium rider. What this means to you is that should you become disabled, the company will pay the premium for you. This will give you the peace of mind of knowing that if you cannot work because of a disability, your premium will be paid and your life insurance coverage will remain in effect, protecting your family in the event of your death.

To effectively present benefits, you should go through a mental review before meeting with your client. Put yourself in your client's shoes to see things from his or her point of view. See how your solution and the benefits of your product or service help your client get what he or she wants (benefits).

In summary, when you explain a recommendation, stress the benefits that the client will receive. Clients respond to benefits. Focus your presentation on the benefits—what a feature will do for a client that he or she cares about. Concentrate on the benefits that matter most to your client—those you uncovered in the fact-finding process.

Keep Your Client Involved

It is important to maintain your client's participation and involvement in the selling/planning process for several reasons:

- It helps clients feel responsible for solving their own problems.
- It lets you know whether you are on target with your presentation.
- It builds agreement one step at a time.
- It clarifies any misunderstanding by either party.
- It helps lead to a logical and successful close—a conclusion to implement.
- It provides opportunities to deal with client concerns and objections before asking the client to implement a recommendation.

The simplest and most effective way to keep your client involved is to ask questions throughout the presentation. Use questions to help your client express his or her feelings and to confirm that he or she understands what you are saying. For example, after explaining asset allocation to your client, you could ask, "What would an asset allocation that is consistent with your tolerance for risk taking mean to you?" This will reveal not only if the client understands the concept of asset allocation but also how he or she feels about it.

Insist That All Decision Makers Are Present

If applicable, both spouses should be present at the meetings. Experienced advisors know they need to have all decision makers present for a positive outcome.

Remember That Presentations Involve Hypothetical Projections

Client presentations normally involve preparing and presenting illustrations of the projected performance of financial products that are proposed to meet the plan recommendations. This may involve illustrations of life insurance, disability income or long-term care insurance, annuities, mutual funds, equity investments, and so on. Presentation projections are normally produced with financial planning software.

Presenting Recommendations Summary
Before making your actual presentation, be sure to do the following:
• Script the presentation (written) and then outline it (as a guide to the actual presentation).
• Prepare and review standard presentation materials for a typical client.
• Deliver the standard presentation to at least two different people who will offer feedback.
• Summarize your observations, including an assessment of your client's current situation, needs, desired changes, and goals.
• Summarize each recommendation's benefits and possible shortcomings as they specifically address your client's needs and goals.
• Practice handling anticipated questions and objections and explaining more difficult to understand recommendations. Avoid reading directly from the outline or prepared presentation materials; also avoid jargon or using concepts that your client may not understand without an adequate explanation.
• Include opportunities to involve the client, where he or she can express his or her views, ask questions, and provide feedback on his or her understanding and acceptance of the recommendation.
• Include opportunities to ask questions to confirm the client's position such as "How does that sound to you?" or "Could this help your situation?"
• Be prepared to summarize with questions such as "Has everything been addressed?" or "Do you have any further questions about this?"
• Assuming all issues are resolved, be ready to ask the client to implement the recommendation. Confirm the next action steps at the conclusion of the presentation.

There are a few guidelines to keep in mind to present these projections in an ethical and realistic manner. It is important to stress that projections are only that—hypothetical projections—and actual performance will vary from these projections in almost all cases. All projections are based on assumptions about the future that will invariably change over time. It is nearly impossible to expect that actual future financial results and life events will develop exactly as shown in the financial plan. This is not a fault of the plan but simply a fact of the uncertainties of life. It is important to stress with your client that annual reviews are the mechanism to adjust for changes in the environment and in the client's personal life. These assumptions and projections simply serve as the framework from which adjustments will be made as time goes on.

Illustrations and projections are tools to assist you in explaining the intangible, abstract, and in many cases highly complex and sophisticated concept of financial planning. It is essential to keep in mind, and to communicate to your client that what is projected will most likely not happen.

Financial Planning Presentation Example

The following is a sample presentation of a financial plan.

Financial Plan for Barb Dwyer

Goals

Risk Management

Life Insurance—You own $650,000 of life insurance protection, and our analysis reveals that this amount is adequate for now.

Disability Income Insurance—You are interested in increasing your coverage and the analysis reveals that you have an additional protection need.

Property and Liability—You are concerned about liability exposure, and an umbrella liability policy will provide a large amount of additional protection at a reasonable cost.

Investment Planning

Education Funding—It appears you are falling short in providing funds to educate your children and that this is a priority area for you.

Risk Tolerance—You are a moderate risk taker and we will have to recommend investments that you are comfortable with. You admit you are not too knowledgeable in investing but would be willing to risk a small amount of your funds.

Retirement Planning

You want to retire at age 62 and you are 45 years old today. You indicate you would like to plan to live on 80 percent of your income in today's dollars. This would be 80 percent of $100,000, or $80,000.

Recommendations

Risk Management

- The analysis determined that you need another $1,000 a month of disability income insurance. This amount would bring you up to 75 percent of your current income.
- You need to purchase a $1 million personal umbrella liability policy. I can get a quote for you on this from my associate who is licensed in this area of insurance.
- Your should update your beneficiary designations.
- You should consider long-term care insurance coverage.
- You should review your homeowners policy and increase your limits.

Investment Planning

- Education planning is one of your most important objectives. We have determined that you will need to save an additional $300 per month to achieve that objective for your 10-year-old son. We will review the analysis in detail. You should consider purchasing a Sec. 529 plan.
- You should increase your investment in mutual funds.

Retirement Planning

- You wish to retire at age 62. As you know, there are many questions today about the future solvency of Social Security and private company pension plans. We will need to be conservative here, especially in light of your risk tolerance.
- You will need to increase your contribution to your 401(k) plan considerably. Our analysis shows that you will need to raise your monthly contribution by $535. That may create a conflict with contributing to your college fund, so we will need to discuss this issue in greater depth.
- You will need to increase your rate of return by 2 percent or your monthly deposits by $100, or a combination of both.

CHAPTER REVIEW

Key Terms and Concepts are explained in the Glossary. Answers to the Review Questions and Self-Test Questions are found in the back of the book in the Answers to Questions section.

Key Terms and Concepts

client goals	recommendations
identification of concerns and problems	feature
planning assumptions	benefit

Review Questions

6-1. Describe the basic format for and process involved in developing a personal financial plan.

6-2. What 13 factors should you address in developing a personal financial plan?

6-3. List the steps in the preparation of the financial plan presentation.

6-4. Broadly speaking, how should the financial plan be presented to your client?

6-5. List the four techniques you can use to enhance the effectiveness of your presentation.

6-6. Explain the differences between features and benefits and why this is important to the presentation of the personal financial plan.

Self-Test Questions

Instructions: Read the chapter first, then answer the following questions to test your knowledge. There are 10 questions; circle the correct answer, then check your answers with the answer key in the back of the book.

7. Financial planning recommendations should be consistent with the

(A) client's goals, needs, and priorities
(B) quantitative information given to the client
(C) personal and financial planning assumptions you establish
(D) analysis and evaluation of the client's future situation

8. One of the recommended ways to fill the retirement income gap for your client is to

    (A) increase the amount of money being saved and invested each month at the current assumed rate of return
    (B) increase the inflation assumption being used in the calculation of the amount of retirement income needed
    (C) earn a lower rate of return on the current contribution level of savings and investment
    (D) reduce the number of years your client expects to be alive during retirement

9. Which of the following statements concerning the development of estate planning recommendations is correct?

    (A) Even if you lack the requisite estate knowledge, you should develop strategies for your clients.
    (B) Only nonfinancial vehicles can solve the estate problems uncovered when analyzing your client's information.
    (C) Life insurance is the only product that can be used to simultaneously create an estate and help provide for its conservation.
    (D) When owned by a person or entity other than the insured, life insurance can be used to pay estate taxes but will increase the taxable estate.

10. Which of the following statements concerning the plan presentation is (are) correct?

    I. In presenting the plan, summarize your observations about the current plan's inability to accomplish your client's objectives.
    II. During the presentation, outline the recommendations that you propose to meet the client's needs and goals.

    (A) I only
    (B) II only
    (C) Both I and II
    (D) Neither I nor II

11. Keeping your client involved in the plan presentation accomplishes which of the following?

    I. It helps clarify any misunderstanding between you and your client.
    II. It provides opportunities to deal with objections before asking the client to implement your recommendation.

    (A) I only
    (B) II only
    (C) Both I and II
    (D) Neither I nor II

12. Which of the following statements concerning insurance planning and risk management solutions for your client's financial plan is (are) correct?

    I. Catastrophic risks should be insured against even when the probability of loss is slight. Most solutions require the purchase of individual, group, or association insurance products.
    II. Small risks should generally be insured against even when the probability of the occurrence of loss is high.

    (A) I only
    (B) II only
    (C) Both I and II
    (D) Neither I nor II

READ THE FOLLOWING DIRECTIONS BEFORE CONTINUING

The questions below differ from the preceding questions in that they all contain the word EXCEPT. So you understand fully the basis used in selecting each answer, be sure to read each question carefully.

---

13. All the following are reasons for keeping your client involved in the presentation EXCEPT

    (A) It helps you stay on target with your presentation.
    (B) It builds agreement one step at a time.
    (C) It lets you close much faster than otherwise would be possible.
    (D) It helps your client feel responsible for solving his or her own problems.

14. All the following statements concerning employee benefits planning are correct EXCEPT

    (A) Employee benefits can have a direct effect on developing recommendations for the other major areas of financial planning.
    (B) Recommendations developed for the other major areas of planning can have a direct effect on employee benefits planning.
    (C) The client's existing benefits should be organized to show employer and employee contributions to benefits within each planning area.
    (D) Including a summary of recommended changes to employee benefits is optional in developing the financial plan.

15. All the following statements concerning the content of personal financial plans are correct EXCEPT

    (A) They should address the current status of all the major planning areas.
    (B) They should be based on planning assumptions determined by the clients.
    (C) They should be structured around strategies to achieve the clients' goals.
    (D) They should be based on goals set by the clients.

16. All the following are acceptable income tax-saving techniques EXCEPT

    (A) using deductions and credits when available
    (B) shifting the tax burden to others who are in lower brackets
    (C) taking returns as ordinary income rather than long-term capital gains
    (D) postponing or deferring income taxation

7

Implementing and Servicing the Plan

Learning Objectives

An understanding of the material in this chapter should enable the student to

7-1. Explain the implementation of the financial plan.

7-2. Describe the financial advisor's responsibilities in plan implementation.

7-3. Explain the advisor's use of and relationship with a team of professional advisors.

7-4. Explain the advisor's role in monitoring the financial plan.

7-5. Identify what should be monitored in a financial plan.

7-6. List the objectives of servicing the plan.

7-7. Identify the key components of servicing the plan.

The first part of this chapter focuses on implementing the plan, step 7 of the selling/planning process. To implement the plan, the advisor must respond to client concerns, points of resistance, and objections if they arise; obtain the client's approval to take action on the plan recommendations; work with other advisors if necessary; and finally put the plan into effect. The second part of the chapter discusses the advisor's ongoing role in servicing the plan once it has been implemented. Servicing the plan is step 8, the final step of the selling/planning process.

IMPLEMENTING THE PLAN

Implementing the plan is in many ways the most important step of the selling/planning process. It involves giving birth to the recommendations that you presented in the action plan discussed in the previous chapter. Without implementation of the plan, your clients are no better off for having worked with you than they were before they met you. In fact, they may be worse off. Before they met you, they may not have realized the extent of their financial problems, let alone what to do about them. Now they know what their financial shortcomings are and may feel disturbed or even overwhelmed about what they have to do to overcome them and/or to achieve their goals. In other words, without implementation, the best recommendations will fail and the client will not realize his or her goals.

To be an effective financial advisor, you must be able to motivate clients to implement your plan recommendations. Although your clients clearly recognize that they are under no obligation to adopt your plan recommendations, they must also recognize that for them to derive any benefits from your recommendations, they must implement them in a timely manner. As an advisor, you have a moral and professional obligation to assist your clients in implementing your recommendations once they decide to take action and adopt them.

The approach to financial planning that has been our focus throughout this book is sequential multiple-purpose financial planning. It has been described as a series of multiple-purpose financial planning consultations that take place over a period of years. Some advisors even refer to this approach as a less pure form of comprehensive financial planning because the ultimate goal is for the client to have a comprehensive financial plan in place after the final multiple-purpose planning meeting.[18] Other advisors point out that in order for financial planning to be true to the process, it never ends. There is no final discussion because the last step in the process requires you to service the plan. This calls for an ongoing advisor-client relationship in which you periodically review your client's situation and adjust the plan, if needed, as the client progresses through the stages of his or her financial life cycle.

client-focused selling

Client-Focused Selling and Plan Implementation

The sale of financial products and/or services by advisors who are true professionals is client focused. *Client-focused selling* is a sales philosophy that rejects high pressure and hard-sell methods and supports the counselor model of an advisor, which is deeply embedded within the selling/planning process. Client-focused selling emphasizes helping clients by providing solutions to their financial problems and assisting them in achieving their goals. Advisors who embrace the selling/planning process are, in reality, practicing client-focused selling. They approach clients with a willingness to listen carefully because clients can best provide the information regarding their own financial problems and goals. To this end, advisors should keep clients focused on articulating their financial problems and goals so they can help advisors to develop plans to solve those problems and achieve those goals.

However, if an advisor is unable to convince his or her client to take action and implement the plan, applying pressure is not the answer. What is necessary is more specific communication about what the client needs and what the advisor has to offer. By asking open-ended questions like "Where do we go from here?" "How should we proceed?" or "What do you see as our next step?" the advisor is reaching out to the client and asking the client what he or she needs to move the process forward so the plan can be implemented. Because the selling/planning process is client focused, it requires the advisor and client to work together.

18. As you may recall, the pure form of comprehensive financial planning occurs when the financial advisor (and his or her team of specialists) completes a comprehensive plan for the client all at one meeting or, more realistically, at several meetings that take place over a relatively short period of time.

Motivating the Client to Take Action

People need help in managing their personal finances to achieve their financial goals. Many people seem to realize that they would benefit from the professional help you have to offer; with greater knowledge about financial planning, many others would reach the same conclusion. The problem is that they fail to take action. A major part of your challenge as a financial advisor is to help people overcome this obstacle by teaching them about financial planning and motivating them to use this knowledge to take control of their finances.

Merely giving financial advice, no matter how solid the foundation on which it is based, does not constitute financial planning. A financial plan is useful to your client only if the client puts it into action. Therefore, part of your responsibility as an advisor is to motivate your client to take action and authorize the plan to be implemented.

Preparing for the Implementation Meeting

To prepare for the implementation meeting (which often is part of the same meeting in which you present the plan), review the recommendations you are making. Analyze each recommendation and be ready to discuss its benefits and drawbacks with your client. This will give your client the information he or she needs to decide which recommendations are best.

Mentally walk through your meeting presentation, anticipating all client concerns, points of resistance, and objections that may arise. This will sharpen your focus on the pros and cons of each recommendation. Be sure to have any materials you wish to show your client ready for the meeting. Review these materials so that everything is fresh in your mind. Finally, check your briefcase to be sure that all materials you need for the meeting are there.

Conducting the Implementation Meeting

Implementation means carrying the selling/planning process to its natural conclusion by putting the whole plan or some of its selected components into action. As an advisor, you must know when and how to ask the questions that motivate clients to go forward. Remember, it is a matter of commitment for clients to accept your recommendations. You need to be skilled at asking them to proceed, avoiding any perception that you are acting primarily for your own benefit.

If you have completed all the previous steps of the selling/planning process with honesty and thoroughness, your clients should accept the implementation step as both a professional and logical result of their adopting your plan recommendations. Way back in the initial meeting, you introduced yourself to your client, explained your products and services, defined the nature of the advisor-client relationship, established rapport and credibility, and reached a preliminary consensus regarding the work you would do together. Your client must have accepted this foundation or the relationship would have ended well before now. Your client made a commitment to continue the process and engage in fact finding, and you assisted your client in establishing and prioritizing goals. You discussed resources to apply to the plan and obtained agreement on the goals to address. Your client made a commitment again when he or she signed the agreement letter. Next, you developed several recommendations to solve your client's financial problems and/or achieve his or her financial goals. With this sequence of events as the backdrop, the implementation meeting should culminate in your client's taking action.

A large part of the implementation meeting involves you and your client reviewing the plan recommendations to make sure that he or she understands them. After a thorough review, your client must choose those recommendations that he or she wishes to implement. This approach makes your client a participant in the process, enabling your client to reach decisions about his or her life and family, while receiving your support and advice. Your client may adopt some recommendations immediately and postpone others or set them aside for further consideration and clarification. You should review any recommendations other advisors developed as part of the plan in draft form so you can determine if there are any misunderstandings about the recommendations and/or the planning goals they address.

After your client chooses those recommendations that he or she wishes to implement, you both must agree on the implementation responsibilities. As an advisor, your implementation responsibilities may include, but are not limited to, the following:

- identifying activities necessary for implementation
- determining the division of activities between you and the client
- referring the client to other professionals if necessary
- coordinating duties and information with other professionals
- sharing information as authorized
- selecting and securing appropriate products and/or services

Agreeing to a plan of action is just the first step in implementing a financial plan. There is still plenty of work to make sure your client actually implements the plan. You may implement a single-purpose or multiple-purpose financial plan entirely for your client if it is limited in scope and complexity. For other plans, however, you will likely need additional professional expertise. Financial planning often requires the coordinated efforts of a number of professionals. No one person can be expected to have expertise in all the component parts of a comprehensive plan. For example, legal instruments such as wills and trusts may need to be drafted, both life and property/liability insurance policies may have to be purchased, and/or investment securities may need to be acquired. Part of your responsibility as your client's advisor is to motivate and assist him or her in completing each of the steps necessary for full plan implementation.

The execution of an action plan is not usually a task that is accomplished quickly. Many times, you or other professionals will need to research various issues to determine what techniques are available, to understand how they operate, and to uncover possible constraints that may affect their use. Moreover, as an advisor you must select products and/or services that are consistent with your client's goals and priorities. You must use your professional judgment to select the products and/or services that are in your client's best interest. Although there may be several products and/or services suitable for achieving your client's goals, you should discuss the strengths and weaknesses of each with your client, explaining why it is either well suited or poorly suited to his or her situation. You should state your recommendation of choice for achieving a particular goal and why you feel that your client should adopt it.

Although you have made your recommendations based on your best professional judgment, do not expect your client to accept them on faith. Part of your challenge as an advisor is to teach your clients how to make informed decisions, however limited they may be.

If your client accepts the plan, it is time to begin to implement it. Implementation requires that all the necessary documents be drafted, agreements signed, and products purchased. This may take a considerable amount of time. Implementation, in fact, is an ongoing process that never really ends. While servicing the plan, you may determine that several changes are needed, and these changes, too, will have to be implemented.

Disclose Conflicts of Interest

If you have not already done so in previous meetings with your client, it is imperative that you set aside time in the implementation meeting to disclose any situations that may involve a personal conflict of interest. Conflicts of interest are situations in which you use the influence of your position as an advisor to benefit yourself at the expense of your client. An area of potential danger is self-interested advice, where you advise your client to purchase a financial product only because you would benefit. For example, if you recommend the wrong kind of insurance or an unsuitable investment just because you stand to receive a large commission, you are violating your fiduciary duty to your client. This is especially significant where you are receiving both a fee for advice and a commission for a sale. A breach of fiduciary duty may exist if you fail to inform your client of the potential conflict of interest. In other words, if there are conflicts of interest or any other items such as sources of compensation or material relationships with other professionals that you have not previously disclosed (in the disclosure statement or when they first appeared), you should disclose them now before proceeding with implementation of the plan.

Identify Obstacles Confronting the Client

As an advisor, you will encounter situations where clients hesitate to take action and implement plan recommendations. In fact, there are many households that have neither the discipline nor the proper motivation to seize control of their financial destinies. Although the reasons for this state of affairs are many and varied, perhaps they can all be categorized to fit into one of the following:

- the natural human tendency to procrastinate. Delaying the task of establishing a financial plan may result from a hectic lifestyle, the seeming enormity of the task of getting finances under control, and the belief that there is still plenty of time to prepare for achieving financial goals.
- living up to or beyond current income. This is a common tendency of many people. The pressure in households to overspend for current consumption is enormous, and many families have no funds left with which to implement plans to achieve future goals.
- consumers' lack of financial knowledge. Although in recent years there has undoubtedly been some growth in people's financial sophistication, there is still widespread ignorance about how to formulate financial goals and evaluate all the strategies that might be used to achieve them.

Ask Checking Questions

checking questions

You may want to stop at appropriate points in the presentation and/or implementation meetings to elicit feedback from your client by asking a few *checking questions.* These help you verify what your client is thinking and feeling about your plan recommendations. You can use either open-ended or closed-ended questions for this purpose, although closed-ended questions prevent your client from exploring thoughts, ideas, and feelings, and therefore you should use them with the utmost caution.

Here are a few examples of (open-ended and closed-ended) checking questions:

- Is what I am saying making sense?
- Can you see where we are headed with this line of reasoning?
- What do you think about these recommendations so far?
- Did the point I just made raise an issue? (This works well as a response to a frown or facial expression that demonstrates a reaction other than understanding or agreement.)
- Wouldn't you agree? (This is one of the most powerful questions you could pose regarding your recommendations. It asks your client to make a judgment about what you have said. By asking this and similar checking questions like "Isn't that right?" and "Is that the way you see it?" and "Does that coincide with your thinking?" you continually keep pace with your client and help your client stay on track with your recommendations.)
- Just suppose this wasn't a concern, then would there be any other reason why we couldn't put this plan into effect today? (This checking question is designed to find out what your client's true objection is. Once you know it, you can handle it.)
- What interests you most about this plan?
- Do you think that adopting this plan will enable you to achieve your goals?

Welcome Your Client's Objections
Expect and welcome objections. Some advisors say the worst appointment they can imagine is one without objections. The client who sits straight-faced in complete silence is impossible to communicate with. You need the feedback of your client's opinions; be sure he or she does not let you down. Encourage your client to give you feedback regarding your ideas and recommendations.

Using checking questions throughout the presentation and implementation meetings can help you get feedback from your client regarding each plan recommendation. This feedback gives you valuable information about what your client wants from and likes about your plan recommendations. The use of these questions can also ease your client into taking action when you request that the plan be implemented. In fact, if you have asked several checking questions during the course of the implementation meeting, you should be able to convince your client to implement the plan by summarizing his or her responses to the questions and then asking him or her to take action.

Look for Approval Signals

approval signals

Approval signals are signs that your client is interested in something you are saying or presenting to him or her. They may be expressed verbally or nonverbally. They are like "green" traffic lights that tell you to proceed without hesitation. If the signal from your client is like a "yellow" or "red" light, you should continue with caution or stop and ask open-ended questions to see what is causing your client's concern. If the signal is "green," your client is responding positively, and you should confirm that with a checking question. Speaking up and participating in the conversation with you is a verbal approval signal. The following statements by the client are also examples of verbal approval signals:

- I feel good about including that in the plan.
- I see what you mean.
- I appreciate the thoroughness of your presentation.

Some examples of nonverbal approval signals are

- leaning forward
- listening attentively
- making good eye contact
- nodding and showing appreciation

Approval signals and checking questions go hand in hand. If you observe an approval signal, ask a checking question to confirm the observation.

Support the Decision to Take Action

One of your greatest challenges in your relationship with clients is in plan implementation. Clients often approach decisions that cost them money with anxiety and mixed emotions. You have probably felt this when you have made an important buying decision. You ask yourself, "Is this the right decision?" "Can I afford it?" "Should I spend this much money?" "Are there better alternatives that are just as effective but less expensive to implement?" Many clients who feel confused and unsure regularly look to their advisors for help in making up their minds.

If your client asks you, "How much will this plan cost me?" he or she may be looking for an excuse or a justification not to spend the money. Do not let this line of questioning intimidate you. It may indicate that your client has mixed emotions based on confusion and uncertainty. It does not necessarily mean that price alone is the final determinant in his or her decision. Reassure your client that implementing the plan is the right decision and that it will help solve his or her financial problems and/or achieve his or her financial goals.

Remember that the goal of plan implementation really started with the first meeting when your objective was to establish credibility with your client as quickly as possible. Although plan implementation is thought of as the culmination of the selling/planning process, every step along the way is a critical part of the process that leads to your client's decision to take action and implement the plan.

Ask for Commitment to the Plan

At times your client may want to procrastinate and not deal with important financial issues. Although high-pressure tactics and hard-sell techniques are not part of the client-focused selling/planning process and are ultimately counterproductive, you may sometimes need to exert a small amount of pressure on your client. As stated earlier in this chapter, your role as an advisor is to motivate your client to take action and implement the plan. If you find a small amount of pressure is necessary, the following techniques can help you.

assumed or implied consent

Assumed or Implied Consent. With this technique, the decision to take action and implement the plan is assumed or implied; it is not the result of your client's telling you to begin the implementation process. Many clients simply need a gentle nudge to start the implementation process, and you can provide this nudge by beginning the process for them. If your client does not approve of your actions, he or she will state an objection and you will know where you stand.

This technique is considered by many advisors to be the most powerful one because it concludes the process without being forceful. It allows the implementation decision to happen easily, with gentle persuasion, with finesse, but never with aggressive force. Some advisors feel that every implementation decision should begin with an assumed or implied consent.

Alternative Choice. This is a variation on the implied consent technique. Instead of asking your client to say yes or no to a recommendation, present two or three alternatives and ask him or her to select one. You assume that your client's choice of the alternative implies consent. You should be able to use this technique in most client situations because there are almost always alternatives from which to choose, each having advantages and disadvantages.

Silence. When you use this technique, do not speak again after you ask your client to take action. Wait in silence until your client reacts. Deal with his or her reaction to you and your idea—your call to action.

Do not lose the impact of this technique by reacting to yourself. Remain perfectly silent, watching your client's face. Smile. Take a deep breath and let it out slowly. This is a critical moment. Wait for your client's response. The answer will tell you if he or she has agreed to your recommendations or not.

Direct Question. Perhaps the most straightforward technique is to ask your client if he or she has decided to implement your plan recommendations. Simply say, "Are you ready to start this plan?" or "Isn't this plan right for you?" or ask any other direct question that gets to the heart of the matter. Simply waiting for your client to take action may result in his or her procrastination. If this happens, plan implementation will not begin soon, if at all. You need to make it clear that now is the time to act, so give him or her a gentle nudge. Other examples of direct questions that you can ask to accomplish this are as follows:

- Do you have enough information to make a decision, or would you like to review anything we have discussed?
- What would you like the next step to be?
- If you don't have any other questions, can we begin to implement the plan?
- Since you seem positive about this plan, why don't we take the next step?
- Do you have any questions, or are you ready to take the next step?

It is a good idea to review some direct questions before the implementation meeting. Write down the questions you might ask your client and practice asking them. This way, you can ask them with confidence and conviction. It is easier for your client to say no to you if you are unprepared.

Why Question. Asking the why question shifts the pressure back to your client. This technique enables you to regain control of the meeting and/or go on the offense. However, a word of caution is in order when you ask why questions. They carry a connotation of implied disapproval, thus forcing your client to justify or defend his or her thoughts, ideas, or actions. Furthermore, you do not want to get into a debate with your client. Therefore, it is generally better to avoid why questions unless there is a valid reason for asking one and no other type of question will suffice. Consequently, if you need to ask one, actively listen to your client's response and determine if you are dealing with an excuse or an objection. In any event, you should use the why question sincerely, though sparingly, and not as a challenge to your client's position.

Ben Franklin Balance Sheet. Benjamin Franklin supposedly used this technique when faced with difficult decisions. Have your client draw a "T" on a piece of paper and write "pro" on the left side of the "T" and "con" on the right side. Under "pro," your client should list all the reasons favoring the decision; under "con" he or she should list the reasons opposed to the decision. After identifying all the reasons both pro and con, your client should weigh each one and, if possible, rank it in terms of its importance. By identifying the reasons, writing them down, and ranking them, the decision should become easier.

As your client's advisor, you can help him or her work through this process, but you should be cautious not to manipulate or bias the results. If you try to influence your client by encouraging him or her to list more positive reasons than negative ones, you may jeopardize both your credibility and your client's trust. Do not debate the con reasons with your client. In an advisor-client relationship, your status as an advisor depends on your client's trust.

Similar Situation. This technique involves telling your client about a situation similar to his or hers, so the client can reflect on the possible consequences of taking or not taking action. A story about the outcome of a person in a similar situation can be powerful.

Telling specific emotional stories (that is, something bad happened because someone did not take action, or something good happened because someone did) is often all you need to communicate the idea. The primary requirement is to be honest and tell only true stories, whether they are your own experiences or not. Just remember, however, that some people may view this technique as manipulative and high pressure, so be careful not to summon a fearful response from your client.

Call for Action
(Client's name), as we have determined, you want to be able to (restate the goals). I think you will agree with me that you cannot reach these goals unless you make some changes. Because the changes I recommended to you will allow you to attain your goals, am I correct in assuming that you would be interested in implementing them?

The "Let Me Think it Over" Response

Your client's saying, "Let me think it over," thus delaying the implementation decision, is a common response. Often, what your client really means is "goodbye." You must determine if your client's response is a genuine need to think over what you have recommended or simply an excuse to end the implementation process or delay making a decision.

Procrastination is a normal human reaction to making an important decision to spend money, which can be traumatic for clients. They are tense, uneasy, and afraid of making the wrong decision. You should recognize that most clients have an interest in implementing your recommendations; otherwise, they would give you an outright rejection. Answering all your clients' questions may not really get to the core of their concerns if they are stalling for time.

Procrastination is natural. Nevertheless, you need to work through your clients' excuses and move toward motivating them to act. The following example is one way to respond to a client who says, "Let me think it over."

Example

"That's fine. Obviously you wouldn't take your time to think this over unless you were really interested, would you? So, may I assume that you will give it very careful consideration? Just to clarify my thinking, what aspect of the plan do you want to think over? Is it the expense? The benefits it provides?"

If your client says, "The whole thing," try to narrow it down to some specific aspect(s), because most likely it is only one or a few specific aspects that your client needs to think over.

Try to get your client to take action now or, if that is not possible, at least to indicate when he or she will make a decision. If additional information or consultation with other advisors is needed, be sure to provide it on a timely basis. At this point, you are walking a fine line between trying to motivate your client with a gentle nudge to act now and being seen as exerting more than a small amount of pressure on the client. If your client postpones making a decision and you are able to get another appointment with him or her, review what you discussed in the previous meeting but do not ask if the client has thought it over—this might simply invite another postponement.

Many of your clients' initial objections and/or concerns are just delaying tactics—excuses not to make a decision. They are reflexive responses to preserve their freedom and control of the situation and to prevent you from altering their agenda. Other objections and/or concerns may be automatic responses, defensive comebacks, or knee-jerk reactions. These responses are more about "don't ask me to deal with something until I'm ready" than real responses to an action request. They give your clients an opportunity to equalize the situation and take the initiative in pursuit of their goals.

To effectively deal with the "I want to think it over response" (objection), you need to understand where this response is coming from. There are five primary sources:

1. For some reason, your client wants to think about it.
2. Your client is concerned about the cost and is unsure of the plan's value.
3. Your client is a procrastinator or is analytical and never makes a fast decision.
4. Your client has no interest in implementing your plan and wants you to go away.
5. Your client needs someone else's input to make a decision.

Addressing these sources in reverse order, you should have encountered reason number 5 early on in the process when you asked your client "Besides you, who else will be involved in making the final decision?" If number 4 is the reason, you will need to determine if it is worth your effort to attempt to gain the client's interest. If it is not worth your effort, you should comply with the client's wishes and go away. If number 3 is the reason and you push too hard, the reason becomes number 4. With respect to reason number 2, if cost is your client's concern, you will need to review the benefits of implementing the plan. You can do this by having your client state the benefits he or she perceives from implementing the plan. In this way, you can try to build momentum for your client to make a decision now.

Another Way to Handle Objections

Some advisors say that the best way to handle objections is not to get any. This is easier said than done. However, any advisor who listens carefully during fact finding can reduce the number of objections that his or her clients raise later. If your client has told you that money is a problem, bring it up immediately in your presentation meeting. "(Client), this is what we can do. . . ."

Keep track of the types of objections your client makes; they may show a pattern that you can correct. Thus, if you are able to anticipate your client's objections, you can bring them up before your client does.

In the case of reason number 1, you need to determine exactly what your client wants to think about. This requires that you ask him or her the right question and listen actively to his or her answer. Acknowledge the answer by saying, "I understand how you feel. If I were in your shoes, I'd probably want to think about it myself" (displaying empathy). However, because the only person who can truly overcome your client's concern is your client, you need to get him or her to talk openly. By discussing the concern with you, your client may be able to resolve it and remove the final barrier. If this happens, your client should be ready, willing, and able to take action and implement your plan recommendations now.

Dealing with Concerns and Resistance

If your client resists implementing your plan recommendations, you should listen to what he or she is saying. Do not try to out-talk your client; you will not hear what he or she is saying while you are talking. Besides, no one likes to be interrupted or feel that he or she is not being listened to, so encourage your client to tell you what he or she is thinking and stop trying to figure out what you are going to say in response. If you are busy formulating your response, you are not listening to your client.

Each step in the selling/planning process supports the one that follows. Therefore, by the time you reach the implementation stage you should know enough about your client's personal and financial situation to respond directly and honestly to his or her concerns. Confirm your understanding of your client's concerns by restating or rephrasing them. By doing this, you are letting your client know not only that you received his or her message correctly but also that you care about his or her concerns.

Allow your client to respond to your version of what he or she said. If your client's response is on target, you can begin to work with him or her to resolve the issues that are causing his or her concerns. You can best do this by taking a straightforward, honest, problem-solving approach. Answer your client's questions while focusing on his or her concerns. Remember that your client is making an important decision. Comments, concerns, and questions are a natural and expected part of this process. In answering your client's questions, you are showing that you understand his or her concerns, explaining how your recommendations meet those concerns, and demonstrating the urgency of acting now to put your recommendations in force.

Acknowledge, Clarify, Resolve

Another common technique for responding to a client's concern is to take the following steps:

- **Acknowledge** your client's concern. You should validate your client's thoughts and feelings on the topic. If you do not acknowledge your client's concern, but instead take it head-on and try to resolve it without his or her input, all you will succeed in doing is putting more distance between you and your client. Responses such as "I understand how you feel" or "I can appreciate that" show your client that you are listening and care about what he or she is saying.
- **Clarify** your client's concern. It is necessary that you clarify a vague or negative response from your client before you can effectively resolve it. Clarify any statement that is too global, vague, or overreaching by saying something like "Could you please explain that?" or "I don't understand what you mean." Make sure your client clearly states his or her concern. Do not attempt to address the concern if it is not clear and specific. It is impossible to resolve your client's concern unless you know exactly what it is. Sometimes even your client may not be completely sure what his or her concern is. In these cases, it is your job to help your client work through the issues that are disturbing him or her.

  Often, you may think you know what your client is saying only to find out later that he or she meant something altogether different. To avoid this problem, rephrase your client's concern and repeat it to him or her in the form of a question. This will help to ensure that both you and your client are on the same page.
- **Resolve** your client's concern. Once you understand your client's concern, you can help to resolve it by making appropriate recommendations. After you have satisfied your client's concern and he or she agrees there are no other obstacles, there is no reason why he or she cannot take action and implement the plan.

Think of your client's expression of resistance as an issue that needs greater clarification. Do not allow objections to stress you out. Overcoming objections is about staying relaxed and listening. Develop a system for handling them that you can easily follow.

"Feel, Felt, Found"

Yet another method for responding to a client's concern is the "feel, felt, found" technique. This technique, similar to the acknowledge, clarify, resolve technique, can be expressed as follows:

- "I understand exactly how you **feel**."
- "Many of my clients **felt** the same way."
- "Until they **found** that . . .(state an appropriate response, such as "my recommendations were a good solution for their concerns").

This technique begins by using the acknowledgement step of the technique above to empathize with your client. Empathetic acknowledgment puts your client at ease by telling him or her that this is a feeling many people have. Feeling like you are part of the crowd is reassuring to most people. It is reassuring to know that others felt the same way when faced with similar concerns. It also neutralizes the situation and gives you an opportunity to address your client's concerns by explaining how your recommendations will alleviate them.

The Cost of Waiting

cost of waiting

A strategy designed to emphasize the advantage of implementing a financial plan now versus sometime in the future is called the cost of waiting. It is based on demonstrating the effects of the time value of money. It shows that the sooner your client starts saving, the less he or she will have to save to achieve his or her financial goals. Because of the magic of compound interest, if your client starts saving at a young enough age, he or she will be able to accumulate more money by putting less money aside than if he or she starts saving at an older age.

Example

As illustrated in the table, if a client deposits $2,000 a year in an account for 9 years starting at age 22 (and ending at age 30), he or she will have deposited a total of $18,000. If this account earns 8 percent compound annual interest, it will be worth $398,807 when the client is age 65.

If a second client deposits $2,000 a year in an account for 35 years starting at age 31 (and ending at age 65), he or she will have deposited a total of $70,000. Again, if the account earns 8 percent compound annual interest, it will be worth $372,204 when the second client is age 65. Even though the first client deposits $52,000 less than the second client, he or she will have accumulated $26,603 more at age 65.

Table 7-1
Starting Early Pays Off

Age	Deposits Made Early	Age	Deposits Made Early	Age	Deposits Made Late	Age	Deposits Made Late
22	$2,000	44	—	22	—	44	$2,000
23	$2,000	45	—	23	—	45	$2,000
24	$2,000	46	—	24	—	46	$2,000
25	$2,000	47	—	25	—	47	$2,000
26	$2,000	48	—	26	—	48	$2,000
27	$2,000	49	—	27	—	49	$2,000
28	$2,000	50	—	28	—	50	$2,000
29	$2,000	51	—	29	—	51	$2,000
30	$2,000	52	—	30	—	52	$2,000
31	—	53	—	31	$2,000	53	$2,000
32	—	54	—	32	$2,000	54	$2,000
33	—	55	—	33	$2,000	55	$2,000
34	—	56	—	34	$2,000	56	$2,000
45	—	57	—	45	$2,000	57	$2,000
56	—	58	—	56	$2,000	58	$2,000
57	—	59	—	57	$2,000	59	$2,000
38	—	60	—	38	$2,000	60	$2,000
39	—	61	—	39	$2,000	61	$2,000
40	—	62	—	40	$2,000	62	$2,000
41	—	63	—	41	$2,000	63	$2,000
42	—	64	—	42	$2,000	64	$2,000
43	—	65	—	43	$2,000	65	$2,000
Total amount deposited: $18,000				**Total amount deposited: $70,000**			
Total amount available at age 65: $398,807				**Total amount available at age 65: $372,204**			

This table illustrates two savings programs with annual deposits of $2,000. One client starts to make deposits at age 22 and stops making them at age 30. The other client starts making deposits at age 31 and stops making them at age 65. The numbers prove a point. If your client starts saving at a young age, he or she can accumulate more money with a smaller total amount deposited than if he or she starts savings at an older age. These figures are based on a hypothetical rate of return of 8 percent. Of course, not every client can deposit $2,000 each year beginning at age 22. However, any amount saved at an early age will make a dramatic difference later. The longer your client's dollars are allowed to grow and compound, the more he or she will accumulate. The message: Your client needs to put time on his or her side.

Selling versus Helping

To perform financial planning and counseling successfully, you must look not at how you will benefit from working with your client but at how your client can benefit from you. Measure your success by how much you help your clients. Focus on how your recommendations can make your client's life better, instead of focusing on how your client can make your life better.

Managing Implementation

Financial matters are becoming increasingly complex. Tax laws are frequently changing, new investment vehicles are being developed, and insurance coverages are continually evolving. Add to this the already complex subject matter of each of the major planning areas, and it is easy to see why even the most experienced advisors encounter client situations beyond their individual expertise. Because of the wide range of expertise required to develop comprehensive financial plans or, for that matter, multiple-purpose financial plans, you should have arrangements with other advisors that allow you to draw upon their expertise if needed. In those cases when the expertise of other advisors is needed, your role is to coordinate their plan development efforts and to contribute expertise in your own field of specialization. Once your plan recommendations are agreed to by the client, your role shifts to making sure the plan is implemented.

Relationships With Other Advisors

strategic alliances

Strategic alliances are relationships you develop with other professionals that enable you to have at your disposal an established complementary team of advisors to whom to refer a client when his or her financial situation requires their expertise and services. These relationships are typically mutually beneficial; clients receive services from professionals who are competent, cooperative, and trusted, and the alliance provides additional clients for each advisor.

If your client already has a relationship with another advisor, it may be unrealistic to expect the client to make a decision without first consulting that advisor. If this other advisor is important to your client, that advisor should be involved in the planning process as soon as it is apparent that he or she will influence your client's decision.

Strategic Alliances
Strategic alliances are relationships you develop with other advisors who provide you with an established complementary team of professionals. You can refer clients to these other advisors when your clients' financial situations require expertise and services beyond your capabilities. These relationships are mutually beneficial because they make the expertise and services of each team member available to the clients of the other team members.

Referrals

When referring your client to other professionals, you should indicate the basis for the referral. Any referral to an advisor should be done with the client's permission and within the scope of the planning activities required by the plan recommendations. You have an obligation to keep client information confidential. By the same token, other professionals have the same obligation. Therefore, you should not expect them to share or discuss information with you about the client's financial planning matters without his or her permission.

You also need to be careful when referring a client to a specialist because, in many states, the person who makes the referral can be as liable as the specialist if the specialist makes an error. You can give your client a listing of specialists and suggest that he or she pick one from it, without recommending a particular specialist. Before using a specialist for your clients or including this person on your team of specialists, perform due diligence and know the specialist's areas of competence and expertise. Ask all specialists about their experience, how long they have been in the business, how many cases similar to ones you might refer to them that they have worked on, and whether they have malpractice or errors and omissions insurance.

Mentoring
Joint work with specialists who are more knowledgeable in other disciplines is an excellent way to gain experience, learn from experts, and provide competent, professional advice to clients who have needs and concerns outside of your area of expertise. These specialists can serve as mentors to you to enhance your practice. They can be from your own financial services area or from another area.

Besides you, your financial team should include specialists in investments, insurance (life, health, and property liability), estate planning, retirement planning, and income taxation. These specialists' professions may be attorney, accountant, insurance agent, investment broker, and banker. The financial advisor is usually regarded as the quarterback who leads the advisory team, taking responsibility for implementing and coordinating the specialties of the various advisors.

Once the plan recommendations have been agreed upon, your client may take all or part of the plan to other advisors, or to those who work with you for implementation. It is a good idea to prepare an additional copy of the plan for the client to give to these advisors so that they can review the recommendations directly rather than depending on the client to explain them, thus reducing the chances of misunderstanding. In addition, a well-prepared and documented plan is less likely to meet with resistance from your client's existing advisors.

SERVICING THE PLAN

Once the financial plan is implemented, the relationship between you and your client should be an ongoing one because your client's personal and financial situation will change over time as he or she moves through the stages of the financial life cycle. Financial planning is a never-ending process, which takes us to the eighth and final step in the selling/planning process—servicing the plan. By servicing the plan we mean two things. The first is monitoring the progress of the plan. The second is delivering promised services to the client. Together, they work to satisfy your present clientele and provide you with referrals, a key ingredient in building a practice.

Monitoring the Plan

After the plan is implemented, you should periodically review its progress in solving your client's problems and/or achieving your client's goals. Normally, this would require you to meet with your client once each year. However, if the circumstances warrant it or your client requests it, you may have to meet more frequently.

If the periodic plan review shows that satisfactory progress is being made toward solving the client's financial problems and/or achieving the client's financial goals, no action needs to be taken. If, however, performance is unacceptable and/or there has been a significant change in your client's personal and/or financial situation, his or her goals, or in the economic and financial environment, you should repeat the selling/planning process, beginning with step 3. (It will most likely take less time and effort to update the plan than it took to develop the original one.)

Defining Responsibilities

Together, the financial advisor and client must define their monitoring responsibilities. As the advisor, you must clarify and delineate your role in the monitoring process. You and your client may have different perceptions and expectations about monitoring responsibilities.

When monitoring is included within the scope of the advisor/client relationship, the advisor should identify which monitoring activities are appropriate. He or she should define and communicate those activities that he or she is able and willing to provide. The advisor and client must agree on the extent, frequency, and duration of the monitoring activities, if any, to be provided by the advisor. The scope of the advisor/client relationship, as originally defined, may need to be modified.

Monitoring responsibilities may include but are not limited to

- identifying changes in conditions that would affect the current plan and existing recommendations
- obtaining information from the client to determine changes in personal circumstances
- reviewing work done by other professionals or providers
- evaluating the client's progress toward achieving financial goals

The monitoring process may reveal the need to re-initiate steps 3 through 8 of the selling/planning process. Changing needs and circumstances often make this necessary.

Changing Needs and Circumstances

The monitoring process requires that we look at the components of the financial plan. To refresh our memories and focus this discussion, we will list them again here. The monitoring process parallels the development and presentation of the financial plan, because the major planning areas represent the planning process, the resulting recommendations, and the implementation actions. Consequently, you and your client need to review all of the following plan components to evaluate performance, discern changes in needs or circumstances, and determine continued suitability:

1. client's goals
2. identification of concerns and problems
3. planning assumptions
4. financial position statement
5. cash flow statement
6. insurance planning and risk management
7. employee benefits planning
8. specialized financial planning goals
9. investment planning
10. income tax planning
11. retirement planning
12. estate planning
13. recommendations

The following discussion outlines some of the points that a periodic review should monitor.

1. Client's Goals

- Determine whether or not your client's goals or priorities changed since the last review.
- Find out if your client has any new goals or objectives.
- Establish whether the time frames or amounts needed to achieve goals have changed.

2. Identification of Concerns and Problems

- Identify any changes in your client's personal concerns or problems or in the personal concerns or problems of any people associated with your client that may affect the financial plan.
- List any changes in financial concerns and problems that affect the client.
- Determine whether any of these concerns or problems affect the direction or specifics of the financial plan as it was developed.

3. Planning Assumptions

- Review any assumptions used in developing the plan, such as inflation rate, investment growth rate, personal and family plans, and so on, to see if there have been changes that require adjustment in the plan.
- Be aware that many of the concepts on which plan recommendations are based may be affected by tax law changes. Monitoring can ensure that the plan will perform as anticipated; needed changes can be made. The most common areas affected are income tax planning, retirement planning, and estate planning. You need to keep abreast of developments in tax law not only because lack of knowledge may pose a threat to both you and your clients but also because tax law changes can provide new planning opportunities.

4. Financial Position Statement

- Note any changes in your client's net worth.
- Determine if your client's assets and liabilities have changed appreciably.

5. Cash Flow Statement

- Determine if your client's cash flows in or out have changed in a significant way.
- Also ascertain if his or her sources or uses of funds have changed in any important way.

6. Insurance Planning and Risk Management

There is an ongoing need to review your client's risk exposures and to ensure that the amount of coverage is adequate to protect your client's financial needs. A change in coverage could occur for various reasons, including

- additional needs uncovered but not insured—for example, a need for more life insurance, liability, or disability income protection that the original needs analysis revealed but that your client could not afford to cover at the time

- additional needs due to life events—for example, a need for additional life insurance, disability income insurance, or homeowners coverage triggered by marriage, the birth or adoption of a child, a divorce, a promotion, or the purchase of a new home
- increase in the amount of current needs—for example, a need for plan adjustment if inflation spikes for several years, salary and expenses increase, or the original amount was underestimated
- changing or decreasing needs due to life events—for example, a diminished financial need if your client's children are all out of the house, coupled with a greater need for long-term care insurance
- changes in property and liability risks—for example, a need to update coverages if there have been any changes in property ownership, business interest, or motor vehicle ownership

7. Employee Benefits Planning

- Identify any changes in your client's employee benefits since your last review.
- Discover whether there have been any changes in your client's, his or her spouse's, or family employment or dependency status that may require a review of employee benefit options.

8. Specialized Financial Planning Goals

- Determine if your client has any special needs, such as education goals or caring for a special needs individual, about which you were unaware.
- Find out if there are any charitable giving objectives that you and your client need to address.

9. Investment Planning

- Review your client's investment portfolio to see if it has changed in any substantial way since the last review.
- Determine whether it is necessary to reevaluate your client's asset allocation or rebalance his or her portfolio.
- Reexamine your client's risk tolerance, investment objectives, and liquidity needs, and evaluate his investments as to their suitability and diversification.

10. Income Tax Planning

- Review the client's income tax situation to determine if there is any need to examine more tax-efficient methods regarding income.

- Make sure you are up-to-date on any new laws that may affect your client and that you know how prior law provisions might benefit him or her.

11. Retirement Planning

- Calculate whether the retirement accumulation needs are on pace for the projected retirement date.
- Determine whether the assumptions regarding your client's retirement need revision.
- Identify any changes in your client's circumstances regarding retirement.

12. Estate Planning

- Find out if there have been any changes in the client's situation that would warrant a review of the estate plan.
- Determine whether provisions in your client's estate plan regarding control, disposition, and taxation need to be updated.

13. Recommendations

- Review recommendations to see if the plan is effectively addressing your client's identified goals and objectives and his or her and concerns and problems.
- Ascertain whether or not each aspect of the plan is progressing in an appropriate manner.
- Reevaluate any recommendations that were not implemented to see if it is appropriate to implement or change them now.

Conducting the Periodic Review

Monitoring is integral to the ultimate success of a financial plan and to your ongoing relationship with your client. A properly developed and implemented financial plan should be monitored and revised to ensure that it is doing what your client intends for it to do. Therefore, monitoring should be part of the basic service package you offer to all planning clients. There are several key points to consider in conducting a periodic review.

Set the Expectation. Build your client's expectations regarding the value of your service throughout the selling/planning process. This is one important benefit that can distinguish you from your competitors. Lay the groundwork for your service commitment early in the planning process—in the first interview when you explain how you work and the services you offer. Position yourself as someone who helps your clients uncover their financial goals, create and implement a plan to achieve them, and then continues to monitor their plans and make adjustments as needed. Demonstrating your commitment to service by regularly monitoring your client's plan shows your client the importance you place on helping your client realize his or her financial planning goals.

Set the Appointment at the Implementation Meeting. Your goal after step 7 of the selling/planning process (implement the plan) should be to schedule a meeting with your client for step 8 of the process (service the plan). Remember, however, that different clients have different needs and expectations of the process, so never try to force your client into a predetermined timetable. Rather, determine a mutually agreeable schedule for reviews.

Resistance to Reviews

Your client may display resistance to scheduling a periodic plan review, or even to hearing from you. Responses such as "Why are you calling me?" or "I'm not ready to buy anything else right now" can be disappointing and unnerving when you are sincerely trying to provide good service for its own sake. The reason for this kind of response is that your client perceives that your sole motive is to earn another fee or commission. You must change your client's perception.

You should contact your client at least annually to touch base and say hi, to wish him or her a happy birthday or anniversary, or for some other reason that is unrelated to the financial services business. Some successful advisors who do this refuse to discuss business at all, even if the client raises the topic, so that the message is that this is clearly a relationship call, not a business call.

Your client's perception should be that you care about him or her as a person; your contact is sincere. As you plan your calendar, see that every one of your clients has contacts from you to build the relationship and show you care.

Of course, besides social contacts, there should be periodic reviews to make sure your client's plan is still on target and reaching his or her goals. Therefore, each year, you should schedule two kinds of visits to your clients—one geared toward service and the other toward strengthening your personal relationship with him or her.

Keep Good Records. Record keeping is extremely important. Keeping good records will shorten your preparation time for the review and enable you to present a more professional image. It will boost your confidence, which will, in turn, enhance your credibility with clients. Make sure that your records contain information about the client's family such as his or her children's names and ages, the names and ages of any grandchildren, and so forth. Some advisors record the client's personal interests to help them reestablish rapport and further the advisor-client relationship. You should also update any information on your client's investment performance, insurance values, retirement plan values, and the like. In addition, you should maintain records of insurance coverage renewal dates and keep copies of your client's recent income tax returns.

Moreover, financial services companies today have file inspection and maintenance requirements as a routine part of the compliance process. In all cases, follow your company procedures, which may require that you keep records of such things as the following:

- fact-finding forms
- written notes describing the basic events and discussions with the client
- contact log with dates and topics discussed
- copies of quotes or illustrations
- copies of applications and related materials
- copies of correspondence with the client

Generally, no original documents or blank signed documents should be in a file. Original documents should be submitted to the company; blank signed documents are strictly forbidden.

Confirm the Appointment. Call to confirm the appointment. You can let your client know at this time what documentation he or she may need to bring to the review. If you are making changes to the client's disability income plan, for example, you will need him or her to bring a W-2 form and a Social Security benefits statements to the meeting. You may also need to ask your client to bring other information such as tax returns, investment performance statements, and employee benefit and retirement plan annual statements to the review.

If you have not set the appointment in advance, you can treat this as you would a prospecting call, except, of course, that you already have a relationship with the client. Some advisors send a preapproach letter to remind the client of the review and monitoring service that they offer and then follow up with a phone call to set a date for the appointment.

Prepare for the Appointment. If you have kept good records, preparing for the appointment will be much easier. Refresh your memory by reviewing the fact finder. Reexamine the information you gathered on your client's attitudes, values, and goals. Review plan recommendations: Which were implemented? Which were not? Why were they not implemented? Put together a game plan of areas where you feel client needs may exist.

Conduct the Review. Review the client's financial plan, and evaluate the plan's progress in relation to your client's goals. If appropriate, recalculate needs and note any shortfalls. Using a client-focused selling approach, inquire about any changes in your client's current or future personal or financial situation. Listen carefully and note any planning opportunities. Implement any plan changes and/or arrange for any necessary follow-up appointments.

Ask for Referrals. A periodic review is a perfect opportunity to ask your client if he and she knows anyone who shares the same values and goals. There is a high probability that your client trusts you; otherwise, your client would not have agreed to have you review his or her financial plan. Therefore, it is likely that your client realizes your value and the value in what you do and will want to refer you to his or her family and friends. You do not become referable by selling a product. You become referable by providing excellent and dedicated service that demonstrates your trustworthiness, professionalism, and competence.

Checklist for Financial Planning Review

You can use the financial planning checklist on the next page to review the many areas of the financial plan in order to monitor progress toward your client's goals.

Figure 7–1 Checklist For Financial Planning Review

Change in	Has Occurred	Is Expected
1. Marital status		
Marriage	☐	☐
Separation	☐	☐
Divorce	☐	☐
Remarriage	☐	☐
2. Number of dependents		
Increase	☐	☐
Decrease	☐	☐
3. Health status		
Client	☐	☐
Spouse	☐	☐
Dependent	☐	☐
4. Residence	☐	☐
5. Occupation		
Client	☐	☐
Spouse	☐	☐
Dependent	☐	☐
6. Family financial status		
Borrowing	☐	☐
Lending	☐	☐
Gifts over $1,000 received	☐	☐
Gifts over $1,000 made	☐	☐
Purchase of property	☐	☐
Sale of property	☐	☐
Investments	☐	☐
Inheritance	☐	☐
Deferred income	☐	☐
Pension plan	☐	☐
Tax-deferred annuity	☐	☐
Dependent's income	☐	☐
7. Sources of income		
As employee	☐	☐
From self-employment	☐	☐
From tax-exempt employer	☐	☐
From investments	☐	☐
Inventions, patents, copyrights	☐	☐
Hobbies, avocations	☐	☐
8. Income tax status		
From single to joint return	☐	☐
From joint to single return	☐	☐
Capital gains	☐	☐
Capital losses	☐	☐
Charitable contributions	☐	☐
Unreimbursed casualty loss	☐	☐
Sick pay received	☐	☐
Unreimbursed medical expenses	☐	☐
Tax-impact investment(s)	☐	☐
9. Property ownership		
Purchase in joint ownership	☐	☐
Purchase, client owned	☐	☐
Purchase, spouse owned	☐	☐
Purchase, dependent owned	☐	☐
Transfer to joint ownership	☐	☐
Transfer to client	☐	☐
Transfer to spouse	☐	☐
Transfer to dependent	☐	☐
Transfer to trustee	☐	☐
10. Liabilities		
Leases executed	☐	☐
Mortgage increase	☐	☐
Lawsuit against	☐	☐
Judgment against	☐	☐
Unsecured borrowing	☐	☐
Cosigning of notes	☐	☐
11. Business ownership		
New business formation	☐	☐
Interest purchase	☐	☐
Sale of interest	☐	☐
Transfer of interest	☐	☐
Reorganization among owners	☐	☐
Liquidation	☐	☐
Change of carrier	☐	☐
Termination or lapse	☐	☐
Surrender	☐	☐
12. Legal document status		
Change in last will	☐	☐
Change in trust	☐	☐
Buy-sell agreement	☐	☐
Agreement to defer income	☐	☐
Advance medical directives	☐	☐
Powers of attorney	☐	☐
Nuptial agreements	☐	☐
13. Insurance status		
Life insurance	☐	☐
Health insurance	☐	☐
Long-term care insurance	☐	☐
Disability income insurance	☐	☐
Annuities	☐	☐
Group insurance	☐	☐
Other employer plan	☐	☐
Property insurance	☐	☐
Liability insurance	☐	☐
Change of plan	☐	☐
14. Attitudes toward others		
In family	☐	☐
In business	☐	☐
In accepting professional advice	☐	☐
15. Interest in		
Idea previously discussed	☐	☐
Plans seen or heard about	☐	☐

Servicing the Plan

Servicing the plan is the key to long-term success for all parties involved in the selling/planning process. It presents a number of responsibilities for the advisor, as well as a number of opportunities. It is the key to client building by strengthening the advisor-client relationship and developing the client as a source of continued business opportunities.

Objectives of Service

Your success at client building through service will accomplish these objectives:

- maintain/increase level of client business
- generate referrals
- lower expenses

Maintain/Increase Level of Client Business. A strong client relationship can distinguish you from your competitors. In today's competitive climate, providing good service is a necessary defensive strategy. Maintaining a high profile with clients through your service activities and other contacts will help them feel loyal to you and committed to the business you have done together. A client who feels no such loyalty or commitment is not likely to think twice about accepting the next attractive proposal that comes along. Your practice will suffer unless you take steps to keep your clients in the fold.

Relationship building is fostered by regular client contact—both business contacts and contacts that show your client that you care about him or her personally. Exemplary service is based on timely reviews and prompt response to client requests. Changes in the financial plan should be made to conform to changes in the client's situation.

Retaining clients can have a huge effect on your bottom line. Research shows that profits can grow by 100 percent from a 10 percent increase in retention. Overall U.S. businesses typically lose from 10 to 30 percent of their customers each year; yet most of those customers would not have left if they had received more responsive attitudes and a passion to make things right. How can you sustain significant growth when you have to replace 20 percent of your clients each year just to stay even? The cost to acquire a new client is five to seven times higher than the cost to retain a current one. It is cheaper and easier to keep your existing clients than it is to win new ones. Here's how:

- Relate one-to-one. Remember that all business is personal and no relationship is static.
- Reinforce relationships. Seize every opportunity to learn about your client's needs, realities, and dreams. Reinforce the reasons why your client chose you. People do business with people, not companies.
- Exceed expectations. Meeting clients' expectations is the price of admission into today's market. To generate clients' commitment and loyalty, you must strive to exceed their expectations. Expect to lose

business if you deliver merely what the client needs, because he or she probably has many avenues from which to get it. Instead, discover and deliver what your clients' want. If you do not add value, you are no longer necessary.

- Be an expert listener. Demonstrate your knowledge and gain the clients' loyalty by asking the right questions and listening closely to the answers.
- Differentiate yourself. Do not compete on price, but rather on the benefits and the value of your expertise and that of your products and/or services. Differentiate your services in clients' minds by adding choice, specialization, research, responsiveness, technology, and knowledge. Most clients do not buy on price alone. Your job is to offer the best overall value, not the lowest price. Educate clients about the value of your financial planning products and/or services.
- Establish strategic alliances. Look to specialists, other clients and even competitors for joint opportunities that will add value for your client.
- Become referable. To get referrals, you need to be referable. That means you must offer more than a product. You have to offer a process and, even better, a memorable experience. You have to earn your clients' trust.

Generate Referrals. Client building is also a result of a well-developed selling/planning process. Experienced advisors will tell you that as much as 75 percent of their new business comes from existing clients or referrals provided by these clients. Remember that people have a tendency to refer those like themselves. Thus, if your client values your products and services, there is a good chance that the people your client refers will value them as well.

Lower Expenses. Another consideration in your practice is the cost of developing clients. What are your marketing and sales costs to find one qualified client and go through a multiple-interview sales process? Factor them all in: the cost of the lead, sales promotion, telephone, secretarial and mail expenses, other overhead expenses, automobile costs, meals, computer time, and presentation materials. Multiply that total by the number of clients it takes to make a sale. By being able to sell primarily to clients, you will be able to lower your sales and marketing costs.

Proactive Service

Most successful advisors have an automated system to assure regular contact and communication with clients and potential clients on a year-round basis. Each advisor's system can be tailored to his or her individual personality, clientele, budget, manner of doing business, and a variety of other factors. There is no right or wrong way to accomplish this, but all advisors should devote some attention to this broad area of client communications. Remember, though, that there is no satisfactory substitute for face-to-face contact.

The purpose of the communication pieces described below is to demonstrate your knowledge and to keep clients informed of current events in the financial world. Keeping your client aware of possible financial needs and how your services and products can address those needs is just another aspect of providing service.

Brochure. A brochure can be a simple black-and-white résumé, or it can be a beautiful multicolored piece printed on high-quality paper. Many companies provide a template that you can complete with your own personal information that meets compliance standards. There are many business services and printers who also do this type of work, for a wide range of charges. In addition to your business card, you should have a descriptive piece that promotes your expertise, products, services, education, business philosophy, community involvement, personal background, and any other information that helps build your relationship with clients. The brochure can be used as part of an initial contact, a handout at your first meeting, or at any point in your developing advisor-client relationship.

Product branding has received a lot of attention in recent years. A brochure can help communicate your personal image. Here, you can market yourself, rather than your products or services. You can explain your mission or value statement. You can focus on a benefit of working with you—for example, helping a client plan for a financially secure retirement or finance children's college educations.

Newsletter. Newsletters are a good way to stay in contact with your clients, keep your name in front of them, and provide interesting items of financial interest that may also serve as prospecting ideas. Some companies provide subscription services that offer newsletter options on a continuum from full-service, direct delivery of newsletters to clients, to do-it-yourself delivery. There are also numerous industry services and associations that offer newsletters. Or you can write your own. The newsletter should include your name, address, phone number, and e-mail address; photos are optional.

Greeting Card. Sending a birthday card to your client is a way of saying, "I'm thinking of you and I care about you." Sending calendars and greeting cards at the holidays also help you to stand out. In addition, they bring your name in front of the client. Many advisors use other gifts like pocket diaries, pen sets, and so on to keep in contact with clients. Consider sending Thanksgiving (or some other holiday) cards as a way to differentiate yourself.

A handwritten note is an especially "high-touch" technique in this day of technology and rapid-paced life. It is such a rare occasion that we receive a note that someone has written by hand that it creates a special impression.

Keeping in touch by various methods is an important part of the relationship-building process. Moreover, newsletters, birthday or anniversary phone calls, and periodic mailings about topics of interest continue to put you in front of the client, build prestige, and enhance your practice.

Customers versus Clients

All clients are customers, but not all customers are clients. Clients are people who have bought from you, but they are also people with whom you have developed, or are in the process of developing, a strong interpersonal business relationship. Because of this relationship, the client will look to you for direction if he or she has any problems in areas relevant to your expertise. You are a trusted advisor. An advisor finds comfort in knowing that he or she can call or visit the client for a private meeting at almost any time.

The goal of the selling/planning process is to turn prospects into clients. The intermediate result is the creation of a financial plan owner, where the client has purchased a product but may not yet have "bought" you—that is, you have not yet been able to establish a firm advisor-client relationship. Each step in the selling/planning process contributes to the creation of a client. You cannot have a client without creating a customer, and you cannot have a customer unless you execute an effective financial selling/planning process. In step 8, service the plan, a customer becomes a client—someone who looks to you for advice, consistently follows your suggestions and recommendations, and enthusiastically recommends your services to others. He or she believes in you and the products and services you provide. To build a lifetime career on client relationships, it is essential for you to convert customers to clients.

Developing advisor-client relationships is mutually beneficial. The advisor recognizes the importance of the relationship as a building block in the development of a long-term career. The client knows the advisor will deliver promised services and will be available when he or she is needed.

In client building, the sale is not the end; it is the beginning. The advisor must fulfill all of the promises of service made during the selling/planning process and at implementation. Client expectations and advisor promises should be exceeded, if possible. There should be frequent contacts and information updates. This entails more work than servicing a customer, but it is more rewarding. As clients grow, the advisor grows, and more doors are opened through referrals and the development of clients' other financial needs and objectives.

Your clients are your most valuable business inventory. You can achieve total success in the financial services business when your established client base and the referrals and repeat business they provide enable you to reach your personal goals as you help clients achieve theirs. What can you do to cement that advisor-client relationship and protect your customers from the competition as you develop them into clients? The following four tips should help:

- Try to broaden the product portfolio you can offer to customers, and develop strategic alliances with other producers and professionals who offer products and services you do not.

- Broaden your areas of expertise. Pursue professional designations, add additional licenses, and generally improve your expertise and skills that make you more valuable to clients.
- Be sure to inform your clients and prospective clients frequently, through mail and personal contact, about your total product and service portfolio.
- Go back to every client, at least for his or her periodic plan review, and explain your total portfolio, particularly in areas you may not have previously addressed.

CHAPTER REVIEW

Key Terms and Concepts are explained in the Glossary. Answers to the Review Questions and Self-Test Questions are found in the back of the book in the Answers to Questions section.

Key Terms and Concepts

client-focused selling	assumed or implied consent
checking questions	cost of waiting
approval signals	strategic alliances

Review Questions

7-1. Explain what is involved in the implementation of a financial plan.

7-2. Describe the financial advisor's role in plan implementation.

7-3. Describe what a financial planning team is, and explain why one may be created.

7-4. Explain strategic alliances and how they can benefit the advisor and the client.

7-5. Explain why approval signals are like green traffic lights for the advisor.

7-6. Identify techniques the advisor can use to exert a small amount of pressure on the client to get him or her to take action and implement the plan.

7-7. Describe techniques the advisor can use to answer client concerns.

7-8. Describe the advisor's responsibilities in monitoring the financial plan.

7-9. Describe advisor activities in servicing the financial plan.

Self-Test Questions

Instructions: Read the chapter first, then answer the following questions to test your knowledge. There are 10 questions; circle the correct answer, then check your answers with the answer key in the back of the book.

10. The first step in dealing with client resistance is to

    (A) listen to what the client has to say
    (B) tell the client to think it over
    (C) consider it an approval signal
    (D) ignore it because it probably is an excuse

11. A sales idea comparing the cost and values of a plan started today and one to start 5 or 10 years from now is an example of

    (A) premium maximization
    (B) the cost of waiting
    (C) assumed consent
    (D) the alternate choice

12. "What interests you most about this proposal?" is an example of what type of question?

    (A) progressive "yes"
    (B) closed-ended
    (C) disturbing
    (D) checking

13. A situation where an advisor uses his or her influence with a client to benefit his or her own interest, usually at the expense of the client, is known as a(n)

    (A) fiduciary relationship
    (B) strategic alliance
    (C) conflict of interest
    (D) assumed consent

14. Which of the following is a type of verbal approval signal?

    (A) making good eye contact
    (B) commenting on the thoroughness of the presentation
    (C) listening attentively
    (D) nodding and showing appreciation

15. Which of the following statements concerning the advisor-client relationship is (are) correct?

    I. An effective advisor must be able to motivate the client to implement the plan.
    II. A client is obligated to implement the plan through the advisor who developed it.

    (A) I only
    (B) II only
    (C) Both I and II
    (D) Neither I nor II

16. Which of the following statements concerning techniques that motivate the client to take action and implement the plan is (are) correct?

    I. Under the implied consent technique, the advisor assumes the client is ready to implement the plan and begins the process for the client.
    II. Under the direct question technique, the advisor asks the client if he or she is ready to implement the plan.

    (A) I only
    (B) II only
    (C) Both I and II
    (D) Neither I nor II

17. Which of the following statements concerning the Ben Franklin balance sheet technique for motivating the client to take action and implement the plan is (are) correct?

    I. The client should weigh each pro and each con reason and rank it in terms of its importance.
    II. The advisor should encourage the client to list more pro reasons than con reasons.

    (A) I only
    (B) II only
    (C) Both I and II
    (D) Neither I nor II

READ THE FOLLOWING DIRECTIONS BEFORE CONTINUING

The questions below differ from the preceding questions in that they all contain the word EXCEPT. So you understand fully the basis used in selecting each answer, be sure to read each question carefully.

18. All the following are objectives of client service EXCEPT

    (A) To maintain/increase the level of client business
    (B) To discredit the competition
    (C) To lower expenses
    (D) To generate referrals to new clients

19. Implementation responsibilities of the advisor may include all the following EXCEPT

    (A) To identify activities necessary for implementation
    (B) To refer the client to other professionals if necessary
    (C) To select and secure appropriate products and/or services
    (D) To evaluate client problems and/or goals

8

College Funding and the Regulation of Advisors

Learning Objectives

An understanding of the material in this chapter should enable the student to

8-1. Identify the two funding requirements associated with financing a college education.

8-2. Describe the process for calculating the resources required to fund a college education.

8-3. List and describe the characteristics of the types of investments typically considered for use in funding a college education.

8-4. Describe the various tax deductions, tax credits, and penalty waivers that are available to encourage saving for college education.

8-5. Explain how a college student's financial need is determined for purposes of obtaining federal student aid.

8-6. Describe the characteristics of the various types of federal student aid available to college students.

8-7. Explain how the role of the Financial Industry Regulatory Authority (FINRA) relates to the SEC's oversight of registered representatives and investment advisors.

8-8. Describe the tests that determine whether a financial advisor must register with the Securities and Exchange Commission (SEC) as an investment advisor.

8-9. Describe the procedure for becoming a registered investment advisor and the types of requirements imposed on one who does register.

8-10. Explain the role of a financial advisor as a fiduciary to his or her client.

This chapter covers two basic financial planning topics—funding a college education and the regulation of financial advisors. Education funding was selected to illustrate the application of concepts covered in earlier chapters because of its importance to financial advisors in their ability to provide professional financial planning services to clients. For example, helping parents plan funding for their child's college education requires estimating future costs that increase with time due to inflation and periodic amounts of savings that decrease with time due to investment returns. Given the influence of time, inflation, and investment return on college funding, you as a financial advisor must apply several time-value-of-money concepts—the future value of a single sum, the present value of a single sum, and the present value of an annuity or an annuity due—to determine the amount your client must save periodically to accumulate the funds required to pay for the college education.

This chapter uses some of the steps in the sales/planning process to explain the concepts involved in developing an educational funding module for your client's financial plan. Let us assume that you have met with your client and through your discussions and the fact-finding process, you have determined that the top priority is college funding for your client's children. We will go through the process that you would perform with your client to determine the need and how to fund it properly.

FUNDING A COLLEGE EDUCATION

Most clients understand the need to save for college and are aware that college costs have risen at a faster pace than the consumer price index. Still, the vast majority of families accumulate far too little money for college by the enrollment date. This may be due to a variety of factors, but two common causes are (1) procrastination in establishing and following a savings plan in the case where the client survives until funds are needed to pay college expenses, and (2) failure to provide for the creation of a fund needed to pay future college costs in the case where the client dies before an adequate savings plan can be completed. Instead, most families have to cut back on living expenses, borrow money, tap into retirement assets, or seek additional employment to meet the funding need. Often, they lower their sights and target a school that is less expensive rather than the one best suited to their child's needs.

Financial advisors who can calculate college funding requirements in the event of a client's survival and recommend appropriate investment alternatives to meet those requirements, who can calculate funding requirements in the event of the client's death and recommend appropriate life insurance products, and who can explain important aspects of financial aid provide an invaluable financial planning service to their clients.

THE COST OF A COLLEGE EDUCATION

College education costs vary widely. In addition to such factors as public versus private, in-state versus out-of-state, residential versus commuter, and local versus distant, some schools are simply more expensive to operate while others may be more successful at generating gifts and endowments. The following table shows average undergraduate costs for 2008–2009 as calculated by the College Board.

These data provide some insight regarding costs, but there are two critical factors to consider. First, your client's expectation or goal may deviate substantially from "average." Perhaps one of your clients anticipates sending his or her child to a premier college with correspondingly high tuition. By contrast, another client may anticipate that the student will attend an in-state public college with particularly low costs. The point is that each case involves estimating a cost that is appropriate for your client rather than one that is average. Second, the estimated cost for a year of education today will increase by inflation in the future.

Table 8-1
Average Estimated Undergraduate Budgets: 2008–2009 (Enrollment-Weighted)

	Public Colleges (In-State) Four-Year On-Campus	Public Colleges (Out-of-State) Four-Year On-Campus
Tuition and fees	$6,585	$17,452
Books and supplies	1,077	1,077
Room and board	7,748	7,748
Transportation	1,010	1,010
Other	1,906	1,906
Total	$18,326	$29,193
	Private Colleges Four-Year On-Campus	**Public Colleges Two-Year Commuter**
Tuition and fees	$25,143	$2,402
Books and supplies	1,054	1,036
Room and board	8,989	7,341*
Transportation	807	1,380
Other	1,397	1,895
Total	$37,390	$14,054

Note: The figures are weighted by enrollment to reflect the charges incurred by the average undergraduate enrolled at each type of institution.
* Room and board costs for commuter students are average expenses for students living off campus but not with parents.

Source: *Trends in College Pricing 2008*. Copyright © 2008 by the College Board. Reproduced with permission. All rights reserved. collegeboard.com.

Education Inflation

During the past 10 years (from 1999 through 2008), inflation as measured by the consumer price index has averaged 2.8 percent per year. For the same period, inflation in published tuition and fees for 4-year private colleges has been 5.2 percent, and it has been 7.0 percent for 4-year publicly funded colleges.

Will both private and public college costs, especially those of 4-year institutions, continue to rise much more rapidly than the prices of other goods and services as they have over the past decade? Many people think they will and point to enrollment projections that indicate continuing growth in demand.

Calculating the Funding Requirement

As mentioned above, you need to show your client the amounts required to meet the education objective under two possible circumstances—your client's death and your client's survival. These two funding requirements can be stated as follows:

- the lump sum required to fund the college education if the client were to die on the date his or her plan is implemented
- the monthly savings required to fund the college education if the client survives until enrollment begins

The calculation of these two funding requirements lends itself to time-value-of-money concepts discussed in chapter 4. A worksheet that provides a good approximation of the required college funding should contain the following five inputs:

- current cost of a year of college
- education inflation rate
- number of years of college attendance
- number of years until enrollment
- investment rate of return

The following figure shows the steps to calculate the two funding requirements and presents an example. This example assumes that the current annual college cost is $25,000, the inflation rate is 5 percent, and the length of time until the child's college enrollment is 14 years. Applying the concept of determining the future value of a single sum (FVSS), the first step is to calculate the cost of each of the 4 years of the child's college education. The table below shows the calculator inputs and resulting college costs.

Most likely you have computer software that can produce these calculations, but it important for you to understand the concepts in deriving these results so that you can (1) recognize when a calculation does not make sense and is therefore inaccurate and (2) be able to explain the concepts in general terms accurately to your client.

The cost of the child's first year of college is estimated by multiplying the current annual cost of the type of college the client seeks by the FVSS factor for an education inflation rate of 5 percent (i = 5%) and 14 years until enrollment (n = 14). The cost of the first year of college, $49,497.50 is calculated as follows:

$$\text{FVSS} = \text{PVSS} \times (1 + .05)^{14}$$

$$\text{FVSS} = (\text{current annual cost of college}) \times \text{factor})$$

$$\text{FVSS} = \$25{,}000 \times 1.9799$$

$$\text{FVSS} = \$49{,}497.50$$

Figure 8–1 Funding Requirements Using Time-Value-of-Money Concepts

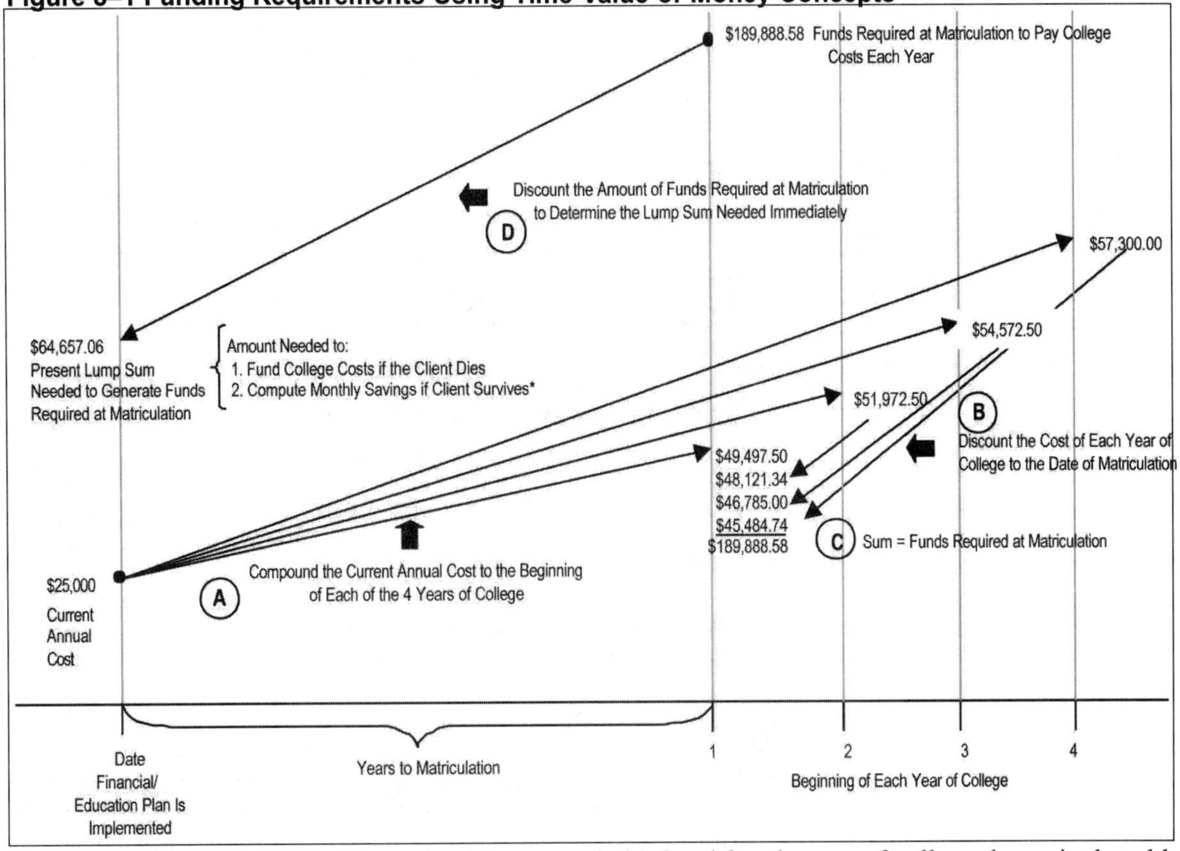

The costs of the second, third and fourth years of college shown in the table are calculated as follows using the appropriate factors where i =5% and n=15, 16, and 17 years respectively:

FVSS second year	=	$25,000 × 2.0789	=	$51,972.50
FVSS third year	=	$25,000 × 2.1829	=	$54,572.50
FVSS fourth yea	=	$25,000 × 2.2920	=	$57,300.00

The second step involves discounting the costs for each of the 4 years of college to determine their present value on the date of enrollment. This is done by computing the present value of a single sum (PVSS) for the costs of each of the 4 years of college by multiplying the FVSS for a given year by the factor, for an 8 percent investment return (i = 8%) and the number of years (n) from the date of enrollment until the beginning of that year. The present values of the costs of each of the 4 years of college on the date of enrollment are calculated as follows:

Table 8-2
Estimated College Funding Requirements for 4 Years

	Freshman	Sophomore	Junior	Senior
Years until (N)	14	15	16	17
Education inflation (I/YR)	5%	5%	5%	5%
Current college cost (PV)	$25,000.00	$25,000.00	$25,000.00	$25,000.00
Estimated cost (FV)	$49,497.50	$51,972.50	$54,572.50	$57,300.00
Note: These are four separate FV calculations.				

PVSS first year	=	$49,497.50 × 1.0000*	=	$49,497.50
PVSS second year	=	$51,972.50 × 0.9259	=	$48,121.34
PVSS third year	=	$54,572.50 × 0.8573	=	$46,785.00
PVSS fourth year	=	$57,300.00 × 0.7938	=	$45,484.74
Amount required by enrollment date to pay each year's cost as it comes due			=	$189,888.58

Note: Because the first year is the year of enrollment, n = 0 and thus the PVSS factor = 1.0000.

This step calculates the amount that must be available by the enrollment date to be able to pay each year's cost as it comes due. As shown above, this amount, $189,888.58, is the total of the present values of the costs for each of the 4 years of college as of the enrollment date.

In a final third step, the total amount of funds required as of the enrollment date, $189,888.58, is then discounted to the date the financial/education plan is implemented to determine the lump sum needed at that time to generate the $189,888.58 in 14 years, assuming an 8 percent investment return. Again, the present value factor for an 8 percent investment return (i = 8%) and 14 years (n = 14) is 0.3405. The lump sum required at the time of plan implementation is $64,657.06 ($189,888.58 × 0.3405).

This lump sum of $64,657.06 is the amount of the first of the two education funding requirements mentioned earlier—that is, it is the lump sum required to fund the college education if your client were to die on the date his or her plan is implemented. Because this sum would be needed immediately if your client were to die at the time the plan is implemented, you should ensure that the client either has an adequate amount of life insurance on his or her life or has existing savings not allocated to other planning goals to meet this need.

The lump sum of $64,657.06 also serves as the basis for calculating the amount needed to achieve the second education funding requirement—the monthly savings required to fund the college education if your client survives until enrollment begins. Assuming the monthly payments to an accumulation vehicle earning an annual 8 percent investment return are to be made at the beginning of each month, the amount of each of the 168 monthly payments (14 years × 12 months = 168 payments) is calculated by dividing the $64,657.06 present lump sum by the present value of an annuity due (PVAD) factor for i = .67% (8% ÷ 12) and n = 168.

Because factor values for i = .67% and n = 168, the amount of monthly savings must either be computed directly using a financial calculator, or the two components of the PVAD factor must be computed using a calculator. Then they must be multiplied by one another to compute the PVAD factor. Finally, they must be divided into the lump sum of $64,657.06 to obtain the desired result. The results of the latter approach are illustrated below:

PVAD = monthly payment × PVA factor × (1 + i)
PVAD factor = 100.6451 × 1.0067 = 101.3194
Amount needed to be saved at the beginning of each month =
($64,656.06 ÷ 101.3194) = $638.15

Thus, if your client saves $638.15 at the beginning of each month over the next 14 years and earns 8 percent annual interest, $189,888.58 would be available at the time of enrollment to pay the costs of college as they come due over the 4 years. Ideally, this figure is attainable. Otherwise, lowering aspirations or seeking financial aid, probably in the form of loans, is likely.

INVESTING FOR COLLEGE

The previous section explained the use of time-value-of-money concepts in calculating the college funding requirements in the event of both the client's death and the client's survival. This section focuses on the key considerations in designing an appropriate accumulation plan to achieve the college funding objective in the event the client survives until a specified future date, generally the date of enrollment.

Once you and your client have established the financial goal, you can consider the best methods of accumulation. There are many aspects to investment accumulation for college, but two are especially important. The first is selecting a portfolio of assets that is consistent with achieving the funding goal. The second is selection of investment vehicles and techniques. This latter aspect of investing considers tax effects and financial aid formulas.

Selecting a Portfolio for College Funding

To select a portfolio for college funding, it is important to understand some basic investment concepts.

The first step in investing funds for college is selection of an asset allocation consistent with your client's risk tolerance and the amount of time until the funds are needed. Asset allocation refers to the proportion of assets invested in broad asset categories, typically stocks, bonds, and money market instruments. For example, a risk-tolerant client saving for a very young child is likely to emphasize stock investments over money market instruments. A client investing the college savings for a high school junior is apt to take the opposite approach.

The second step in investing funds for college is selecting specific investments for the portfolio consistent with the asset-allocation decision. Although the portfolio's risk-reward characteristics must be consistent with the client's asset-allocation decision, the individual risk-reward characteristics of each investment will not necessarily be uniform. Indeed, standard concepts of diversification dictate that they not be uniform.

The types of investments typically considered for use in funding a college education are

- certificates of deposit (CDs)
- Series EE U.S. savings bonds
- zero coupon bonds
- baccalaureate bonds
- cash value life insurance
- common stocks
- mutual funds
- CollegeSure® CDs
- Sec. 529 plans

Certificates of deposit (CDs) from banks and other financial institutions are a common choice because they are easy to purchase, simple to understand, and can be bought in small denominations. They have a guaranteed rate of return and are federally insured, but they usually carry early withdrawal penalties. Because the income is taxable as it is received, your client has no control over the timing of the income, nor does it qualify for lower capital gains rates. Worst of all, the rate of return is low. The funds are likely to lose ground to education inflation.

modified adjusted gross income

Series EE U.S. savings bonds are considered default risk free. Because the federal income tax can be deferred until redemption, they can be placed in the name of the child and circumvent the so-called kiddie tax, which is discussed later. Another benefit is that Series EE bonds are exempt from state income tax, making them especially appealing to higher-bracket clients. Interest from these bonds is either totally or partially exempt from federal income taxation if used for tuition and fees. The tax-exempt feature phases out for joint filers with modified adjusted gross income of $104,900 to $134,900 and for single taxpayers between $69,950 and $84,950 for 2009, and it is indexed for inflation. *Modified adjusted gross income* is an intermediate calculation that is made to determine an individual's tax liability. It is derived from gross income, minus "above the line" deductions in determining adjusted gross income (AGI). The term modified means that each tax provision may have different items that are included in the AGI calculation. The downside for EE bonds, as with CDs and other fixed-income investments, is that they are a poor hedge against inflation.

Zero coupon bonds are sold at a substantial discount and pay off the face amount at maturity. This offers the advantage of locking in a return for the life of the bonds, which are usually selected so that their maturity matches the child's college years. Their disadvantages are that their price is more volatile than bonds that pay interest currently, your client must report interest income each year even though he or she actually receives none, and zeros are a poor inflation hedge.

Baccalaureate bonds are zero coupon bonds issued by states for the purpose of accumulating funds for education. The bonds have the same characteristics as regular zeros, but their interest is exempt from federal income taxation as well as income taxation in the state of issue. The interest rate is lower to reflect the tax advantage.

Cash value life insurance offers tax deferral on earnings while the policy is in force and allows your client to package education funding with a needed death benefit. Earnings on life insurance policies are competitive with long-term fixed-income investments, and variable life insurance policies, whose returns are based on the stock market, provide an excellent inflation hedge. Clients can borrow money from the policy at moderate rates for extended periods, keeping the policy in force. As with many other investments, a premature surrender of the policy will result in loss to the client.

Common stocks represent an excellent inflation hedge because of their appreciation potential, which also takes advantage of preferential capital gains taxation. Most stocks generate income in the form of dividends. The trade-off your client makes for the possible growth is significantly greater risk of capital, especially if the time periods until the funds are needed is short. Additional disadvantages are that many clients are uncomfortable investing in individual stocks and brokerage fees that reduce the actual investment.

Mutual funds are the best avenue for most clients to invest money in the stock market for a child's college education. Your client gains safety through diversification and can select the type of mutual fund most suitable for his or her risk-taking propensity. For example, there are money market funds, government bond funds, tax-free bond funds, taxable bond funds, growth funds, and balanced funds. Clients typically place most, if not all, of their mutual fund money in a mutual fund family, a company that permits the client to move money from fund to fund. That makes it easier and less expensive to shift investments as circumstances change.

CollegeSure® CDs are federally insured up to $250,000 per depositor through December 31, 2013 and pay an interest rate that is linked to the inflation rate in college costs as measured by the College Board's cost index for 500 independent colleges. They offer maturities ranging from 3 to 22 years. These CDs are purchased in units or parts of units that reflect college costs existing at the time they are purchased. At maturity, one unit is equal to one full year's average tuition, fees, and room and board at a 4-year private college as measured by the Independent College 500 Index. The purchase price per unit exceeds the value of the Independent College 500 Index on the date of deposit. The College Savings Bank provided the following example and the illustration in Figure 8-2 showing how these CDs work.

Example

If today's cost for 10 percent of one year of private college is $3,720, Mary Client would deposit $5,736 to purchase .10 units of a CollegeSure® CD for her 3-year-old child to guarantee the future cost of college in 15 years. At the CD's maturity, she would receive 10 percent of one year of whatever the average private college costs are in 15 years, no matter how high college costs rise. Over the term to maturity of each CollegeSure® CD, the annual percentage yield (APY) is not less than the college inflation rate less 3.00 percent.[19]

In the example above, the difference between the $5,736 and the $3,720 is explained by this 3.00 percent reduction in return. The future value of $3,720 compounded at 5.49 percent, the 2008 college inflation rate, annually over the next 15 years is $8,295, but the present value of $8,295 discounted at an annual rate of 2.49 percent over 15 years is a present value of $5,736. The depositor pays a 54.20 percent premium over the current cost for a unit, or fraction of a unit, to allow for the spread between the college inflation rate and the rate earned on the CollegeSure CD.

Sec. 529 plans, named for the section of the Internal Revenue Code that authorizes them, provide tax-advantaged approaches to saving for college expenses. These programs are sponsored by states or qualified educational institutions and are also called qualified tuition programs (QTPs). Available in almost all states, they can take two forms: prepaid tuition plans and savings plans.

prepaid tuition plans

Approaches vary, but *prepaid tuition plans* typically allow parents to purchase tuition credits at current prices, thus locking in a child's tuition rate years in advance of enrollment. It should be emphasized that prepaid tuition plans do not guarantee admission to college. The plan beneficiary still has to qualify for admission to the college of his or her choice. If the child does not go to college, plans generally offer refunds of the amounts paid without interest. In the event of death, disability, or the child's receiving a scholarship, most plans not only provide a refund but also pay interest (generally at a relatively low rate). Although they will not cover the same share of college costs as would be prepaid for a 4-year university or community college located in the same state as the plan, plans can often be used for private schools as well as various types of out-of-state schools.

19. The CollegeSure® CD, College Savings Bank, Princeton, NJ. Retrieved April 17, 2009, from collegesavings.com/csb/collegesure_cd.asp.

Figure 8–2 CollegeSure® CD

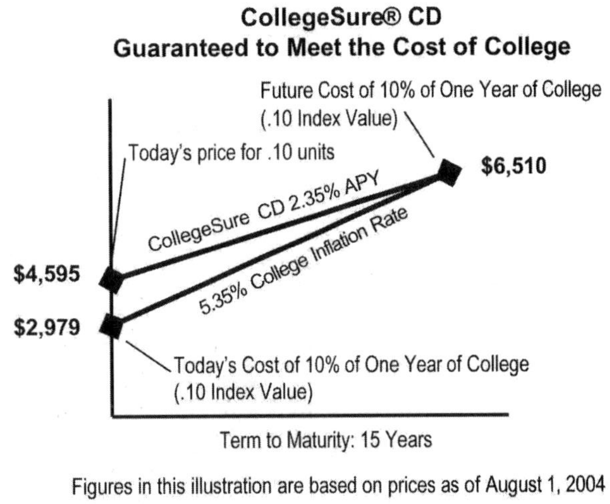

Source: About the CollegeSure® CD, College Savings Bank, Princeton, NJ. Retrieved October 21, 2004, from collegesavings.com/basics.shtml. Reprinted with permission.

Sec. 529 plans

Sec. 529 savings plans typically allow investment in mutual funds. Their returns are not tied directly to tuition inflation at a particular college, but the potential returns exceed the inflation protection offered by prepaid tuition plans.

Funds from Sec. 529 savings accounts can be applied to qualified higher education expenses, which include tuition, fees, books, supplies, and equipment required for enrollment or attendance at an eligible educational institution, as well as reasonable costs of room and board, specified by the institution, for a beneficiary who is at least a half-time student.

Benefits of Sec. 529 plans include the following:

- Earnings are tax deferred.
- Distributions are federal income tax free if the amount is no greater than the beneficiary's adjusted qualified education expenses.
- There are no income restrictions.
- Contribution limits are high.
- Proceeds can be used nationwide.
- There are estate and gift tax benefits.
- Plans are open to residents of any state.
- Initial minimum investment is low.
- Funds can be transferred from one plan to another once in every 12 months.
- Hope or Lifetime Learning credits (described later in this chapter) can be claimed in the same year as a qualified distribution from a Sec. 529 plan as long as the same expenses are not used for both benefits.

SavingforCollege.com provides reviews and rankings of Sec. 529 offerings by state, discusses other college savings vehicles, and is a ready resource for investment advisors.

Titling Accounts in the Child's Name

For many clients, saving money in an account in their child's name is a common practice. This helps them to segregate the funds and keep track of progress, and it may result in lower taxation. However, there are shortcomings to this approach. First, the kiddie tax reduces the tax advantage somewhat, although only for large amounts. Second, the child may elect to skip college and use the funds for other purposes after reaching majority. Third, financial aid formulas reduce aid availability substantially more for each dollar of the child's assets than for each dollar of the parent's assets. (A subsequent section covers this topic in detail.)

Legislative Benefits

The Taxpayer Relief Act of 1997 and subsequent legislation have contained several provisions beneficial to families saving for postsecondary education. These provisions relate to tax deductions, tax credits, and penalty waivers that were designed specifically to encourage saving.

FOCUS ON ETHICS
Assets under Management and Ethics

A potential conflict for the advisor who charges the client based on an assets-under-management model is in providing advice that allows the advisor to retain assets even if that is not in the client's best interests. The potential conflict when recommending a Sec. 529 plan to a client is a good example.

Sec. 529 college savings plans typically are not closed to nonresidents, but there may be tax or tuition reasons why your client would be better served by investing in his or her home state's offering than in another state's plan. If you recommend an out-of-state plan for compensation reasons when tax or tuition advantages exist in the home state plan, there is a problem. This has happened often enough that the Financial Industry Regulatory Authority (FINRA) has issued an Investor Alert* warning investors against investing in out-of-state plans without comparing them with in-state and other college savings alternatives.

* FINRA Investor Alert, College Savings Plans—School Yourself Before You Invest. Available online at: finra.org/Investors/ProtectYourself/InvestorAlerts/529plans/PV010756

Changes in Individual Retirement Accounts

Individuals who receive taxable distributions from IRAs before age 59½ no longer must pay a 10 percent early withdrawal tax if they use the funds for qualified education expenses. The student on whose behalf the expenses are incurred can be the taxpayer, the taxpayer's spouse, or any child or grandchild of the taxpayer or the taxpayer's spouse.

Qualified education expenses include tuition, fees, books, supplies, and equipment required for enrollment in a postsecondary education institution. Qualified higher education expenses also include room and board if the student is enrolled at least half-time. In determining the amount of the distribution that is not subject to the 10 percent additional tax, total qualified education expenses are reduced by any tax-free educational assistance such as payments from a Pell Grant or other tax-free scholarships, a tax-free distribution from a Coverdell education savings account (see below), or tax-free employer-provided educational assistance. However, qualified higher education expenses paid with an individual's earnings, a loan, a gift, an inheritance given to the student or the individual claiming the credit, or personal savings (including savings from a qualified state tuition program) are not deducted from total qualified education expenses to determine the amount not subject to the 10 percent early withdrawal tax.

Roth IRA

The *Roth IRA*, which requires after-tax contributions but allows tax-free withdrawals after age 59½, provides some benefit in college funding. First, as with other IRAs, no early withdrawal tax applies to withdrawals for qualified education expenses. Second, withdrawals may be made up to the amount of the total contribution without taxation. In effect, your client pulls those after-tax contributions back out. He or she can leave the earnings in the IRA to accumulate on a tax-free basis for retirement or withdraw the earnings for education purposes, although they will be taxed at the taxpayer's marginal rate. Tax deferral is the primary advantage of Roth IRAs, which are phased out in 2009 for individual taxpayers with modified adjusted gross income (MAGI) between $105,000 and $120,000 and for joint filers with MAGI between $166,000 and 176,000.

Coverdell education savings accounts

Coverdell education savings accounts, formerly known as education IRAs, allow donors (parents, grandparents, or anyone else) to contribute up to $2,000 per child into an education fund. However, the maximum amount that can be contributed on behalf of an individual child from all sources cannot exceed $2,000 per year. Although the contribution is not deductible, earnings are not taxed as long as the funds are used to pay elementary, secondary, or postsecondary education expenses. The availability of Coverdell education savings accounts is phased out for individual taxpayers with modified adjusted gross income of $95,000 to $110,000 and for joint filers with MAGI of $190,000 to $220,000.

Despite the tax advantages related to earnings, Coverdell education savings accounts have potential disadvantages. First, while either the Hope credit or the Lifetime Learning credit can be claimed in the same year the beneficiary takes a tax-free distribution from a Coverdell education savings account, the same expenses cannot be used for both benefits. Second, using this type of account may also limit or eliminate the amount of financial aid available to a student. Because Coverdell education savings accounts are considered to be the student's assets, which are given more weight in calculating the expected family contribution, student eligibility for financial aid will be reduced.

Tax Credits

The Taxpayer Relief Act of 1997 established two tax credits for education—the Hope scholarship credit and the Lifetime Learning credit. The following table compares key features of these two tax credits.

Hope Scholarship tax credit

The Hope Scholarship tax credit allows a tax credit of up to $1,800 per student per year for tuition and related expenses incurred during the first 2 years of postsecondary education. The credit equals 100 percent of the first $1,200 of qualified tuition and related expenses, and 50 percent of the next $1,200 of tuition and fees.

Table 8-3
Comparison of Education Tax Credits

Hope Credit	Lifetime Learning Credit
Up to $1,800 credit per eligible student	Up to $2,000 credit per return
Available only until the first 2 years of postsecondary education are completed	Available for all years of postsecondary education and for courses to acquire or improve job skills
Available **only** for 2 years per eligible student	Available for an unlimited number of years
Student must be pursuing an undergraduate degree or other recognized education credential	Student does not need to be pursuing a degree or other recognized education credential
Student must be enrolled at least half-time for at least one academic period beginning during the year	Available for one or more courses
Source: *Tax Benefits for Education*, IRS Publication 970 (for use in preparing 2008 returns)	

Lifetime Learning tax credit

The Lifetime Learning tax credit provides a credit of up to $2,000, calculated as 20 percent of the first $10,000 of tuition and other qualified education expenses.

Claiming the Hope Scholarship tax credit and the Lifetime Learning tax credit in the same year for the same student is not allowed, but clients who pay qualified expenses for more than one student can elect to claim the Hope Scholarship tax credit for one student and the Lifetime Learning tax credit for the other. (In 2009, both credits were phased out for modified adjusted gross incomes from $50,000 to $60,000 for single filers and $100,000 to $120,000 for joint filers.)

Tax Deductions

Deductibility of Interest on Education Loans

Another benefit to your client from the Taxpayer Relief Act of 1997 is that some interest on education loans is now deductible even if your client does not itemize deductions. The available deduction is a maximum of $2,500. In 2009, the deduction is subject to a phaseout for single filers between $60,000 and $75,000 of modified adjusted gross income and for joint filers between $120,000 and $150,000 of MAGI. Note that borrowing through a home equity loan is a viable alternative because these loans not only tend to carry relatively low interest rates but also in most cases, interest is deductible.

Deductibility of Higher Education Expenses

Beginning in 2004, your clients are able to deduct qualified tuition and related expenses even if they do not itemize deductions. The amount of qualified education expenses that can be taken into account in figuring the deduction is $4,000 for individual taxpayers with MAGI not more than $65,000 and joint filers whose MAGI is $130,000 or less. If MAGI is greater than $65,000 ($130,000 for joint filers) but not more than $80,000 ($160,000 for joint filers), the maximum deduction is $2,000. No deduction is permitted if the taxpayer's MAGI is larger than $80,000 ($160,000 for joint filers). There are also provisions that limit deductibility if a Hope or Lifetime Learning credit is declared and that require coordination with other education tax benefits, including U.S. savings bonds, Coverdell education savings accounts, and distributions for qualified tuition programs.

Integrating Education Planning with Retirement Planning

One way that clients can save for a child's education is to increase their 401(k) or 403(b) contribution to the maximum allowable. There are good reasons for taking this approach. First, these balances are not included in the parents' asset base in the financial aid formula, so it is easier to qualify. (However, the contribution does not reduce the parents' income in the formula.) Second, the contributions reduce taxable income, and savings accumulate on a tax-deferred basis. In many plans, your client can then borrow part of the account balance to pay for the child's education, and the interest paid will be credited to the 401(k) or 403(b) account.

In general, loans from qualified retirement plans can finance a child's education if the plan permits education loans and these requirements are met:

- The loan is amortized in substantially level payments over a period no longer than 5 years.
- The loan does not exceed half of the vested amount (with some exceptions).

- The loan does not exceed $50,000 (reduced by amounts outstanding from the prior year).

Another consideration is that many older clients reach age 59½ while their children are in college. At that point, your client can withdraw retirement plan balances without any penalty even if he or she remains with the same employer. Of course, income taxes will be due just as if money were withdrawn for retirement.

Clients sometimes find that by the time their child is in college, they have accumulated enough in their retirement plan that they can forego contributions while their child is in college. The budget allocation that was going into the retirement plan can then be used to fund some college expenses out-of-pocket.

You should discuss with clients who are already maximizing their 401(k) and Roth IRA contributions that they consider a deferred annuity. They will not be allowed a deduction and the money will not be accessible. But they can take advantage of the retirement plan as a college-funding vehicle and use the deferred annuity as a retirement supplement. When the child is in college, your client can eliminate the annuity contribution to make room in the budget for tuition payments. A cash value life insurance policy can be used in the same way with increased flexibility.

Integrating Education Planning with Estate Planning

Clients who have enough assets, and for whom estate conservation and distribution is a concern, should generally avoid giving education funds directly to their children. For example, they may already be pursuing a gifting plan in which husband and wife give $26,000 per year to their child, staying within the annual gift tax exclusion ($13,000 per individual in 2009, as indexed for inflation; $26,000 per married couple via gift splitting). Any gift for education funding will count toward the exclusion. However, because expenses paid as parental support obligations are not gifts, parents typically do not incur gift taxes for the payment of education expenses for their children through the college years. Thus, if parents pay for their child's education directly out of their own pockets, they can still make the $26,000 gift protected by the annual gift tax exclusion, thereby distributing even more of their estate tax free.

A technique that is especially useful to well-heeled grandparents who wish to help their cash-strapped children by paying their grandchildren's college tuition involves the use of the Sec. 2503(e) exclusion from taxable gifts. This unlimited exclusion provides that gifts made directly to the provider of services on behalf of the donee (in this case a grandchild) for certain education or medical expenses are not treated as taxable gifts. In the case of education expenses, the exclusion is limited to tuition payments; payments for books, meals, and lodging may be taxable gifts. The tuition payments must be made directly to educational institutions described in the charitable organization rules—that is, schools that normally have a regular faculty and curriculum and an enrolled student body regularly engaged in educational activities. This exclusion applies independently of and in addition to the annual gift tax exclusion. Thus, by paying for a grandchild's tuition expenses directly, grandparents (or other donors) can pay for a major portion of a college education while removing assets from their taxable estates without incurring gift taxation. Moreover, the annual gift tax exclusion is still available to allow an additional $26,000 (if the grandmother and grandfather split the gift) to be gifted tax free to the grandchild in the same year.

Shifting Wealth and Income

One popular tax planning strategy is the shifting of income to a taxpayer who is subject to a lower marginal rate. Since parents generally have more income than young children, investment assets are often transferred to children by parents in order to gain the benefit of lower marginal tax rates. Custodial accounts, such as those created under the Uniform Gifts to Minors Act (UGMA) or the Uniform Transfers to Minors Act (UTMA), or certain trusts can be used for this purpose.

kiddie tax

Under current tax law, however, this planning strategy is significantly curtailed. Families are prevented from shifting large amounts of unearned income to children and making the shift effective for income tax purposes. The provision that limits such income shifting is referred to as the *kiddie tax*.

The kiddie tax applies to dependent children who are either age 18 at the end of 2009 or who are full-time students over age 18 and under age 24 at the end of 2009. It also applies to children who are under age 18 regardless of their dependency status.

If a child who falls into one of these categories has unearned income above a specified amount, the excess is taxed at the highest marginal rate applicable to the child's parents for the year rather than at the child's marginal rate. The child's excess unearned income above the specified amount is called net unearned income. The specified amount is the amount of a dependent child's regular standard deduction ($950 as adjusted for inflation in 2009) plus another $950, or $1,900 for 2009. Therefore unearned income in excess of $1,900 is net unearned income and is taxed at the parents' rates for 2009. If a child does not have more than $1,900 in unearned income for 2009, the child will not be subject to the kiddie tax.

However, for students who have taxable investments in their own names or in UGMA/UTMA accounts, the kiddie tax could have an effect if those investments are used to pay college bills. In any event, children who have Sec. 529 plans in their own names will not be affected by the kiddie tax. The kiddie tax makes using either a Sec. 529 plan or a Coverdell education savings account a very attractive way to save for college because the earnings are distributed tax-free when used to pay qualified education expenses. A downside of these two savings vehicles is that the same qualified education expenses cannot also be used to claim Hope or Lifetime Learning credits.

To find out if a currently enrolled college student over the age of 18 is subject to the kiddie tax, it is necessary to calculate the child's total support, then cut that number in half, and compare the resulting amount to the child's earned income.

If the child's earned income is higher than one-half of the child's total support, the child will not be considered dependent and therefore subject to the kiddie tax for the year.

As a technique that limits income-shifting, the kiddie tax generally applies to income generated by any asset the child owns, regardless of whether the asset was received from the child's parents or from another source. It also applies regardless of when any income-producing assets were transferred to the child. If the income is unearned and is included in the child's taxable income, it is subject to the kiddie tax rules.

In addition to the kiddie tax, there are several other things you must caution your client about in transferring wealth to a child. First, most experts advise against naming the client custodian of an UGMA/UTMA account because, if he or she dies while the child is a minor, the value of the account can be included in his or her taxable estate. Second, as with any gift, clients run the risk that their child may decide that the best use of the money is not education. The child could leave the money in the account until the age of majority and then squander it. (Of course, the child may reconsider if he or she understands that the client's reaction will be to change the child's status in the client's will!) But as we will see in the discussion of financial aid for college funding, transferring assets to a student can have a negative effect on the student's eligibility for financial aid. Additionally, if the grantor of the gift is also the custodian of the gifted asset(s), the account value of the property remains in that individual's estate, which can have an unintended effect on any estate reduction planning.

Trusts

In general, high taxation makes trusts less beneficial for college funding. Nevertheless, trusts provide investment expertise, management, flexibility, and unification unequaled with other investment ownership vehicles. Your client can plan for a number of beneficiaries with one trust, and each of those beneficiaries—and the trust itself—helps to lower the rates at which investment income will be taxed. Alternatively, your client can create multiple trusts for each beneficiary to provide even more flexibility and income splitting and shifting potential. You, as the advisor, must be conscious of the costs incurred in administering and preparing tax returns for multiple trusts. If the trusts have the same terms, beneficiaries, and grantors, they all will be taxed as if they were one trust.

The 2503(c) trusts are useful to take advantage of the annual gift tax exclusion. A married couple can contribute up to $26,000 year per child to a 2503(c) trust gift tax free. Because this type of trust can accumulate income, delay payment of principal, and then allow disbursements during the college years, it is an ideal method where larger amounts are involved.

The 2503(b) trusts require that all income be paid at least annually to the beneficiaries. This type of trust is also eligible for the annual gift tax exclusion and allows delayed payment of principal until college funding is needed. It differs from the 2503(c) trust in two ways. First, the 2503(b) trust requires that all income be paid out each year while the trustee of a 2503(c) trust can decide to accumulate it. Second, the 2503(b) trust can retain funds beyond the beneficiary's age of majority while the 2503(c) trust requires that all principal and income be distributed to the minor at age 21. Thus, the 2503(b) trust makes sense if the beneficiary is aged 18 or older, or if the amount in the trust is very large and the client wants to be sure payment of the principal can be delayed far longer than when the child reaches age 21.

In addition to high taxation and setup and administration costs, the use of trusts has an unfavorable impact on the determination of a family's expected contribution to college expenses when computing a child's eligibility for financial aid. The value of a trust is treated as an asset of the student, rather than of the parents, for purposes of determining the amount of the family's expected contribution to college expenses and, thus, the amount of financial aid needed. Although only 5.6 percent of the parents' unprotected assets are earmarked for inclusion in the expected family contribution to college costs, 35 percent of the child's unprotected assets are counted in determining the amount that the family is expected to contribute to higher education expenses.

Thus, in education planning, you and your client should consider that the use of trusts in funding a college education reduces the amount of federal aid for which your client's child is eligible. (See section titled "Understanding the Aid Formula" for more information on expected contribution.)

Investing in College Housing

Many parents with ample resources elect to provide college housing by buying a multifamily dwelling near the child's college for investment and/or quality-of-life purposes. By making the college student into a landlord's agent who is hired to manage and care for the property and collect fair rents from other tenants, the parent can deduct reasonable salary payments to their college student son or daughter, depreciation (subject to the passive activity loss rule), and travel expenses the parents incur to inspect and maintain their investment property. Ideally, the property will appreciate over time and will either be sold at a profit after the child graduates or be the subject of a future deductible gift to the college upon the child's graduation.

OBTAINING FINANCIAL AID

As a financial advisor, you should have a basic understanding of how to obtain financial aid for higher education. Some of the more complex aspects are best left to competent college financial aid counselors. Still, you must be aware that qualifying for financial aid is sometimes a function of the structure, rather than the size, of assets and income.

Understanding the Aid Formula

FAFSA

The federal need-analysis formula dictates how much the student and the student's parents are expected to contribute per academic year for higher education. The formula is applied to data requested in the U.S. Department of Education's Free Application for Federal Student Aid (FAFSA), which is available from high school guidance counselors or online (fafsa.ed.gov).

expected family contribution

The formula calculates the *expected parent contribution* and the *expected student contribution* and combines them to equal the *expected family contribution* (EFC). After submitting the FAFSA, the student receives a student aid report (SAR) by mail, specifying the EFC. The EFC is subtracted from the cost of attendance (COA) to determine financial need. The cost of attendance is specific to each individual college and includes tuition and fees, on-campus room and board, and allowances for books, supplies, transportation, loan fees, and certain other costs.

Deriving Expected Parent Contribution

expected parent contribution

In the FAFSA formula, parental income includes wages, interest and investment income, housing and living allowances, tax-exempt interest income, child support received, Social Security benefits, unemployment compensation, and contributions to qualified retirement plans and deductible IRAs. Then it adjusts for federal, state, and Social Security taxes and family expenses.

The formula considers assets to include all cash, bank accounts, stocks and bonds, mutual funds, commodities, precious metals, real estate, and trust funds. Employer-sponsored retirement plans, IRAs, annuities, life insurance, and primary residence are excluded. The formula then subtracts education savings and asset-protection allowances. What remains is multiplied by 12 percent to calculate the parents' contribution from assets.

Available income and available assets are now added. Even if the total is negative, your clients may be expected to contribute something. If there is more than one family member (other than a parent) attending college during the year, the parents' total contribution is divided by the number of attendees to determine the expected parent contribution for each of them.

The good news is that most people can exclude most of their assets through exclusions and allowances, and only 12 percent of the remainder is considered available assets. Even then, the formula earmarks at most only 47 percent of this total for the child's education. Parents are expected to kick in an amount equal to 5.6 percent of unprotected assets during each year of school.

Deriving Expected Student Contribution

expected student contribution

The child's available income is calculated after subtracting federal, state, and Social Security taxes and an income-protection allowance. The formula dictates that 50 percent of the remainder be contributed to the child's education. Students are also expected to contribute an amount equal to 35 percent of their assets each year. Because the 35 percent is calculated on a declining balance, the formula theoretically allows the student to retain almost 18 percent of his or her assets after 4 years.

What Can We Learn from the Formula?

In spite of differential tax rates, shifting assets to the child, a standard technique in estate planning, may be counterproductive. First, only 5.6 percent of the parents' unprotected assets are earmarked for inclusion in the expected contribution to college costs, compared to 35 percent of the child's. Second, rather than shifting assets to the child, clients could move their assets into, for example, annuities or cash value life insurance. This removes them from the formula in addition to providing tax deferral. Even so, it might not be worth the effort because if loans are the only form of aid available, hiding assets may only allow the client to borrow money that he or she does not really need to borrow.

Clients who do qualify for financial aid should spend the child's assets first because they count more heavily in the formula. Eliminating a dollar of the child's assets reduces the financial aid formula's required family contribution six times as much as eliminating a dollar of the parents' assets. This should help the family qualify for more aid in subsequent years.

Income is the critical variable. The first year of income that figures into the formula is the one that ends in the child's senior year of high school. Clients considering taking capital gains may want to declare them in the year that ends in the child's junior year—before they count in the formula.

Obtaining Government Money

The federal government, through the Department of Education, plays a significant role in providing funds for college students. Federal student aid includes work-study and other campus-based programs, grants (which do not require repayment), and loans, which together account for approximately two-thirds of all student financial aid.[20] In addition to these sources of federal student aid, which are discussed below, many states have their own grant and loan programs with which you should be familiar.

federal Pell grant

The primary grant program for undergraduate students who qualify under the need-analysis formula is the *federal Pell grant.* Pell Grants are available in amounts of up to $4,731 per year (2008–2009). The amounts students actually receive depend on their financial need, their costs to attend school, their status as a full-time or part-time student, and their plans to attend school for a full academic year or less.

Three additional federal programs—Federal Supplemental Education Opportunity Grants (FSEOGs), Federal Work Study, and Federal Perkins Loans—are referred to as campus-based programs because they are

20. Student Aid on the Web, U.S. Department of Education, Washington, D.C. Retrieved April 29, 2009 from studentaid.ed.gov.

administered directly by the financial aid office at each participating school. FSEOGs are available in amounts up to $4,000 per year for students who show exceptional financial need. Most states have similar programs, which use different eligibility formulas. The Federal Work Study Program provides jobs for undergraduate and graduate students with financial need. The program allows students to earn money to help pay their education expenses.

federal Perkins loans

Federal Perkins loans are another source of funds for students who can show exceptional financial need. A dependent undergraduate student, for example, can qualify for up to $5,500 per year and $27,500 cumulatively. The loan is made with federal government funds, although the school also contributes a share. The school is the lender and the student must eventually repay the loan to his or her school. Interest is only 5 percent and, in general, does not accrue until the student leaves college or drops below half-time status. Payments also begin after the student leaves school and typically can be spread over several years.

Stafford loans

Stafford loans are the major source of education borrowing from the federal government. They are available through the Direct Loan Program, in which funds come directly from the federal government, or through the Federal Family Education Loan (FFEL) program, in which participating banks, credit unions, and other lenders serve as intermediaries. For dependent undergraduate students, loans are available in amounts up to $5,500 for freshman, $6,500 for sophomores, and $7,500 for juniors and seniors.

Stafford loans are subsidized for students with financial need, as determined by subtracting the EFC, Pell grants, and other aid from the cost of attending the college. This means that interest does not accrue until 6 months after the student leaves college. Unsubsidized Stafford loans are available even if there is no need under the aid formula. (Keep in mind that the formula's determination of need may deviate significantly from reality.) A student can receive both a subsidized loan and an unsubsidized loan for the same enrollment period as long as the student does not exceed the annual loan limits.

The interest rate for all unsubsidized Stafford loans first disbursed on or After July 1, 2006, is fixed at 6.8 percent. The interest accrues from the time the funds are disbursed and can be paid as incurred or added to the principal of the loan. The interest rate for subsidized Stafford loans first disbursed on or after July 1, 2008 starts at 6 percent but is reduced over a 4-year period. Stafford loans are subject to a fee of up to 2 percent of the loan.

PLUS loans

PLUS loans (parent loans for undergraduate students) are available through both the Direct and FFEL programs for all family incomes and asset levels, but the borrower cannot have a bad credit history. Applicants can borrow up to the entire cost of the education, less any other financial aid received. For PLUS loans disbursed on or after July 1, 2006, the interest rate is fixed (at 7.9 percent for Direct and 8.5 percent for FFEL PLUS loans), and interest accrues from the time of the first disbursement. Repayment must begin either 60 days after the loan is fully disbursed or 6 months after the student ceases to be enrolled on at least a half-time basis. There is a fee of up to 4 percent of the loan amount.

federal loan consolidation programs

Federal loan consolidation programs are available under both the Direct and FFEL loan programs. Under these programs, a student's or parents' loans are repaid and a new consolidation loan is created. Stafford loans, PLUS loans, and federal Perkins loans are eligible for consolidation. The consolidated loan has a fixed interest rate equal to the weighted average of the interest rates of the loans being combined at the time of consolidation, although the interest rate will never exceed 8.25 percent. In addition, no fees can be charged in connection with the consolidation of eligible student loans.

You and your client should investigate consolidating student loans. With a consolidation loan, your client will:

- receive a fixed interest rate on a Direct or FFEL consolidation loan
- have only one lender and one monthly bill
- be able to take a longer time to repay (up to 30 years) if the consolidation loan is under the Standard or Graduated Repayment Plans and total student loan debt is $60,000 or more. The maximum repayment period for a consolidation loan is based on the total amount of the consolidation loan and other student loan debt.
- likely have lower monthly payments. Because repayment terms can be extended under consolidation loans, the monthly payment can be reduced to a more manageable amount. Whenever the repayment term on a loan is lengthened at a given interest rate, the total amount of interest paid increases if the loan is not fully paid off until the end of the repayment term.

Moreover, the cost of repayment unconsolidated loans should be compared with the cost of repaying a consolidation loan. Things to consider are:

- whether borrower benefits, such as interest rate discounts or principal rebates, will be lost if loans are consolidated. These borrower benefits can significantly reduce the cost of repaying loans.
- whether discharge and cancellation benefits will be lost if a Perkins loan is included in the consolidation loan

Tapping the College's Resources

You should encourage your clients to pursue funding options directly through college resources. Academic scholarships and grants continue to be available to needy and/or talented students at most institutions. There are literally thousands available and many can be obtained even by children of upper-middle-income families. Many colleges also have their own loan funds.

Scholarships and grants are not taxable income to the extent that

- the money is for tuition, fees, books, supplies, and equipment
- the student is a candidate for a degree at a qualified educational institution (an educational institution that maintains a regular faculty

and curriculum, and normally has a regularly enrolled body of students in attendance at the place where it carries on its educational activities)

To the extent that the scholarship is for room and board, payments will be taxable income to the student. Likewise, if the student is not a degree candidate or if payments are for teaching, research, or other services rendered by the student, payments will be taxable.

Example Your client plans to spend $10,000 per year at a state university, which happens to coincide with the expected contribution calculated by the need-analysis formula. If his child applies and is accepted to a $25,000-per-year private college, financial aid might be available to cover the entire $15,000 difference. If the aid takes the form of loans rather than a "free" grant, however, your client must decide whether the aid is worthwhile.

Life Insurance Policy Loans

Another option for funding college costs that you should discuss with your client is life insurance policy loans. Although not a source of financial aid, life insurance policies with cash values and low or reasonable interest charges have traditionally been sources of funds for college expenses. The funds are quickly available and require no credit analysis. Further, the transaction is very private and the repayment provisions are typically very flexible. Of course, borrowing from a policy reduces the proceeds payable at death.

REGULATION OF ADVISORS

Financial planning as a profession continues to evolve. The growth in the number of financial advisors that started in the late 1970s and continues today makes the regulation of financial advisors an increasingly important topic to consumers, consumer advocates, regulatory authorities, elected officials, and to financial advisors themselves. This section of the chapter reviews federal legislation and regulatory actions that govern the activities of financial advisors.

Federal or state governments do not regulate financial advisors per se. Instead, the activities and conduct of financial advisors are subject to government regulation because most of the individual components of the sales/planning process are regulated. Thus, federal or state securities regulators oversee financial advisors in their capacity as investment advisors; federal or state securities agencies also regulate financial advisors who sell securities.

Additionally, those engaged in financial planning may be subject to state regulation of insurance brokers and agents, accountants, or attorneys.

For example, financial planning often includes an analysis of a client's insurance needs. Financial advisors, therefore, may find themselves subject to state insurance regulations. In some states, financial advisors may even be subject to regulation if they recommend a generic insurance product or a specific amount of insurance without referring the client to a licensed insurance agent. On the other hand, a few states make obtaining an insurance license easier for individuals who hold the CLU®, ChFC®, CFP® or some other professional designation.

What laws and rules apply to the profession of financial planning? As a financial advisor, you want to play fair and refer to yourself and what you do in a way that will not get you into trouble or mislead others. Unfortunately, there is no single body of law that can serve as a guideline of standards for financial advisors.

Statutes and organizations vary widely in the way they do or do not distinguish among financial planners, financial advisors, and investment advisors. Your professional duties may subject you to lawsuits in one state but not another. In some states, an insurance agent may be treated legally as a financial planner. Often, state and federal regulations may not agree. This section will provide an overview of some of the issues in registration, licensing, and compliance.

Laws That Govern the Securities Industry

- Securities Act of 1933
- Securities Exchange Act of 1934
- Investment Advisers Act of 1940

Federal Regulation of Registered Security Products

Historical Background

It has been many years since the 1929 stock market crash, but the regulatory responses to this crisis remain with us. Federal investigations at the time of the 1929 crash recognized that market manipulation, overextension of credit for stock purchases, and unfair dealings with clients were abuses in need of correction. Speculative excess and self-dealings, combined with the financial hardships of the Great Depression, fostered a legislative environment that produced the current foundation of securities law in the United States.

In response, Congress enacted several major laws that changed the structure of the securities markets in the United States. These acts provided a definition of securities, guidelines for the issuance and registration of security products, and rules regarding the conduct of security marketplace operations. These acts also provided for the establishment of self-regulatory organizations such as the

Financial Industry Regulatory Authority (FINRA), formerly called the National Association of Securities Dealers (NASD).

A general familiarity with three of these federal acts—the Securities Act of 1933, the Securities Exchange Act of 1934, and the Investment Advisers Act of 1940—will help you understand what is appropriate conduct in today's financial services marketplace. All three acts share a common statutory theme—providing the proper disclosure, which is necessary to free, fair, and honest dealings in an open marketplace.

Securities Act of 1933

Securities Act of 1933

The *Securities Act of 1933* provides guidelines that a company must follow before it can sell new issues of its stock to the public. These guidelines emphasize disclosure of information through the completion of a registration statement, which must be reviewed by the Securities and Exchange Commission (SEC). Following the filing of the registration statement, a prospectus is prepared. The prospectus summarizes the information contained in the registration statement and must be presented to all interested buyers.

Securities Exchange Act of 1934

Securities Exchange Act of 1934

While the Securities Act of 1933 concerns newly issued securities, the *Securities Exchange Act of 1934* extends federal regulation to the ongoing trading of securities already issued. The 1934 Act charged the SEC with the enforcement of these directives.

Provisions of the 1934 Act require disclosure of information by publicly traded companies, prohibit market manipulation, and restrict the amount of credit that may be extended for the purchase of securities. The 1934 Act also requires security brokers and dealers to register with the SEC. In addition, the 1934 Act provides for SEC supervision of national security exchanges, industry associations, and securities information processors.

The primary function of the SEC is to review information provided in the registration statement and other forms submitted to its offices. The SEC does not give the public investment advice. It is up to individual investors and/or their advisors to evaluate the securities registered with the SEC.

Investment Advisers Act of 1940

Investment Advisers Act of 1940

The *Investment Advisers Act of 1940* seeks to protect the public from harmful and fraudulent conduct of persons who are paid to advise others on buying and/or selling securities. It is aimed at two categories of advisors: (1) those who publish market reports or newsletters for paying subscribers that contain recommendations concerning securities and (2) those who advise individual clients about securities. A major purpose of the law is to reveal conflicts of interests that may cause the advisor to make recommendations more in his or her own interest than in the client's interest.

This Act sets out a system of federal regulation for investment advisors. The key question the Act poses for financial services professionals is whether or not they are considered investment advisors. If they are, they are required to register with the SEC. For example, if an insurance agent is in the business of providing investment advice for compensation in addition to selling insurance, the registration provisions of the Act apply.

There are some instances in which it is unclear whether or not an advisor is an investment advisor. For example, if an insurance agent advertises a financial planning designation, is he or she providing financial advice in the ordinary course of business? In a few cases, state law points to a "yes" answer. In other cases, the answer is unclear; in still others, the answer is "no." Failure to comply with the law's provisions carries heavy penalties, so many legal commentators suggest that advisors should register if in doubt.

Registration under the Investment Advisers Act is not an endorsement of competence or expertise by the SEC. Financial advisors should avoid the temptation to imply SEC endorsement when speaking to clients—this would be unethical and possibly illegal.

Regulation of Financial Planning Professionals

If you are engaged as a financial planner, be aware that a broader scope of ethical responsibility is involved, and that there is federal monitoring of your behavior. Your ethical responsibility is that of a fiduciary acting on behalf of your clients. Your services are likely to fall under the jurisdiction of the SEC, and your behavior should be guided by the dictates of the Investment Advisers Act of 1940. This requires you to register as an investment advisor with the SEC and agree to abide by strict standards of ethical conduct.

Financial Industry Regulatory Authority (FINRA)

The SEC is not the sole source of rules and regulations under the federal securities laws. Congress recognized that the nation's stock exchanges had long been regulating the trading activities of their own members. With this in mind, self-regulatory organizations (SROs) were incorporated into the regulatory structure of the securities industry.

Financial Industry Regulatory Authority (FINRA)

The *Financial Industry Regulatory Authority (FINRA)* [formerly known as the National Association of Securities Dealers (NASD)] is part of this self-regulatory structure. It was established under authority granted by the Securities Exchange Act of 1934 to provide voluntary self-regulation of broker/dealers under SEC oversight.

The FINRA has the power to require and monitor compliance with standardized rules of fair practice for the industry. FINRA regulatory responsibilities include registration and testing of securities professionals, review of members' advertising and sales literature, and services such as arbitration of investor disputes. Registered representatives must provide the

FINRA with personal information including prior employment and any history of securities-related disciplinary action.

FINRA Rules of Conduct

The FINRA sets forth its expectations for the ethical treatment of customers in its Rules of Conduct. These rules spell out two fundamental steps, which the advisor must follow in order to fairly deal with clients. The advisor must understand the client's

- current financial status
- financial goals

Only with these two pieces of information is it possible for you as a financial advisor to offer appropriate advice to a client. For example, an older client who has accumulated a relatively modest retirement nest egg and who seeks some income along with preservation of capital would be an unlikely candidate for a financial product that stresses high-risk emerging growth funds.

Changing client circumstances are also part of the fair dealings equation. For example, in mid-life, successful clients have accumulated more assets and may be able to tolerate greater risk in order to seek higher return. On the other hand, clients near the end of their working careers may find that the high-risk strategies, which enabled them to achieve earlier financial success, no longer fit their needs.

Under the 1934 Act, the FINRA must promulgate rules designed to

- prevent fraudulent practices and promote equitable principles of trade
- safeguard against unreasonable profits, commissions, or other charge
- prevent unfair discrimination between customers, issuers, or broker/dealers
- provide for appropriate discipline for the violation of its rules (for example, censure, suspension, and expulsion)

The FINRA Rules of Conduct require that member broker/dealers and associated persons of broker/dealers observe high standards of commercial honor and just and equitable principles of trade. The rules regulate a wide range of activities relating to such areas as the sale of securities, suitability of such sales, confirmation of transactions, and supervision.

The rules of conduct govern the following activities:

- supervision. A broker/dealer must establish and maintain a system of specified written oversight and review procedures to supervise the activities of each registered representative.
- private securities transactions. This area involves any securities transactions beyond the regular scope of an associated person's relationship with a broker/dealer such as new offerings of securities, which are not registered with the SEC. Thus, it is the responsibility of the broker/dealer to train and continually remind its registered representatives that the definition of a security is very broad and any

activity even remotely resembling a securities transaction should be brought to the brokers-dealer's attention for approval.

- outside business activities of associated persons. FINRA Rules prohibit an associated person of a broker/dealer from accepting employment or compensation concerning any business activity outside the scope of the broker/dealer employment relationship unless the person provides the broker/dealer with prompt written notice.
- suitability and fair dealing with customers. FINRA Rules provide that in recommending to a customer the purchase or sale of any security, a member shall have reasonable grounds for believing that the recommendation is suitable for that customer upon the basis of the facts, if any, disclosed by that customer as to his or her other securities holdings and as to his or her financial situation and needs.

  This determination should be based on customer disclosures as to income, net worth, securities holdings, life insurance, real estate holdings, customer financial sophistication, investment objectives, and financial needs. Registered principals of the broker/dealer make the final determination as to suitability and the acceptance of the transaction.

  The SEC recognizes a broker/dealer obligation of fair dealing under the general antifraud provisions of the federal securities laws. The commission maintains that a violation of the suitability doctrine may constitute a violation under the Securities Exchange Act of 1934, which is the SEC's general antifraud rule under the act. This position is based on the premise that when a broker/dealer holds itself out as a broker/dealer (solicits business), it implicitly represents that it will recommend securities only when it has a reasonable basis that they are suited to the customer's needs.
- sales literature, advertising, and communications with the public. A series of SEC and FINRA rules and guidelines has evolved to govern advertising, sales literature, and communications with the public concerning the distribution of equity products.
- communications with the public. The FINRA Rules of Conduct mandate that every item of advertising and sales literature (the definition of which is quite broad) be approved by a registered principal of the broker/dealer prior to its use. This material must contain a broker/dealer's name, the identity of the preparer of the material, and the date first published. Advertisements and sales literature must also be filed with the FINRA within 10 days of their first use. These materials can be disapproved for failure to meet FINRA guidelines.

  For example, the FINRA has established a Variable Life Insurance Marketing Guide. Prior to 1990, FINRA policy emphasized that the primary attribute of a variable life insurance (VLI) policy is its death benefit, even though VLI also contains an important investment aspect in its cash value. The FINRA insisted that VLI should not be described as an investment. With the advent of single-premium VLI policies, the FINRA revised its position to permit broker/dealers to give more weight to the investment element of policies or contracts. By 1990, the FINRA further relaxed its position and moved to imposing no absolute requirement that broker/dealers maintain a "balance" in describing the insurance and investment elements of a VLI policy, only that communications should describe both elements. By early 1994, the FINRA had in place SEC-approved guidelines covering variable products to govern the preparation of and communication with the public through advertising and sales literature. These guidelines prohibit referring to variable products as mutual funds. Communications concerning variable products must clearly identify the product as either a variable life insurance policy or a variable annuity contract; avoid implying that the underlying product is a mutual fund; avoid presenting variable products as short-term liquid investments; disclose the impact of early withdrawal such as sales loads, tax penalties, and potential loss of principal in references to liquidity; and avoid suggestion that guarantees apply to investment returns.

Registration As an Investment Advisor

Who Is Subject to the Investment Advisers Act?

registered representative
investment advisor representative
registered investment advisor (RIA)

To sell securities products and work as a financial advisor, you need to register with a governmental regulator. There are three basic ways to become registered:

- *registered representative* (RR). When you work for a broker/dealer, your supervisor, manager, or employer will tell you what licenses, exams, and registrations you need to be able to sell the services and products the broker/dealer offers. The broker/dealer will instruct you on what forms, agreements and records to keep, and what payouts, commissions, or salary you will receive. You will be a registered representative under your broker/dealer's FINRA registration. If you change your broker/dealer, you will need to transfer your registration to your new broker/dealer.
- *investment advisor representative (IAR)*. If you join an independent firm, you will register as an investment advisor representative (IAR) of the independent advisory firm. Again, your supervisor will tell you how and where to register.
- *registered investment advisor (RIA)*. Registration as an investment advisor is discussed in detail below.

The SEC takes the position that the Investment Advisers Act of 1940 governs the regulation of financial planners. The Act defines an investment advisor as any person who, for compensation, engages in the business of advising others as to the value of securities or the advisability of acquiring or disposing of securities. Any person who falls within the Advisers Act's definition of an investment advisor and who makes use of the mails or any instrumentality of interstate commerce is required to register with the SEC pursuant to the Act.

The Supreme Court defined what constitutes a security in the 1946 landmark case *SEC v. T.W. Howey Co.* In that case, the Court ruled,

The test is whether the scheme involves an investment of money in a common enterprise with profits to come solely from the efforts of others.

security

Under this test, virtually every investment that a financial planner might recommend for his or her client would appear to qualify as a security. The term *security* has been interpreted to include not only marketable securities traded on an organized exchange (such as the New York Stock Exchange) but also such instruments as limited partnerships, mutual funds, certificates of deposit, commercial paper, variable annuities, and variable life insurance, as well as other types of interest-sensitive life insurance products.

However, merely dealing with a security does not, by itself, make someone an investment advisor. In the 1980s, the SEC issued three tests to determine whether or not individuals must register as an investment advisor. If all three tests are answered in the affirmative, registration is required. If any of the tests is answered in the negative, there is no need to become a registered investment advisor. According to the SEC's three tests, the individual or entity must

security advice test
security business test
compensation test

- give advice or analysis concerning securities (*security advice test*)
- be engaged in the business of advising others regarding securities (*security business test*)
- be in receipt of compensation (*compensation test*)

It is important to remember that the purpose of the SEC in devising the three tests is to protect clients from fraud and other abusive situations. The SEC does not guarantee the competence or investment abilities of any individuals who register under the Act; it merely seeks to provide a mechanism for discouraging unethical behavior, principally via full disclosure to clients.

The three elements that must be met if persons or entities want to qualify as investment advisors under the Act are defined more fully below.

Security Advice Test

To determine whether or not an individual must become an RIA, the SEC looks first at the type of services being provided. If an individual provides advice about the purchase or sale of securities, this indicates that registration is necessary.

If you provide advice or issue reports or analyses regarding specific securities, clearly you meet this test. The advice need not relate to specific securities but may focus on the advisability of investing in securities in general. The SEC has determined that a person who deals with securities in general or who advises as to the advantages and disadvantages of investing in securities vis-a-vis other financial vehicles (for example, life insurance) meets this test. Virtually any person who presents himself or herself as a financial planning professional will render advice concerning securities.

Security Business Test

Are you engaged in the business of providing such services about securities? Providing advice with some regularity, even when it is not the person's primary business activity, is an important factor in subjecting the person to the Act. A person is deemed to be "in the business" if he or she does any of the following:

- holds himself or herself out as an investment advisor
- receives separate or additional compensation that is a clearly definable charge for providing advice about securities
- provides specific investment advice in other than isolated instances

Another way of looking at this is to examine how you present your business to the public. For example, what name and type of business description appear in the telephone book or on the front door? How is the telephone answered? Does your business card or letterhead suggest that you are an investment advisor or stockbroker? If the way you present your business to the public suggests that you provide investment advice, this indicates the need for you to be a registered investment advisor.

Compensation Test

Do you provide such services for compensation? The compensation can be in any form and from any source. Even though you do not charge a separate fee for advice concerning a security, if you receive some form of advisory fee, a fee relating to total services rendered, a commission, or some combination thereof in connection with this advice, you meet the compensation test. In meeting this test, it is not necessary that the advisor's compensation be paid directly by the person receiving the services, but only that he or she receive compensation from some source (for example, an insurance company) for such services.

Under this three-pronged definitional test, all of the elements must be present to classify as an investment advisor under the Act. Given the broad scope of each of the definitional elements, those engaged in financial planning activities are highly likely to be included in the Act's definition of an investment advisor.

Regulation under the Investment Advisers Act

The basic regulatory mechanism of the Investment Advisers Act is the requirement that any person who falls within the definition of an investment advisor must register with the SEC. A financial planner, as an investment advisor, is subject to a number of legal responsibilities in addition to the registration requirement, as shown in the following figure.

Avoiding Registration as an RIA for Insurance Advisors

Many insurance advisors involved in the sale of variable products will find it difficult not to answer the compensation test in an affirmative manner. Therefore, the second test (security business) becomes the key issue. If you do not wish to be an RIA, do not present yourself as a full-fledged financial planner to the public. Exercise caution when developing a name for your business. Get approval for any business name from your insurance company or broker/dealer.

Example Consider the case of an independent insurance agent named Maria M. Conte. Maria may wish to lend a greater professional tone to her business by printing cards and stationery with MMC Investment Advisors, Ltd. after her name. This may sound very professional, but it may also mislead the public into thinking Maria is providing services beyond the sale of insurance.

Also, take a look at your state's law. Some states, such as Maryland and Washington, have very strict criteria as to what constitutes being a financial planner. For instance, using designations such as Chartered Financial Consultant (ChFC) can be enough to trigger registration. Insurance advisors who wish to avoid registration should also keep four other factors in mind:

- Make it clear to your clients that you are a financial advisor who is selling insurance. Do not try to hide the identity of the product. Trying to recast an insurance policy as a mutual fund is one example not only of a violation of ethics, but also of a legal matter that indicates the need for compliance with SEC registration requirements.
- Up-front fees may be a tempting source of income, but if you want to avoid registration, do not charge clients for your professional advice.
- Base your income on regular commissions. Again, to avoid registration, do not charge advisory fees.
- Follow your company guidelines. If your company is affiliated with a broker/dealer, in all likelihood it has specified methods of operating the business in a manner that can avoid the necessity of registering as an investment advisor. Ignoring these guidelines is an invitation to becoming an RIA.

Table 8-4
Responsibilities of a Registered Investment Advisor (RIA)

The major responsibilities of an RIA are as follows: • registration. The first step in becoming an RIA is to register with the SEC. Registration involves the completion of a detailed questionnaire (Form ADV) and the submission of a one-time filing fee. • records. RIAs are required to keep extensive records regarding the many aspects of their practices. This record keeping involves retention of sales brochures, client communications, and recommendations. It also involves maintenance of financial records in accordance with generally accepted accounting principles. • fee restrictions. RIAs are subject to the fee restrictions developed under SEC rules. As a general rule of thumb, the fee restrictions tend to be stricter for clients with assets of less than $1 million. • designation prohibition. The term "RIA" cannot be used as a designation as one would use LUTCF, CLU, or ChFC. This is because it merely represents a registration, not an educational achievement. However, the rules do permit those registered to fully spell out and refer to their status as registered investment advisor when dealing with clients. • informational brochure. RIAs must develop and distribute a brochure to clients that includes substantial information about their education, business background, and clientele. The brochure must also indicate the type of informational sources used and the investment strategies pursued. • Client reassignment. RIAs cannot arbitrarily reassign their clients to other RIAs. Clients must clearly consent to any reassignment. This rule stresses the personal nature of the relationship and the uniqueness of services RIAs provide. (This is also a factor that RIAs must keep in mind when planning for their retirement. Simply put, RIAs cannot decide to sell their practices without notifying clients. Preretirement succession planning thus becomes an important element for any RIA. In this way, clients can get to know the newcomer during a transition period and can then make informed decisions as to how they wish their accounts handled.) • fiduciary role. The Investment Advisers Act of 1940 contains strict antifraud provisions. These provisions have the effect of recognizing RIAs as fiduciaries who owe their clients affirmative duties. These duties include the obligation to deal in good faith and to provide full and fair disclosure of all material facts that surround an investment recommendation. As fiduciaries, RIAs must also be careful not to place themselves in ethically questionable situations that involve a conflict of interest.

Investment Advisor Tests

If any of these tests are answered in the negative, there is no need to become a registered investment advisor:

- securities advice test
- securities business test
- compensation test

RIA: Weighing the Responsibilities, Advantages, and Disadvantages

An individual who becomes an RIA assumes a series of responsibilities. For some individuals, the advantages offered by RIA status outweigh any potential disadvantages. For others, these responsibilities outweigh the advantages of being an RIA.

Whether or not you choose to register as an investment advisor depends in part on the type of practice you wish to develop and the guidelines drafted by your company. Some companies discourage their advisors from being RIAs because of the potential for added legal liability that the company and the advisor share. Other companies leave registration up to the discretion of their individual advisors.

Summarized below are some of the advantages and disadvantages you may wish to take into consideration before deciding whether or not to conduct your practice as an RIA.

Advantages

If you are a registered investment advisor, you have the ability to charge fees for your professional advice and planning services. For those who wish to move away from a dependence on commissions, this can be a substantial reason to become an RIA.

Registering as an investment advisor also affords you far greater latitude in how you advertise and promote your practice. Your cards and letterhead can indicate that you are engaged in providing investment advice. As an RIA, you can indicate that you develop financial planning programs and investment achievement strategies for clients. You can expand your practice in investment planning and asset management, and you can move into markets calling for a wider array of product and service needs.

Disadvantages

To register as an investment advisor, you must pay application fees. Although these are not onerous, they are a factor to be considered.

Being an RIA also involves substantial paperwork. As an RIA, you must maintain meticulous records regarding the advice you give to clients, and you must also comply with regulatory reporting requirements. Perhaps the greatest disincentive to being an RIA is the potential for substantial legal liability. You are clearly inviting clients to rely on your expertise and investment advice. If your expertise is limited or your investment advice imprudent, you are likely to find yourself named in a lawsuit. In addition, an RIA is legally held to a higher professional standard than that normally applied to an individual who is engaged solely in the sale of insurance.

State Regulation in the Securities Marketplace

Federal securities laws do not necessarily preempt state authority. In fact, various federal securities laws specifically preserve the regulatory power of the states, and all states have so-called blue sky laws [21] regulating securities activities in their respective states.

For example, most states follow the broad definition of advertising set forth in the National Association of Insurance Commissioners (NAIC) model legislation. At the same time, the FINRA has also developed rules regarding advertising and the literature that may be used in the sale of registered products such as variable annuities. The FINRA rules do not override the state rules; they supplement them.

Another example is that both state laws and FINRA rules apply to sales practices of variable products. Both state and federal regulators have guidelines as to what you say and what you do as part of your interaction with a client. Simply using approved materials is not enough. You must use them in a proper fashion that will not mislead your clients.

The overlap of state and FINRA guidelines means that you must consider two sets of rules as you develop strategies involving the sale of today's sophisticated financial products. How can you retain all this information when securities laws vary greatly from state to state? The answer lies in studying the three common themes in most state statutes:

- The laws prohibit fraud in the sale of securities.
- There are state registration requirements for those involved in the sale of securities.
- There are registration and disclosure requirements for securities sold within the state.

Insider Information

insider information

Another consideration, *insider information*, places ethical and legal obligations on the financial services advisor because many financial services professionals have access to important financial information before it becomes available to the public.

Example You may have clients with considerable sums of money in highly responsible positions. As part of the selling/planning process, your clients may be privy to confidential information regarding the companies for which they work or in which they hold substantial ownership positions. Hence, they may obtain important financial information before it becomes generally available to the public.

21. The name "blue sky" comes from a statement made by a U.S. Supreme Court justice, who referred to "speculative schemes that have no more basis than so many feet of blue sky." The Uniform Securities Act (USA) serves as model legislation that each state may follow or adapt to its own needs.

This important (material) information might indicate, for instance, an upcoming loss or profit decline. On the other hand, it might indicate the expansion of a new product line with the likelihood of increased and significant profitability. In each instance, the information may involve a firm whose shares are publicly traded and from which sizable personal profits could arise. This type of financial data is considered "insider" information. Personal stock purchases or sales based on this data constitute insider trading and are considered illegal under federal securities laws.

The courts have broadly applied the insider-trading laws. In one case, insider-trading issues arose when a printer read reports that he was preparing for publication. In other cases, people who have received information from corporate executives have been held in violation of the law.

As a financial advisor, you must treat financial information you receive as confidential information. This is another example of combining good ethics with good business. Clients need to know they can trust you with private matters. You will receive more information through fact finding, which in turn will enable you to satisfy a greater number of needs as a financial services advisor.

The Advisor as Fiduciary

fiduciary

A *fiduciary* has a duty to the client to act in a responsible manner when it comes to the financial management of that client's affairs. Registered investment advisors, including many financial planners, have a fiduciary duty, whereas registered representatives and insurance advisors may not. A fiduciary may be a person who has discretionary control over a client's assets, or is in a position of trust as a professional who renders investment advice. You do not have to have discretionary control to be considered a fiduciary.

When a financial advisor has a fiduciary duty, failure to perform that duty can be grounds for civil or criminal proceedings against the advisor. This can also trigger disciplinary actions by an advisor's professional society or organization. As a fiduciary, you must not only act to do what is in your client's best interest, but also do what a "prudent person" would do in that situation. Fiduciaries must always act in complete fairness and never exert any influence or pressure or deal in a way for self-benefit. Utmost good faith is required in all dealings.

YOUR FINANCIAL SERVICES PRACTICE: UNAUTHORIZED ENTITIES

Regulation of insurance products and services varies from state to stare. In Florida, for example, regulations prohibit doing business with an unauthorized insurance entity. An unauthorized entity is an insurance company that has not gained approval to place insurance in the jurisdiction where it or a producer wants to sell insurance. These carriers are unlicensed and prohibited from doing business in that state. In most cases where these carriers have operated, they have characterized themselves as one of several types that are exempt from state regulation. It is the financial planner's responsibility to exercise due diligence to make sure the carriers for whom they are selling are approved by the department of insurance in that state.

CHAPTER REVIEW

Key Terms and Concepts are explained in the Glossary. Answers to the Review Questions and Self-Test Questions are found in the back of the textbook in the Answers to Questions section.

Key Terms and Concepts

modified adjusted gross income
prepaid tuition plans
Sec. 529 plans
Roth IRA
Coverdell education savings accounts
Hope Scholarship tax credit
Lifetime Learning tax credit
kiddie tax
FAFSA
expected family contribution
expected parent contribution
expected student contribution
federal Pell grant
federal Perkins loans
Stafford loans
PLUS loans
federal loan consolidation programs
Securities Act of 1933
Securities Exchange Act of 1934
Investment Advisers Act of 1940
Financial Industry Regulatory Authority (FINRA)
registered representative
investment advisor representative
registered investment advisor (RIA)
security
security advice test
security business test
compensation test
insider information
fiduciary

Review Questions

8-1. Identify the two funding requirements associated with financing a college education.

8-2. What types of investments typically are considered for use in funding a college education?

8-3. Compare and contrast the availability of scholarships, grants, and loans for college funding.

8-4. Describe the financial aid process from filling out the FAFSA form to establishing the expected family contribution (EFC).

8-5. Describe the federal regulation of registered security products.

8-6. Describe the regulation of financial planning professionals.

8-7. Describe the role of the Financial Industry Regulatory Authority (FINRA) in the regulation of financial planning professionals.

8-8. Explain the three tests used to determine if an advisor must register as a registered investment advisor (RIA).

8-9. List the advisor's responsibilities as an RIA.

8-10. Describe the advantages and disadvantages of becoming an RIA.

8-11. Explain the rules regarding insider trading.

8-12. Explain the role of an advisor as a fiduciary.

Self-Test Questions

13. Which of the following statements concerning education inflation in recent years is correct?

    (A) Education inflation has far exceeded the general inflation rate.
    (B) Education inflation has been very similar to the general inflation rate.
    (C) General inflation has been slightly higher than education inflation.
    (D) Inflation has had a small impact on the cost of a college education.

14. Which of the following statements concerning transferring wealth to a child is correct?

    (A) Transferring assets to a child can have a negative effect on the child's eligibility for financial aid.
    (B) If a client gives money to a child through an UGMA account and acts as custodian, the value of the account is not included in his or her estate.
    (C) The kiddie tax applies to all children until they reach the age of 21.
    (D) Spending restrictions on a UGMA account can ensure that account proceeds are used for education expenses.

15. Which of the following would be the best strategy for parents (clients) who qualify for financial aid for their children's educations and want to maximize their financial aid in subsequent years?

    (A) Parents should spend their own assets before spending their children's.
    (B) Children's assets will not count in the financial aid formula.
    (C) Parents should shift their assets to their children to avoid kiddie tax.
    (D) Parents should spend their children's assets before spending their own.

16. For an insurance advisor to avoid registration as a registered investment advisor (RIA), he or she must do which of the following?

    (A) avoid receiving commissions for sales of registered insurance or annuity products
    (B) avoid presenting himself or herself as a full-fledged financial planner to the public
    (C) charge clients for professional advice
    (D) charge advisory fees in addition to regular commissions

17. Which of the following statements concerning registration under the Investment Advisers Act as an RIA is correct?

    (A) It is an endorsement of competence by the SEC.
    (B) It requires that extensive records be maintained.
    (C) It allows for the sale of all financial products
    (D) It is an educational achievement displayed as a designation.

18. A financial advisor may be required to register as a registered investment advisor if which of the following questions is (are) answered in the affirmative?

    I. Does the financial advisor provide advice or analysis about securities?
    II. Does the financial advisor hold himself or herself out as an investment advisor?

    (A) I only
    (B) II only
    (C) Both I and II
    (D) Neither I nor II

19. Which of the following statements concerning college student financial aid is (are) correct?

    I. Required contributions from parental assets are a lower percentage than required contributions from the student's assets.
    II. The federal need-analysis formula calculates the expected family contribution.

    (A) I only
    (B) II only
    (C) Both I and II
    (D) Neither I nor II

READ THE FOLLOWING DIRECTIONS BEFORE CONTINUING

The questions below differ from the preceding questions in that they all contain the word EXCEPT. So you understand fully the basis used in selecting each answer, be sure to read each question carefully.

---

20. The benefits of Sec. 529 plans for college funding include all the following EXCEPT

    (A) Earnings are tax deferred.
    (B) Qualified withdrawals are free from federal income tax.
    (C) Contributions are tax deductible.
    (D) There are no income restrictions.

21. All the following statements concerning an advisor's fiduciary role are correct EXCEPT

    (A) You must have discretionary authority over a client's investments to be a fiduciary.
    (B) You must act in the client's best interest as a "prudent person" would.
    (C) Failure to perform a fiduciary duty can be grounds for civil or criminal proceedings.
    (D) As a fiduciary, you may be in a position of trust as a professional who renders investment advice.

22. All the following statements concerning the kiddie tax are correct EXCEPT

    (A) It applies to dependent children who are full-time students over age 18 but under age 24.
    (B) It applies to children who are under age 18 regardless of their dependency status.
    (C) It makes using a Sec. 529 plan a very attractive way to save for college.
    (D) It prohibits children from being taxed at their parents' marginal rate.

Appendix A

Comprehensive Financial Planning Fact Finder

Comprehensive Financial Planning Fact Finder

Client's Name ______________________________

Spouse's Name ______________________________

Date Compiled ______________________________

The information collected and maintained in this document will be held in the utmost confidentiality. It will not be shared except as may be required by law or as may be authorized in writing by the client.

____
(Client's Signature)

____
(Spouse's Signature)

____
(Advisor's Signature)

THE AMERICAN COLLEGE
THE LEADER IN FINANCIAL SERVICES EDUCATION

PERSONAL DATA

Client's name	
Spouse's name	
Home address	
Mailing address (if different from home address)	
Business address	Client:
	Spouse:
Phone numbers	Home: Cell: Client Spouse Business: Client Spouse
E-mail address(es)	Home: Client Spouse Business: Client Spouse

Other Advisors

		* ✓	Name	Address	Phone
Attorney	personal				
	business				
Accountant	personal				
	business				
Trust officer					
Other bank officer					
Life insurance agent					
Property and liability insurance agent					
Investment advisor (securities broker)					
Primary financial advisor					

* Please check the names of those with whom we can share information about your financial affairs.

Notes

Client and Spouse*

	Date of Birth	Social Security Number	Occupation	Amount of Support by Client/Spouse	Health Problems/ Special Needs
Client[1]					
Spouse[1]					

1. If not U.S. citizen, indicate nationality.

Children[2]/Grandchildren

2. Indicate whether by prior marriage, adopted or stepchild.

Client's Parents, Siblings

Spouse's Parents, Siblings

* If possible, obtain addresses, phone numbers, and Social Security numbers of family members, especially those who are, or may become, beneficiaries, executors, guardians, etc.

Notes

Marital status	Check appropriate status: ☐ Married ☐ Divorced ☐ Widowed Date: ☐ Never married
	Any former marriages? ☐ Yes ☐ No If yes, to whom? Client: Spouse:
	Client: Are you paying alimony? ☐ Yes ☐ No If yes, amount: Are you paying child support? ☐ Yes ☐ No If yes, amount: Is your spouse paying alimony? ☐ Yes ☐ No If yes, amount: Is your spouse paying child support? ☐ Yes ☐ No If yes, amount:
Nuptial agreements	Does a prenuptial or postnuptial agreement exist? ☐ Yes ☐ No If yes, describe briefly.
Wills	Do you have a will? ☐ Yes ☐ No Date of will:
	Does your spouse have a will? ☐ Yes ☐ No Date of will:
Estate plan	Do you have a basic estate plan? ☐ Yes ☐ No If yes, describe briefly.
Executor nominations	Who has been named as executor in your will? in your spouse's will? Name: Name: Address: Address: Phone: Phone:
Guardian nominations	Have guardians been named for your children? ☐ Yes ☐ No If yes, who? Name: Address: Phone:
Trust/trustee nominations	Have you created grantor, insurance, or testamentary trusts? ☐ Yes ☐ No If yes, who is the trustee?
	Who are the beneficiaries?
	Has your spouse created grantor, insurance, or testamentary trusts? ☐ Yes ☐ No If yes, who is the trustee?
	Who are the beneficiaries?
Custodianships	Have you or your spouse ever made a gift under the Uniform Gifts to Minors Act or Uniform Transfer to Minors Act? ☐ Yes ☐ No If yes, in which state?
	Who is the custodian?
	Who are the donees?
Trust beneficiary	Are you or any members of your immediate family beneficiaries of a trust? ☐ Yes ☐ No If yes, who? Amount expected:
Gifts/inheritances	Do you or your spouse expect to receive gifts/inheritances? ☐ Yes ☐ No If yes, who? How much? From whom? When?
Education	What is the level of your education?
	What is the level of your spouse's education?
Military or government service benefits	Are you or your spouse eligible for any benefits deriving from military or government service? ☐ Yes ☐ No If yes, explain.

Notes

FINANCIAL OBJECTIVES

Rank from 1 to 9 the importance of being able to do the following:

- ________ Maintain/expand standard of living/family income.
- ________ Enjoy a comfortable retirement/retirement planning.
- ________ Take care of self and family during a period of long-term disability.
- ________ Invest and accumulate wealth/investment planning.
- ________ Reduce income tax burden/income tax planning.
- ________ Provide college educations for children.
- ________ Take care of family in the event of my death/insurance planning.
- ________ Develop an estate distribution plan/estate planning.
- ________ Other important financial planning goals. Specify:

Do you have a formal monthly budget? ☐ Yes ☐ No	If yes, indicate amount:	
How much do you save/invest annually?	In what form?	Why?
How much do you think you should be able to save/invest annually?	For what purpose?	

FACTORS AFFECTING YOUR FINANCIAL PLAN

Have you or your spouse ever made substantial gifts to family members or to tax-exempt beneficiaries? ☐ Yes ☐ No If yes, give details.
What special bequests do you or your spouse intend to make (including charitable bequests)?
Are you dissatisfied with your previous saving/investment results? ☐ Yes ☐ No Explain.
Are there any savings/investments you feel committed to (for past performance, family, or social reasons)? ☐ Yes ☐ No If yes, explain.
Is your spouse good at handling money? ☐ Yes ☐ No
If you die, would your spouse be able to manage family finances? ☐ Yes ☐ No
At what age would you like to retire? At what age would your spouse like to retire?
Tax considerations aside, in what manner would you (or your spouse) want your estate(s) distributed? Explain.
What do you think financial planning should do for you?

Notes

OBJECTIVES REQUIRING ADDITIONAL INCOME/CAPITAL

Do your children attend public or private schools?

If private, annual cost: (elementary) (secondary)

Do you plan for your children to attend private schools later? ☐ Yes ☐ No

If yes, when?

Education Fund

Name of Child	Age	No. Years until College	Estimated 4-Year Cost		Estimated Graduate School Costs	Capital Allocated	Monthly Income Allocated
			If Private	If Public			

Support for Family Member(s)

Name	Age	Relation	Estimated Cost	Estimated Period of Funding	Capital Allocated	Monthly Income Allocated

Other Objectives

Objective	Target Date	Estimated Cost	Estimated Period of Funding	Capital Allocated	Monthly Income Allocated

Notes

SOURCES OF INCOME

Annual Income

	Client	Spouse*	Dependents*
Wages, salary, bonus, etc.			
Income as business owner (self-employment)			
Real estate rental			
Dividends			
Investments (public stock, mutual funds, etc.)			
Close corporation stock			
Interest			
Investments (bonds, money market funds, T-bills, etc.)			
Savings accounts, certificates of deposit			
Loans, notes			
Trust income			
Life insurance settlement options			
Child support/alimony			
Annuities			
Other sources (specify)			
Other sources (specify)			
Other sources (specify)			
Total annual income			

*If spouse or dependents are employed, give details here.

Income Tax Last year

Federal			
State			
Local			
Total income tax paid last year			
Estimated quarterly tax this year			

Future Annual Income Estimate

Next year			
Three years			
Five years			
How often do you expect a salary increase or bonus?			
On average, how much of a salary increase or bonus do you expect annually?			
Has your total annual income fluctuated significantly during the past three years?			

CASH FLOW STATEMENT

Annual Income

	Current Yr.	Projections for Subsequent Years				
	20___	Assumptions	20___	20___	20___	20___
Wages, salary, bonus, etc.: Client						
Wages, salary, bonus, etc.: Spouse						
Income as business owner (self-employment)						
Real estate rental						
Dividends—investments						
Dividends—close corporation stock						
Interest on bonds: Taxable						
Interest on bonds: Tax exempt						
Interest on savings accts., CDs						
Interest on loans, notes, etc.						
Trust income						
Life insurance settlement options						
Annuities						
Child support/alimony						
Other sources (specify)						
Total annual income						

Fixed Expenses

Housing (mortgage/rent)						
Utilities and telephone						
Food, groceries, etc.						
Clothing and cleaning						
Income and Social Security taxes						
Property taxes						
Transportation (auto/commuting)						
Medical/dental/drugs/health insurance						
Debt repayment						
House upkeep/repairs/maintenance						
Life, property and liability insurance						
Child support/alimony						
Current education expenses						
Total fixed expenses						

Discretionary Expenses

Vacations/travel/etc.						
Recreation/entertainment						
Contributions/gifts						
Household furnishings						
Education fund						
Savings/investments						
Other (specify)						
Total discretionary expenses						
Total annual expenses						
Net cash flow (total annual income minus total annual expenses)						

INVENTORY OF ASSETS

Cash, Near-Cash Equivalents

Items	No. Units or Shares	Date Acquired	Amount, Cost, or Other Basis	Market Value and Titled Owners					
				Client	Spouse	Joint (survivor rights)	Joint (no survivor rights)	Com-munity Property	Other*
Checking accounts/cash									
Savings accounts									
Money-market funds									
Treasury bills									
Commercial paper									
Short-term CDs									
Cash value, life insurance									
Accum. dividends, life insurance									
Savings bonds									
Other (specify)									
Subtotal									

U.S. Govt., Municipal, Corporate Bonds, and Bond Funds: Issuer, Maturity, Call Dates

Subtotal									

Preferred Stock: Issuer, Maturity, Call Dates

Subtotal									

Common Stock: Issuer, Listed (L), Unlisted (U), Nonmarketable (NM)

Subtotal									

Warrants and Options: Issuer, Expiration Date

Subtotal									

Mutual Funds and Type: Growth (G), Income (I), Balanced (B), Indexed (IX), Speculative (S)

Subtotal									

*Life estate, leasehold or term interest, future interest, tenancy in common, powers, children, custodial accounts, trusts, etc.

Cash, Near-Cash Equivalents

Annual Yield		Amount Available for Liquidity	Amount of Indebtedness	Location, Description, Client's Reasons for Holding Asset, etc.	Items
%	$				
					Checking accounts/cash
					Savings accounts
					Money-market funds
					Treasury bills
					Commercial paper
					Short-term CDs
					Cash value, life insurance
					Accum. dividends, life insurance
					Savings bonds
					Other (specify)
					Subtotal

U.S. Govt., Municipal, Corporate Bonds, and Bond Funds: Issuer, Maturity, Call Dates

					Subtotal

Preferred Stock: Issuer, Maturity, Call Dates

					Subtotal

Common Stock: Issuer, Listed (L), Unlisted (U), Nonmarketable (NM)

					Subtotal

Warrants and Options: Issuer, Expiration Date

					Subtotal

Mutual Funds and Type: Growth (G), Income (I), Balanced (B), Indexed (IX), Speculative (S)

					Subtotal

Real Estate

Items	No. Units or Shares	Date Acquired	Amount, Cost, or Other Basis	Market Value and Titled Owners					
				Client	Spouse	Joint (survivor rights)	Joint (no survivor rights)	Com-munity Property	Other*
Personal residence									
Seasonal residence									
Investment (residential)									
Investment (commercial)									
Land									
Other (specify)									
Subtotal									

Long-Term, Nonmarketable Assets

Long-term CDs									
Vested retirement benefits									
Life insurance cash values									
Annuities (fixed/indexed/variable)									
HR-10 plan (Keogh)									
IRAs (Roth/traditional)									
Mortgages owned									
Land contracts									
Limited partnership units									
Other (specify)									
Subtotal									

Personal Assets

Household furnishings									
Automobile(s)									
Recreational vehicles									
Boats									
Jewelry/furs									
Collections (art, coins, etc.)									
Hobby equipment									
Other (specify)									
Subtotal									

Miscellaneous Assets

Interest(s) in trust(s)									
Receivables									
Patents, copyrights, royalties									
Other (specify)									
Subtotal									
Totals of all columns									

*Life estate, leasehold or term interest, future interest, tenancy in common, powers, children, custodial accounts, trusts, etc.

Real Estate

Annual Yield %	Annual Yield $	Amount Available for Liquidity	Amount of Indebtedness	Location, Description, Client's Reasons for Holding Asset, etc.	Items
					Personal residence
					Seasonal residence
					Investment (residential)
					Investment (commercial)
					Land
					Other (specify)
					Subtotal

Long-Term, Nonmarketable Assets

					Long-term CDs
					Vested retirement benefits
					Life insurance cash values
					Annuities (fixed/indexed/variable)
					HR-10 plan (Keogh)
					IRAs (Roth/traditional)
					Mortgages owned
					Land contracts
					Limited partnership units
					Other (specify)
					Subtotal

Personal Assets

					Household furnishings
					Automobile(s)
					Recreational vehicles
					Boats
					Jewelry/furs
					Collections (art, coins, etc.)
					Hobby equipment
					Other (specify)
					Subtotal

Miscellaneous Assets

					Interest(s) in trust(s)
					Receivables
					Patents, copyrights, royalties
					Other (specify)
					Subtotal
					Totals of all columns

BUSINESS INTEREST

General Information

Full legal name	Phone
Address	
Business now operates as ☐ proprietorship ☐ partnership ☐ corporation ☐ S corporation ☐ other (specify)	
When does the fiscal year end?	
What accounting method is used?	
What is the principal business activity?	
In what year did this business begin operation?	
If it began other than as a corporation, what was the date of incorporation?	State of incorporation?
Classes of stock No. authorized shares	No. outstanding shares
What is your function in the business?	
Do you have an employment contract?	

Present Owners*

		Insurability Problem?			Form of Business		
					Corporation		Partnership
		Yes	No				
(A)	*Client*	☐	☐	owns	____% common	____% preferred	____% ________
(B)	________	☐	☐	owns	____% common	____% preferred	____% ________
(C)	________	☐	☐	owns	____% common	____% preferred	____% ________
(D)	________	☐	☐	owns	____% common	____% preferred	____% ________
(E)	________	☐	☐	owns	____% common	____% preferred	____% ________

* Indicate relationship to client by blood or marriage.

Key Employees (other than present owners)

	Insurability Problem			Insurability Problem	
	Yes	No		Yes	No
________	☐	☐	________	☐	☐
________	☐	☐	________	☐	☐
________	☐	☐	________	☐	☐
________	☐	☐	________	☐	☐

Disposition of Business Interest

Do you want your business interest retained or sold if you
retire? ☐ retained ☐ sold   become disabled? ☐ retained ☐ sold   die? ☐ retained ☐ sold

IF RETAINED
Who will own your interest and how will the person(s) acquire it?

Who will replace you in your job?

IF SOLD
Who will buy your interest?

How is purchase price to be determined?

What is the funding arrangement?

Do you have a buy-sell agreement? ☐ Yes ☐ No

If yes, is it a cross-purchase, entity-purchase, or "wait-and-see" type of agreement?

Where is it located?

Valuation of Business Interest

Estimate the lowest price for which the entire business might be sold as a going concern today.

What is the lowest price you would accept for your interest today?

If you were not an owner, what is your estimate of the highest price you would pay today for the entire business as a going concern?

What is the highest price you would pay today to buy the interest of your coowners?

Has an impartial valuation of the business been made? ☐ Yes ☐ No If yes, when?
What valuation method was used?   What value was established?

What is the average business indebtedness?
Estimate the highest it has ever been.   Estimate the lowest it has ever been.

Are there patents, special processes, or leased equipment/real property used by, but not owned by, the business?
☐ Yes ☐ No If yes, who owns what, and under what terms is each used or leased?

What are the prospects for growth, sale, merger, or going public?

Survivor Control (letters in parentheses refer to owners named on page 14)

IF (A) DIES	IF (B) DIES	IF (C) DIES	IF (D) DIES	IF (E) DIES
B wants ____% control	A wants ____%	A wants ____%	A wants ____%	A wants ____%
C wants ____% control	C wants ____%	B wants ____%	B wants ____%	B wants ____%
D wants ____% control	D wants ____%	D wants ____%	C wants ____%	C wants ____%
E wants ____% control	E wants ____%	E wants ____%	E wants ____%	D wants ____%
__ wants ____% control	__ wants ____%	__ wants ____%	__ wants ____%	__ wants ____%

It is suggested that the client request this data directly from the bookkeeper or other appropriate person.

EMPLOYEE CENSUS DATA*

			Name			Date of Birth			Date Em-ployed†						Earnings			
	Sex	Marital Status	Last	First	M.I.	Month	Day	Year	Month	Day	Year	Full-time‡	Hourly	Salaried	Annual Salary or Wage	Additional Compen-sation	Member of Collective Bargaining Unit?	Occupation or Job Title
1																		
2																		
3																		
4																		
5																		
6																		
7																		
8																		
9																		
10																		
11																		
12																		
13																		
14																		
15																		
16																		
17																		
18																		
19																		
20																		
21																		
22																		
23																		
24																		
25																		

*It is suggested that the client request this data directly from the bookkeeper or other appropriate person.
†The date of its incorporation is also the date of employment of former proprietors or partners of a business.
‡A full-time employee is one who works 1,000 or more hours per year.

INVENTORY OF LIABILITIES

Outstanding Obligations of Client or Spouse	Original Amount	Maximum Credit Available	Present Balance	Monthly/ Annual Repayment	Effective Interest Rate	Payments Remaining/ Maturity Date	Secured?	Insured?
Retail charge accounts								
Credit cards								
Family/personal loans								
Securities margin loans								
Investment liabilities								
Bank loans								
Life insurance policy loans								
Income tax liability								
Federal								
State								
Local								
Property taxes								
Mortgage(s)								
Lease(s)								
Family member support								
Child support/alimony								
Other (specify)								
Total								

Are there any other liabilities your estate might be called on to pay? ☐ Yes ☐ No If yes, explain.

Do you foresee any future liabilities (business expansion, new home, etc.)? ☐ Yes ☐ No If yes, explain.

Policies and most recent policy anniversary premium notices should be examined for the information recorded on this page.

INDIVIDUALLY OWNED INSURANCE*

Life Insurance

Item	Policy 1	Policy 2	Policy 3
Policy number			
Name of insurance company			
Issue age			
Insured			
Owner of policy			
Type of policy			
Annual premium			
Net annual outlay by client			
Current cash value			
Extra benefits (for example, waiver of premium, accidental death, etc.)			
Amount of base policy			
Dividends (value & option)			
Term rider(s)			
Loan outstanding			
Net amount payable at death			
Primary beneficiary and settlement option elected			
Secondary beneficiary and settlement option elected			

Long-Term Care Insurance

Item	Policy 1	Policy 2	Policy 3
Policy number			
Name of insurance company			
Issue age			
Insured			
Owner of policy			
Type of policy (Qualified/Nonqualified)			
Annual premium			
Inflation protection			
Nonforfeiture benefit			
Third party notification Name:			
Issued prior to January 1, 1997	☐ Yes ☐ No	☐ Yes ☐ No	☐ Yes ☐ No
Level of care			
Term rider(s)			
Elimination period (days)			
Maximum duration (years)			
Restoration	☐ Yes ☐ No	☐ Yes ☐ No	☐ Yes ☐ No
Spousal coverage	☐ Yes ☐ No	☐ Yes ☐ No	☐ Yes ☐ No
Maximum benefit day/cumulative			

*Policies and most recent policy anniversary premium notices should be examined for the information recorded on this page.

Medical/Dental Insurance

Item	Policy 1	Policy 2	Policy 3	Policy 4
Type of policy				
Policy number				
Name of insurance company or other provider				
Insured				
Annual cost to client				
Type of continuance or renewal provision				
Deductible				
Percentage participation				
Stop-loss limit				
Inside limits				
Overall maximum				

Disability Income Insurance

Item	Policy 1	Policy 2	Policy 3	Policy 4
Policy number				
Name of insurance company or other provider				
Insured				
Annual cost to client				
Type of continuance or renewal provision				
Definition of disability				
Monthly disability income				
Accident				
Sickness				
Partial disability provision				
Waiting period				
Accident				
Sickness				
Benefit period				
Accident				
Sickness				

*Policies should be examined for the information recorded on this page.

Homeowners Insurance

Item	Principal Residence	Seasonal Residence	Other Property
Policy number			
Name of insurance company			
Address of property			
HO form # (or other type of policy)			
Coverage on dwelling			
Replacement cost of dwelling			
Replacement cost of contents			
Liability limits			
Endorsements			
Deductibles			
Annual cost			

Automobile Insurance

Item	Auto #1	Auto #2	Auto #3 (or other vehicles, trailers)
Policy number			
Name of insurance company			
Automobile make/year			
Liability limits			
No-fault/medical benefits			
Uninsured motorist			
Collision/deductible			
Comprehensive/deductible			
Annual cost			

Other Property/Liability Insurance

Item	Policy 1	Policy 2	Policy 3
Type of policy			
Policy number			
Name of insurance company			
Property covered			
Limits			
Annual cost			

Umbrella Liability Insurance

Item	Policy
Policy number	
Name of insurance company	
Liability limits	
Retention	
Annual cost	

*Policies should be examined for the information recorded on this page.

EMPLOYMENT-RELATED BENEFITS CHECKLIST

Name and address of client's employer ____________________

Name and address of spouse's employer ____________________

Who can provide detailed information on employee benefits for you and your spouse?

Client	*Spouse*
Name ____________	Name ____________
Title ____________	Title ____________
Department ____________	Department ____________
Phone ____________	Phone ____________

	Benefit now provided for client?		Benefit now provided for spouse?		Information/Comments
Life and Health Insurance	Yes	No	Yes	No	
Death benefits	☐	☐	☐	☐	
Accidental death/dismemberment	☐	☐	☐	☐	
Travel accident	☐	☐	☐	☐	
Medical expense benefits	☐	☐	☐	☐	
Short-term disability income (sick pay)	☐	☐	☐	☐	
Long-term disability income	☐	☐	☐	☐	
Retirement Benefits/ Deferred Compensation*					
Qualified pension plan	☐	☐	☐	☐	
Qualified profit-sharing plan	☐	☐	☐	☐	
Nonqualified deferred-compensation plan	☐	☐	☐	☐	
Salary reduction plan [§401(k)]	☐	☐	☐	☐	
Simplified employee pension (SEP)	☐	☐	☐	☐	
Stock bonus plan	☐	☐	☐	☐	
Employee stock-ownership plan (ESOP)	☐	☐	☐	☐	
Employee stock-purchase plan	☐	☐	☐	☐	
Incentive stock-option plan [§422]	☐	☐	☐	☐	
Restricted stock plan [§83(b)]	☐	☐	☐	☐	
Phantom stock plan [§83(a)]	☐	☐	☐	☐	
Tax-deferred annuity plan [§403(b)]	☐	☐	☐	☐	
Salary continuation after death	☐	☐	☐	☐	
Other (specify)	☐	☐	☐	☐	
Miscellaneous Benefits					
Excess medical reimbursement plan	☐	☐	☐	☐	
Split-dollar life insurance	☐	☐	☐	☐	
Auto/homeowners insurance	☐	☐	☐	☐	
Legal expense	☐	☐	☐	☐	
Company car	☐	☐	☐	☐	
Education reimbursement	☐	☐	☐	☐	
Club membership	☐	☐	☐	☐	
Other (specify)	☐	☐	☐	☐	

*Describe appropriate benefits on page 22.

EMPLOYMENT-RELATED RETIREMENT BENEFITS/DEFERRED COMPENSATION

Type	Employee's Annual Contribution	Benefits to Client			Benefits to Survivors			
		Lump-sum Pmts.	Monthly Income		Beneficiary	Lump-sum Pmts.	Monthly Income	
			Amount	Beginning/ Ending			Amount	Beginning/ Ending
Qualified pension plan								
Qualified profit-sharing plan								
Nonqualified deferred-compensation plan								
Salary reduction plan [§401(k)]								
Stock bonus plan								
Employee stock-ownership plan (ESOP)								
Employee stock-purchase plan								
Incentive stock-option plan [§422]								
Restricted stock plan [§83(b)]								
Phantom stock plan [§83(a)]								
Tax-deferred annuity plan [§403(b)]								
Salary continuation after death								
Other (specify)								
Other (specify)								

Explain and describe pertinent details for planning purposes here (for example, anticipated benefits not yet in place; client's views on relevance, need, and feasibility of these benefits; problems associated with implementing benefits; etc.).

Social Security Benefits

What are the estimated retirement benefits (in current dollars)?

Client only: Client and spouse:

What are the estimated disability benefits the client is eligible for if disabled today?

Client only: Client and spouse:

What are the estimated survivor's benefits payable to the client's family if death should occur today?

RISK/RETURN PROFILE

On a scale from 0 to 5, with 5 representing a strong preference and 0 representing an aversion, indicate your preference for the following instruments of savings and investment by circling the appropriate number.

Savings account	0	1	2	3	4	5
Money-market fund	0	1	2	3	4	5
U.S. government bond	0	1	2	3	4	5
Corporate bond	0	1	2	3	4	5
Mutual fund (growth)	0	1	2	3	4	5
Common stock (growth)	0	1	2	3	4	5
Mutual fund (income)	0	1	2	3	4	5
Municipal bond	0	1	2	3	4	5
Real estate (direct ownership)	0	1	2	3	4	5
Variable annuity	0	1	2	3	4	5
Limited partnership unit (real estate, oil and gas, cattle, equipment leasing)	0	1	2	3	4	5
Commodities, gold, collectibles	0	1	2	3	4	5

On a scale from 0 to 5, circle the number to the right of each of the items below that most accurately reflects your own financial concerns; 5 indicates a very strong concern and 0 indicates no concern.

Liquidity	0	1	2	3	4	5
Safety of principal	0	1	2	3	4	5
Capital appreciation	0	1	2	3	4	5
Current income	0	1	2	3	4	5
Inflation protection	0	1	2	3	4	5
Future income	0	1	2	3	4	5
Tax reduction/deferral	0	1	2	3	4	5

Advisor's comments and observations

INCOME AND LUMP-SUM NEEDS FOR DISABILITY, RETIREMENT, AND DEATH

	Client	Spouse/ Children
Disability Income Needs		
Monthly income needed in current dollars	$ ______	$ ______
Retirement Income Needs		
Monthly income needed in current dollars	$ ______	$ ______
Survivors' Income Needs*		
Monthly income needed in current dollars for surviving family members during the following periods after death:		
Adjustment period (adjustment of standard of living in a transitional period, as needed)	$ ______	$ ______
Until youngest child is self-supporting (number of years __________)	$ ______	$ ______
After youngest child is self-supporting	$ ______	$ ______
Survivors' Lump-sum Needs*		
Last expenses (final illness and funeral)	$ ______	$ ______
Emergency fund	$ ______	$ ______
Mortgage cancellation fund (if appropriate)	$ ______	$ ______
Notes and loans payable	$ ______	$ ______
Accrued taxes (income, real estate, etc., if not withheld)	$ ______	$ ______
Children's education (if not already funded)	$ ______	$ ______
Estate settlement costs and taxes (if not provided by liquidity)	$ ______	$ ______
Other (specify)	$ ______	$ ______
Total lump-sum needs in current dollars	$ ______	$ ______

* Some survivors' needs may be met by either periodic income or lump-sum payments or by some combination of the two approaches. Double counting in both categories should be avoided.

Notes

AUTHORIZATION FOR INFORMATION

TO: ______________________________

____

____

Please provide any information that is in your possession and that is asked for in connection with a survey of my/our financial affairs to ______________________________

____
(client's signature)

____
(spouse's signature)

____
(date)

TO: ______________________________
(company)

Please provide any information that is in your possession and that is requested by ______________________________

______________________________ concerning the following policies of which I am the owner:

______________________________ ______________________________

______________________________ ______________________________

______________________________ ______________________________

____
(policyowner's signature)

____
(date)

RECEIPT FOR DOCUMENTS

Insurance Policies: Life, Long-Term Care, Medical/Dental, Disability Income, and Property/Liability

Company	Policy Number	☑	Company	Policy Number	☑
____________	________	☐	____________	________	☐
____________	________	☐	____________	________	☐
____________	________	☐	____________	________	☐
____________	________	☐	____________	________	☐
____________	________	☐	____________	________	☐

Original policies checked ☑ above have been received for review and analysis; they will be returned upon completion of analysis or client request.

____
(advisor)

____
(address)

____
(phone)

____
(date)

All original policies and documents checked in this receipt have been returned to me.

____
(client)

____
(date)

Personal/Family Documents (copies)	Date	Business Documents (copies)	Date
☐ Tax returns (3–5 years)	______	☐ Tax returns (3–5 years)	______
☐ Wills (client and spouse)	______	☐ Financial statements (3–5 years)	______
☐ Trust instruments	______	☐ Deferred-compensation plan	______
☐ Financial statements	______	☐ HR-10 plan (Keogh)	______
☐ Personal/family budgets	______	☐ IRAs (Roth/traditional)	______
☐ Sale/purchase contract	______	☐ Simplified employee pension (SEP)	______
☐ Current insurance offers	______	☐ Pension/profit-sharing plan	______
☐ Current investment offers	______	☐ §401(k) or §403(b) plan	______
☐ Deeds, mortgages, land contracts	______	☐ Stock-option/purchase agreement	______
☐ Guardian nominations	______	☐ Buy-sell agreements	______
☐ Leases (as lessor or lessee)	______	☐ Employment agreement	______
☐ Notices of awards, elections	______	☐ Employee benefits booklet	______
☐ Power of attorney/appointment	______	☐ Articles of incorporation	______
☐ Separation/divorce/nuptial	______	☐ Merger/acquisition agreement	______
☐ Patents/copyrights/royalties	______	☐ Partnership agreement	______
☐ Employee benefits statement	______	☐ Company patents	______
☐ Other (specify)	______	☐ Equipment leasing agreement(s)	______
☐ Other (specify)	______	☐ Other (specify)	______

OBSERVATIONS FROM PLANNING SESSIONS

As soon after planning sessions as possible the financial advisor should record observations and impressions about the client in terms of the following:

Personal interests (sports, hobbies, music, etc.) ____________________

____

____

Civic-mindedness ____________________

____

Financial sophistication ____________________

____

College ties ____________________

____

Condition of health ____________________

____

____

Financial risk-taking propensity ____________________

____

Investment decisions client has made and why ____________________

____

____

Observations and impressions

All code section references are to the Internal Revenue Code of 1986 as amended.

TAX-PLANNING CHECKLIST*

Individual Planning

		At Present Yes	At Present No	Advisable Yes	Advisable No
1.	Does the client itemize rather than utilize the standard deduction?	☐	☐	☐	☐
2.	Are all personal and dependency exemptions being taken (children, parents, foster children, etc.)? [§§151, 152]	☐	☐	☐	☐
3.	Are maximum deductions for all expenses related to the production of income being taken?	☐	☐	☐	☐
4.	a. Is optimum utilization being made of retirement plans for tax advantage?	☐	☐	☐	☐
	b. Has the appropriate type of plan or plans been chosen?	☐	☐	☐	☐
5.	Are contributions to c haritable and other tax-exempt organizations being used as fully as the client is disposed to use them? [§170]	☐	☐	☐	☐
6.	Are the client's real property investments being fully used for tax advantages?	☐	☐	☐	☐
7.	Is the impact of the alternative minimum tax being considered for transactions involving tax-preference items? [§55]	☐	☐	☐	☐
8.	Are income and deductions being directed to specific years to avoid drastic fluctuation by				
	a. accelerating income	☐	☐	☐	☐
	b. postponing deductions	☐	☐	☐	☐
	c. postponing income	☐	☐	☐	☐
	d. accelerating deductions	☐	☐	☐	☐
	e. avoiding constructive receipt	☐	☐	☐	☐
		☐	☐	☐	☐
9.	To reduce estate taxes				
	a. Have incidents of life insurance ownership been assigned?	☐	☐	☐	☐
	b. Is a life insurance trust being used? [§§2035, 2042]	☐	☐	☐	☐
10.	Have installment sales of investments or property been arranged to minimize tax? [§453]	☐	☐	☐	☐
11.	Is investment in tax-exempt instruments being used?	☐	☐	☐	☐
12.	Is income being shifted to lower-bracket taxpayers through outright gifts or other lifetime transfers such as family partnerships or irrevocable trusts?	☐	☐	☐	☐
13.	Is a qualified minors [§2503(c)] trust being used effectively for income shifting or other tax advantage?	☐	☐	☐	☐
14.	Have gifts been made under the Uniform Gifts to Minors Act (UGMA) or the Uniform Transfers to Minors Act (UTMA)?	☐	☐	☐	☐
15.	Are gift/sale leasebacks being used?	☐	☐	☐	☐

*All code section references are to the Internal Revenue Code of 1986 as amended.

Individual Planning (continued)

		At Present Yes	At Present No	Advisable Yes	Advisable No
16.	Have alternative distribution methods for qualified plans been analyzed for tax consequences?	☐	☐	☐	☐
17.	Are capital-loss offsets being used to reduce total income subject to tax?	☐	☐	☐	☐
18.	Are qualified plan distributions, rollovers to another qualified plan, or IRAs advisable for the client in the near future?	☐	☐	☐	☐
19.	Are contributions to a new or existing IRA advisable if				
	a. the client can make deductible contributions?	☐	☐	☐	☐
	b. the client can make only nondeductible contributions?	☐	☐	☐	☐
20.	Have like-kind exchanges of property been compared with sale and repurchase and utilized when more advantageous? [§1031]	☐	☐	☐	☐
21.	Is the client paying substantial amounts of nondeductible loan interest that should be consolidated under deductible home equity loans? [§163]	☐	☐	☐	☐
22.	Have returns of capital on investment been distinguished from taxable income? (For example, has the client's basis in the investment been ascertained and any special tax treatment to which that investment is entitled determined?)	☐	☐	☐	☐
23.	Is the client suited for tax-advantaged investments?	☐	☐	☐	☐
24.	Indicate any situation unique to this client that does not appear above.				

Business Planning

		At Present Yes	At Present No	Advisable Yes	Advisable No
1.	Are maximum allowable deductions for all expenses being taken?	☐	☐	☐	☐
2.	Are expiring carryovers of credits, net operating losses, and charitable contributions being effectively used through timing of income and deductions? [§§39, 170, 172]	☐	☐	☐	☐
3.	a. Is optimum use being made of retirement plans for tax advantage?	☐	☐	☐	☐
	b. Has the appropriate type of plan or plans been chosen?	☐	☐	☐	☐
4.	Are contributions to charitable and other tax-exempt organizations being used as fully as the client is disposed to use them? [§§170, 501]	☐	☐	☐	☐
5.	a. Is the form of client's business or investment being fully utilized to maximize personal deductions and credits (for example, corporation, partnership, trust, S corp.)?	☐	☐	☐	☐
	b. Are the business's investments being fully used to maximize deductions and credits to the shareholder(s)?	☐	☐	☐	☐
6.	Are income and deductions being directed to specific years to avoid drastic fluctuation by				
	a. accelerating income	☐	☐	☐	☐
	b. postponing deductions	☐	☐	☐	☐
	c. postponing income	☐	☐	☐	☐
	d. accelerating deductions	☐	☐	☐	☐
	e. avoiding constructive receipt	☐	☐	☐	☐
7.	Is the full range of deductible employment fringe benefits being explored and used within the client's limits?	☐	☐	☐	☐
8.	Are gift/sale leasebacks appropriate for this client?	☐	☐	☐	☐
9.	Have alternative distribution methods for qualified plans been analyzed for tax consequences?	☐	☐	☐	☐
10.	Is sale-or-exchange treatment preferable for redemption of equity in a closely held corporation? [§§301, 302, 303, 318]	☐	☐	☐	☐
11.	Have nonqualified retirement or deferred-compensation plans been considered? [§83]	☐	☐	☐	☐
12.	Are stock options possible and advantageous? [§422]	☐	☐	☐	☐
13.	Have simplified employee pensions (SEPs) been compared with other forms of deferred compensation?	☐	☐	☐	☐
14.	Are qualified plans designed for maximum employee advantage during employment as well as at retirement? (For example, do they permit loans and rollovers from other plans, etc.?)	☐	☐	☐	☐

Business Planning (continued)

		At Present Yes	At Present No	Advisable Yes	Advisable No
15.	a. Have buy-sell plans to take effect at death been developed and formalized by legal agreements?	☐	☐	☐	☐
	b. If yes, have they been appropriately funded?	☐	☐	☐	☐
16.	Have lifetime transfer methods been considered to facilitate the orderly continuation of the business, for example, in case of disability?	☐	☐	☐	☐
17.	Are employment contracts being used effectively to support the reasonableness of executive compensation?	☐	☐	☐	☐
18.	Indicate any situation unique to this client that does not appear above.				

Estate Planning

		At Present Yes	At Present No	Advisable Yes	Advisable No
1.	Have the client and spouse considered electing not to fully use the marital deduction if such an election is tax advantageous to their cumulative estates? [§2056]	☐	☐	☐	☐
2.	Have life insurance policies been properly positioned to minimize estate taxes?	☐	☐	☐	☐
3.	Does the estate appear to have sufficient liquidity to fund postmortem expenses and estate/inheritance tax liabilities?	☐	☐	☐	☐
4.	Has optimum use been made of generation-skipping transfer exemptions? [§§2601–2664]	☐	☐	☐	☐
5.	Have testamentary charitable dispositions and their advantages been explored? [§2055]	☐	☐	☐	☐
6.	a. Are lifetime gifting programs being used to shift ownership of assets from the client's estate? [§§2503(b), 2503(c)]	☐	☐	☐	☐
	b. Have gifts been made under the Uniform Gifts to Minors Act (UGMA) or the Uniform Transfers to Minors Act (UTMA)?	☐	☐	☐	☐
7.	a. Is the client's will current?	☐	☐	☐	☐
	b. Does the will dispose of estate assets in accordance with the client's wishes?	☐	☐	☐	☐
8.	Has the value of each estate asset been explored in order to obtain an estimate of potential estate tax liability?	☐	☐	☐	☐
9.	Has it been determined that the client can qualify for estate tax deferral? [§6166]	☐	☐	☐	☐
10.	If the client qualifies for the requisite percentage of ownership in a corporation, can §303 be utilized to assure sale-or-exchange treatment for stock redeemed to pay administration expenses and estate taxes?	☐	☐	☐	☐
11.	Have the client's personal planning objectives, feelings, and thoughts been given equal weight with tax planning?	☐	☐	☐	☐
12.	Has an existing estate plan been evaluated as to the impact of the current applicable credit amount, marital deduction, and gift tax exclusion? [§§2010, 2056, 2503, 2523]	☐	☐	☐	☐
13.	Has the impact of state death taxes on the client's estate been evaluated?	☐	☐	☐	☐
14.	Has consideration been given to the potential consequence of certain transfers made within 3 years of death? [§2035]	☐	☐	☐	☐
15.	Have rules on valuation of certain property (for example, family farms and real property used in a closely held business) been considered? [§2032A]	☐	☐	☐	☐
16.	a. Does the client have any reversionary interests or hold any powers of appointment?	☐	☐	☐	☐
	b. If so, have they been examined for their potential tax impact? [§§2037, 2041]	☐	☐	☐	☐
17.	a. Does the client have an incapacity plan in place?	☐	☐	☐	☐
	b. Does the client have a durable power of attorney?	☐	☐	☐	☐
	c. Has consideration been given to appropriate health care and advance medical directive documents?	☐	☐	☐	☐
18.	Indicate any situation unique to this client that does not appear above.				

FINANCIAL POSITION STATEMENT

Assets		Projections for Subsequent Years			
Cash, Near-Cash Equivalents	**Current Value**	**Assumptions**	**20____**	**20____**	**20____**
Checking accounts/cash					
Savings accounts					
Money-market funds					
Treasury bills					
Commercial paper					
Short-term CDs					
Life insurance/annuity cash values					
Life insurance, accumulated dividends					
Savings bonds					
Other (specify)					
Subtotal					
Other Financial Assets					
U.S. government bonds					
Municipal bonds					
Corporate bonds					
Preferred stock					
Common stock					
Nonmarketable securities					
Warrants and options					
Mutual funds					
Investment real estate (residential/commercial)					
Long-term CDs					
Vested retirement benefits					
Annuities (fixed/indexed/variable)					
HR-10 plan (Keogh)					
IRAs (Roth/traditional)					
Mortgages owned					
Land contracts					
Limited partnership units					
Interest(s) in trust(s)					
Receivables					
Patents, copyrights, royalties					
Value of business interest (from page 15)					
Other (specify)					
Subtotal					

Assets (continued)

Personal Assets	Current Value	Projections for Subsequent Years: Assumptions	20___	20___	20___
Personal residence					
Seasonal residence					
Automobile(s)					
Recreation vehicles					
Household furnishings					
Boats					
Jewelry/furs					
Collections (art, coins, etc.)					
Hobby equipment					
Other (specify)					
Subtotal					
Total assets					

Liabilities

Charge accts./credit cards					
Family/personal loans					
Margin/bank/life ins. loans					
Income taxes (fed., state, local)					
Property taxes					
Investment liabilities					
Mortgage(s)					
Lease(s)					
Child support					
Alimony					
Other (specify)					
Other (specify)					
Other (specify)					
Total Liabilities					

Net Worth

Total assets minus total liabilities					

INCOME AND LUMP-SUM RESOURCES FOR DISABILITY, RETIREMENT*, AND DEATH

Sources of Funds	For Disability			For Retirement			For Death		
	Lump-sum Pmts.	Monthly Income		Lump-sum Pmts.	Monthly Income		Lump-sum Pmts.	Monthly Income	
		Amount	Beginning/ Ending		Amount	Beginning/ Ending		Amount	Beginning/ Ending
Continuing income†									
Income of spouse									
Social Security benefits‡									
Qualified pension plan									
Qualified profit-sharing plan									
HR-10 plan (Keogh)									
IRAs (Roth/traditional)									
Nonqualified deferred compensation									
Salary reduction plan [§401(k)]									
Tax-deferred annuity plan [§403(b)]									
Other retirement benefits*									
Group life insurance									
Personal life insurance									
Annuities (fixed, indexed, variable)									
Group short-term disability income									
Group long-term disability income									
Personal disability income insurance									
Asset liquidation									
Proceeds of sale of business interest									
Other (specify)									
Other (specify)									
Other (specify)									
Totals									

*See page 22 of the Fact Finder for a complete listing of Employment-Related Retirement Benefits/Deferred Compensation.
†Be sure to adjust for income sources from page 8 of the Fact Finder that will terminate or decrease if client or spouse dies, retires, or is disabled.
‡See the bottom of page 22.

CHECKLIST FOR FINANCIAL PLANNING REVIEW

Change in	Has Occurred	Is Expected
1. Marital status		
Marriage	☐	☐
Separation	☐	☐
Divorce	☐	☐
Remarriage	☐	☐
2. Number of dependents		
Increase	☐	☐
Decrease	☐	☐
3. Health status		
Client	☐	☐
Spouse	☐	☐
Dependent	☐	☐
4. Residence	☐	☐
5. Occupation		
Client	☐	☐
Spouse	☐	☐
Dependent	☐	☐
6. Family financial status		
Borrowing	☐	☐
Lending	☐	☐
Gifts over $1,000 received	☐	☐
Gifts over $1,000 made	☐	☐
Purchase of property	☐	☐
Sale of property	☐	☐
Investments	☐	☐
Inheritance	☐	☐
Deferred income	☐	☐
Pension plan	☐	☐
Tax-deferred annuity	☐	☐
Dependent's income	☐	☐
7. Sources of income		
As employee	☐	☐
From self-employment	☐	☐
From tax-exempt employer	☐	☐
From investments	☐	☐
Inventions, patents, copyrights	☐	☐
Hobbies, avocations	☐	☐
8. Income tax status		
From single to joint return	☐	☐
From joint to single return	☐	☐
Capital gains	☐	☐
Capital losses	☐	☐
Charitable contributions	☐	☐
Unreimbursed casualty loss	☐	☐
Sick pay received	☐	☐
Unreimbursed medical expenses		
Tax-impact investment(s)	☐	☐
	☐	☐
9. Property ownership		
Purchase in joint ownership		
Purchase, n client owned		
Purchase, spouse owned	☐	☐
Purchase, dependent owned	☐	☐
Transfer to joint ownership	☐	☐
Transfer to client	☐	☐
Transfer to spouse	☐	☐
Transfer to dependent	☐	☐
Transfer to trustee	☐	☐
10. Liabilities		
Leases executed	☐	☐
Mortgage increase	☐	☐
Lawsuit against	☐	☐
Judgment against	☐	☐
Unsecured borrowing	☐	☐
Cosigning of notes	☐	☐
11. Business ownership		
New business formation	☐	☐
Interest purchase	☐	☐
Sale of interest	☐	☐
Transfer of interest	☐	☐
Reorganization among owners	☐	☐
Liquidation	☐	☐
Change of carrier	☐	☐
Termination or lapse	☐	☐
Surrender	☐	☐
12. Legal document status		
Change in last will	☐	☐
Change in trust	☐	☐
Buy-sell agreement	☐	☐
Agreement to defer income	☐	☐
Advance medical directives	☐	☐
Powers of attorney	☐	☐
Nuptial agreements	☐	☐
13. Insurance status		
Life insurance	☐	☐
Health insurance	☐	☐
Long-term care insurance	☐	☐
Disability income insurance	☐	☐
Annuities	☐	☐
Group insurance	☐	☐
Other employer plan	☐	☐
Property insurance	☐	☐
Liability insurance	☐	☐
Change of plan	☐	☐
14. Attitudes toward others		
In family	☐	☐
In business	☐	☐
In accepting professional advice	☐	☐
15. Interest in		
Idea previously discussed	☐	☐
Plans seen or heard about	☐	☐

Appendix B

Survey of Financial Risk Tolerance

Client Name/ID ____________________

FINANCIAL

PLANNING

Survey of Financial Risk Tolerance

The Survey of Financial Risk Tolerance (hereinafter referred to as the Survey) is a 40-item questionnaire that takes approximately 15 to 20 minutes to complete. Each individual question on the Survey is based on one of the approaches to assessing risk tolerance.

The Survey relies on direct measures of risk tolerance as well as proxy measures of this characteristic. Please understand, however, that this questionnaire, like all others, is meant to complement rather than serve as a substitute for a more comprehensive assessment. Always be sure to compare the impressions you gain using this questionnaire with other more objective evidence. For instance, one section of the questionnaire asks the client to indicate his or her preference for various investment vehicles. You should determine whether the expressed preferences match the client's actual portfolio of past and current investments.

Remember too that other factors besides the person's characteristic level of risk tolerance can influence the amount of risk he or she may be willing to take. Research suggests that people treat money differently depending on how it was acquired. Generally money that was easily earned, especially if acquired through a windfall (other than by an inheritance from a beloved relative), is more apt to be exposed to risk than money that was earned through hard labor. Likewise, since investments are likely to vary in their value and returns more sharply in the short run than in the long run, the client's investment horizon is a critical consideration. If a client is able to adopt a long-term horizon, there may be a correspondingly greater willingness to take a risk.

The financial advisor therefore needs to determine the suitability of the assessment procedure for the particular client and the client's unique situation. The Survey is intended only as a tool to assist the advisor in assessing a client's attitudes toward risk taking as part of a comprehensive review of appropriate investment choices. The Survey is not intended to substitute for the advisor's professional judgment of the client's level of risk tolerance and financial ability to sustain a loss.

How the Survey Can Be Used

There are two ways to use the Survey in the financial planning process, and both ways are described below.

As an Interview Discussion Aid

It is possible to use the Survey as a list of questions to ask the client during the course of a face-to-face interview, allowing the client to respond in his or her own words. For example, "How do you react to unexpected bad financial news?" can be answered by the client in a variety of ways. The answer, of course, needs to be analyzed by the financial advisor for the degree of risk aversion it conveys. This procedure imposes minimal restraints on the client's answers and allows the advisor to explore in depth through further questioning the reasons underlying them. But the costs are the amount of time it takes to ask the number of questions necessary to get a feel for the pattern of the client's answers and the potential for ambiguity in the answers.

As an Information-Gathering Device

The second way to use the Survey is to have the client complete the Survey by answering the questions. The advisor will then be able to obtain some sense of the client's risk tolerance by examining his or her answers to see if they follow a consistent pattern. This is possible because, with the exception of question 32, the answers for each question are arranged on a continuum, reflecting a progression from risk-averse to risk-tolerant behaviors. The use of standardized options provides a uniform basis for interpreting the client's responses. The more risk-taking options the client selects, the more risk taking he or she is likely to be.

The Importance of Risk Tolerance Questionnaires

Although understanding the risk tolerance of a client is so critically important to proper investment and financial planning, there is no simple formula, tool, or technique that allows an advisor to identify the client's financial risk tolerance and then relate it to an investment portfolio. The fact that measurement of financial risk tolerance is not perfect, however, does not mean it cannot or should not be done. For this reason, The American College developed the Survey of Financial Risk Tolerance. While the Survey can be used to assist financial advisors in assessing their clients' attitudes toward risk taking, its purpose in being included in this book is to show just how important risk tolerance questionnaires are to the financial planning process.

Most financial advisors use risk tolerance questionnaires that are designed to be used with specific financial planning software. Moreover, many large financial services companies have developed their own risk tolerance questionnaires to satisfy compliance departments, and they fully expect their advisor-representatives to use them. Therefore, even though other questionnaires are available and even required, the real value of The College's Survey lies in providing an example of the types of questions that advisors need to ask in their assessment of clients' risk tolerances.

Whether engaged in single purpose, multiple-purpose, or comprehensive financial planning, a financial advisor should make the use of a risk tolerance questionnaire a top priority in data gathering (for step 2 of the financial planning process). The type of information provided by a risk tolerance questionnaire is necessary in order for an advisor to develop a financial and/or investment plan (in step 4 of the financial planning process) for his or her client. When the questionnaire has been completed and analyzed (in step 3 of the financial planning process), it provides the advisor with information that can help in assessing the client's risk tolerance. In other words, this type of information is intended to complement and reinforce the advisor's judgment about the client's level of risk tolerance.

Financial advisors are under a legal and an ethical obligation to help clients make investment choices that are suitable for their particular circumstances. Determining suitability requires consideration of the client's goals (as determined in step 2 of the financial planning process), his or her ability to sustain a financial loss, and his or her psychological attitudes toward risk taking.

Developing a suitable financial and/or investment plan for the client should lead to a lasting and profitable relationship with the client. Not only will the client be happy, but the advisor will come away with a sense of personal satisfaction and professional pride from having fulfilled the client's expectations.

Client Name/ID________________

Survey of Financial Risk Tolerance

Directions: *Please answer all questions by circling the number in front of the answer that indicates your response.*

1. Do you experience "anxiety" or "thrill" when awaiting the outcome of an important investment decision?

1 Always anxiety
2 Most frequently anxiety
3 Neither anxiety nor thrill
4 Most frequently thrill
5 Always thrill

2. How do you react to unexpected bad financial news?

1 Always overreact
2 Frequently overreact
3 Rarely overreact
4 Almost never overreact
5 Never overreact

3. Assume you're an executive. Your company offers you two ways of collecting your bonus: either the cash equivalent of 6 months' salary or a stock option with a 50-50 chance of either doubling in value or becoming worthless in the next year. Which would you take?

1 Definitely the cash
2 Probably the cash
3 Not sure
4 Probably the stock option
5 Definitely the stock option

4. Once you have made an investment decision, how sure do you usually feel that your choice was the correct one?

1 Very unsure
2 Somewhat unsure
3 Somewhat sure
4 Very sure

5. Which of the following investment portfolios do you find most appealing?

1 60 percent in low-risk
30 percent in medium-risk
10 percent in high-risk investments

2 30 percent in low-risk
40 percent in medium-risk
30 percent in high-risk investments

3 10 percent in low-risk
50 percent in medium-risk
40 percent in high-risk investments

6. When you think of the word risk in an investment context, which of the following words comes to mind first?

1 Danger
2 Uncertainty
3 Opportunity
4 Thrill

7. How often have you invested a large sum in a risky investment primarily for the "thrill" of seeing whether it went up or down in value?

1 Never
2 Very rarely
3 Somewhat rarely
4 Somewhat frequently
5 Very frequently

8. How easily do you adapt to unfavorable financial changes in your life?

1 Very uneasily
2 Somewhat uneasily
3 Somewhat easily
4 Very easily

Survey of Financial Risk Tolerance

9. You are considering an investment that amounts to 25 percent of the funds you have allocated for investment purposes. The expected return on this investment is about twice the return you would get by placing the money into a savings account at your local bank. However, this investment, unlike a bank account, is not protected against loss of the principal. What would the chance of loss have to be in order for you to make this investment?

1 Zero
2 Very improbable
3 Low chance
4 Even chance

10. Compared with other investors, how sophisticated are you about investing money?

1 Very unsophisticated
2 Somewhat unsophisticated
3 Somewhat sophisticated
4 Very sophisticated

11. If your friends were interviewed, how would *they* describe *your* evaluation of financial risks?

1 Severely overestimates the risks
2 Somewhat overestimates the risks
3 Estimates the risks correctly
4 Somewhat underestimates the risks
5 Severely underestimates the risks

12. You are faced with a choice between (a) greater job security with a small pay raise and (b) a high pay raise but less job security. Which would you select?

1 Definitely greater job security
2 Probably greater job security
3 Not sure
4 Probably higher pay raise
5 Definitely higher pay raise

13. An investment decision involves the possibility of making an amount of money as well as the possibility of losing all or some portion of the funds invested. Some people focus more on the possibility of making money, whereas others focus more on the possibility of losing money as a result of the decision. When making an important investment decision, what dominates your thinking?

1 The potential loss, by far
2 The potential loss, somewhat more
3 The potential gain, somewhat more
4 The potential gain, by far

14. In the past what have been the outcomes of your high-risk investment decisions?

1 Almost always unfavorable
2 Usually unfavorable
3 Equal mix of favorable and unfavorable outcomes
4 Usually favorable
5 Almost always favorable

15. How long does it take you to make an important financial decision?

1 Very long time
2 Long time
3 Average amount of time
4 Short time
5 Very short time

16. Compared with other people you know, how would you rate your ability to tolerate the stress associated with important financial matters?

1 Very low
2 Low
3 Average
4 High
5 Very high

Survey of Financial Risk Tolerance

17. Some people view financial losses as personal failures. Others consider these same consequences as merely setbacks. How do you tend to view these issues?

1 Almost always as personal failures
2 Mainly as personal failures
3 Sometimes as personal failures and sometimes as merely setbacks
4 Mainly as just setbacks
5 Almost always as just setbacks

18. If you were to become unemployed, which of the following would you be most likely to do?

1 Definitely take the first job offered, even if it was not exactly what I was looking for
2 Probably take the first job offered, even if it was not exactly what I was looking for
3 Not sure
4 Probably hold out for the kind of job I really wanted
5 Definitely hold out for the kind of job I really wanted

19. What is your general outlook on the eventual outcome of your financial decisions after you make them?

1 Very pessimistic
2 Somewhat pessimistic
3 Somewhere in the middle
4 Somewhat optimistic
5 Very optimistic

20. Which of the following comes closest to your ideal employment compensation structure involving some mix of *salary* and *commissions*?

1 Entirely salary
2 Primarily salary
3 Equal mix of salary and commissions
4 Primarily commissions
5 Entirely commissions

21. What degree of risk have you assumed on your investments in the past?

1 Very small
2 Small
3 Medium
4 Large
5 Very large

22. Do you consider yourself reflective or impulsive when making investment decisions?

1 Very reflective
2 Somewhat reflective
3 Neither reflective nor impulsive
4 Somewhat impulsive
5 Very impulsive

23. You are applying for a mortgage. The interest rates have been coming down over the last several months, and there's a possibility that they may drop another percentage point in the next month. However, the possibility also exists that the rates will start climbing again. It's unclear which of the two possibilities is more likely since economists disagree in their forecasts. You have the option of locking in on the current interest rate or letting it float. If you lock in, you will get the current rate, even if interest rates go up. If the rates go down, though, you'll have to settle at the higher rate. What would you do?

1 Definitely lock in
2 Probably lock in
3 Probably let it float
4 Definitely let it float

Survey of Financial Risk Tolerance

24. Assume you are a contestant on a TV game show. After winning a prize that's equivalent to one year's salary, you are offered the option of walking away with this prize money or taking a chance on either doubling it or losing it all. What are the odds of success that you would require before agreeing to accept this gamble?

1 Would not take the bet no matter what the odds
2 9 in 10
3 8 in 10
4 7 in 10
5 6 in 10
6 5 in 10
7 4 in 10
8 3 in 10
9 2 in 10
10 1 in 10

25. Have you ever borrowed money in order to make an investment (other than a home-mortgage loan)?

1 No
2 Yes

26. How much confidence do you have in your ability to make money?

1 Very low confidence
2 Low confidence
3 Average level of confidence
4 High confidence
5 Very high confidence

27. Compared with other people you know, how much time do you spend reading about financial and investment matters?

1 Much less than most
2 Somewhat less than most
3 About the same
4 Somewhat more than most
5 Much more than most

28. Suppose that 5 years ago you bought stock issued by a company highly recommended by your financial advisor. That same year the company experienced a severe decline in sales due to poor management. The price of the stock dropped drastically, and you sold your shares at a substantial loss. The company is now restructured under new management, and most analysts expect its stock to produce better-than-average returns. Given your bad experience with this stock in the past, how likely are you now to purchase shares of this stock?

1 Definitely would not buy
2 Probably would not buy
3 Not sure
4 Probably would buy
5 Definitely would buy

29. Is it more important to be protected from inflation or to be assured of the safety of your principal?

1 Much more important to be assured of the safety of principal
2 Somewhat more important to be assured of the safety of principal
3 Somewhat more important to be protected from inflation
4 Much more important to be protected from inflation

30. What percent of your funds are you willing to place in investments that are of above-average risk?

1 0 percent
2 1–9 percent
3 10–19 percent
4 20–29 percent
5 30–39 percent
6 40–49 percent
7 50–59 percent
8 60–69 percent
9 70–79 percent
10 80–89 percent
11 90–99 percent
12 100 percent

Survey of Financial Risk Tolerance

31. In some instances you are faced with a choice between (a) earning a certain amount of money for sure and (b) taking a risk and earning either a larger amount of money or nothing at all.

For example, consider an investment choice between a certain gain of $50 and an 80 percent chance of earning $100. If you take the certain choice, you will get $50 for sure (no more, no less). On the other hand, if you take the 80 percent probability of earning $100, you also stand a 20 percent chance of earning nothing at all.

For the choices shown below please indicate whether you would take the sure gain or some probability of earning twice as much (or nothing at all). Be sure to select one option for each pair, A through F.

Pair A: 1 A certain gain of $10,000
2 80 percent probability of gaining $20,000 (with a corresponding 20 percent chance of earning nothing)

Pair B: 1 A certain gain of $10,000
2 50 percent probability of gaining $20,000 (with a corresponding 50 percent chance of earning nothing)

Pair C: 1 A certain gain of $30,000
2 80 percent probability of gaining $60,000 (with a corresponding 20 percent chance of earning nothing)

Pair D: 1 A certain gain of $30,000
2 50 percent probability of gaining $60,000 (with a corresponding 50 percent chance of earning nothing)

Pair E: 1 A certain gain of $50,000
2 80 percent probability of gaining $100,000 (with a corresponding 20 percent chance of earning nothing)

Pair F: 1 A certain gain of $50,000
2 50 percent probability of gaining $100,000 (with a corresponding 50 percent chance of earning nothing)

Survey of Financial Risk Tolerance

32. How likely is it that you would be willing to place one-fourth of your net wealth into each of the following classes of investments?

LOW RISK

	Very Unlikely	Somewhat Unlikely	Not Sure	Somewhat Likely	Very Likely
(a) 90-day U.S. Treasury bill	1	2	3	4	5
(b) Deposit account (savings, CD)	1	2	3	4	5
(c) Money market fund	1	2	3	4	5
(d) U.S. government bond	1	2	3	4	5
(e) Municipal bond	1	2	3	4	5
(f) Corporate bond	1	2	3	4	5
(g) Blue-chip common stock	1	2	3	4	5
(h) Convertible security	1	2	3	4	5
(i) Aggressive-growth common stock	1	2	3	4	5
(j) Venture capital	1	2	3	4	5
(k) Limited-partnership unit	1	2	3	4	5
(l) Junk bond	1	2	3	4	5
(m) Options/commodities	1	2	3	4	5

HIGH RISK

33. Diversification is typically the soundest investment strategy. However, suppose an eccentric uncle left you an inheritance of $75,000, stipulating in his will that you invest *all* the money in only *one* of the following investments. Which one would you select?

1 Savings account
2 Mutual fund (moderate growth)
3 Blue-chip common stock
4 Limited partnership
5 Naked option/commodities futures contract

34. Investments can go up and down in value. What is the maximum drop in the value of your total investment portfolio that you could tolerate before feeling uncomfortable?

1 0 percent
2 1–9 percent
3 10–19 percent
4 20–29 percent
5 30–39 percent
6 40–49 percent
7 50–59 percent
8 60–69 percent
9 70–79 percent
10 80–89 percent
11 90–99 percent
12 100 percent

35. A long-lost relative dies and leaves you her house. The house is in disrepair but is located in a neighborhood that's being rehabilitated. As is, the house would probably sell for about $75,000, but if you were to spend about $25,000 on renovations, the selling price would be approximately $150,000. However, there's some talk about constructing a major highway next to the house, which would lower its value considerably. What would you do?

1 Sell it as is.
2 Keep it as is, but rent it out.
3 Take out a $25,000 mortgage for the necessary renovations.

36. You are offered an investment in which you stand an even chance of either losing half of your personal net worth or making a certain amount of money. What's the lowest return you would need in order to make such an investment?

1 I would not make the investment no matter what the rate of return.
2 Quadruple my net worth
3 Triple my net worth
4 Double my net worth
5 Less than double my net worth

Survey of Financial Risk Tolerance

37. What types of changes have you made in your investment portfolio in the past?

1 Always toward less risky investments
2 Mostly toward less risky investments
3 No changes or changes with no clear direction
4 Mostly toward more risky investments
5 Always toward more risky investments

38. How often have you used "short selling" or "margin buying" in stock market investments?

1 Never
2 Seldom
3 Frequently
4 Very frequently

39. Suppose you are the beneficiary of a $100,000 life insurance policy from a beloved relative. You are considering various investment possibilities, including some of very high risk. How much of this money could you lose *forever* without feeling that you were betraying your relative's motive for leaving you this sum?

1 $0
2 $1,000–$9,000
3 $10,000–$19,000
4 $20,000–$29,000
5 $30,000–$39,000
6 $40,000–$49,000
7 $50,000–$59,000
8 $60,000–$69,000
9 $70,000–$79,000
10 $80,000–$89,000
11 $90,000–$100,000

40. How do you rate your willingness to take investment risks in comparison with the general population?

1 Extremely low risk taker
2 Very low risk taker
3 Low risk taker
4 Average risk taker
5 High risk taker
6 Very high risk taker
7 Extremely high risk taker

Client Name/ID ____________________

Survey of Financial Risk Tolerance ***Demographic Data Form***

The following information will allow your risk-tolerance score to be classified by relevant demographic categories. Please be assured that this information, like your responses to the risk-tolerance questions, will remain confidential. Circle the number in front of the answer that indicates your response.

1. Sex 1 Male
   2 Female

2. Age ______

3. Marital status

   1 Single
   2 Married
   3 Divorced
   4 Widowed

4. Number of dependents, including yourself

   ______

5. Highest education level

   1 Less than high school
   2 High school
   3 Some college
   4 Bachelor's degree
   5 Master's degree
   6 Law degree
   7 Doctorate

6. Occupation

   1 An employee of a private company or business, or an individual working for wages, salary, or commissions
   2 A government employee (federal, state, county, or local)
   3 Self-employed in your own business, professional practice, or farm
   4 Retired

7. If you are an employee, how many years have you been with the same employer?

   ______

8. Approximate income, before taxes, from all sources. Please indicate your own income *and* total household income.

	a. Your income	b. Household income
Under $50,000	1	1
$50,000 to $99,000	2	2
$100,000 to $149,000	3	3
$150,000 to $199,000	4	4
$200,000 to $249,000	5	5
$250,000 to $500,000	6	6
Over $500,000	7	7

9. Which category describes your approximate net wealth?

   1 Under $250,000
   2 $250,000 to $499,000
   3 $500,000 to $999,000
   4 $1,000,000 to $2,499,000
   5 $2,500,000 to $5,000,000
   6 Over $5,000,000

10. Which of the following investments do you presently own? (Circle all that apply.)

    1 Life insurance
    2 Savings account or CDs
    3 Money market funds
    4 Bonds
    5 Stocks
    6 Real estate (other than primary residence)
    7 Options or futures
    8 Other (list)

    ____
    ____
    ____

Appendix C

Time-Value-of-Money Tables

Table C-1
FUTURE VALUE OF A SINGLE SUM FACTORS

FVSS Factor = $(1 + i)^n$ where i = rate and n = periods

i =	0.5%	1%	1.5%	2%	2.5%	3%	3.5%	4%	4.5%	5%
n = 1	1.0050	1.0100	1.0150	1.0200	1.0250	1.0300	1.0350	1.0400	1.0450	1.0500
2	1.0100	1.0201	1.0302	1.0404	1.0506	1.0609	1.0712	1.0816	1.0920	1.1025
3	1.0151	1.0303	1.0457	1.0612	1.0769	1.0927	1.1087	1.1249	1.1412	1.1576
4	1.0202	1.0406	1.0614	1.0824	1.1038	1.1255	1.1475	1.1699	1.1925	1.2155
5	1.0253	1.0510	1.0773	1.1041	1.1314	1.1593	1.1877	1.2167	1.2462	1.2763
6	1.0304	1.0615	1.0934	1.1262	1.1597	1.1941	1.2293	1.2653	1.3023	1.3401
7	1.0355	1.0721	1.1098	1.1487	1.1887	1.2299	1.2723	1.3159	1.3609	1.4071
8	1.0407	1.0829	1.1265	1.1717	1.2184	1.2668	1.3168	1.3686	1.4221	1.4775
9	1.0459	1.0937	1.1434	1.1951	1.2489	1.3048	1.3629	1.4233	1.4861	1.5513
10	1.0511	1.1046	1.1605	1.2190	1.2801	1.3439	1.4106	1.4802	1.5530	1.6289
11	1.0564	1.1157	1.1779	1.2434	1.3121	1.3842	1.4600	1.5395	1.6229	1.7103
12	1.0617	1.1268	1.1956	1.2682	1.3449	1.4258	1.5111	1.6010	1.6959	1.7959
13	1.0670	1.1381	1.2136	1.2936	1.3785	1.4685	1.5640	1.6651	1.7722	1.8856
14	1.0723	1.1495	1.2318	1.3195	1.4130	1.5126	1.6187	1.7317	1.8519	1.9799
15	1.0777	1.1610	1.2502	1.3459	1.4483	1.5580	1.6753	1.8009	1.9353	2.0789
16	1.0831	1.1726	1.2690	1.3728	1.4845	1.6047	1.7340	1.8730	2.0224	2.1829
17	1.0885	1.1843	1.2880	1.4002	1.5216	1.6528	1.7947	1.9479	2.1134	2.2920
18	1.0939	1.1961	1.3073	1.4282	1.5597	1.7024	1.8575	2.0258	2.2085	2.4066
19	1.0994	1.2081	1.3270	1.4568	1.5987	1.7535	1.9225	2.1068	2.3079	2.5270
20	1.1049	1.2202	1.3469	1.4859	1.6386	1.8061	1.9898	2.1911	2.4117	2.6533
21	1.1104	1.2324	1.3671	1.5157	1.6796	1.8603	2.0594	2.2788	2.5202	2.7860
22	1.1160	1.2447	1.3876	1.5460	1.7216	1.9161	2.1315	2.3699	2.6337	2.9253

23	1.1216	1.2572	1.4084	1.5769	1.7646	1.9736	2.2061	2.4647	2.7522	3.0715
24	1.1272	1.2697	1.4295	1.6084	1.8087	2.0328	2.2833	2.5633	2.8760	3.2251
25	1.1328	1.2824	1.4509	1.6406	1.8539	2.0938	2.3632	2.6658	3.0054	3.3864
26	1.1385	1.2953	1.4727	1.6734	1.9003	2.1566	2.4460	2.7725	3.1407	3.5557
27	1.1442	1.3082	1.4948	1.7069	1.9478	2.2213	2.5316	2.8834	3.2820	3.7335
28	1.1499	1.3213	1.5172	1.7410	1.9965	2.2879	2.6202	2.9987	3.4297	3.9201
29	1.1556	1.3345	1.5400	1.7758	2.0464	2.3566	2.7119	3.1187	3.5840	4.1161
30	1.1614	1.3478	1.5631	1.8114	2.0976	2.4273	2.8068	3.2434	3.7453	4.3219
35	1.1907	1.4166	1.6839	1.9999	2.3732	2.8139	3.3336	3.9461	4.6673	5.5160
40	1.2208	1.4889	1.8140	2.2080	2.6851	3.2620	3.9593	4.8010	5.8164	7.0400
45	1.2516	1.5648	1.9542	2.4379	3.0379	3.7816	4.7024	5.8412	7.2482	8.9850
50	1.2832	1.6446	2.1052	2.6916	3.4371	4.3839	5.5849	7.1067	9.0326	11.4674

Table C-2
FUTURE VALUE OF A SINGLE SUM FACTORS

FVSS Factor = $(1 + i)^n$ where i = rate and n = periods

i =	5.5%	6%	6.5%	7%	7.5%	8%	8.5%	9%	9.5%	10%
n = 1	1.0550	1.0600	1.0650	1.0700	1.0750	1.0800	1.0850	1.0900	1.0950	1.1000
2	1.1130	1.1236	1.1342	1.1449	1.1556	1.1664	1.1772	1.1881	1.1990	1.2100
3	1.1742	1.1910	1.2079	1.2250	1.2423	1.2597	1.2773	1.2950	1.3129	1.3310
4	1.2388	1.2625	1.2865	1.3108	1.3355	1.3605	1.3859	1.4116	1.4377	1.4641
5	1.3070	1.3382	1.3701	1.4026	1.4356	1.4693	1.5037	1.5386	1.5742	1.6105
6	1.3788	1.4185	1.4591	1.5007	1.5433	1.5869	1.6315	1.6771	1.7238	1.7716
7	1.4547	1.5036	1.5540	1.6058	1.6590	1.7138	1.7701	1.8280	1.8876	1.9487
8	1.5347	1.5938	1.6550	1.7182	1.7835	1.8509	1.9206	1.9926	2.0669	2.1436
9	1.6191	1.6895	1.7626	1.8385	1.9172	1.9990	2.0839	2.1719	2.2632	2.3579
10	1.7081	1.7908	1.8771	1.9672	2.0610	2.1589	2.2610	2.3674	2.4782	2.5937
11	1.8021	1.8983	1.9992	2.1049	2.2156	2.3316	2.4532	2.5804	2.7137	2.8531
12	1.9012	2.0122	2.1291	2.2522	2.3818	2.5182	2.6617	2.8127	2.9715	3.1384
13	2.0058	2.1329	2.2675	2.4098	2.5604	2.7196	2.8879	3.0658	3.2537	3.4523
14	2.1161	2.2609	2.4149	2.5785	2.7524	2.9372	3.1334	3.3417	3.5629	3.7975
15	2.2325	2.3966	2.5718	2.7590	2.9589	3.1722	3.3997	3.6425	3.9013	4.1772
16	2.3553	2.5404	2.7390	2.9522	3.1808	3.4259	3.6887	3.9703	4.2719	4.5950
17	2.4848	2.6928	2.9170	3.1588	3.4194	3.7000	4.0023	4.3276	4.6778	5.0545
18	2.6215	2.8543	3.1067	3.3799	3.6758	3.9960	4.3425	4.7171	5.1222	5.5599
19	2.7656	3.0256	3.3086	3.6165	3.9515	4.3157	4.7116	5.1417	5.6088	6.1159
20	2.9178	3.2071	3.5236	3.8697	4.2479	4.6610	5.1120	5.6044	6.1416	6.7275
21	3.0782	3.3996	3.7527	4.1406	4.5664	5.0338	5.5466	6.1088	6.7251	7.4002
22	3.2475	3.6035	3.9966	4.4304	4.9089	5.4365	6.0180	6.6586	7.3639	8.1403

23	3.4262	3.8197	4.2564	4.7405	5.2771	5.8715	6.5296	7.2579	8.0635	8.9543
24	3.6146	4.0489	4.5331	5.0724	5.6729	6.3412	7.0846	7.9111	8.8296	9.8497
25	3.8134	4.2919	4.8277	5.4274	6.0983	6.8485	7.6868	8.6231	9.6684	10.8347
26	4.0231	4.5494	5.1415	5.8074	6.5557	7.3964	8.3401	9.3992	10.5869	11.9182
27	4.2444	4.8223	5.4757	6.2139	7.0474	7.9881	9.0490	10.2451	11.5926	13.1100
28	4.4778	5.1117	5.8316	6.6488	7.5759	8.6271	9.8182	11.1671	12.6939	14.4210
29	4.7241	5.4184	6.2107	7.1143	8.1441	9.3173	10.6528	12.1722	13.8998	15.8631
30	4.9840	5.7435	6.6144	7.6123	8.7550	10.0627	11.5583	13.2677	15.2203	17.4494
35	6.5138	7.6861	9.0623	10.6766	12.5689	14.7853	17.3796	20.4140	23.9604	28.1024
40	8.5133	10.2857	12.4161	14.9745	18.0442	21.7245	26.1330	31.4094	37.7194	45.2593
45	11.1266	13.7646	17.0111	21.0025	25.9048	31.9204	39.2951	48.3273	59.3793	72.8905
50	14.5420	18.4202	23.3067	29.4570	37.1897	46.9016	59.0863	74.3575	93.4773	117.391

Table C-3
FUTURE VALUE OF A SINGLE SUM FACTORS

FVSS Factor = $(1 + i)^n$ where i = rate and n = periods

i =	10.5%	11%	11.5%	12%	12.5%	13%	13.5%	14%	14.5%	15%
n = 1	1.1050	1.1100	1.1150	1.1200	1.1250	1.1300	1.1350	1.1400	1.1450	1.1500
2	1.2210	1.2321	1.2432	1.2544	1.2656	1.2769	1.2882	1.2996	1.3110	1.3225
3	1.3492	1.3676	1.3862	1.4049	1.4238	1.4429	1.4621	1.4815	1.5011	1.5209
4	1.4909	1.5181	1.5456	1.5735	1.6018	1.6305	1.6595	1.6890	1.7188	1.7490
5	1.6474	1.6851	1.7234	1.7623	1.8020	1.8424	1.8836	1.9254	1.9680	2.0114
6	1.8204	1.8704	1.9215	1.9738	2.0273	2.0820	2.1378	2.1950	2.2534	2.3131
7	2.0116	2.0762	2.1425	2.2107	2.2807	2.3526	2.4264	2.5023	2.5801	2.6600
8	2.2228	2.3045	2.3889	2.4760	2.5658	2.6584	2.7540	2.8526	2.9542	3.0590
9	2.4562	2.5580	2.6636	2.7731	2.8865	3.0040	3.1258	3.2519	3.3826	3.5179
10	2.7141	2.8394	2.9699	3.1058	3.2473	3.3946	3.5478	3.7072	3.8731	4.0456
11	2.9991	3.1518	3.3115	3.4785	3.6532	3.8359	4.0267	4.2262	4.4347	4.6524
12	3.3140	3.4985	3.6923	3.8960	4.1099	4.3345	4.5704	4.8179	5.0777	5.3503
13	3.6619	3.8833	4.1169	4.3635	4.6236	4.8980	5.1874	5.4924	5.8140	6.1528
14	4.0464	4.3104	4.5904	4.8871	5.2016	5.5348	5.8877	6.2613	6.6570	7.0757
15	4.4713	4.7846	5.1183	5.4736	5.8518	6.2543	6.6825	7.1379	7.6222	8.1371
16	4.9408	5.3109	5.7069	6.1304	6.5833	7.0673	7.5846	8.1372	8.7275	9.3576
17	5.4596	5.8951	6.3632	6.8660	7.4062	7.9861	8.6085	9.2765	9.9929	10.7613
18	6.0328	6.5436	7.0949	7.6900	8.3319	9.0243	9.7707	10.5752	11.4419	12.3755
19	6.6663	7.2633	7.9108	8.6128	9.3734	10.1974	11.0897	12.0557	13.1010	14.2318
20	7.3662	8.0623	8.8206	9.6463	10.5451	11.5231	12.5869	13.7435	15.0006	16.3665
21	8.1397	8.9492	9.8350	10.8038	11.8632	13.0211	14.2861	15.6676	17.1757	18.8215
22	8.9944	9.9336	10.9660	12.1003	13.3461	14.7138	16.2147	17.8610	19.6662	21.6447

23	9.9388	11.0263	12.2271	13.5523	15.0144	16.6266	18.4037	20.3616	22.5178	24.8915
24	10.9823	12.2392	13.6332	15.1786	16.8912	18.7881	20.8882	23.2122	25.7829	28.6252
25	12.1355	13.5855	15.2010	17.0001	19.0026	21.2305	23.7081	26.4619	29.5214	32.9190
26	13.4097	15.0799	16.9491	19.0401	21.3779	23.9905	26.9087	30.1666	33.8020	37.8568
27	14.8177	16.7386	18.8982	21.3249	24.0502	27.1093	30.5414	34.3899	38.7033	43.5353
28	16.3736	18.5799	21.0715	23.8839	27.0564	30.6335	34.6644	39.2045	44.3153	50.0656
29	18.0928	20.6237	23.4948	26.7499	30.4385	34.6158	39.3441	44.6931	50.7410	57.5755
30	19.9926	22.8923	26.1967	29.9599	34.2433	39.1159	44.6556	50.9502	58.0985	66.2118
35	32.9367	38.5749	45.1461	52.7996	61.7075	72.0685	84.1115	98.1002	114.338	133.176
40	54.2614	65.0009	77.8027	93.0510	111.199	132.782	158.429	188.884	225.019	267.864
45	89.3928	109.530	134.082	163.988	200.384	244.641	298.410	363.679	442.840	538.769
50	147.270	184.565	231.070	289.002	361.099	450.736	562.073	700.233	871.514	1083.66

Appendix D

Answers to Review and Self-Test Questions

Chapter 1

Review Answers

1. Financial planning is a process in which the client's financial problems and/or goals are determined and a plan is developed to solve those problems and achieve those goals.
2. The steps of the selling/planning process are to

    - identify the prospect
    - approach the prospect
    - meet the prospect
    - gather information and establish goals
    - analyze the information
    - develop and present the plan
    - implement the plan
    - service the plan

3. The major planning areas to include in a comprehensive financial plan are

    - general principles of financial planning
    - insurance planning and risk management
    - employee benefits planning
    - investment planning
    - income tax planning
    - retirement planning
    - estate planning

4. The multiple-purpose approach to planning addresses more than a single client problem or goal but something less than the full range of client problems and/or goals.
5. The advantages of creating an ideal client profile are as follows:

    - You can avoid those prospects with whom a relationship would be difficult.
    - You will receive more referrals, which makes your job easier.
    - You will work with prospects who have a high probability of becoming clients.
    - Your business will be more profitable.

6. The following are steps to identify target markets:

- Identify and segment your natural markets.
- Research potential target markets.
- Write a description of your potential target markets.
- Test potential target markets.

7. Seven questions to answer when studying your competition are as follows:

    - Who is your competition?
    - What are they identifying as their unique value? In other words, what are they giving as the reason to do business with them?
    - How long have they been targeting this market?
    - How are they gaining access to the target market?
    - How are they building prestige within the target market?
    - What are their strengths and weaknesses?
    - How does the target market view them?

8. Nine ways to build prestige and create awareness are as follows:

    - Enhance your public persona.
    - Develop a personal brochure.
    - Create a 10-second commercial.
    - Get involved in local organizations.
    - Make yourself available to local media.
    - Mail to your target market.
    - Speak to groups or teach classes.
    - Advertise to your target market.
    - Set up an Internet website.

9. Four prospecting methods are

    - referrals
    - centers of influence
    - networking
    - seminars

10. The four categories of objections are

    - no hurry
    - no money
    - no need
    - no trust

Self-Test Answers—Chapter 1

Question	Answer
11.	A
12.	B
13.	A
14.	C
15.	C
16.	A
17.	B
18.	C
19.	C
20.	D

Chapter 2

Review Answers

1.
    - Interviewing can be defined as a process of communication with a predetermined and specific purpose, usually involving asking and answering questions designed to gather meaningful information.
    - Counseling involves providing assistance to clients as they explore their present financial situations, begin to understand where they are in relation to where they would like to be, and develop a plan to get from where they are to where they want to be.
    - Advising is giving specific guidance or suggestions to clients.
2. Structuring serves to determine both the format and the subject matter of a client session.
3. The four social styles and the characteristics of each are as follows:
    - driver—forceful, direct; will not waste time on small talk; wants power
    - expressive—outgoing, enthusiastic; enjoys telling about personal projects and dreams; wants recognition
    - amiable—easy-going, dependent; enjoys telling about personal relationships; wants approval
    - analytical—logical, quiet; is uncomfortable with small talk; wants respect
4. The sources of client resistance behavior are

- death and dying
- marital tensions, including separation/divorce, parent-child disputes, sex, the empty nest syndrome, and mid-life crises
- failure to attain the expected degree of professional success

5. The types of information clients want to know about their advisors include

   - educational background
   - professional certifications and licenses held
   - professional experience
   - business philosophy
   - training
   - method of compensation
   - possible conflicts of interest

6. The attributes of an effective advisor are

   - unconditional positive regard
   - accurate empathy
   - genuineness
   - self-awareness

7. Advisors who are aware of their own value systems have a better chance of avoiding imposing their values onto their clients. This quality is of vital importance, because we want to help our clients make decisions that stem from their own value systems, rather than from ours. Values, while deeply internalized, are not immutable. Advisors need to remind themselves of this as they work with clients who are confused and afraid in approaching important decisions. Advisors must have enough faith in the client's worth as a unique human being to permit that client to make value choices that fit his or her value system. The financial advisor can and should provide information that will help the client make the choice, but the choice ultimately belongs with the client, not the advisor.
8. The basic principles of communication are the following:

   - Communication is learned through experience, but experience itself does not necessarily make a person an effective communicator.
   - The meaning of words is illusory; words do not mean—people do. Words are merely symbols, and a word can have almost as many meanings as there are people who use it.
   - Language is learned; thus, in a sense, we are programmed, and the meaning of words stays within us for future reference. This programming is extremely helpful because, once we learn a word, it usually remains ours for a lifetime.
   - No two people are programmed alike; therefore, no symbol can always be interpreted the same way. Individuals differ in

the nature and degree of their understanding. They perceive things differently, from their own frame of reference, so meanings differ.

- It is impossible for any individual to encode or process all parts of a message. Besides the fact that words are often inadequate to describe accurately what we are feeling or thinking, there is the problem of distortion—that is, an individual's altering the event to suit his or her own purposes.
- Some experts claim that the single greatest problem with communication is the assumption of it. Too many people assume that their messages are automatically understood. Where human communication is concerned, no assumptions can or should be made.
- We are constantly communicating. Anything we say or do can be interpreted in a meaningful way as a message. Even during periods of silence, communication takes place. Nonverbal behaviors, such as eye contact, facial expressions, gestures, body posture, voice inflections, hesitations, and the like, all speak volumes.
- Listening is communication, too. Unfortunately, not everyone is a good listener; that should not be surprising, because listening as a communication skill is rarely, if ever, formally taught. To speak precisely and to listen carefully present a real challenge to all of us.
- The most effective communication occurs when the receiver of a message gives understanding responses, sometimes called paraphrases.
- Personalizing messages enhances the communication process and the advisor-client relationship. The hallmark of personal statements is the use of the personal pronouns I, me, and my. Using generalized pronouns, such as everyone, anyone, or somebody, to refer to your own ideas only tends to confuse clients and, hence, results in ambiguity and faulty understanding.

9. The ways that nonverbal behaviors are communicated by the body and the voice are

   - body positions
   - body movements
   - gestures
   - facial expressions
   - eye contact
   - voice tone
   - voice pitch

10. The meaning of both verbal and nonverbal behaviors must be assessed because both types of behaviors communicate. If the two types of

communication are not consistent with each other, the advisor must delve further to determine the true meaning. Nonverbal behaviors are clues or indicators of the client's true feelings. Most sociological research claims that approximately two-thirds of a person's total message is communicated via nonverbal channels, especially where human emotions are concerned.

11. The five basic attributes associated with physical attending are to
    - face the other person squarely
    - adopt an open posture
    - lean toward the other person
    - maintain good eye contact
    - be relaxed while attending

12. The following are types of understanding responses:

    a. "Well, let's see what we've concluded then. You want to set aside about $3,000 per year to save for a down payment on a vacation house at the shore, and safety is your prime consideration in the investment of that money." (summarization response)
    b. "I'm not sure I'm following you. Tell me again what your plan is for disposing of your interest in the partnership." (clarifying response)
    c. "From what you just told me, then, I gather that you want to stay away from the limited partnership and put the money into the stock market instead." (restatement-of-content response)

13. The four types of leading responses are as follows:

    - An explanatory response is a relatively neutral description of the way things are. It deals in logical, practical, and factual information.
    - An interpretive response can be an extremely effective response because it often cuts to the heart of the matter. When the interpretation makes sense to the client, it definitely accelerates the session.
    - A reassuring response offers sympathy. It is designed to make the client feel better, to bolster his or her spirits, and to offer support in a time of need.
    - A suggestive response essentially involves telling the client what he or she should do. When advice is given, it should be in the form of a suggestion. However, in a financial planning relationship, the best kind of advice is self-advice.

14. The questioning techniques are as follows:

    a. "Why haven't you started converting some of that term insurance to whole life?" (open-ended question, why question)

b. "Don't you think your present portfolio of investments is pretty illiquid?" (closed-ended question, leading question)
c. "What goals do you have with respect to the education of your children?" (open-ended question)
d. "Do you plan to hold on to your mutual fund?" (closed-ended question)
e. "Don't you think you should put $4,000 into an IRA this year? That isn't much money for you, is it? After all, don't you have at least that much in your passbook savings account right now? Or am I mistaken on that point?" (question bombardment, leading question, closed-ended question)
f. "You were born in 1946, right?" (closed-ended question, true-false question)

Self-Test Answers—Chapter 2

Question	Answer
15.	A
16.	B
17.	C
18.	D
19.	C
20.	B
21.	A
22.	D
23.	D
24.	B

Chapter 3

Review Answers

1. The client should understand that meaningful financial planning can be accomplished only with complete information about his or her personal and financial situation. The client should also understand the need to furnish financial records and documents and to participate in fact-finding and planning meetings with you, during which time his or her financial situation, problems, and goals will be thoroughly discussed. You should make the client aware that he or she will have to invest time, perhaps a significant amount of time, in the information-gathering stage of financial planning. Finally, you should be sure the client understands that he or she probably will have to

provide you with some information that is highly confidential, perhaps even sensitive or painful to reveal.

2. Assembling complete, accurate, and up-to-date information about the client is the single most important task in financial planning. It is therefore imperative that the fact finder used to gather information for financial planning purposes be sufficiently comprehensive to enable the advisor to

    - evaluate the client's total financial condition
    - identify what type of person the client really is
    - determine where the client wants to be
    - formulate the most appropriate strategies for getting there

3. The major information-gathering sections of the Fact Finder are Personal Data; Future Goals and Objectives; Factors Affecting Your Financial Plan; Objectives Requiring Additional Income/Capital; Retirement Planning; Estate and Gift Planning; Sources and Uses of Cash; Cash Flow Statement; Inventory of Assets and Liabilities; Individually Owned Insurance; Employment-Related Benefits Checklist; Employment-Related Benefits/Deferred Compensation; Risk/Return Profile; Income and Lump-Sum Needs and Resources for Disability, Retirement, and Death; and Observations and Goals from Planning Sessions.
4. The Case Management Checklist consists of three subsections that are exclusively for the use of the financial advisor. The Scope of Planning Agreement subsection at the top of the checklist lists the different subject areas for which advisors may do planning. For each client, depending on the scope of the planning agreement, the advisor should circle only those subject areas that apply. The Planning Tasks Completed subsection in the middle of the checklist is a scoreboard that allows the advisor to keep track of certain documents that have been sent to and received from the client, as well as when each remaining step of the selling/planning process has been completed. The Confidential Client Summary Information subsection at the bottom of the checklist provides a quick summary of the client's current financial position.
5. Goal setting is critical to creating a successful financial plan because it sets the tone for the entire planning process. The client's personal values and attitudes shape his or her goals and the priority placed on them. Accordingly, the client's goals and their priorities must be consistent with his or her values and attitudes in order for him or her to make the commitment necessary to accomplish them.

    Prioritized goals provide focus, purpose, vision, and direction for the planning process. In the areas of planning being addressed, it is important, therefore, to establish clear and measurable goals that are both relevant and realistic.

    Thus, as part of the goal-setting process, a financial advisor should

- facilitate the goal-setting process by making sure that the client's goals are relevant and realistic
- when necessary, explain to the client the implications of his or her trying to adopt unrealistic goals
- help clients rank the importance of competing goals such as saving for retirement and saving for education

6. The major topic areas for identifying a client's specific personal financial goals and objectives include

    - life planning
    - insurance planning and risk management
    - employee benefits planning
    - specialized financial planning goals
    - investment planning
    - income tax planning
    - retirement planning
    - estate planning

7. The content of the agreement letter should

    - specify the purpose of the letter
    - indicate the client's current status, including facts, observations, and understandings about his or her current situation, attitudes, values and major areas of concern
    - state the client's goals and desired situation
    - specify the client's assessed level of risk tolerance
    - disclose the available capital and/or income resources that may be allocated toward reaching the client's financial goals
    - indicate specific areas of financial planning that you will address in your recommendations such as insurance planning and risk management, income tax planning, retirement planning, and college education planning
    - acknowledge the areas you will not address in your recommendations because you are not qualified or licensed to do so such as legal or tax advice (you may discuss alternative resources you can make available to the client to provide these services)
    - specify the fees for your services, if any apply, and/or other types of compensation you will receive such as commissions on financial products you may sell
    - request that the client correct and/or clarify any of statements made in the letter
    - specify what the next step is and how it will be conducted, and schedule the next advisor-client meeting

Self-Test Answers—Chapter 3

Question	Answer
8.	B
9.	C
10.	A
11.	C
12.	C
13.	C
14.	B
15.	D
16.	B
17.	C

Chapter 4

Review Answers

1. It would be in your best interest to pay the bill at the end of the 30-day period. By doing so, you would retain the ability to use the money for your own benefit by either spending it or investing it to earn interest. By paying immediately, you would incur an opportunity cost, which is the value you would be forgoing.
2.

   a.

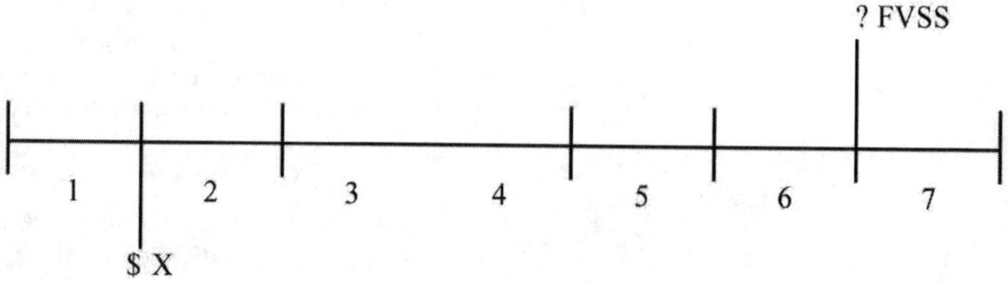

b.

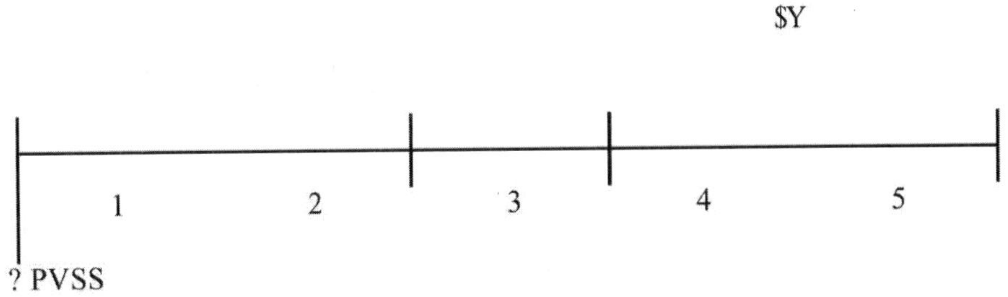

3. The interest rate is 7 percent per year. The number of years of compounding is 6.
4.
   a. The future value of a particular single sum increases as the interest rate used in the calculation increases, and it decreases as the interest rate decreases.
   b. The future value of a particular single sum increases as the number of years used in the calculation increases, and it decreases as the number of years decreases.

5. According to the Rule of 72, it will take about 18 years for a sum of money to double in value if it earns a compound annual interest rate of 4 percent (72 ÷ 4 = 18).
6. The discount rate is 11 percent per year. The number of years of discounting is 7.
7.
   a. The present value of a particular single sum decreases as the discount rate used in the calculation increases, and it increases as the discount rate decreases.
   b. The present value of a particular single sum decreases as the number of years used in the calculation increases, and it increases as the number of years decreases.

8.

   a.

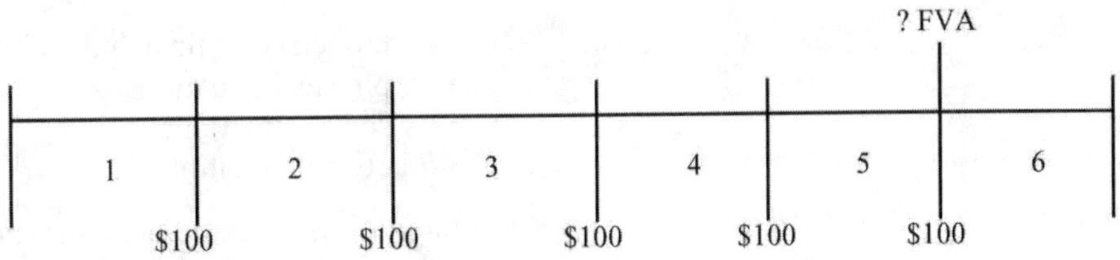

b.

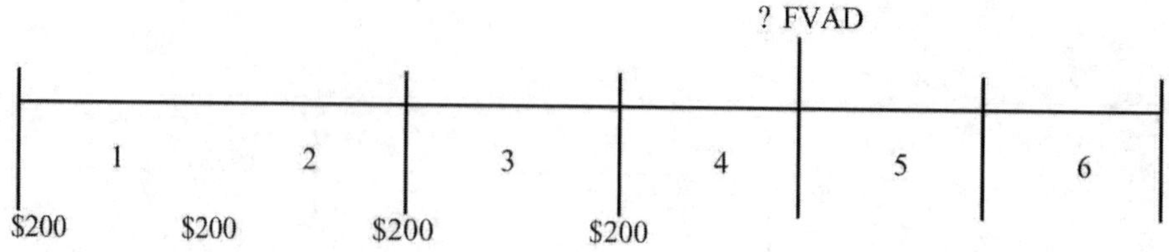

9.

a.

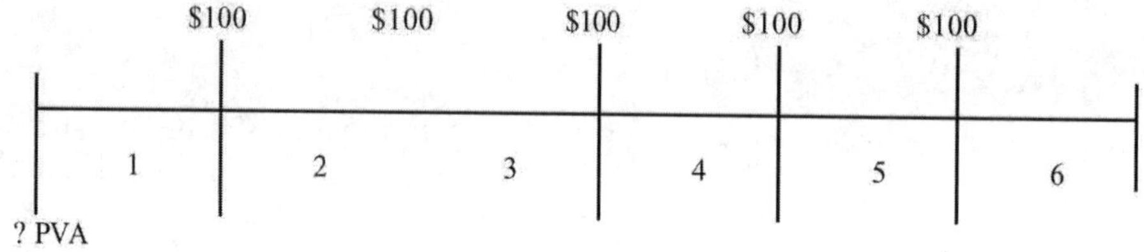

b.

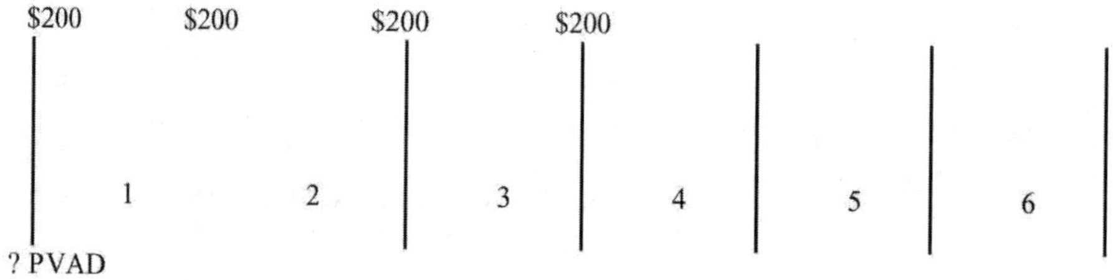

10. In general, the investment portfolio that, on average, produces higher rates of return also has greater variability in its returns. Risk refers to the possibility that an investment will experience variations in its returns over time. Return refers to the increase or decrease in the value of an investment. To earn the highest potential returns, it is necessary to put money in those investments with the highest risk.

11.

a. The four major types of life situations that involve risk taking are

- monetary or financial situations
- physical situations
- social situations
- ethical situations

b. Research on risk taking demonstrates that a person's level of risk tolerance for types of risky situations other than monetary or financial ones is not a good gauge of risk taking in situations involving the potential loss of money such as investment decisions.

12. It is difficult to assess an individual's level of financial risk tolerance for the following reasons:

    - It is an elusive, ambiguous concept to most people. If they have no previous investment experience, it is especially hard for them to specify how risk tolerant they are.
    - The results of the various approaches to assessing financial risk tolerance are often discrepant.
    - It is not a fixed characteristic of the individual. The particulars of a given situation are as strong an influence on the person's willingness to accept a risk as are his or her natural predispositions to be risk taking or risk averse.
    - Demographic characteristics should serve primarily as a means for developing some hunches about an individual's risk tolerance level.
    - Many individuals find it difficult to open up and provide the information needed to assess their risk tolerance.

13. Most measurement devices were not developed scientifically and do not have norms. In some, the wrong questions are asked, or they are presented in an incorrect format. Many devices are too short, failing to contain an adequate representation of questions. Also, because answers to similar questions about risk tolerance may not concur, it is important to ask enough closely related questions to get a good reading. Some questionnaires do not separate the different contexts of risk taking, so a high score on such a questionnaire is probably better at identifying tendencies toward thrill seeking rather than high risk tolerance for investment matters. It is strongly recommended that the financial advisor examine the content of the questionnaire. A questionnaire, checklist, or inventory purporting to assess risk tolerance may, in fact, be measuring some other attribute.

14.

    a. The client may be asked to indicate how important the following investment objectives are to him or her: liquidity, safety of principal, appreciation, protection from inflation, current income, and tax reduction. Typically, the client will be asked to rank the objectives in terms of importance.
    b. In its simplest form, the client is presented with available investment alternatives and is then asked how he or she wishes to distribute available assets among these options. The products are usually presented in some rank order ranging from very safe investments to very risky investments.
    c. Factual information about the client's life is gathered and evaluated. In general, the following lifestyle characteristics can be used to gauge a client's disposition toward monetary risk: composition of the present investment portfolio, debt ratio, ratio of life insurance to annual salary, size of deductibles

on property-liability coverage, percentage of net wealth used for recreational gambling, job tenure, variations in income, and type of mortgage.

d. Clients are asked to rank themselves on global questions such as, "On a 10-point scale, where 1 is an ultimate risk averter and 10 is an ultimate risk taker, where would you place yourself?" They may also be asked their specific reactions to risk such as "Do you experience anxiety or thrill when awaiting the outcome of an important investment decision?"

e. Three approaches are used in this technique. First, the client may be asked to choose between a certain payoff and an uncertain payoff (gamble). Second, the client may be asked to specify the minimum probability of success that would cause him or her to take a particular risky action. Third, the client may be asked to specify the minimum rate of return that he or she would require to make an investment that has a specified set of probabilities.

15. Guidelines that the financial advisor should observe when attempting to assess clients' risk tolerances include the following:

- Diversify your methods of assessment, and compare the results for inconsistencies.
- Use the information you collect to start a dialogue with the client about risk tolerance.
- The greater the number of questions asked on a questionnaire, the more accurate the results are likely to be.
- Average the results from different approaches to obtain a best estimate.
- Consider the results of the assessment to be an overestimate of the client's true level of risk tolerance unless you have evidence to the contrary.
- Remember that a client's propensity for risk taking does not necessarily remain constant throughout his or her lifetime. It is prudent to reassess the client's risk tolerance periodically.
- Using a formal procedure (such as a questionnaire) to assess a client's risk tolerance permits you to standardize the assessment process.
- In the final analysis, it is the client who must decide what level of financial risk he or she is willing to bear.

16.

a. Smaller stock categories may include

- large cap value stocks
- large cap growth stocks
- small cap value stocks
- small cap growth stocks

- international value stocks
- international growth stocks

b. Smaller bond categories may be determined by

- length of maturing (long-term, intermediate, and short-term)
- type of issuer (corporate, municipal, government/agency, and foreign)
- type of bond (inflation-protected, zero-coupon, callable, high-yield, and so on)

Self-Test Answers—Chapter 4

Question	Answer
17.	B
18.	C
19.	A
20.	D
21.	A
22.	B
23.	D
24.	C
25.	B
26.	D

Chapter 5

Review Answers

1. A financial position statement is used to show an individual's (or family's) wealth at a specified time and reflects the results of the individual's (or family's) past financial activities. Another name for this statement is the balance sheet.
2. The key components of a financial position statement are assets, liabilities, and net worth; together they make up the accounting equation: Assets = Liabilities + Net worth. Assets are the items that the client owns. They are often subdivided into financial assets and nonfinancial (personal) assets and are shown on the statement at their fair market values. Liabilities are the client's debts. They are often subdivided into short-term (due in 1 year or less), intermediate-term (due in more than 1 year but not more than 5 years), and long-term (due in more than 5 years). Net worth measures the client's wealth or

equity at the date of the statement. It is calculated by subtracting the client's liabilities from his or her assets.

3. Other things being equal, a client's net worth can increase during a period of time as a result of any of the following:

    - appreciation in the value of the client's assets
    - addition to the client's assets through retention of income
    - addition to the client's assets through gifts or inheritances
    - decrease in the client's liabilities through debt forgiveness

4.

    a. Paying off a debt has no effect on a client's net worth because the cash account declines by the same amount that the liability declines, leaving the difference between total assets and total liabilities unchanged.
    b. Buying an asset with cash has no effect on a client's net worth because total assets remain unchanged. Cash declines by the same amount that the other asset category increases.

5. Financial assets consist of cash and cash equivalents (or liquid assets) and other financial (or investment) assets. Cash and cash equivalents are liquid in the sense that they are either already cash or can be converted into cash relatively quickly with little, if any, loss in value. Assets classified as other financial assets represent a variety of assets with wide-ranging degrees of risk in which clients may invest in an effort to earn a return.

    Nonfinancial (personal) assets consist of items bought primarily for the creature comforts they provide. They include such things as the client's primary residence, his or her vehicles, and other tangible personal assets like clothes, household furnishings, appliances, jewelry, antiques, and hobby equipment. However, in addition to items bought primarily for creature comforts, nonfinancial assets include the client's net equity in nonresidential real estate and in privately held businesses.

6. A cash flow statement is used to summarize a client's financial activities over a specified period of time by comparing cash inflows and cash outflows, and indicating whether the net cash flow for the period is positive or negative.

    The cash flow statement has three basic components—income, expenses, and net cash flow. They are related as follows: Income − Expenses = Net Cash Flow.

7.

    a. Cash flow analysis or income and expense analysis is the process of gathering data concerning the client's cash flow situation; presenting the data in an organized format; and identifying strengths, weaknesses, and important patterns. In addition, it reveals inefficient, ineffective, or unusual utilization of resources; highlights alternative courses of action; provides motivation for the client; and makes family members aware of the need to conserve resources.

b. Cash flow planning identifies courses of action that will help optimize net cash flow. A positive net cash flow is available for any use—consumption, investment, or gifting—although in most financial planning situations, the primary benefit of a positive net cash flow is to provide a source of investable funds. Any new investments, however, represent a financial commitment that raises expenses and lowers net cash flow. If there is any positive net cash flow remaining, the client may consider another alternative.

c. Budgeting is the process of creating and following an explicit plan for spending and investing the resources available to the client. In simplest terms, the process works via the establishment of a working budget model followed by a comparison of actual and expected results. By constantly monitoring the budget, the advisor and client can recognize problems as they occur and even anticipate them. Budgeting offers both a means of financial self-evaluation and a guideline to measure actual performance.

8.

a. Fixed expenses are payments the client makes for products and services essential to meet basic needs (for example, food and clothing) and/or to meet obligations established by contract or law (for example, mortgage payments or rent and income tax payments).

b. Discretionary expenses are expenses the client has considerable choice about whether or not to incur (for example, payments for vacations, other forms of recreation, charitable contributions, and education).

9. A positive net cash flow for a given period can be used to increase assets and/or reduce liabilities, the net result of which is an increase in the client's net worth.

10. The 13 components of the personal financial plan are

a. client's goals
b. identification of concerns and problems
c. planning assumptions
d. financial position statement
e. cash flow statement
f. insurance planning and risk management
g. employee benefits planning
h. specialized financial planning goals
i. investment planning
j. income tax planning

k. retirement planning
l. estate planning
m. recommendations

11. The 13 guidelines for analyzing and developing a personal financial plan are as follows:

    a. *client's goals*. The financial plan should list the client's stated goals and objectives, indicating the priority of each one and the time frame for it, where applicable. The client's goals and needs should bc expressed in as specific and precise language as possible.
    b. *identification of concerns and problems*. The plan should identify and discuss all the relevant concerns and problems that you, other advisors, and/or the client may have as they relate to the development of the plan.
    c. *planning assumptions*. All assumptions that you will use to prepare your recommended strategies should be explicitly spelled out in the plan and should include future inflation rates, investment yields, level of risk tolerance, and life expectancy.
    d. *financial position statement*. This statement lists your client's assets and liabilities in itemized schedules when appropriate. Net worth is what is left over after liabilities are subtracted from assets.
    e. *cash flow statement*. This statement includes the client's sources and uses of funds for the current year and for all other relevant years, both past and future. It subtracts the client's uses of funds from his or her sources to determine net cash flow.
    f. *insurance planning and risk management*. This entails an analysis of the client's financial exposure relative to mortality, morbidity, and liability and property risk exposures, including business, as appropriate. All current insurance policies should be listed and analyzed to make sure that they cover the financial exposures they are supposed to cover. If any coverage gaps exist, they should be promptly closed if the exposures cannot be budgeted for or handled with some other risk management technique.
    g. *employee benefits planning*. The plan should contain a statement of the current status, use of, and cost of the client's employee benefits, as well as the probability of continuation of relevant aspects of the plan. This analysis should include the types of benefits available and their relationship to other components of the plan such as insurance and risk management, retirement planning, and estate planning.
    h. *specialized financial planning goals*, The plan should analyze any future capital needs that the client will have for special

purposes such as college education or other special needs. The analysis should include a projection of resources expected to be available to meet these needs, as well as the time horizon required for funding each goal.

i. *investment planning*. All securities in your client's investment portfolio should be listed. The portfolio should then be analyzed with respect to its marketability, liquidity, degree of diversification, overall performance, and so on. The suitability of the investments in relation to your client's needs, goals, and objectives—including risk tolerance, risk management of investments, and relevant concerns and problems—should also be addressed.

j. *income tax planning*. This includes an analysis of your client's income tax returns for the current year and for recent past years. It should also include projections for several years into the future. Projections should show the nature of the income and deductions in sufficient detail to permit the calculation of the tax liability. The analysis should identify the marginal tax rate for each year and any special situations, such as the alternative minimum tax, passive loss limitations, and so on, that may affect your client's income tax liability.

k. *retirement planning*. This involves an analysis of the capital needed at some future time to provide for your client's financial independence and/or a desirable retirement lifestyle. The analysis should include a projection of resources expected to be available to meet these needs at that time.

l. *estate planning*—The financial plan should address the client's estate plan. This typically involves the identification of assets that can be included in the client's estate and an analysis of the control, disposition, and taxation of those assets.

m. *recommendations*. The plan should include a list of specific recommendations to deal with your client's concerns and problems identified earlier and to achieve his or her goals and objectives. Recommendations should also address actions that would be required to compensate for any shortfalls.

12. A client with a negative net cash flow may increase income or reduce expenses by

- reallocating some assets from low-yielding cash and cash equivalents to other financial assets with higher potential returns
- reducing the amount of discretionary expenses
- lowering the amount of certain fixed expenses to the extent possible
- refinancing his or her home mortgage at a lower interest rate

- reducing income taxes through greater use of tax-advantaged retirement accounts and tax-exempt bonds

Self-Test Answers—Chapter 5

Question	Answer
13.	B
14.	C
15.	C
16.	D
17.	C
18.	D
19.	C
20.	A
21.	B
22.	C

Chapter 6

Review Answers

1. A personal financial plan, whether comprehensive or not, is essentially a written report to the client regarding the advisor's findings and recommendations. This report results from the application of the financial planning process to the client's present situation in an effort to assist the client in meeting his or her financial goals. Every financial plan should

   - address the current status of all the major planning areas even if recommendations are not included for every one of them
   - be based on reasonable, achievable goals set by the client
   - be structured around strategies to achieve the client's goals
   - be developed around information gathered during a fact-finding process

   In addition, a personal financial plan should be built according to the three stages of the financial planning pyramid discussed in chapter 1. This type of plan typically requires several meetings with the client over a period of years. At the first stage of plan development, the advisor should concentrate on protecting the client against unexpected occurrences that could cause financial hardship. At the second stage, the advisor should focus on the client's wealth accumulation objectives. At the third and final stage, the advisor should address retirement and estate concerns.

2. The considerations to factor into developing recommendations are as follows:
    - The plan should list your specific recommendations for dealing with the concerns and problems identified previously and for achieving the client's goals and objectives.
    - Recommendations should also determine the actions necessary to compensate for any shortfalls.
    - Recommendations should be clear and stated straightforwardly.
    - If several alternative techniques are available, the plan should discuss the advantages and disadvantages of each of them, identify the recommendation of choice to achieve the client's objective, and indicate any additional reasons why the client should adopt your recommendation.
    - Whenever possible, planning recommendations should include citations to any authority or data (tax code sections, case names, numbers, assumptions, and so on) that were considered in formulating, explaining, or illustrating that recommendation.

3. In preparing for the presentation, you should do the following:
    - Analyze your client.
    - Create a summary of the fact-finding interview that you can use as an outline when you present your recommendations.
    - Check your suggested alternatives.
    - Collect any company-approved sales material you will use in the presentation.
    - Create projections for all of your recommendations.
    - Create comparisons for the probable outcome of current plans and those of the recommended alternatives.
    - Create and organize any written proposals you will use with your presentation.
    - Confirm the appointment time and location with the client.

4. The plan can be organized in a comprehensive or modular approach, summarizing the following: where the client is now (current situation), where the client wants to be (desired situation), and your recommendations to get the client to where he or she wants to be. Your presentation of the financial plan should include the following steps:
    - Describe your client's present personal and financial situation.
    - Identify your client's goals and desired situation.
    - Spell our your planning assumptions.
    - Summarize your observations.
    - Present your recommendations.
    - Outline the implementation plan.

5. You can use the following four techniques to enhance the effectiveness of your presentation:
   - Focus on relevant product features and benefits.
   - Keep the client involved.
   - Insist that all decision-makers are present.
   - Remember that presentations involve hypothetical projections.

6. Features are characteristics of the product itself—what it is or a fact about the product. Features are descriptive and are not given values. A benefit is what the client gets as a result of the feature. It is what the product does for the client and why he or she wants it. Benefits are value laden and subjective. They are the solutions that the client wants. When presenting a recommendation, you need to explain what it is and how it solves the client's problem. The delivery of benefits is essential to the client's acceptance and purchase of your product and/or service.

Answers to Self-Test Questions—Chapter 6

Question	Answer
7.	A
8.	A
9.	C
10.	C
11.	C
12.	A
13.	C
14.	D
15.	B
16.	C

Chapter 7

Review Answers

1. Implementation puts a financial plan into effect. The advisor reviews the plan, explains its pros and cons, determines what steps the client should take to implement it, and motivates the client to take action. The advisor manages the implementation, which may involve the creation of a financial planning team. In addition to the financial advisor, the team members include other professionals in disciples that complement the financial advisor's and thus can address all areas of the financial plan.

2. The financial advisor should present the recommendations and help the client determine what plan of action to take to implement the plan. The advisor may need to respond to objections and concerns that the client may pose in relation to plan implementation. Advisor responsibilities include identifying activities for implementation, determining the division of activities between the advisor and client, referring the client to other professionals (if appropriate), coordinating duties and information with other professionals, sharing information as authorized, and selecting and securing products and services.
3. The financial planning team should be made up of professionals in specialties whose expertise is needed to implement the plan. The advisor who creates the team should have an ongoing relationship with team members, including those members who are already the client's advisors and thus need to be brought in to work on their aspect of the plan. The financial advisor typically serves to coordinate and integrate the activities of team members for the client.
4. Strategic alliances are relationships developed with other professionals to create a financial planning team that can implement a plan. Because of the complexity and breadth of a financial plan, it is often necessary for professionals in different fields to collaborate to best meet the client's needs. The alliance is a network that can be used to increase market penetration, enhance competitiveness and product development, develop new business opportunities, and expand market development.
5. Approval signals are like "green" traffic lights because they tell the advisor to proceed without hesitation. They are signs that the client is responding positively and is interested in something the advisor is saying or presenting. If the signal from the client is "yellow" or "red," the advisor should continue with caution or stop and ask checking questions to see what is causing the client's concern.
6. Techniques to help motivate the client include the following:

    - assumed or implied consent—presuming the client wants to take action without actually asking the client
    - alternative choice—giving the client two or more choices and asking the client to make a choice
    - silence—saying nothing after asking a closing question and waiting for the client's reaction
    - direct question—asking the client if he or she is ready to start the plan and then seeking clarification if he or she is not ready
    - why question—asking the client, "Why . . . ?" to shift the pressure back to the client and regain control of the meeting (However, because why questions carry a connotation of implied disapproval, they should be used sparingly and only when no other question will suffice.)
    - Ben Franklin balance sheet—comparing and weighing the pros and cons of each alternative

- similar situation—telling the client about another client in a situation similar to the client's

7. When a client expresses a concern, the advisor should listen carefully to what the client is saying and then confirm his or her understanding by restating or rephrasing what the client has said. The advisor should communicate sincerity and build trust. Two ways to do this are the "acknowledge, clarify and resolve" technique and the "feel, felt, found" technique.
8. The advisor should monitor the continued soundness and appropriateness of the plan and its progress toward achieving the client's specific financial goals. The advisor should also check to see if the client's situation has changed—for example, any change in his or her objectives or overall personal and financial situation—or if there have been any changes in the national economic and tax environment affecting the client. Revisions should be made whenever warranted by situational changes or unsatisfactory plan performance. These responsibilities should be well defined and communicated to the client. Work by other professionals should also be reviewed.
9. The objectives of plan service are to maintain/increase the level of client business, generate referrals, and lower expenses. These activities enhance the advisor-client relationship and lead to additional business. Brochures, newsletters, and greeting cards keep the advisor's name in front of the client. Maintaining good records will facilitate this process and help keep clients up-to-date. It will also demonstrate the advisor's professionalism and interest in the client.

Self-Test Answers—Chapter 7

Question	Answer
10.	A
11.	B
12.	D
13.	C
14.	B
15.	A
16.	C
17.	A
18.	B
19.	D

Chapter 8

Review Answers

1. The two funding requirements associated with financing a college education are the lump-sum requirement and the monthly savings requirement.
2. College cost inflation has historically outpaced consumer price inflation. Conservative investment allocations are not likely to keep up with college cost inflation, which is influencing clients to select college funding strategies that are tax advantaged like prepaid tuition programs and Sec. 529 college savings plans.
3. Loans are more widely available than grants, which are more widely available than scholarships. Need-based aid versus merit-based aid also is a consideration.
4. Parental assets and income combined with student assets and income, less any exclusions or allowances, determines the parental and student contributions, which combined is the expected family contribution.
5. Three federal legislative acts form the basis for the regulation of securities products:

    - *Securities Act of 1933*—provides statutory guidelines that a company must follow before it can sell new issues of its stock to the public
    - *Securities Exchange Act of 1934*—extends federal regulation to the ongoing trading of securities that have already been issued
    - *Investment Advisers Act of 1940*—seeks to protect the public from harmful and fraudulent conduct of persons who are paid to advise others on buying and/or selling securities

6. The SEC is not the sole source of rules and regulations under the federal securities laws. Congress recognized that the nation's stock exchanges had long been regulating the trading activities of their own members. With this in mind, self-regulatory organizations (SROs) were incorporated into the regulatory structure of the securities industry.
7. The FINRA has the power to require and monitor compliance with standardized rules of fair practice for the industry. FINRA regulatory responsibilities include registration and testing of securities professionals, review of members' advertising and sales literature, and services such as arbitration of investor disputes. Registered representatives must provide the FINRA with personal information, including prior employment and any history of securities-related disciplinary action. The FINRA sets forth its expectations for the ethical treatment of customers in its Rules of Conduct. These rules spell out two fundamental steps, which must be followed in order to fairly deal with clients. The advisor must understand the client's

current financial status and the client's financial goals. The rules of conduct govern (1) the supervision of the salespersons, (2) private securities transactions, (3) outside business activities of associated persons, (4) suitability and fair dealing with customers, (5) influencing or rewarding employees of other broker/dealers and finder's fees, and (6) sales literature, advertising, and communications with the public.

8. The first test asks if the practitioner provides "advice or analysis" about a security. Because the term security is broadly defined for federal securities law purposes, it can include many financial instruments in addition to the best-known securities like common stocks or bonds. The second test is the business standard, which asks if the financial services professional is presented to the public as being "in the business" of providing advice about securities. The third test is the compensation test, which asks if the practitioner receives compensation, and the test is met regardless of the source of payment.
9. A financial planner, as an investment advisor, is subject to a number of legal responsibilities in addition to the registration requirement. (1) Under its rule-making authority, the SEC has imposed extensive recordkeeping and reporting requirements. (2) An investment advisor is subject to inspection and examination by the SEC. Inspections are of two types—routine and "for cause." (3) An investment advisor is prohibited from entering into an investment advisory contract if the contract provides for compensation based on a share of the capital gains or capital appreciation of the client's funds. (4) Every investment advisor must deliver a written disclosure statement (the "brochure rule") to the prospective client at least 2 days before the advisory contract is entered into or at the time of entering into the contract if the client can terminate the contract within 5 days. This statement must include information concerning the advisor's background, education, experience, types of services offered, and the investment techniques to be employed. (5) The Act prohibits an investment advisor from representing that he or she is an "investment counsel" unless his or her principal business consists of action as an investment advisor and a substantial portion of the business consists of providing investment advisory services. (6) An investment advisor is permitted to pay finder's fees, but only if certain conditions are met. There must be a written agreement between the advisor and the finder of the business. (7) The Act contains an antifraud section detailing various types of conduct considered to be in violation of the fiduciary nature of the investment advisory relationship.
10. *Advantages*. A registered investment advisor has the ability to charge fees for professional advice and planning services. Registering as an investment advisor affords an advisor far greater latitude in how he or she advertises and promotes his or her practice. Business cards and letterhead can indicate that you engage in providing investment advice, and develop financial planning programs and investment achievement

strategies for clients. You can expand your practice in investment planning and asset management, and you can move into markets calling for a wider array of product and service needs.

Disadvantages. You must pay application fees, and there is substantial paperwork. As an RIA, you must maintain meticulous records regarding the advice you give to clients. You must also comply with regulatory reporting requirements. Perhaps the greatest disincentive to being an RIA is the potential for substantial legal liability. You are clearly inviting clients to rely on your expertise and investment advice. If your expertise is limited or your investment advice imprudent, you are likely to find yourself named in a lawsuit. In addition, an RIA is legally held to a higher professional standard than other financial advisors are.

11. You may have clients with considerable sums of money in highly responsible positions. As part of selling/planning process, they may be privy to confidential information regarding the companies for which they work or in which they hold substantial ownership positions. They may obtain important financial information before it becomes generally available to the public. This important (material) information might indicate, for example, an upcoming loss or profit decline. On the other hand, it might indicate the expansion of a new product line with the likelihood of increased and significant profitability. In each instance, the information may involve a firm whose shares are publicly traded and from which sizable personal profits could arise. This type of financial data is considered "insider" information. Personal stock purchases or sales based on this data constitute insider trading and are considered illegal under federal securities laws.
12. A fiduciary has a duty to the client to act in a responsible manner when it comes to the financial management of that client's affairs. Registered investment advisors, including many financial advisors, have a fiduciary duty, whereas registered representatives and insurance advisors may not. A fiduciary may be a person who has discretionary control over a client's assets or is in a position as a professional held in the capacity of trust who renders investment advice. You do not have to have discretionary control to be considered a fiduciary.

Self-Test Answers—Chapter 8

Question	Answer
13.	A
14.	A
15.	D
16.	B
17.	B
18.	C
19.	C
20.	C
21.	A
22.	D

GLOSSARY

accurate empathy • a bonding that occurs when the financial advisor's sense of the client's world fits the client's self-image; it gives clients the sense that the advisor is in touch with them

active listening • the act of putting together a speaker's words and nonverbal behaviors to get the essence of the communication being sent. With active listening, you become involved in the inner world of another person while, at the same time, maintaining your own identity and responding meaningfully to the person's messages.

advising • one form of structured communication; an expert (advisor) giving specific guidance or suggestions to a client, who in turn may use this knowledge to help reach a decision

agreement letter • a written confirmation that the advisor sends to the client after the fact-finding meeting(s), in which the advisor and the client acknowledge the client's financial problems and goals. It serves as a basis for proceeding to the next step of the selling/planning process where the advisor analyzes the client's current situation and, in conjunction with his or her goals, develops several appropriate recommendations.

annuity • a finite stream of equal payments made at the end of each of a number of consecutive periods

annuity due • a series of equal payments made at the beginning of each of a number of consecutive periods

approval signals • verbal or nonverbal signs that the client is interested in something the advisors is saying or presenting to him or her

asset allocation • a portfolio management technique, which typically divides the portfolio among three broad asset categories (stocks, bonds, and cash equivalents) and specifies the percentage of total portfolio assets to be invested in each category

assumed or implied consent • the advisor's assumption that the client's decision to proceed is implied, without directly asking or confronting the client

balance sheet • a financial report that shows the status of an individual's assets, liabilities, and net worth on a given date. The balance sheet is a listing of the items that make up the two sides of the basic accounting equation, which states that assets equal (or balance) liabilities plus net worth. *See also* financial position statement.

benefit • what the client receives as a result of a product feature; what the product does for the client and why he or she wants it. Benefits are value laden and subjective.

budgeting • the process of creating and following an explicit plan for spending and investing the resources available to the client, which works via the establishment of a working budget model followed by a comparison of actual and expected results. It provides a means of financial self-evaluation and a guideline to measure actual performance.

cash flow analysis • the process of gathering cash flow information, presenting the data in an organized format (the cash flow statement), and identifying strengths, weaknesses, and important patterns (also called income and expense analysis)

cash flow management • the budget planning and control process, which consists of three components—cash flow analysis, cash flow planning, and budgeting

cash flow planning • identifying courses of action that help to optimize net cash flow (the difference between income and expenses)

cash flow statement • a statement that summarizes a client's financial activities over a specified period of time by comparing cash inflows and cash outflows and indicating whether the net cash flow for the period is positive or negative. The cash flow statement contains three basic classifications— income, expenses, and net cash flow—that are related in an equation, which states that income minus expenses equals net cash flow. *See also* income statement.

center of influence (COI) • an influential person who knows an advisor favorably and agrees to introduce or recommend him or her to others

checking questions • questions the advisor asks to elicit the prospect's or client's thoughts and tune into his or her feelings

clarifying response • a type of understanding response associated with active listening to enhance communication. There are two forms of clarifying response. In the first, the listener attempts to restate or clarify what the speaker has had difficulty in expressing clearly. In the second, the listener asks the speaker to clarify what he or she means.

client goals • the first component of a personal financial plan. The client's personal and financial goals should be listed, indicating the priority of each one and the time frame for achieving it.

closed-ended question • a type of question that solicits singular facts or a yes or no response

compensation test • one of three tests to determine if an individual must become a registered investment advisor. An individual who charges a fee or receives a commission on the sale of securities meets this test.

components of a personal financial plan • 13 areas relating to the client that should be addressed in creating a personal financial plan: client goals, identification of concerns and problems, planning assumptions, financial position statement, cash flow statement, insurance planning and risk management, employee benefits planning, specialized financial planning goals, investment planning, income tax planning, retirement planning, estate planning, and recommendations. These 13 components form the basis for the procedure that advisors can use to analyze, develop, present, implement, and service a client's personal financial plan.

compound interest • interest computed by applying the interest rate to the sum of the original principal and the interest credited to it in earlier time periods

compounding • the process by which money today (present value) grows over time to a larger amount (future value)

comprehensive approach • the approach to financial planning that occurs when an advisor uses the selling/planning process to develop a comprehensive financial plan that addresses a client's financial problems and goals. The plan considers all aspects of a client's financial position, which typically includes financial problems from all the major planning areas. In addition, the plan usually encompasses several integrated and coordinated planning strategies that can be used to help solve the client's problems and achieve his or her goals.

conflict of interest • a situation in which an advisor uses the influence of his or her position to benefit the advisor's own interest, usually at the expense of the client

consumer price index (CPI) • the index that measures the change in consumer purchasing power due to price inflation (deflation), as determined by a monthly survey of the U.S. Bureau of Labor Statistics (also referred to as the cost-of-living index)

continuing response • a type of understanding response associated with active listening. It is a relatively unobtrusive response that encourages a speaker to continue talking. Examples include "uh-huh," "mmmm," "and. . . ?" and "then?" They communicate to the speaker, "Go on, I'm with you."

cost of waiting • a comparison between the costs and values of a financial plan started today and one started in the future. Such a comparison reveals a dramatic difference in the amount a given deposit or ongoing deposits can accumulate, depending on when they are made, and demonstrates the concept of the time value of money.

counseling • one form of structured communication. It provides assistance to clients as they explore their present situations, begin to understand where they are in relation to where they want to be, and act to get from where they are to where they want to be. It evolves over a period of time, and an interpersonal relationship often develops between the counselor (advisor) and the client.

Coverdell education savings accounts • education funds that allow donors to contribute up to $2,000 per year per child. Contributions are tax deferred and earnings are tax free as long as funds are used to pay for qualified educational expenses (formerly known as education IRAs).

debt-service ratio • total annual loan payments (that is, mortgage and consumer debt payments) divided by gross income. The ratio (which can also be calculated on a monthly basis) indicates the percentage of the client's income required to cover existing loan payments.

directive interview • a type of communication in which the interviewer (advisor) directs and controls the pace and content to be covered; it is a formalized, structured form of interaction. Its advantages are that it can be brief and that it provides measurable data; its disadvantages are that it is often inflexible and does not allow the interviewee (client) to choose topics for discussion.

disclosure statement • a form that discloses information about the advisor to his or her clients. It provides information about the advisor's educational background, professional certifications and licenses held, professional experience, business philosophy, training, method of compensation, and possible conflicts of interest with a consultation.

discounting • the process by which money due in the future (future value) is reduced over time to a smaller amount today (present value)

diversification • a portfolio management technique to minimize the impact of any one security, investment, or asset category on overall portfolio performance. It occurs when a portfolio is composed of several asset categories, each one of which is designed for investments with risk and return profiles that are dissimilar to the profiles of investments in other categories, so that a downward movement of investments in one asset category is offset by an upward movement of investments in another asset category.

either/or question • a relatively ineffective type of question in which the client's answer is limited to only two options

employee benefits planning • the integration and coordination of all employer- and government-provided benefits—such as those provided for medical expenses, death, disability, retirement, and unemployment—with all other areas of financial planning

estate planning • the process of accumulation, management, conservation, and transfer of wealth, considering legal, tax, and personal objectives

expected family contribution (EFC) • the amount of postsecondary expenses the family is expected to pay (derived from the FAFSA application) based on the parent's (or parents') and student's assets and the cost of attendance at the selected school. The EFC is a combination of the amounts determined for the parent(s) and the student.

expected parent contribution • the amount of postsecondary expenses the parent or parents are expected to pay (derived from the FAFSA application) based on the parent's (or parents') assets and the cost of attendance at the selected school

expected student contribution • the amount of postsecondary expenses the student is expected to pay (derived from the FAFSA application) based on the student's assets and the cost of attendance at the selected school

explanatory response • a type of leading response in which the advisor explains something to the client in a simple, concise, and comprehensible way

fact-finder form • an information-gathering form that a financial advisor and/or client needs to complete as part of the selling/planning process. It includes both quantitative and qualitative information about the client's current financial position and personal circumstances.

FAFSA • the U.S. Department of Education's Free Application for Federal Student Aid, used to submit financial information to obtain financial aid. The federal need-analysis formula dictates how much the student and the student's parent or parents are expected to contribute per academic year for higher education.

feature • a fact about a product; a feature is descriptive and is not given a value

federal loan consolidation programs • programs that pay a student's or parent's college loans when the student leaves full-time student status; a new consolidation loan is created with a favorable interest rate and repayment terms

federal Pell grant • a federal grant for undergraduate students who qualify under a need-analysis formula, available in amounts up to $4,731 per year (2008–2009)

federal Perkins loan • a loan of up to $4,000 per year ($20,000 cumulatively) for students who show exceptional need. The program is administered by colleges but uses federal funds; interest is only 5 percent, and payments can be spread over 10 years after the student leaves school.

fiduciary • a person who holds another's trust or confidence. A financial advisor engaged in financial planning is a fiduciary who owes the client an affirmative duty of utmost good faith and full and fair disclosure of all the material facts. He or she must act in the best interest of the client and put the client's interest before his or her own.

financial assets • assets that consist of cash and cash equivalents (or liquid assets) and other financial (or investment) assets. Cash and cash equivalents are liquid in the sense that they are either already cash or can be converted into cash relatively quickly with little or no loss in value. Other financial assets represent a variety of assets with wide-ranging degrees of risk in which clients may invest in an effort to earn a return. *See also* nonfinancial assets.

Financial Industry Regulatory Authority (FINRA) • the successor to National Association of Securities Dealers (NASD); part of the self-regulatory structure established under the authority granted by the Securities Exchange Act of 1934 to provide voluntary self-regulation of broker/dealers under SEC oversight. The FINRA has the power to require and monitor compliance with standardized rules of fair practice for the industry. FINRA regulatory responsibilities include registration and testing of securities professionals, review of members' advertising and sales literature, and services such as arbitration of investor disputes.

financial life cycle • the approach to financial planning that occurs when an advisor uses the selling/planning process to develop a comprehensive financial plan that solves a client's financial problems. The plan considers all aspects of a client's financial position, which typically includes financial problems from all the major planning areas. In addition, the plan usually encompasses several integrated and coordinated planning strategies that can be used to help solve the client's problems and achieve his or her goals.

financial life planning • a client-centered approach that explores life issues as they relate to money. It involves discussing the client's money as it pertains to each aspect of the client's life.

financial planning • a process that focuses on determining a client's financial problems and/or goals and then developing a plan to help the client solve the problems and achieve the goals

financial planning pyramid • a widely accepted approach for developing a comprehensive financial plan over time. It prioritizes financial goals by categorizing them into three levels. Level 1 goals provide protection against risks, level 2 goals focus on accumulating wealth, and level 3 goals address retirement and estate concerns.

financial planning team • a team of professional advisors with expertise in different areas who can address all the major planning components of a financial plan

financial position statement • an organized list of the components of an individual's or family's wealth at a specified time. It reflects the results of past financial activities and covers three basic classifications: assets, liabilities, and net worth. *See also* balance sheet.

framing • the way in which a question is structured with regard to the issue being evaluated. For example, the same objective facts can be described either in terms of the probability of success or the probability of failure.

future value of an annuity (FVA) • the amount to which an annuity would accumulate by the end of its term if the payments earned a specific rate of return during the entire time period

future value of an annuity due (FVAD) • the amount to which an annuity due would accumulate by the end of its term if the payments earned a specific rate of return during the entire time period

future value of a single sum (FVSS) • an amount determined by compounding a present value at a particular interest rate for a particular length of time

FVA factor • a factor used to determine the future value of an annuity. The FVA factor is $(1 + i)^n - 1 \div i$. , where i is the periodic interest rate expressed as a decimal and n is the number of time periods.

FVA formula • a formula, FVA = periodic payment $\times (1 + i)^n - 1 \div i$, where FVA is the future value of an annuity, periodic payment is the amount of each payment, i is the periodic interest rate expressed as a decimal, and n is the number of periods over which the annuity is paid

FVAD formula • a formula, FVAD = FVA formula × (1 + i), where FVAD is the future value of an annuity due, FVA formula is the formula for the future value of an annuity, and i is the periodic interest rate expressed as a decimal. *See also* FVA formula.

FVSS factor • a factor used to determine the future value of a single sum. The FVSS factor is $(1 + i)^n$, where i is the periodic interest rate expressed as a decimal and n is the number of periods during which compounding occurs.

FVSS formula • a basic formula, FVSS = PVSS $\times (1 + i)^n$, where FVSS is the future value of a single sum, PVSS is the present value of a single sum, i is the periodic interest rate expressed as a decimal, and n is the number of periods during which compounding occurs

genuineness • a quality necessary to be an effective advisor. Financial advisors who are genuine are aware of themselves and their feelings, thoughts, values, and attitudes; always express themselves openly and honestly; do not play roles; communicate expressively without concealing anything; and are consistent.

goal setting • in financial planning, the process of establishing clearly definable, measurable, achievable, and realistic financial and personal goals toward which a client's effort, resources, plans and actions can be targeted

goal prioritization • the process of ranking goals according to their order of importance for the purpose of deciding the order for their achievement

Hope Scholarship tax credit • an education tax credit of up to $1,500 per student per year for tuition and related expenses incurred during the first 2 years of postsecondary education; the credit equals 100 percent of the first $1,000 of tuition and fees and 50 percent of the next $1,000 of tuition and fees. The credit may be reduced (phased out) based on modified adjusted gross income.

identification of concerns and problems • the second component of a personal financial plan. Financial concerns should be listed and rated in order of importance by the client. Common financial concerns include liquidity, safety of principal, capital appreciation, current income, inflation protection, future income, and tax reduction/deferral.

income statement • summary of the various income and expense items of an individual or company during an accounting period, which is typically 1 year. *See also* cash flow statement.

income tax planning • the analysis, evaluation, and client acceptance of the income tax consequences of every capital and financial transaction before the transaction is made

insider information • material, nonpublic information about a security. Under Securities and Exchange Commission rules, trading on the basis of such insider information is not allowed.

insurance planning and risk management • a category of financial planning goals that recognizes most people's desire to protect themselves and their families against the risks they face in everyday life that can arise because of premature death, disability, medical care, long-term care, property and liability losses, and unemployment

interpretive response • a type of leading response in which the advisor cuts to the heart of the matter, "translating" what the client has said

interviewing • a form of structured communication, most often between two people, with a predetermined and specific purpose, usually involving asking and answering questions designed to gather meaningful information

Investment Advisers Act of 1940 • the statutory body of law that controls the regulation of investment advisors. With certain exceptions, it requires that firms or sole practitioners compensated for advising others about securities investments register with the SEC and conform to regulations designed to protect investors.

investment advisor representative • an investment advisor who joins an independent advisory firm and must register under the Investment Advisers Act. The firm will provide supervisory services and registration assistance.

investment planning • the selection of financial products for the accumulation of capital, taking into consideration a person's goals, time horizon, risk tolerance, and means to invest. Asset-allocation, diversification, and market-timing strategies may be used in the process, and the impact that income taxation has on net results is usually considered.

kiddie tax • a tax that applies to children under age 14. It allows up to $950 (in 2009) of unearned income to be received tax free, it taxes the next $950 at the child's tax rate, and it applies the parents' rate to additional amounts. The kiddie tax is an attempt to make income shifting from parents to children less attractive.

leading question • a question that steers the client toward a conclusion that the advisor, not the client, has already formulated. This type of question is considered ineffective, dishonest, and manipulative.

leading response • a type of response in which the financial advisor takes the lead (to a certain extent) and deviates somewhat from the client's preceding responses

life cycle financial planning • a financial planning process that is ongoing and occurs throughout a client's financial life. The advisor who monitors this type of planning is practicing life cycle financial planning

life planning • a comprehensive approach to planning founded on the philosophy that the most successful and satisfying experiences are based on a series of thoughtful, future-focused decisions made throughout a person's adult life. Skills, values, attitudes, resources and relationships that are developed and honed during one stage of life all contribute to meeting the challenges and recognizing the opportunities of the next stage of life.

Lifetime Learning tax credit • an education tax credit of up to $2,000, calculated as 20 percent of the first $10,000 of tuition and related expenses paid for an eligible student. The credit may be reduced based on modified adjusted gross income.

liquidity ratio • liquid assets (cash and cash equivalents) divided by total current debts (current liabilities plus annual loan payments). The ratio indicates the percentage of liquid assets the client has available to pay current (1-year) debt.

market segment • a group of people with common characteristics and needs

modified adjusted gross income • an intermediate calculation made to determine an individual's tax liability. It is derived from gross income, minus above-the-line deductions in calculating adjusted gross income (AGI). The term modified means that each tax provision may have different items that are included in the AGI calculation.

multiple-purpose approach • the approach to financial planning that occurs when an advisor follows the selling/planning process to develop a plan that solves two or more financial problems or meets two or more goals for a client. The plan may focus on solving several problems from one of the major planning areas, or it may focus on problems from two or three major planning areas.

natural market • a group of people to whom an advisor has a natural affinity or to whom an advisor has access because of similar values, lifestyles, experiences, attitudes, and so on

net cash flow • the difference between income and expenses. A positive net cash flow is available for any use, whether for consumption, investment, or gifting. However, in most financial planning situations, the primary benefit of a positive net cash flow is to provide a source of investable funds.

networking • the mutual sharing of ideas and clients with other professionals whose work does not compete with the advisor's

nondirective interview • a type of structured communication that allows both the interviewer (advisor) and interviewee (client) to discuss a wider range of subject matters; the interviewee (client) usually controls the pacing and purpose of the interview. Its advantages are that there is greater flexibility and more in-depth responses than with a directive interview, and a closer relationship between the interviewer (advisor) and interviewee (client) is established. Its disadvantages are that it consumes more time than a directive interview, and it often provides data that are difficult to measure objectively.

nonfinancial (personal) assets • assets bought primarily for the creature comforts they provide. They include such things as the client's primary residence, his or her vehicles, and other tangible (personal) assets like clothes, household furnishings, antiques, and hobby equipment. Nonfinancial assets also include the client's net equity in nonresidential real estate and in privately held businesses.

nonverbal behaviors • non-linguistic actions that make up a large part of communication. From the two main sources of nonverbal behaviors—the body and the voice—there are seven important types of nonverbal signs of meaning: body position, body movement, gestures, facial expressions, eye contact, voice tone, and voice pitch.

norms • standards of measurement, such as average, that allow comparison of an individual to a representative group. For instance, using a normed measure of risk tolerance, it is possible to see whether the client is more or less risk tolerant than people in general or to compare the client to other people of the same age and gender.

objective information • factual information about a client that is obtained through fact finding, which includes personal and family information, a list of securities holdings, an inventory of assets and liabilities, the client's current estate plan, a list of annual income and expenditures, a summary of present insurance coverages, and the current financial plan

open-ended question • a type of question that encourages expansive responses, especially when soliciting opinions, thoughts, ideas, values, and feelings

opportunity cost • the implied cost of undertaking a financial action, usually represented as the rate that could have been earned by investing in the best alternative activity with the same resources

physical attending • using your body to communicate. The five basic attributes associated with physical attending are to (1) face the other person squarely, (2) adopt an open posture, (3) lean toward the other person, (4) maintain good eye contact, and (5) be relaxed while attending.

planning assumptions • the third component of a personal financial plan. Used to define the client's personal and financial planning problems and challenges, they serve to remind the client of the obstacles and limitations that must be observed throughout the customization of his or her personalized financial plan. Assumptions, which should be explicitly spelled out in the financial plan document, include future inflation rates, investment yields, risk tolerance, and life expectancies.

PLUS loans • parent loans for undergraduate students available through both the Direct Loan and Family Federal Education Loan programs for all families, regardless of income and asset levels, with acceptable credit histories. Applicants can borrow up to the entire cost of the education, less any other financial aid received, at an annually floating interest rate equal to the 91-day Treasury bill rate on July 1 plus 3.1 percent, with a maximum of 9 percent. Interest accrues from the time of the first disbursement. Payments must begin within 60 days after the loan is fully disbursed, and the loan must be paid within 10 years.

present value of an annuity (PVA) • the present value of a series of equal periodic payments made at the end of each period and discounted at an appropriate rate

present value of an annuity due (PVAD) • the present value of a series of equal periodic payments made at the beginning of each period and discounted at an appropriate rate

present value of a single sum (PVSS) • an amount determined by discounting a future value at a particular interest rate for a particular length of time

presentation checklist • 13 questions financial advisors should ask and answer to prepare themselves for the presentation of the personal financial plan to the client

presentation techniques • four skills that financial advisors can use to enhance the effectiveness of the presentation of the financial plan to the client: Focus on relevant product features and benefits, keep the client involved, insist that all decision-makers are present, and remember that presentations involve hypothetical projections.

pro forma • projected. Pro forma financial statements represent the advisor's best estimate of how the statements will look at a future point in time.

PVA factor • a factor used to determine the present value of an annuity. The PVA factor is $1 - [1 \div (1 + i)^n] \div i$, where i is the periodic interest rate expressed as a decimal and n is the number of time periods.

PVA formula •

a formula, PVA = periodic payment × 1 – [1 ÷ $(1 + i)^n$] ÷ *i*, where PVA is the present value of an annuity, periodic payment is the amount of each payment, i is the periodic interest rate expressed as a decimal, and n is the number of periods over which the annuity is paid

PVAD formula • a formula, PVAD = PVA formula × (1 + i), where PVAD is the present value of an annuity due, PVA formula is the formula for the present value of an annuity, and i is the periodic interest rate expressed as a decimal. *See also* PVA formula.

PVSS factor • a factor used to determine the present value of a single sum. The PVSS factor is 1/(1 + i)n, where i is the periodic interest rate expressed as a decimal and n is the number of periods over which discounting occurs.

PVSS formula • a basic formula, PVSS = FVSS × 1 ÷ $(1 + i)^{n}$], where PVSS is the present value of a single sum, FVSS is the future value of a single sum, i is the periodic interest rate expressed as a decimal, and n is the number of periods during which discounting occurs

question bombardment • a faulty questioning technique in which the advisor asks two or more questions without giving the client a chance to respond

rapport • a relationship marked by harmony or accord. Rapport between a financial advisor and client can be aided by the advisor's friendly, interested concern; an unhurried, leisurely pace; an accepting, nonjudgmental attitude; attentive, active listening; and an egalitarian relationship.

reassuring response • a type of leading response that is intended to reassure or encourage the client. Although reassuring responses can make the client feel better and enhance rapport with the advisor, they do not address the underlying situation.

rebalancing • a portfolio management technique. A portfolio can become unbalanced over time because some asset categories will outperform others, throwing off the carefully planned asset-allocation percentages. The portfolio can be brought back in line through rebalancing by selling assets that have appreciated and buying those that have fallen in price.

recommendations • the 13th and final component of a personal financial plan. Definitive written recommendations that meet the client's goals should be formulated, clearly identified, and stated straightforwardly in the plan. They should specifically address the client's problems and goals identified in the plan, as well as determine the actions necessary to compensate for any shortfalls.

referral • a person to whom an advisor is introduced by someone who knows the advisor and values his or her work

reflection-of-feeling response • a type of understanding response associated with active listening. It shows the listener's understanding of the speaker's experience by responding to the speaker's feelings. By paraphrasing the speaker's feelings, the listener enables the speaker to get in closer touch with those feelings. This, in turn, facilitates working through the speaker's problem.

registered investment advisor (RIA) • an investment advisor who has registered with either the SEC or the appropriate state agency as an investment advisor

registered representative • an individual who has the legal status of an agent and is licensed to sell securities, having passed the Series 7 and Series 63 examinations; usually works for a broker/dealer licensed by the SEC, NYSE, or FINRA

resistance • in an advisor-client relationship, behavior by the client being counseled that impedes the counseling process. It is often expressed as overt or covert hostility toward the advisor.

restatement-of-content response • a type of understanding response associated with active listening. By paraphrasing what the speaker has just said, the listener encourages the speaker to delve more deeply into the situation because he or she feels the listener is "on the same wavelength."

retirement planning • the dynamic process aimed at achieving economic independence and a desired lifestyle after the cessation of an individual's career or major full-time occupation

risk • in an asset-allocation context, the probability that the actual return on an investment portfolio will be lower than the expected return. This risk is measured in terms of the variability in returns.

risk aversion • a preference for certain outcomes with low returns over uncertain outcomes with the possibility of higher returns

risk averter • individuals who are relatively unwilling to take a chance and incur financial risk

risk-free rate • the rate of return that can be achieved by investing in an alternative that has no risk. The usual surrogate for the risk-free rate is the short-term Treasury bill rate, although even Treasury bills are subject to inflation risk.

risk premium • the increment of return required above the risk-free rate that an investor demands to reward him or her for accepting risk. The amount of the risk premium is directly related to the amount of risk undertaken and is typically added to the short-term Treasury bill rate to calculate the required rate of return for the investment.

risk/return trade-off • a trade-off between risk and return. In general, the investment portfolio that, on average, produces higher rates of return also has greater variability in its returns. Risk refers to the possibility that a portfolio will experience variations in its returns over time.

risk seeker • an individual who is willing to take a chance and incur a high degree of financial risk

risk tolerance • a preference for uncertain outcomes with the possibility of high returns over certain outcomes with lower returns

Roth IRA • a type of individual retirement account in which after-tax contributions are required, but earnings and distributions after age 59½ are not taxed. Roth IRAs also have other characteristics that make them more beneficial than traditional IRAs for many people.

Rule of 72 • a quick method to estimate how long it will take for an amount to double in value at various compound interest rates. In this method, the number 72 is divided by the applicable interest rate expressed as a whole number. The quotient is the approximate number of periods until the amount doubles.

savings ratio • net cash flow plus amounts already being saved or invested, divided by annual after-tax income. It indicates the percentage of after-tax income that the client is saving.

Sec. 529 plans • a tax-advantaged approach to funding higher education expenses; types of plans include prepaid tuition programs and savings plans (also called qualified tuition programs)

Securities Act of 1933 • first law Congress enacted to regulate the securities markets and prohibit false representations and disclosures; the Act requires the registration of securities before being sold to the public and disclosure of all pertinent information about the securities in a prospectus

Securities Exchange Act of 1934 • law governing the securities market that outlaws misrepresentation and other abusive practices in issuing securities and that created the Securities and Exchange Commission to enforce both this Act and the Securities Act of 1933

security • one of many financial instruments, including stocks, bonds, certificates of deposit, commercial paper, limited partnerships, variable annuity products, and investment contracts

security advice test • one of three tests to determine if an individual must become a registered investment advisor. If an individual provides advice about the purchase or sale of securities, this indicates that registration is necessary.

security business test • one of three tests to determine if an individual must become a registered investment advisor. A person is deemed to be "in the security business" if he or she holds himself or herself out as an investment advisor, receives separate or additional compensation that is a clearly definable charge for providing advice about securities, or provides specific investment advice in other than isolated instances.

self-awareness • in an advisor-client relationship, the advisor's relative understanding of his or her own value systems. This gives the advisor a better chance to avoid imposing his or her values on clients.

selling/planning process • an eight-step process that advisors follow when they are engaged in financial planning. The steps are (1) identify the prospect, (2) approach the prospect, (3) meet the prospect, (4) gather information and establish goals, (5) analyze the information, (6) develop and present the plan, (7) implement the plan, and (8) service the plan.

simple interest • interest computed by applying the interest rate to only the original principal sum

single-purpose approach • the approach to financial planning that occurs when an advisor follows the selling/planning process to develop a plan that solves a single financial problem or meets a single goal for a client. The plan may be as simple as selling a single financial product or service to the client in order to solve the problem.

social styles • predictable patterns of behavior that people display and that can be observed. The American population is evenly divided among four social styles: driver, expressive, amiable, and analytical. Appropriate responses to the characteristics of each social style indicate how an advisor can best establish rapport with a client who has that style.

solvency ratio • net worth (total assets minus total liabilities) divided by total assets (the sum of all items the client owns). It provides an estimate of the extent to which the market value of a client's total assets can decline before wiping out all of the client's wealth as measured by net worth.

specialized financial planning goals • goals that are subsets of, and generally involve several of, the major planning areas and typically include planning for education funding, divorce, terminal illness, nontraditional families, job or career change, job loss (including severance packages), dependent parents who need long-term care, other dependents with special needs, the purchase of a first home, and the purchase of a vacation or second home

Stafford loans • major source of education borrowing from the federal government; loans are available through the Direct Loan program or the Family Federal Education Loan program from participating banks, credit unions, and other lenders. Stafford loans may be subsidized or unsubsidized and must be paid within 10 years.

strategic alliance • relationship that an advisor develops with another professional that enables the advisor to establish a complementary team of professionals to whom he or she can refer a client when the client's financial situation requires the expertise and services of the team

subjective information • information about the client (and his or her spouse, if applicable) obtained through the fact-finding process that includes his or her hopes, fears, values, preferences, attitudes, financial goals, and nonfinancial goals

suggestive response • a type of leading response in which the advisor gives advice to the client in the form of a suggestion or several suggestions about which the client has the final decision

summarization response • a type of understanding response associated with active listening that can focus and capsulate a series of scattered ideas to present a clear perspective. Summarization permits both the speaker and listener to gauge the accuracy with which messages have been sent and received.

target market • an identifiable and accessible group of people with common characteristics and common needs who regularly communicate with one another. The group must be sufficiently large so that the advisor does not run out of prospects.

thrill seeker • the personality type most likely to be consistently risk seeking in all aspects of life, including financial matters

time value of money (TVM) • the concept that a specific amount of money received (paid) in a specific time period has a different value than the same amount received (paid) in a different time period

true/false question • closed-ended question in which the client's response must indicate whether the question is true or false

unauthorized entity • an insurance company that has not gained approval to place insurance business from a department of insurance in the jurisdiction where it or a producer wants to sell insurance. These carriers are unlicensed and prohibited from doing business in that state.

unconditional positive regard • an attitude of valuing the client or being able to express appreciation of the client as a unique and worthwhile person

unpacking effect • the finding that the perceived likelihood of an event is influenced by how specifically it is described. The more specific the description of the event, the more the event is judged as likely to occur.

why question • a type of question that advisors should generally avoid because asking "why" tends to question the client's motivation or lack of it and thus creates a certain defensiveness. Why questions carry a connotation of implied disapproval, forcing the client to justify or defend his or her thoughts, ideas, or actions.

INDEX